ECLIPSE ASPECTJ

the eclipse series

SERIES EDITORS Erich Gamma ▪ Lee Nackman ▪ John Wiegand

Eclipse is a universal tool platform, an open extensible integrated development environment (IDE) for anything and nothing in particular. Eclipse represents one of the most exciting initiatives hatched from the world of application development in a long time, and it has the considerable support of the leading companies and organizations in the technology sector. Eclipse is gaining widespread acceptance in both the commercial and academic arenas.

The Eclipse Series from Addison-Wesley is the definitive series of books dedicated to the Eclipse platform. Books in the series promise to bring you the key technical information you need to analyze Eclipse, high-quality insight into this powerful technology, and the practical advice you need to build tools to support this evolutionary Open Source platform. Leading experts Erich Gamma, Lee Nackman, and John Wiegand are the series editors.

Titles in the Eclipse Series

John Arthorne and Chris Laffra, *Official Eclipse 3.0 FAQs*, 0-321-26838-5

Kent Beck and Erich Gamma, *Contributing to Eclipse: Principles, Patterns, and Plug-Ins*, 0-321-20575-8

Frank Budinsky, David Steinberg, Ed Merks, Ray Ellersick, and Timothy J. Grose, *Eclipse Modeling Framework*, 0-131-42542-0

Eric Clayberg and Dan Rubel, *Eclipse: Building Commercial-Quality Plug-Ins*, 0-321-22847-2

Steve Northover and Mike Wilson, *SWT: The Standard Widget Toolkit, Volume 1*, 0-321-25663-8

ECLIPSE ASPECTJ

Aspect-Oriented Programming with AspectJ and the Eclipse AspectJ Development Tools

Adrian Colyer,
Andy Clement,
George Harley,
and Matthew Webster

✦ Addison-Wesley

Upper Saddle River, NJ • Boston • Indianapolis • San Francisco •
New York • Toronto • Montreal • London • Munich • Paris • Madrid •
Capetown • Sydney • Tokyo • Singapore • Mexico City

The publisher offers excellent discounts on this book when ordered in quantity for bulk purchases or special sales, which may include electronic versions and/or custom covers and content particular to your business, training goals, marketing focus, and branding interests. For more information, please contact:

U. S. Corporate and Government Sales
(800) 382-3419
corpsales@pearsontechgroup.com

For sales outside the U. S., please contact:

International Sales
international@pearsoned.com

Visit us on the Web: www.awprofessional.com

Library of Congress Number:

2004111870

ISBN 0-32-124587-3
Text printed in the United States on recycled paper at Phoenix Color in Hagerstown, Maryland.
First printing, December 2004

To all the users of AspectJ & AJDT,
past, present, and future.

Contents

Preface   xv

Introduction   xvii

Part I ○ Introducing Eclipse, AspectJ, and AJDT   I

Chapter 1   *Getting Started*   3
             1.1   What Is Eclipse?   3
             1.2   Installing Eclipse   3
             1.3   Eclipse Basics   5
             1.4   Installing AJDT   11
             1.5   Examples for This Book   19
             1.6   Summary   20
Chapter 2   *First Steps in AJDT*   21
             2.1   A Simple Insurance Application   21
             2.2   Tracking Policy Updates   26
             2.3   Creating an AspectJ Project   29
             2.4   Creating the PolicyChangeNotification Aspect   34
             2.5   Stating the Notification Policy   37
             2.6   Implementing the Notification Policy   45
             2.7   Showing Advice In AJDT   50
             2.8   Evaluating the Implementation   54
             2.9   Finishing Touches   61
             2.10 Summary   62
Chapter 3   *Extending the Application*   65
             3.1   The Story So Far   66
             3.2   Serialization-Based Persistence   68
             3.3   Hibernating   84
             3.4   Managing Build Configurations   108
             3.5   Summary   110

Chapter 4   More AJDT   111
          4.1   Building an ASPECTJ Project   111
          4.2   Debugging   116
          4.3   Editor Templates and the Outline View Toolbar   123
          4.4   Generating Documentation (Ajdoc)   125
          4.5   AspectJ Help, Examples, and Cheat Sheets   127
          4.6   Summary   129

Part 2 ○ The AspectJ Language   **131**

Chapter 5   An Overview of AspectJ   133
          5.1   What Is An Aspect?   133
          5.2   Join Points and Pointcuts   136
          5.3   Advice   140
          5.4   Inter-Type Declarations   142
          5.5   Key Design Properties of the AspectJ Language   144
          5.6   Summary   146
                 References   146

Chapter 6   Straight to the Point   147
          6.1   The Calculator Program   147
          6.2   Introduction to Pointcut Designators   148
          6.3   The Method Call Pointcut Designator   149
          6.4   Pointcut Composition   155
          6.5   Patterns and Signatures   157
          6.6   The Method Execution Pointcut Designator   166
          6.7   The *Target* Pointcut Designator   170
          6.8   The *this* Pointcut Designator   176
          6.9   The *get* and *set* Pointcut Designators   179
          6.10 /Capturing Context with the *args*
                 Pointcut Designator   186
          6.11 Extracting Values with *this* and *target*   192
          6.12 The *handler* Pointcut Designator   195
          6.13 Initialization Pointcut Designators   198
          6.14 Static Scoping Pointcut Designators:
                 within, withincode   206
          6.15 Dynamic Scoping Pointcut Designators:
                 cflow, cflowbelow   209
          6.16 The *adviceexecution* Pointcut Designator   216
          6.17 The *if* Pointcut Designator   219
          6.18 How to Write a Good Pointcut   223
          6.19 Common Pitfalls   224
          6.20 Summary   227

Chapter 7   Take My Advice   229
             7.1   The Different Types of Advice   229
             7.2   Advice Parameters and Pointcuts   248
             7.3   Writing Logic in the Body of Advice   250
             7.4   Advice Ordering   256
             7.5   Softening Exceptions   265
             7.6   *declare warning* and *declare error*   267
             7.7   Common Pitfalls   269
             7.8   Summary   271
             References   271
Chapter 8   Inter-Type Declarations   273
             8.1   Fields, Methods, and Constructors   274
             8.2   Scope and Visibility   282
             8.3   Inter-Type Declarations and Interfaces   285
             8.4   Extending Classes   297
             8.5   Using Pointcuts and Advice with
                   Inter-Type Declarations   298
             8.6   Summary   299
Chapter 9   Aspects   301
             9.1   Aspect Definition and Initialization   301
             9.2   Aspect Instantiation   303
             9.3   Aspect Inheritance   318
             9.4   Inner Aspects   323
             9.5   Aspect Privilege   324
             9.6   Common Pitfalls   326
             9.7   Summary   327
Chapter 10   Using the AspectJ API   329
             10.1 Package *org.aspectj.lang*   330
             10.2 Package *org.aspectj.lang.reflect*   342
             10.3 Summary   353

Part 3 ○ Putting It All Together   355

Chapter 11   Adopting AspectJ   357
             11.1 The Adoption Process   357
             11.2 Different Types of Aspects   361
             11.3 Enforcement Aspect Examples   362
             11.4 Infrastructure Aspect Examples   374
             11.5 Core Aspect Examples   401
             11.6 Evaluating the Simple Insurance Application   412
             11.7 Summary   413
             References   413

Chapter 12   *Advanced AJDT*   *415*
            12.1   Aspect Libraries   415
            12.2   Linking Aspects with Compiled .class Files   427
            12.3   Ant Integration   433
            12.4   Aspect Visualization   436
            12.5   Summary   441
Chapter 13   *Aspect-Oriented Design*   *443*
            13.1   Finding Aspects   443
            13.2   What Makes a Good Aspect?   445
            13.3   Closing Thoughts   446
Appendix A   *Command-Line AspectJ*   *447*
            A.1   Installing AspectJ   447
            A.2   Using the Compiler   448
            A.3   Building with Ant   450
Appendix B   *AspectJ Language Quick Reference*   *453*
            B.1   Aspect Declaration   453
            B.2   Pointcuts   454
            B.3   Wildcards   457
            B.4   Advice   457
            B.5   Inter-Type Declarations   459
Appendix C   *Next Steps*   *461*
            C.1   Mailing Lists and FAQ   461
            C.2   Raising Bugs and Enhancement Requests   464
            C.3   Contributing to the Development of
                    AspectJ and AJDT   465
Appendix D   *AJDT Icons Reference*   *467*
            D.1   Objects   467
            D.2   Object Adornments   469
            D.3   Markers   469
            D.4   Build Configuration   470
        Index   471

Acknowledgments

We would like to thank the PARC team that created AspectJ, and especially those whom we have had a chance to work with personally on the AspectJ project: Gregor Kiczales, Jim Hugunin, Erik Hilsdale, Mik Kersten, and Wes Isberg. Mik Kersten has been involved in the development of AJDT since its inception and has made great contributions to both the implementation and the vision of what aspect-oriented development support in an IDE should be. Julie Waterhouse has contributed to the development of AJDT since its very first release. Ron Bodkin helped to organize the first AOP workshop in IBM Hursley that helped us build the initial business case for our investment in AOP.

We also thank all the supporters and users of AspectJ and AJDT; your involvement with the project has been a crucial part of what AspectJ is today. Thank you, too, to the reviewers and editors for making this a much better book than it would otherwise be.

Adrian thanks the IBM management team for showing enough belief in his crazy ideas to let him build a team and go after them. Most of all, he thanks his family—Sara, Rebecca, Elliott, and Derwent—for allowing him the time to work on this project. Like I didn't have enough to do already!

Andy thanks the Hursley AOSD team for helping us build a development tool worth writing about: Sian Whiting, Matt Chapman, Helen Hawkins, and Luzius Meisser. Most of all, he thanks Julie for supporting him while writing this book and even reviewing some of the text when she had no idea what aspects were.

George would like to thank Adrian, Andy, Matthew, Sian, Helen, Matt, and Luzius for putting up with him on a daily basis. Thanks also go out to the AspectJ team for their intelligence, good humor, and, of course, for creating something truly exceptional. An extra special debt of gratitude is owed to the very wonderful Katy, Eleanor, and Dylan, who put up with so much during the making of this book. I don't know where I would be without you.

Matthew would like to thank Adrian for his visionary leadership of the AOSD team and for inviting him to join it. He has learned so much in the past two years and thanks the whole team for their help. Also thanks to Robert Berry for his mentoring support during Extreme Blue 2002, where Matthew got his first real taste for AOP and Eclipse. Most importantly, he thanks Catherine for looking after him during this project.

About the Authors

ADRIAN COLYER is a senior technical staff member at IBM, the leader of the AspectJ Eclipse project, and co-founder of the AspectJ Development Tools (AJDT) for Eclipse project. Currently he leads an IBM team developing and applying aspect-oriented technology.

ANDY CLEMENT is a senior software developer at IBM's Laboratory at Hursley Park, a committer on the AspectJ project, and co-founder of the AJDT project. He is also involved in the use of aspects in J2EE middleware.

GEORGE HARLEY is a senior developer at IBM's Hursley Laboratory currently working on AJDT and deploying aspect technology in enterprise applications.

MATTHEW WEBSTER joined IBM in 1989 and is currently developing aspect-oriented technology for use with IBM products.

Preface

Aspect-oriented programming grew out of research at the *Palo Alto Research Center* (PARC) during the 1980s and 1990s. The first paper to use the term was aptly titled "Aspect-Oriented Programming" (Kiczales 1997) and published in June 1997. The first public release of AspectJ was in March 1998, almost seven years ago. Interest in *aspect-oriented programming* (AOP) and in AspectJ has been growing steadily ever since.

We still recall the excitement of seeing our first aspect-oriented programs run—it felt like magic! Today we spend our time both developing the tools needed for AOP with AspectJ and applying those tools to real-world problems. In the course of our work, we have had the privilege to introduce the ideas of AOP to many developers, architects, and executives. We have learned that seeing AspectJ in use is a vital part of understanding these new ideas. For this reason, when we talk to people about AOP, we also show what it is like to work with an aspect-oriented program using the Eclipse *AspectJ Development Tools* (AJDT). AJDT helps to visualize the behavior of AspectJ programs and reinforces understanding in a way that words alone cannot achieve.

Our goal for this book is to teach you everything you need to understand AOP and to apply it successfully on your own projects. To that end, we introduce the concepts of AOP, the AspectJ language, and the AJDT for Eclipse in a single integrated package. We hope that as you work through the examples in the book you will come to share our excitement at all that AOP has to offer.

References

Kiczales, G. et al., *Aspect-Oriented Programming*, Proceedings of the European Conference on Object-Oriented Programming (ECOOP), June 1997.

Introduction

This book is about AspectJ, the programming language, and *aspect-oriented programming* (AOP), a new way of thinking about program construction.

It is possible to write procedural-style programs in an object-oriented language (and many did), but it does not bring you the full benefit of object orientation. To really exploit object orientation requires changing the way you think about the program. In the same vein, AOP has the most beneficial impact when you allow it to begin changing your thought processes. Changing the way that you think about programs is not something that happens overnight, but we hope to help get you there a little quicker.

The remainder of this Introduction explains the motivation for AOP and gives a framework for thinking about what it is that AOP does. In the subsequent parts of the book, we introduce you to the AspectJ language, an effective way of expressing aspect-oriented programs, and the *AspectJ Development Tools* (AJDT), an efficient way of working with programs written in AspectJ.

Intended Audience

We assume that readers of this book are familiar with the Java programming language, but have little or no experience working with AspectJ. Some basic familiarity with the use of Eclipse for Java development will speed your learning, but is not essential for following the book.

From Requirements to Code

Imagine you are sitting down to write some code. You have some idea (we hope) of what it is the program has to do. You probably have a "design"—if not on paper, then at least in your head—some notion of the main features and functions that the program must support and how you might represent them in code. We argue that in the ideal mapping from these design-level thoughts to their source code implementation, each unique concept, each unique requirement, each unique entity in the problem domain would have a clear and simple one-to-one correspondence with an implementation construct.

For example, if the program needs to deal with monetary amounts, it is a good idea if the concept of money has a one-to-one mapping to a `Money` class. The `Money` class encapsulates everything the program needs to know about working with money. If the program needs to deal with customers, it is a good idea if the concept of a customer has a one-to-one mapping to a `Customer` class. If you have several different kinds of customer, perhaps these map into a `Customer` class hierarchy. In both cases, it is very clear which portions of the implementation correspond to the design-level notions of customers and money.

Having a clear and simple one-to-one mapping from design-level concepts to their source-code implementation helps in a number of ways. First, the program should be much simpler to understand. If you want to know "how does the program handle X," you can go to the X module and find the answer. Second, the program should be much simpler to maintain. The concepts and requirements at the design level correspond closely to the units of change over the program's lifetime. For example, if you need to be able to multiply monetary amounts, you can go to the `Money` class and add a multiply method. If you need to add support for a new kind of customer, you can add a new class to the customer hierarchy. If you no longer need to keep track of your customers' hair color, you can delete the `hairColor` attribute in the `Customer` class.

For some design-level requirements, however, it is very hard to get a clear one-to-one mapping with an implementation construct when using an *object-oriented* (OO) language. Consider, for example, the simple requirement that a view be notified whenever the state of a customer object it is displaying is updated. Typically that would not be implemented in a nicely encapsulated module, but instead would be implemented by fragments of code spread throughout the customer hierarchy. If you were to look inside the `Customer` class, you would see something like the code shown in Listing 1. The portions of the code that correspond to the "view notification" requirement are shown in bold.

Listing 1   Customer Change Notification

```
public class Customer {
  private Address address;
  private String lastName;
  private String firstName;
  private CustomerID id;
  private List listeners;

  public Customer(…) {…} // details omitted
```

```
public void addListener(CustomerListener listener) {
  listeners.add(listener);
}

public void removeListener(CustomerListener listener) {
  listeners.remove(listener);
}

public Address getAddress() { return this.address; }

public String getLastName() { return this.lastName; }

public String setLastName(String name) {
  this.lastName = name;
  notifyListeners(this);
}
// etc.

}
```

The Customer class has methods to add and remove listeners, and has calls to a notifyListeners method after every state-changing operation. The other classes in the customer hierarchy would also need to be sure to call notifyListeners every time they performed a state-changing operation.

What is happening here is that instead of a nice one-to-one mapping, there is a one-to-n mapping. One design-level requirement has ended up as n fragments of code. Sometimes in the AOP community you will hear this described as "scattering." There are lots of examples of one-to-n mappings that occur in real programs. Imagine, for example, a policy about how to handle SQL exceptions in a data access layer. There is one policy that describes what to do when a SQLException is thrown, but the implementation of that policy is spread throughout try-catch-finally blocks all over the code. Or imagine that you want to control concurrent access to a set of resources, allowing multiple readers and a single writer. Although this represents one design-level requirement, it manifests itself in a whole bunch of locks and calls to acquire and release spread throughout the reading and writing operations.

Whenever you see a one-to-n mapping from design-level concepts and requirements to implementation constructs, you can expect a number of problems:[1]

○ **It is harder to understand and reason about the implementation of the requirement**—You need to look in multiple places throughout the source code to get the full picture.

---

1. This list has its origins in the AspectJ Tutorial developed by the AspectJ team.

○ **It is harder to add the implementation of the requirement into the code base**—Care and attention to detail (something humans are not especially good at) is required to remember to add logic in every place it needs to be. Then, at each of these places, the implementation of the requirement needs to be done correctly. It is also harder to write good test cases for the implementation.

○ **It is harder to maintain the implementation**—If we want to change the way that calculations on monetary amounts are done, we can just go to the Money class. If we want to change the way we treat a SQLException in the data access layer, we have to be sure to find all the places that a SQLException is handled, and be sure to change them all consistently and correctly. This process can be both time-consuming and error-prone.

○ **It's harder to remove the implementation from the code base should the requirement go away**—The problems are the same as those involved in maintaining the implementation.

○ **It is harder to give the implementation task to a team member**—It is easy to ask someone to go away and write a Money class, but it is much harder to ask someone to go away and write "view notification" (because it touches on many of the classes that other programmers are working on).

○ **It is harder to reuse the implementation in another system**—It might be possible to reuse the design in another system, and some of the foundation services it relies on, but many of the implementation pieces are not modularized in a way that they can be easily extracted.

It is pretty rare to have a program that does exactly one thing. When you have multiple design concepts and requirements to be implemented, and some of those implementations have one-to-*n* mappings, you inevitably end up with a problem that is the flip side of the coin. You end up with source modules (typically classes in an OO language) that contain logic to do with multiple concepts and requirements. That is, you have an *n*-to-one mapping from design to implementation. The Customer class from Listing 1 exhibits a two-to-one mapping ratio: one single module (the Customer class) is implementing both the core customer concept and the "view notification" requirement. Sometimes in the AOP community you will hear this described as "tangling": The different implementation components have been tangled together inside a single module. The code fragment in Listing 2 is based on the logic for implementing a portion of a single design concept, entity bean passivation, inside one of IBM's application servers.

Listing 2   Entity Bean Passivation

```
try {
  if (!removed) entityBean.ejbPassivate();
  setState(POOLED);
} catch (RemoteException ex) {
  destroy();
  throw ex;
} finally {
  removed = false;
  beanPool.put(this);
}
```

It is easy to follow the logic of the implementation and understand what is going on. Listing 3 shows a version of the same code fragment, which is much closer to the *actual* implementation. Listing 3 illustrates some of the problems of tangling (*n*-to-one mappings). As well as the core passivation logic it has to deal with: the requirement that any exceptions be passed to an analysis engine for diagnosis; the requirement to output statistical information about the number of times the bean has been passivated; and the requirement to write trace records for the entry to and exit from the passivation method.

Listing 3   Tangled Entity Bean Passivation

```
try {
  if (!removed) entityBean.ejbPassivate();
  setState(POOLED);
} catch (RemoteException ex) {
  AnalysisEngine.processException(
      ex,"EntityBean0.ejbPassivate",
      "2078", this);
  destroy();
  throw ex;
} finally {
  if (!removed && (statisticsCollector != null)) {
    statisticsCollector.recordPassivation();
  }
  removed = false;
  beanPool.put(this);
  if (Logger.isEntryExitEnabled) {
    Logger.exit(tc, "passivate");
  }
}
```

Whenever you see an *n*-to-one mapping from design-level concepts and requirements to implementation constructs, you can expect a number of problems:

○ **It is harder to understand and reason about the code**—When you look at the code in Listing 3, it is much harder to see the true logic relating to entity bean passivation than in Listing 2.

○ **It is harder to maintain the implementation**—To maintain the implementation of any one of the concepts or requirements embodied in a source module, we have to disturb the implementations of all of them. This means that a developer maintaining, for example, the Customer class needs to be aware not only of the requirements of the customer, but also of the "view notification" requirement. Because the design-level concepts and requirements tend to represent units of change, and each will have its own rhythm of change, another consequence is that a module with an *n*-to-one mapping will be open for maintenance more often than a module with a one-to-one mapping. Anyone who has ever had cause to say "but I only changed the comments" will understand why this is an issue.

○ **It is harder to test the module**—For example, we want to test the Account class, but because it has logic to do with security checking tangled in its implementation, we need a security manager (or at least a mock version) to test the Account class. Testing the entity bean passivation logic requires the analysis engine, tracing, and statistics-gathering components to be on hand.

○ **It is harder to reuse the implementation of any one design-level concept or requirement, because it has a lot of other dependencies from the current system tangled in with it**—For example, it would be harder to reuse the Account class in a system that had a different security solution (or none at all).

Just as real programs of any size do not implement only a single concept or requirement, real programs of any size also do not consist of only a single module (or if yours does, you have bigger problems to sort out before you start worrying about AOP!). What we end up with then is not a one-to-*n* mapping, or an *n*-to-one mapping, but an *n*-to-*n* mapping between design-level concepts and requirements, and implementation constructs. We have strayed from our goal of a simple, clear, direct one-to-one mapping, and ended up with a complex tangled mess. If this happens to you, it is not your fault.[2] OO does not give us the tools we need to cleanly map all concepts and requirements into modular implementation constructs. This is the problem that AOP helps us to solve. AOP is about getting as close to a one-to-one mapping as we can. When we say that "AOP is about modularity" (rather than, say, interception), this is what we mean.

---

2. Or not entirely your fault anyway. It is still possible to create software with poor modularity even when you have good tools, but it can be very hard indeed to create software with good modularity when you have inadequate tools.

How Does AOP Work?

AOP gives us a new type of module, known as an *aspect*, that turns out to be excellent at taking one-to-*n* implementations of design-level concepts and requirements and turning them into one-to-one implementations. In a single aspect, I can implement the "view notification" requirement, removing the code to do with view notification from the customer hierarchy, and placing it into a module of its own. In a single aspect, I can implement a consistent policy for handling a `SQLException` throughout a data access layer. In another aspect, I can implement the logic required to give multiple readers, single-writer synchronization on resources. I can also use aspects to modularize the failure analysis, statistics gathering, and tracing implementations from Listing 3, and in so doing turn the core module for entity bean passivation back into that shown in Listing 2. Finally, I can use an aspect to implement the security requirements of the banking application, untangling them from the implementation of the `Account` class.

In the AOP community, features such as those previously listed that can be modularized in aspects are sometimes referred to as *crosscutting concerns*. There is one module, the aspect, but its implementation can affect many different points during the runtime execution of the program (every time a `SQLException` is handled, for example). Chapter 4 provides a more complete definition of a crosscutting concern.

Enriching the Programmer's Vocabulary

In OO analysis and design, we are taught to analyze the requirements statements and look for nouns and verbs. Nouns become candidate classes, and verbs become candidate methods on those classes. AOP enriches our vocabulary; among other things, it gives us a new may to modularize the implementation of adverbs and adjectives—a *secure* business transaction, a *permanent* record, a *thread-safe* class, a *billable* event. The reason adverbs and adjectives exist is that they define concepts that have a meaning independent of the nouns and verbs to which they apply. To phrase it another way, adverbs and adjectives represent concepts that can be applied to many different entities; they are a form of crosscutting concern. When you see an adverb or an adjective, you might be looking at a candidate aspect. We are not suggesting you go out and name an aspect "Secured," but the requirement for a *secured* resource might indicate the presence of a "Security" aspect. Likewise if you have a need for a *cached* result, this might indicate the presence of a "Caching" aspect. As in all things in design, this is not a black-and-white mapping—other candidate implementation techniques for adverbs and adjectives are subclasses and interfaces—and you will need to weigh the merits of each case individually. AOP does not replace OOP, it complements it.

Summary

AOP is about improving the modularity of your programs—getting as close to the ideal one-to-one mapping from design-level concepts and requirements to implementation constructs as you can. To help you do this, AOP gives you a new kind of module, known as an *aspect*, which you can use to modularize the implementation of a wide range of crosscutting concerns. AOP does not replace OOP; instead, it complements and builds on what OOP already offers us.

How the Rest of This Book Is Organized

The remainder of this book is divided into three parts. Part 1 is an introduction to AspectJ and AJDT, giving you a feel for what it is like to develop aspect-oriented programs with AspectJ. It introduces the concepts in a tutorial manner. Part 2 goes into more detail about the syntax and semantics of the AspectJ language, building on your knowledge from Part 1 and filling in some of the gaps. In Part 3, we discuss strategies for introducing AspectJ into your projects and your organization, some guidelines for its effective use, and some more examples of AspectJ at work. In the appendixes you will find a quick reference to AspectJ; a list of useful resources for learning more about AspectJ and about AOP in general; and even information on contributing to the development of Eclipse, AJDT, and AspectJ.

PART I

Introducing Eclipse, AspectJ, and AJDT

This part of the book is a practical introduction to Eclipse, AspectJ, and the AspectJ Development Tools (AJDT). It covers how to obtain and install all the software we will be using, and gives you a feel for what it is like to work with AspectJ within Eclipse. Chapter 1 introduces Eclipse and shows you how to install both AJDT and the sample projects that we will be using for the remaining chapters. In Chapter 2 we introduce the Simple Insurance application, write our first aspect, and learn about some of the basics of the AspectJ language. Chapter 3 goes a step further and adds persistence to the application—introducing more features of the language and tools along the way. Chapter 4 concludes this part of the book by looking at some of the AJDT features not already covered—including the answer to everyone's favorite question: "but what about debugging?"

As we work through Part 1, we introduce features of the AspectJ language in the context of the sample application. We explain just enough to enable you to follow along in the text. (Part 2 of the book provides the full details.) By approaching the material this way, the overview that you will gain in this part of the book provides the context for understanding the finer details when we get into them in Part 2 (and it is a lot more interesting than just plunging straight into syntax).

CHAPTER 1

Getting Started

This chapter introduces both the Eclipse platform and the *AspectJ Development Tools* (AJDT). For readers new to Eclipse, we first describe how to install Eclipse and create your first projects. If you are already familiar with installing and using Eclipse, you can skip to Section 1.4. With Eclipse installed, we next cover the addition of the AJDT to your Eclipse environment and show how you can install the samples used in this book.

1.1 What Is Eclipse?

Eclipse is a "universal tool platform—an open extensible IDE for anything and nothing in particular."[1] The Eclipse consortium was founded in November 2001, and grew rapidly in popularity. In early February 2004, it was announced by the Board of Stewards that Eclipse would be reorganized into a fully independent not-for-profit body called the Eclipse Foundation with a membership of more than 50 companies.

Eclipse is now a mature, freely obtainable open source software development platform that provides users with the necessary functionality to develop a wide range of applications. Many third-party tools (called *plug-ins*) work on the Eclipse platform, too. The open source nature of the Eclipse project means users can easily build and customize the platform for whatever purposes they might have.

1.2 Installing Eclipse

The starting point for getting ahold of Eclipse is always the Web site http://www.eclipse.org (see Figure 1.1). As far as all things to do with Eclipse are concerned, this is the center of the universe.

---

1. Eclipse home page, http://www.eclipse.org

Figure 1.1   The Eclipse.org home page.

On this site you can find links for in-depth articles, bug reporting, news groups, project source code repositories, and more, including download sites for the platform itself. The Eclipse project makes a variety of different builds available for download. This book is based on the Eclipse 3.0 release, built on June 25, 2004. Choose a mirror close to you and download the Eclipse SDK for your platform. The file will be named `eclipse-SDK-3.0-platform.archive-format` (for example, `eclipse-SDK-3.0-win32.zip` for Windows).

After the download has completed, just unzip the file into any directory on your local file system. You can find the Eclipse executable in the destination directory. On Windows systems, this is called eclipse.exe. On Linux, it is just called eclipse.

1.3   Eclipse Basics

To run Eclipse, all you need to do is run the eclipse executable in the install directory. Eclipse requires a Java runtime to be located somewhere on your path. If one
cannot be found, you will see a pop-up something like the one shown in Figure 1.2.

Figure 1.2   Missing Java runtime environment.

If you see a message such as this, ensure that you have a Java runtime
installed and have the JAVA_HOME environment variable set appropriately.
When Eclipse starts up, a splash screen like that shown in Figure 1.3 displays,
followed by the arrival of the main Eclipse window as shown in Figure 1.4.

Figure 1.3   Eclipse splash screen.

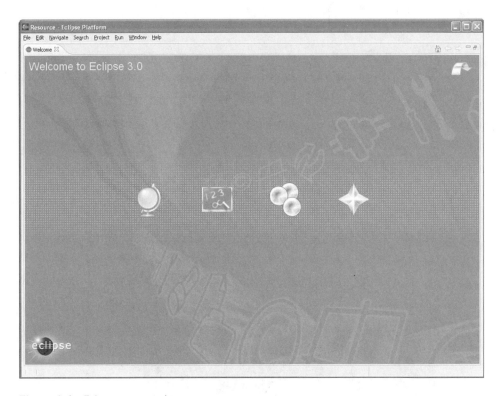

Figure 1.4 Eclipse main window.

If you ever want to get this Welcome page back again, you can do so by clicking **Help > Welcome** on the top menu bar. Clicking the **Overview** icon (the globe in the stand) and then **Workbench basics** will give you an overview of the basic Eclipse workbench. If you have not used Eclipse before, the help pages for the *Java Development Tools* (JDT), also found in the Overview section, will be well worth reading, too. A complete rundown of all the capabilities and configuration options of Eclipse is far beyond the scope of this book. The task at hand here is to quickly get you comfortable working in Eclipse before we move on to using AspectJ. So, with that in mind, let's set out on creating our first Java project.

1.3.1 A Simple Java Project in Eclipse

First we need to make Eclipse switch to using a Java perspective in the workbench so that the appropriate editor and views are visible. On the Welcome page, click the **Workbench** icon to open the workbench. Click the perspective-changer button, which is positioned at the top right of the window and, from the resulting menu, choose the **Java** option. Eclipse will open the Java Development perspective (an arrangement of views for working with Java programs). On the right of the workbench, you will see an Outline view of the source file being edited. On the left is a Package Explorer that enables you to navigate the contents of Java projects. At the bottom is the Problems view where compiler warnings and errors appear should your code step out of line.

Click the **New** button at the far left of the top toolbar to display the pop-up shown in Figure 1.5.

Figure 1.5   New wizard-selector pop-up.

Select the **Java Project** icon and then click the **Next** button. Enter **Hello World** as the project name. Accept the default directory for the project directory and click **Finish**. In the Package Explorer view, you will see that a new icon has appeared for your project. Expand the project-tree structure and you will find that it contains one entry, representing the libraries for the Java runtime to be used for the project.

The next step is to add a Java class to the project. In the Package Explorer view, right-click the "Hello World" project and select **New > Package** from the context menu. In the resulting pop-up dialog box, type in the name **hello**, and then click the **Finish** button (see Figure 1.6).

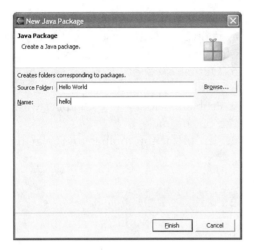

Figure 1.6   New Java Package wizard.

The Package Explorer should now show you that project Hello World contains an (empty) Java package called `hello`. Right-click the **Package** icon and select **New > Class** in the context menu. Give the class the name **HelloWorld** and select the option to create a main method stub (see Figure 1.7).

Figure 1.7   Creating the new Java class *hello.HelloWorld.*

Click the **Finish** button. Eclipse creates a new Java class called `hello.HelloWorld` for you, and opens up a new editor window for it, as shown in Figure 1.8.

```
/*
 * Created on 06-Jul-2004
 *
 * TODO To change the template for this generated file go to
 * Window - Preferences - Java - Code Style - Code Templates
 */
package hello;

/**
 * @author eclipse-user
 *
 * TODO To change the template for this generated type comment
 * Window - Preferences - Java - Code Style - Code Templates
 */
public class HelloWorld {

    public static void main(String[] args) {
    }
}
```

Figure 1.8   Java class *hello.HelloWorld* in the Editor view.

The Outline view should now look like Figure 1.9.

Figure 1.9   Java class *hello.HelloWorld* in the Outline view.

The Java class `HelloWorld` (the C icon tells us it is a class) is in the package `hello` (the full class name is therefore `hello.HelloWorld`), and has one public static method (the green circle signifies public; the small S decoration signifies static) called `main`. The tiny green arrow decoration just next to the C icon signifies that this class may be run because it has a main method.

Edit the Java file to look like the code in Listing 1.1, where we have removed the generated comments for clarity.

Listing 1.1   *hello.HelloWorld*

```
public class HelloWorld {
  public void saySomething(String message) {
    System.out.println(message);
  }

  private String getMessage() {
    return "Hello World!";
  }

  public static void main(String[] args) {
    HelloWorld hw = new HelloWorld();
    hw.saySomething(hw.getMessage());
  }
}
```

Eclipse automatically and incrementally compiles your project. Any compiler errors or warnings show up in the Problems view. Double-clicking a message in this view immediately positions your cursor on the offending line of source in your project.

To run `hello.HelloWorld`, select the class in the Package Explorer, and then click **Run > Run As > Java Application** from the menu bar at the top of the workbench. If it is not already visible, the Console view will open for you just under the Editor view, and the familiar output from the program will be written to it. As its name suggests, the Console view just presents all the data that would normally be written to the console window if your application were running in a command-line environment. To run the program again, just click the **Run** button (⊙).

You can set breakpoints in your code in the editor window by double-clicking in the gutter to the left of the source line you want to breakpoint.

To start the application in Debug mode, just click the **Debug** button on the top toolbar next to the **Run** button. Eclipse switches to the Debug perspective shown in Figure 1.10. The usual step-over, step-into, and so on buttons that you would expect to find in an IDE are located in the Debug view just under the top toolbar. You can inspect variable values in the Variables view to the right of the Debug view.

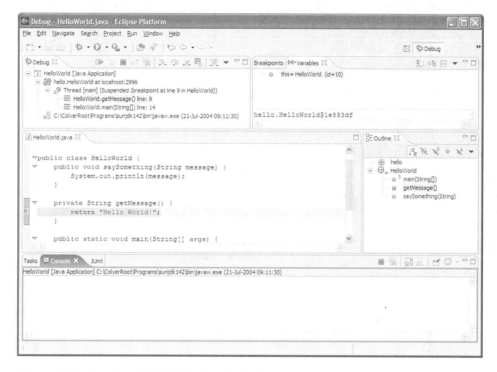

Figure 1.10 Java class *hello.HelloWorld* in the Debug perspective.

1.4 Installing AJDT

This section provides a brief background to the *AspectJ Development Tools* (AJDT) and describes how to install AJDT in your Eclipse environment.

AJDT is one of several subprojects of the Eclipse Technology Project,[2] which fosters the development of new technologies in line with the goals of the Eclipse platform. The AJDT project Web site is at http://www.eclipse.org/ajdt (see Figure 1.11). There you can find information on new releases as well as links to documentation, mailing lists, and even the project CVS repository.

---

2. http://www.eclipse.org/technology/index.html

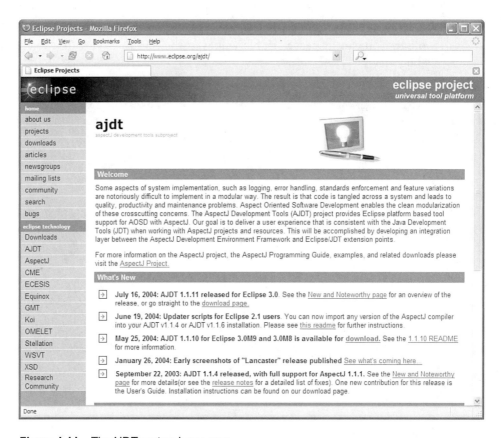

Figure 1.11   The AJDT project home page.

From the download page, you can obtain the latest available version of AJDT. This book is based on AJDT version 1.1.11. AJDT consists of a set of Eclipse modules known as *plug-ins*, which are packaged together into an installable unit called a *feature*, which you can install using the Eclipse Update Manager. Open the Update Manager by clicking **Help > Software Updates > Find and Install** in the top menu bar. A pop-up like that in Figure 1.12 will appear.

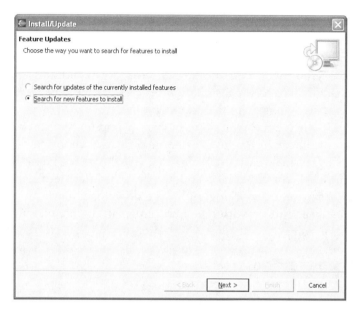

Figure 1.12 First steps in installing a new Eclipse feature using the Update Manager.

Select **Search for new features to install** and then click the **Next** button. In the subsequent panel, click the **New Remote Site** button (see Figure 1.13).

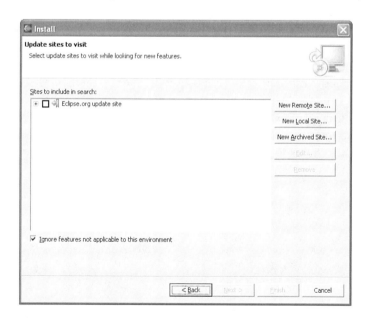

Figure 1.13 Adding a remote update site.

An update site is a location from where you can download and install new Features into your Eclipse. The content of an update site is in a format understood by the Update Manager, enabling it to display detailed information about the features discovered there, and to automate the download and installation process. The steps involved in the installation process are the same regardless of which operating system your Eclipse is running on.

After you click the **New Remote Site** button, a pop-up appears prompting you for the URL of the new site plus a name of your own choosing that can be associated with it (see Figure 1.14). Something like "AJDT Update Site" is a good choice. The URL for the AJDT update site can differ depending on the build of Eclipse that you are working with. The downloads page on the AJDT site will always be kept current with the latest information on which update site URL you should be using.

Figure 1.14   Entering a name and a URL for the new update site.

After clicking the **OK** button, you will see that a new update site location has been created for you. If not, check that your machine has a network connection and that Eclipse is aware of any proxy server settings needed to reach the update site from your current location. If you are behind a proxy server, you can set the server name and port number in an Eclipse preferences panel. Select **Window > Preferences** in the top toolbar and, in the pane on the left, select the **Install/Update** node. This will present you with a preferences page like that in Figure 1.15. The right hand of the panel will change to provide you with a check box for specifying that you have a proxy between you and the Internet. When this option is checked, fields for supplying the host address or name, plus port number, display.

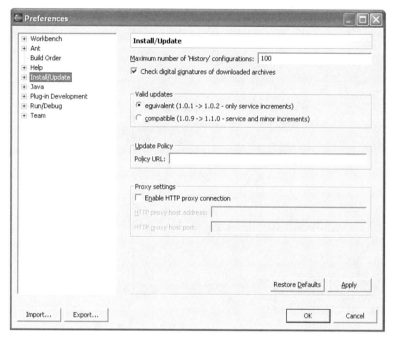

Figure 1.15   Preferences for installs and updates.

Irrespective of whether proxy settings affect you or not, after you have successfully defined the AJDT update site to Eclipse you will be able to select the named location in the **Update sites to visit** panel and expand it to see a list of all updates available at that location, as in Figure 1.16. What we have christened the AJDT Update Site has only one: AspectJ.

Figure 1.16   The AJDT update site.

Check the **AspectJ** site and then click the **Next** button to display all the features that you can install from the site (see Figure 1.17, which shows the AJDT 1.1.11 tools option).

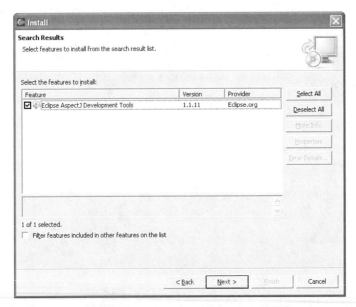

Figure 1.17   The list of features available from the AJDT update site.

Select the check box for the latest version of AJDT and click **Next** to read
and (hopefully) accept the Eclipse license. Provided you accept the terms of the
license, the next panel enables you to choose where to install AJDT, as shown in
Figure 1.18.

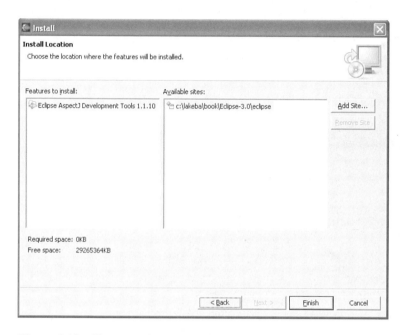

Figure 1.18   Choosing where to install AJDT.

Normally, just clicking the **Finish** button is all that is required here to download and install the features into your running Eclipse environment.

When the managed installation completes, Eclipse should be restarted. (You
will normally be prompted for this.) You can verify the success of the installation
by bringing up the Eclipse Welcome page with **Help > Welcome** and then
clicking the **Overview** icon. The ensuing page will now include an icon for
information on AspectJ development, as in Figure 1.19.

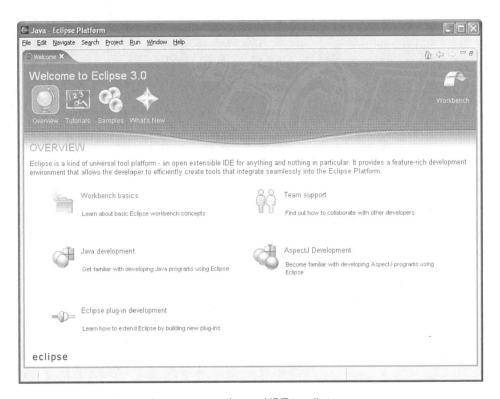

Figure 1.19 The Eclipse Overview page after an AJDT installation.

New entries are also added to the **Tutorials, Samples** and **What's New** pages. The AJDT documentation can be opened from the **Overview** page as shown in Figure 1.20.

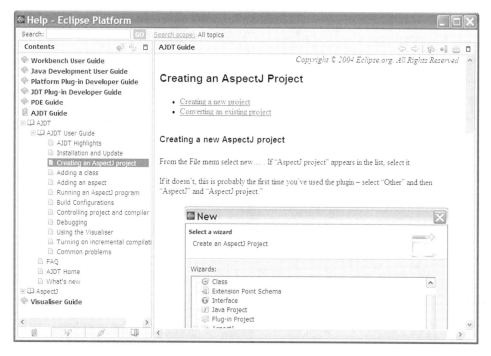

Figure 1.20 The AJDT help pages.

The AJDT documentation is split into two main topics. The first topic is the User Guide for the AJDT tools; the second is devoted to AspectJ itself and includes the AspectJ Programming Guide, the AspectJ Development Environment Guide, the AspectJ API Javadoc reference, and the FAQ. Documentation is also provided for the AJDT Visualiser—which is actually an independent and extensible plug-in in its own right. The Visualiser is discussed in Chapter 12.

1.5 Examples for This Book

Throughout this book you will encounter plenty of examples to aid you in using AspectJ in Eclipse. Because you have better things to do than type all these in by hand, we have created an Eclipse plug-in (what else?) that contains working source for all of these examples, split into their own AspectJ projects. After you deploy this Examples plug-in into your Eclipse, you can install all the contained projects into your workspace ready to investigate, experiment, or just to run them as you see fit.

To install the example, activate the Eclipse Update Manager that was discussed in the section on installing AJDT and add a new update site with the associated URL http://www.awprofessional.com/title/0321245873/update. Then proceed to install the Examples feature at that site as normal. After Eclipse has been automatically restarted, click the **New** button on the top toolbar and you will find a new folder called Eclipse AspectJ Book Examples in the resulting wizard-selector panel. Expand this folder to reveal a list of all the example projects featured in this book. Choose the project you want to work with, click the **Next** button and, after a page that enables you to change the name of the project if you want to (just click **Finish** to keep the default project name), the new AspectJ project will be there in your Package Explorer view.

If you encounter problems following the Update Manager route, the Examples plug-in is also available for downloading using a Web browser. You can find instructions for this on this book's Web site, www.awprofessional.com/title/0321245873.

1.6   Summary

This chapter covered how to install Eclipse and configure it for building Java applications. The AspectJ Development Tools can easily be added to an existing Eclipse installation using the Eclipse Update Manager. As you will discover in the next chapter, with AJDT installed it is trivial to convert an existing Java project to an AspectJ project and begin working with it.

In terms of what AspectJ and Eclipse have to offer, we have only really scratched the surface. To learn more about Eclipse, we encourage you to make use of the resources available at Eclipse.org and the documentation that ships with the platform itself.

CHAPTER 2

First Steps in AJDT

If you've been following along, then at this stage you should have a working Eclipse environment with AJDT installed. What we need now is an application we can use to do some AspectJ development. This chapter introduces a simple insurance application that we can use for this purpose. We show you how to convert the simple insurance Java project into an AspectJ project, discover all the places in the code to do with informing listeners whenever an insurance policy object is updated, and refactor all those code fragments into an aspect to give a modular implementation.

2.1 A Simple Insurance Application

Simple Insurers Inc. are considering going into business as no-frills, bargain-basement insurers. They have been developing a simple insurance application to underpin their new business venture and keep track of customers and policies. It is still early days, and the application is far from complete, but it implements just enough functionality to cover the first few user stories and get feedback from the internal customers to help plan the next iterations.

Figure 2.1 shows the Simple Insurance application project in Eclipse. It is just a regular Eclipse Java project at this stage. Notice in the Package Explorer (the view on the left side of the Eclipse window) that we have two source folders in the project, one named `src` and one named `test-src`. The `src` source folder contains the main application classes, and the `test-src` source folder contains the JUnit test cases.

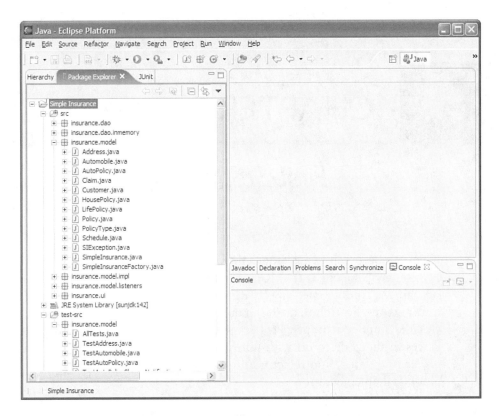

Figure 2.1 The Simple Insurance project in Eclipse.

If you installed the Eclipse AspectJ Examples plug-in following the instructions in Chapter 1, you can create the Simple Insurance project in your own workspace by clicking the **New** icon and selecting the Simple Insurance project from the Eclipse AspectJ Examples category (see Figure 2.2).

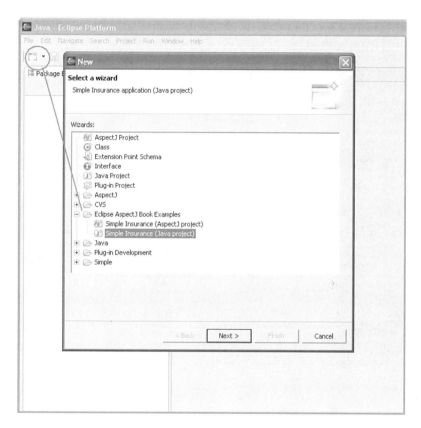

Figure 2.2   Installing the Simple Insurance project into your workspace.

It is a good idea at this point to run the test suite and make sure that nothing is amiss. We will be working primarily with the `insurance.model` and `insurance.model.impl` packages where the domain classes can be found. As shown in Figure 2.3, expand the `insurance.model` package node inside the `test-src` source folder and select the file `AllTests.java`. From the context menu (right-click) select **Run > JUnit Test**. If all goes well, you should be able to click the **JUnit** tab to bring the JUnit view to the foreground, and see a successful result as shown in Figure 2.4.

Figure 2.3 Launching the test suite.

Figure 2.4 A passing test suite—the JUnit view.

Figure 2.5 shows an overview of the classes in the Simple Insurers Inc. domain model (the `insurance.model` package).

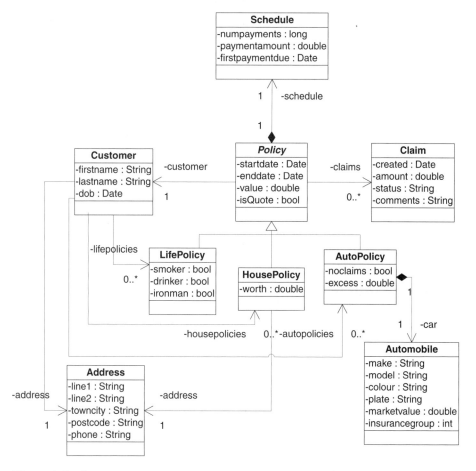

Figure 2.5   Simple Insurers Inc. domain model.

Simple Insurers Inc. will be offering three kinds of insurance policies when they first launch: life insurance, car insurance, and home insurance. Policies are taken out by customers, who pay for their insurance in accordance with some payment schedule. The model also has a facility to record claims made against policies, although worryingly there is no implementation yet to actually pay out on claims.

Simple Insurers Inc. will initially use telesales to market their insurance products, and agents at their company headquarters will have available to them a simple desktop application with which they can create, view, and update information on customers and policies. The user interface for this application is implemented in the `insurance.ui` package. You can launch the application from the Eclipse workbench by selecting the `SimpleInsuranceApp.java` file in the Package Explorer view, and then choosing **Run > Java Application** from the context menu. Figure 2.6 shows how the application looks when running.

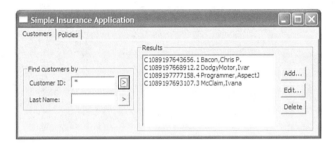

Figure 2.6   The Simple Insurers Inc. application.

2.2 Tracking Policy Updates

The user interface is connected to the model using a simple model-view-controller design. There is a simple `PolicyListener` interface that clients can implement, and after registering themselves with a policy, they will receive a `policyUpdated()` notification whenever the policy is updated. Figure 2.7 shows the `PolicyListener` interface in the editor. Figures 2.8 and 2.9 show excerpts from the `PolicyImpl` class. Notice in Figure 2.8 the calls to `notifyListeners` after updating the state of the `Policy` on lines 86 and 101.

```
PolicyListener.java

    package insurance.model.listeners;

    import insurance.model.Policy;


    public interface PolicyListener {
        void policyUpdated(Policy policy);
    }
```

Figure 2.7   *PolicyListener.*

```java
    /**
     * @param endDate The endDate to set.
     */
    public void setEndDate(Date endDate) {
        this.endDate = endDate;
        notifyListeners();
    }

    /**
     * @return Returns the endDate.
     */
    public Date getEndDate() {
        return endDate;
    }

    /**
     * @param value The value to set.
     */
    public void setValue(double value) {
        this.value = value;
        notifyListeners();
    }

    /**
     * @return Returns the value.
     */
    public double getValue() {
        return value;
```

Figure 2.8 Change notifications.

Figure 2.9 shows the code that keeps track of registered listeners and performs the actual notification.

```java
    /**
     * @param claim
     */
    public void removeClaim(Claim claim) {
        if (claim == null) {
            throw new IllegalArgumentException("Received a null claim!");
        }
        this.claims.remove(claim);
        notifyListeners();
    }

    public void addPolicyListener(PolicyListener l) {
        this.listeners.add(l);
    }

    public boolean removePolicyListener(PolicyListener l) {
        return this.listeners.remove(l);
    }

    protected void notifyListeners() {
        for (Iterator iter = listeners.iterator(); iter.hasNext();) {
            PolicyListener l = (PolicyListener) iter.next();
            l.policyUpdated(this);
        }
    }
}
```

Figure 2.9 Managing the listeners.

The various types of insurance policy all inherit the basic capability of managing a set of listeners from their parent `PolicyImpl` class, but each subclass has to be sure to call the `notifyListeners` method whenever it updates any of its own state. For example, the `AutoPolicyImpl` class keeps track of a no-claims bonus. If we look into the update method for the no-claims bonus, we will see the code shown in Listing 2.1, with a call to `notifyListeners()` duly made after updating the state.

Listing 2.1   Excerpt from *AutoPolicyImpl* Class

```
public void setNoClaims(boolean noClaims) {
    this.noClaims = noClaims;
    notifyListeners();
}
```

So far this strategy has been working okay, but now the business has asked us to consider adding support for pet insurance policies, too. Rather than keep adding more and more calls to `notifyListeners()` spread throughout the hierarchy, is there something better we can do? What we're looking at is a 1-to-*n* implementation: We have one simple requirement, to notify all registered listeners whenever a policy is updated, but an implementation that is scattered in *n* places throughout the policy hierarchy. To quote from the eXtreme programming discipline: "Refactor mercilessly to keep the design simple as you go and to avoid needless clutter and complexity. Keep your code clean and concise so it is easier to understand, modify, and extend. Make sure everything is expressed once and only once. In the end it takes less time to produce a system that is well groomed."[1] We said in the introduction that aspect-oriented programming offered us a new kind of a module, known as an *aspect*, that could help solve problems such as this and turn it back into a one-to-one mapping. In other words, we should be able to modularize the change notification policy inside an aspect. Instead of adding yet more scattered calls to `notifyListeners` in the new `PetPolicyImpl` class, perhaps we should consider refactoring.

---

1. http://www.extremeprogramming.org/rules/refactor.html

2.3   Creating an AspectJ Project

The first thing we need to do before we can start using AspectJ in the Simple Insurance application is to convert the Simple Insurance project from a plain Java project into an AspectJ project. Converting the project to an AspectJ project enables us to use the AspectJ language to implement the application, and the AspectJ compiler to build it.

2.3.1 Converting an Existing Java Project

Converting an existing Java project to an AspectJ project is simple. Select the project in the Package Explorer, and choose **Convert to AspectJ Project** from the context menu (see Figure 2.10). The AJDT Preferences Configuration Wizard may pop up during the conversion process; refer to the next section to learn more about it.

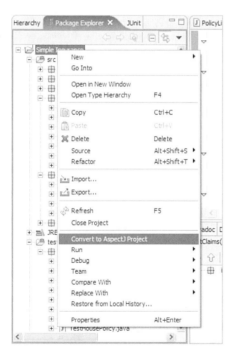

Figure 2.10   Converting from a Java project to an AspectJ project.

After performing the conversion, you will notice a couple of changes in the Package Explorer, as highlighted in Figure 2.11. First, the project icon has changed from the Java project icon (a folder with a J decoration, as shown in

Figure 2.10), to the AspectJ project icon (a folder with an AJ decoration). Second, a new jar file has been added to the project's build path, using the Eclipse path variable `ASPECTJRT_LIB`. This path variable is defined by the AJDT plugins to point to the AspectJ runtime library Jar file (aspectjrt.jar) shipped with AJDT. The AspectJ runtime library is a small library (about 35K) that all AspectJ programs need when they execute. This is the only runtime requirement for AspectJ—that aspectjrt.jar be somewhere on the class path—the AspectJ compiler produces regular Java class files that can be executed on any *Java Virtual Machine* (JVM) and look just like any other Java application to the JVM. Third, a new file called `build.ajproperties` has been created in the project. This file stores configuration information about the building of the project, which we look at in detail later.

Figure 2.11   An AspectJ project.

If you ever want to turn an AspectJ project back into a regular Java project, the process is equally simple: select the project in the Package Explorer and choose **Remove AspectJ Nature** (see Figure 2.12). See the sidebar "Eclipse Builders and Natures" if you are curious as to what goes on when a project is converted to an AspectJ project and back again.

Figure 2.12   Converting an AspectJ project back into a Java project.

Eclipse Builders and Natures

Projects in Eclipse have one or more project natures associated with them. A project nature tells the rest of the world what kind of capabilities the project has. Java projects have the Java nature, and tools that work with Java programs can offer their workbench contributions for working with those projects. AspectJ projects have both the Java nature **and** the AspectJ nature, so Java tools should continue working, but they also benefit from the AspectJ specific tools too. Builders are closely associated with natures. Normally when a nature is added to a project, it installs a project builder. Projects can have multiple builders, just as they can have multiple natures. Java projects use the Java builder (the Eclipse Java compiler), but AspectJ projects use the AspectJ builder. When you convert a Java project to an AspectJ project, the AspectJ nature is **added** to the project, and the Java builder is **replaced** with the AspectJ builder (any other builders defined for the project are left alone). When you remove the AspectJ nature from a project, the AspectJ nature is removed, and the AspectJ builder is replaced with the Java builder. Of course, if you have AspectJ-specific artifacts in your projects, you might get build errors when the Java builder encounters them.

2.3.2 Configuring the Workbench for AspectJ Development

The very first time you activate the AspectJ tools inside a workspace (for example, by converting a project to an AspectJ project, or by creating a new AspectJ project) you will see the AJDT Preferences Configuration Wizard appear (see Figure 2.13).

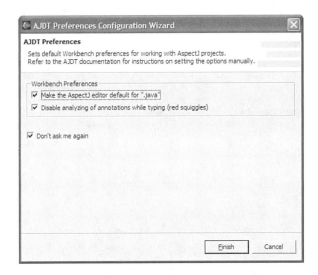

Figure 2.13   AJDT Preferences Configuration Wizard.

This wizard offers to make two configuration customizations for you that will make working with AspectJ inside Eclipse a much more pleasant experience:

Make the AspectJ editor default for ".java"   The standard Java editor that is associated with .java files does not understand the extra keywords that AspectJ introduces, and neither does the Outline view associated with it understand aspect constructs. Choosing this customization makes the AspectJ editor be associated with .java files by default. The AspectJ editor is an extension of the Java editor offering all of the Java editor features, plus the capability to understand AspectJ programs.

Disable analyzing of annotations while typing   The Java Development Tools include an eager parser that analyzes your program as you type, giving you early indications of problems you will have when you compile the code. This eager parser does not understand AspectJ; hence it incorrectly reports errors (the infamous "red squiggles") in your AspectJ program, which can be distracting. Figure 2.14 shows an example of the problem

The eager parser does not recognize the type `AnAspect` (because aspects are not present in the type-space that it uses for name resolution), and so highlights it as a problem when in fact the AspectJ compiler will build the source file perfectly fine. Selecting this customization deactivates the eager parsing. The AJDT development team is working on an update to the tools support that enables the eager parser to understand AspectJ constructs, too. When this new version is available, it will be possible to turn the "analyze annotations while typing" option back on again for AspectJ programs.

```
11▽public class TestLifePolicyChangeNotification extends TestCa
12
 13        private AnAspect a;
14        private LifePolicy policy;
15        private TestPolicyChangeNotification.PolicyChangeListene
16
17
18▽    public void testSmokerNotification() {
```

Figure 2.14 Don't get the red squiggles; disable "analyze annotations while typing."

2.3.3 Creating a New AspectJ Project

Of course, it is also possible to create a new AspectJ project from scratch without converting an existing Java project. To do this, you use the New AspectJ Project Wizard. You can reach the wizard via the Eclipse workbench menus by selecting **File > New > Project**, and then **AspectJ Project**. Alternatively, use the **New** icon on the toolbar and select **AspectJ Project** from there (see Figure 2.15).

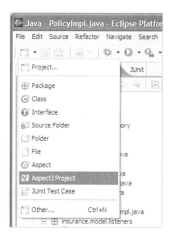

Figure 2.15 Launching the New AspectJ Project Wizard.

When the wizard launches, the dialog box shown in Figure 2.16 displays. It behaves exactly like the New Java Project wizard, except that the project it creates at the end is an AspectJ one.

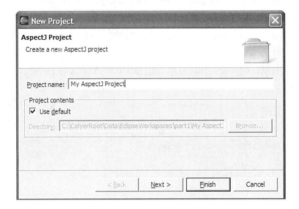

Figure 2.16   The New AspectJ Project Wizard.

2.4   Creating the PolicyChangeNotification Aspect

The Simple Insurance project is now ready for use with AspectJ. It was automatically built by the AspectJ compiler when we converted it to an AspectJ project, so now would be a good time to run the test suite again and verify that the AspectJ compiler has indeed built the project correctly. The tests should all pass correctly.

We are ready to begin the refactoring. Recall that we want to replace the calls to `notifyListeners` that are scattered throughout the policy class hierarchy with a modular implementation in an aspect. Just as to create a new class we would use the New Class Wizard, so to create a new aspect we use the New Aspect Wizard.

2.4.1 The New Aspect Wizard

We want to create an aspect in the `insurance.model.impl` package where the policy implementation classes are defined. Select the `insurance.model.impl` package in the Package Explorer, and from the context menu choose **New > Aspect**. This launches the New Aspect Wizard, as shown in Figure 2.17. (You can also get to this wizard from the **File > New** workbench menu, and the **New** icon on the toolbar.)

New Aspect Wizard

Create a new Aspect
Creates a new aspect within the current project

Source folder:	Simple Insurance/src	Browse...
Package:	insurance.model.impl	Browse...
Enclosing type:		Browse...

Name:	PolicyChangeNotification
Modifiers:	☑ public ☐ abstract ☐ final ☐ privileged ☐ static
Supertype:	java.lang.Object
Interfaces:	

Add...

Remove

Which method stubs would you like to create?
☐ public static void main(String[] args)

Finish   Cancel

Figure 2.17 The New Aspect Wizard.

Notice that the New Aspect Wizard is very similar to the New Class Wizard. The source folder and package fields are prefilled because we launched the wizard from the context menu of the package in the Package Explorer. We just need to provide a name for the aspect and then click **Finish**. Because the aspect is going to encapsulate the implementation of policy-change notification, we have called it `PolicyChangeNotification`. Upon completion of the wizard, the aspect is created and opened in the editor, as shown in Figure 2.18.

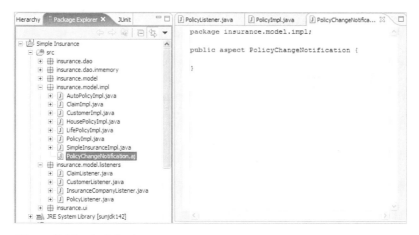

Figure 2.18 A skeletal aspect.

In the Package Explorer, you can see that the wizard has created a new source file called `PolicyChangeNotification.aj`. AJDT uses the .aj extension for source files containing aspects, but you can configure it to use .java instead if you prefer. See the sidebar "Choice of File Suffix: .java or .aj"

In the editor, you can see the basic form of an aspect. Notice that it looks just like a class definition, except that it uses the `aspect` keyword in place of the keyword `class`. In AspectJ, aspects are first class entities in the program just as classes are. There are a lot of similarities between aspects and classes—in fact pretty much anything you can declare in a class you can declare in an aspect, too, but aspects can also do things that classes cannot do. We look at some of those things in Section 2.5.

If you have the Outline view open (**Window > Show View > Outline**), you will see an outline like that shown in Figure 2.19. This shows us that the source file contains no import declarations (the package statement and any import declarations work in exactly the same way for an aspect as they do for a class), and a single aspect with no members.

Figure 2.19   The Outline view.

Chapter 9 provides full details on aspects in AspectJ, but you already know a surprising amount because of your familiarity with classes in Java. You certainly know enough to continue following the examples in this chapter, so let's move on and make our `PolicyChangeNotification` aspect do something useful.

Choice of File Suffix: .java or .aj

The AspectJ compiler doesn't care whether you name your source files with the .aj extension or with the .java extension—it treats them both equally. So you could name all your source files with the .aj extension, or all with the .java extension, or with any combination of the two, and it wouldn't make any difference. It does make a difference, however, if you convert an AspectJ project back to a Java project for some reason. The Java compiler ignores files with an .aj extension, which can make the move easier (but you're still going to have to cope with the fact that all the functions your aspects were implementing are now missing). However, using the .aj extension for files containing regular Java classes has the consequence that the types defined in them are not visible to Eclipse's Java model. By default therefore, AJDT creates new classes in source files with a .java extension, and new aspects in source files with an .aj extension. If you want to change this behavior, you can do so via the AspectJ project Properties page accessible via the **Properties** option in the context menu when a project is selected.

2.5   **Stating the Notification Policy**

How will we know whether our refactoring has succeeded? All the tests will pass, of course, but they do that now. The problem we want to address is the duplication and scattering of calls to `notifyListeners` throughout the policy hierarchy. If our refactoring is a success, there will be no calls to `notifyListeners` left in the policy hierarchy, and they will all have been replaced by a single call in the `PolicyChangeNotification` aspect. AspectJ enables us to capture requirements such as this directly in the code, and in this section you learn how. To do that, we need to introduce you to a couple of new concepts: join points and pointcuts.

2.5.1 *Introducing Join Points*

Programs live to execute, and when they execute, stuff happens. Methods get called, objects get initialized, fields are accessed and updated, constructors are executed, and so on. AspectJ calls these events that happen when a program is running *join points*. If program execution was a spectator sport, and you were commentating on the 2006 world championships, join points are the things that you would highlight in your commentary:

```
Bob: Looks like we're in for a good clean run today.
Jim: Yes Bob, the classes are being fetched from disk now; I
can't wait for this one to get started.
Bob: We're off! The main class is loaded and the static
initializer just ran.
```

```
Jim: A traditional opening, executing the main method now
...
Bob: Hmmm, accessing the "out" field on the old System
class—think he's going for the System.out.println routine
Jim?
Jim: It does look that way, Bob. Ah, yes, look—calling the
println method, and that's a nice String there in the
arguments.
Bob: So, the println method is executing, you can almost
feel the tension. Here it comes … there's an H, an E, …
Jim: It is, it is, it's "Hello, World!". Very nicely done.
Safely back from the call to println.
Bob: Seems like the execution of the main method is just
about done.
Jim: They think it's all over … It is now.
```

AspectJ supports join points for calls made to methods and constructors, for the actual execution of methods and constructors, for the initialization of classes and objects, for field accesses and updates, for the handling of exceptions, and a few more besides. Chapter 5 provides a more thorough introduction to join points.

Join points by themselves aren't all that exciting. Stuff has always happened when programs are executed. What is different in AOP and in AspectJ is that the programmer has a way to refer to join points from within the program. A way to say things such as, "Whenever you update the state of a policy object, notify all of its listeners." To the AspectJ compiler, that sentence looks a little bit more like this: "Whenever a join point that meets these conditions occurs (we'll call that a `policyStateUpdate` shall we?), call the `notifyListeners` method on the policy object."

2.5.2 Writing a Pointcut

The way that we specify which join points we are interested in is to write a *pointcut*. Pointcuts are like filters; as the program executes, a stream of join points occur, and it is the job of a pointcut to pick out the ones that it is interested in.[2] The join points we are interested in right now are those that represent a call to the `notifyListeners()` method. When we make such a call, we are notifying the listeners. Here is what the pointcut declaration looks like in AspectJ:

```
pointcut notifyingListeners() :
  call(* PolicyImpl.notifyListeners(..));
```

---

2. This is just a conceptual model of how it works; the actual implementation as generated by the AspectJ compiler is much more efficient than this.

Figure 2.20 shows the result of typing this into the aspect editor buffer and pressing **Ctrl+S** to save.

Figure 2.20 A pointcut declaration.

The syntax highlighting shows us that `pointcut` and `call` are keywords in the AspectJ language. Also note that the Outline view has updated to show the pointcut as a member of the aspect (just like a field or a method is a member of a class). We can use the Outline view to navigate in the editor buffer by selecting the nodes in the tree. For example, if we click the `notifyingListeners()` node in the Outline view, the selection in the editor is changed to the pointcut declaration, as shown in Figure 2.21.

Figure 2.21 Using the Outline view to navigate in the editor buffer.

The pointcut declaration declares a new pointcut called `notifyingListeners` (the name that appears in the Outline view). After a colon (:), comes the definition of which join points the `notifyingListeners` pointcut should match. In this case we are interested in join points that represent a call to certain methods. Inside the parentheses that follow the `call` keyword, we get to say which particular method calls we want to match: calls to the `notifyListeners` method defined in the `PolicyImpl` class. The first asterisk (*) in the expression is a wildcard that says we don't care what the return type of the method is, and the two periods (..) inside the `notifyListeners(..)` say that we don't care what arguments it takes. We know both of these things: The `notifyListeners` method takes no parameters and returns void, but they are not pertinent to our pointcut—if the definition of the `notifyListeners` method were to change to take a parameter, or to return the number of listeners notified, we would still want the pointcut to match. By not specifying the details we don't care about, we make our program more robust in the face of change.

Chapter 6 explains everything you ever wanted to know about pointcuts and more; all that matters for the time being is that you get a feel for what a pointcut declaration looks like and what it does.

2.5.3 Using Declare Warning

This is all very nice, but the aspect still doesn't actually *do* anything. At the start of this section, we said that if our refactoring is a success, there will be no calls to `notifyListeners` left in the policy hierarchy, and they will all have been replaced by a single call in the `PolicyChangeNotification` aspect. So any call to the `notifyListeners` method that does not occur within the `PolicyChangeNotification` aspect breaks the modularity that we are trying to achieve. It would be useful at this point if we could find all such places. We can use an AspectJ construct known as *declare warning* to do just that. Let's declare it to be a compile time warning if anyone other than the `PolicyChangeNotification` aspect starts `notifyingListeners`. We can write it like this:

```
declare warning :
  notifyingListeners() && !within(PolicyChangeNotification)
  : "Only the PolicyChangeNotification aspect should be
    notifying listeners";
```

Figure 2.22 shows what happens when we type this into the editor buffer and press **Ctrl+S** to save.

```
PolicyListener.java      PolicyImpl.java      PolicyChangeNotification.aj

   package insurance.model.impl;

   public aspect PolicyChangeNotification {

       pointcut notifyingListeners() :
           call(* PolicyImpl.notifyListeners(..));

       declare warning :
         notifyingListeners() && !within(PolicyChangeNotification)
         : "Only the PolicyChangeNotification aspect should be notifying listeners";

   }
```

Figure 2.22   Declare warning in the editor buffer.

We can see again from the syntax highlighting that `declare warning` is a keyword (pair of keywords to be precise) in the AspectJ language. The general form of the statement is this: "Declare it to be a compile-time warning, if any join point matching the following pointcut expression occurs, and this is the warning message I'd like you to use." In this particular case: "Declare it to be a compile-time warning, if any join point occurs that matches the `notifyingListeners` pointcut and is not within the `PolicyChangeNotification` aspect. At such points, issue a compile-time warning with the message 'Only the `PolicyChangeNotification` aspect should be notifying listeners.'"

If we turn our attention to the Outline view, we can see that something very interesting has happened, as shown in Figure 2.23.

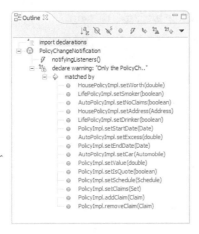

Figure 2.23   Declare warning matches in the Outline view.

First of all, you can see that the declare warning appears in the Outline view
as another kind of member within the aspect. There's also a plus sign (+) next to the
declare warning node, indicating that there is content beneath it. If you expand
this node you see matched by, and if you expand that node you see a list of all the
places that are violating our policy of not calling notifyListeners outside of the
PolicyChangeNotification aspect. There are 15 of them, and these nodes are
actually hyperlinks that will take you directly to the offending statements in the program source code if you click them. Let's click the first entry in the list,
HousePolicyImpl.setWorth. The editor opens on the HousePolicyImpl class, at
the point where the call to notifyListeners is made, as shown in Figure 2.24.

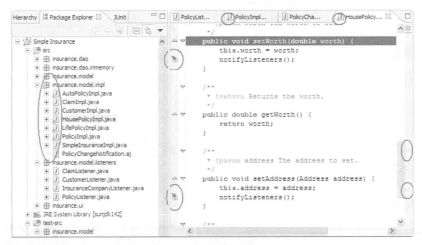

Figure 2.24   Showing warnings in the workbench.

In the gutter of the editor buffer, next to the call to `notifyListeners`, you can see a warning icon. There are also warning decorations on the file icons for all the source files in which warnings have been found, as you can see in the Package Explorer, and in the titles of the files at the top of the Editor window. The gutter to the right of the editor buffer gives an overview of the whole source file. It shows us that there are two warnings in the file, one on the line we are looking at, and one farther down in the source file. Hovering over the warning in the editor brings up the tool tip shown in Figure 2.25.

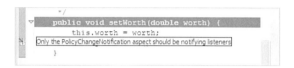

Figure 2.25   Hover help for declared warnings.

You can clearly see the text of our declare warning—a powerful way to get a message across to a programmer who inadvertently violates the intended encapsulation of change notification in the aspect. Having navigated to the `HousePolicyImpl.java` file using the Outline view, we can click the back button on the toolbar (see Figure 2.26) to go back to the `PolicyChangeNotification` aspect again. In this way, we can easily navigate back and forth.

Figure 2.26   Navigating back to the aspect.

Just in case you weren't getting the message that there are violations of the `PolicyChangeNotification` aspect's change notification rule by now, take a look at the Problems view as shown in Figure 2.27. You will see that a compiler warning message has been created for each join point that matches the pointcut we associated with the "declare warning" statement. These are just like any other compiler warning, and you can double-click them to navigate to the source of the problem.

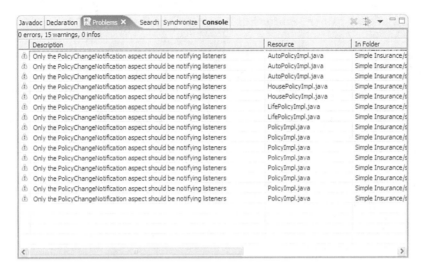

Figure 2.27   We've got problems!

When we have successfully completed the refactoring, none of these warnings should remain.

How Can You Match Join Points at Compile Time?

The more astute readers will have noticed a slight anomaly in the descriptions we just gave in this section. Join points are events that occur during the runtime execution of a program, so how can a pointcut match any join points at compile time when the program isn't running? The answer is that it doesn't; but what the compiler can do, is look at a line of code containing a call to the `notifyListeners` method and say "when this program executes, that line of code is going to give rise to a join point that will match this pointcut." It is the results of this static analysis that display as warnings. Chapter 6 covers some kinds of pointcut expressions that cannot be fully evaluated at compile time. (They require a runtime test to confirm the match.) These kinds of pointcut expressions cannot be used with the declare warning statement (which obviously needs to know at compile time whether or not there is a match).

2.6   **Implementing the Notification Policy**

Section 2.5 showed you how to declare how you would like the world to be. This is the section were we get to make it that way. Remember that when we started on this journey, we had the simple requirement that whenever the state of a policy is updated, we should notify all of its listeners. It seems that a useful next step would be to write a pointcut that captures all the join points where the state of a policy is updated. We could call it `policyStateUpdate`:

```
pointcut policyStateUpdate() :
   execution(* set*(..)) && this(PolicyImpl);
```

This pointcut defines a `policyStateUpdate` to be the execution of any method whose name begins with "set," returning any value and taking any arguments. In addition, the object executing the method must be an instance of `PolicyImpl`. Because we have been following the JavaBeans naming convention in our domain model, this pointcut matches the set of state-updating methods in the policy class hierarchy very well. If we type this pointcut declaration into the editor buffer and save it, the editor should now look like Figure 2.28.

Figure 2.28   Adding the *policyStateUpdate* pointcut.

We have a way of matching all the join points where the state of a policy is updated. Now all we need to do is find a way to specify some action to take at those join points (notifying listeners). What we need is *advice*.

2.6.1 Introducing Advice

Pointcuts match join points, but advice is the means by which we specify what to do at those join points. AspectJ supports different kinds of advice—*before* advice enables you to specify actions to take before a matched join point, *after* advice enables you to specify actions to take after a matched join point, and *around* advice gives you complete control over the execution of the join point. In our case we want to notify listeners after returning from a `policyStateUpdate`:

```
after() returning : policyStateUpdate() {
  // do something
}
```

Figure 2.29 shows what happens when we type this into the editor buffer and save it. You can see that `after` and `returning` are AspectJ keywords. Also notice the similarities between the advice block and a method—both can take parameters (although we have none here yet), and both specify a block of code to execute when they are called. A key difference though is that methods are called explicitly, whereas the advice is implicitly invoked by AspectJ whenever a join point matching its associated pointcut expression occurs. Chapter 7 contains a full discussion of advice in AspectJ.

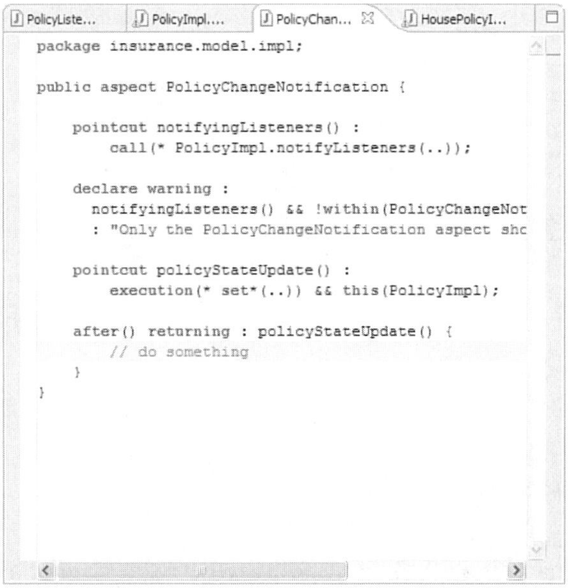

Figure 2.29   Adding advice to the aspect.

2.6.2 Calling the Notify Method

Finally we get to implement the advice body and put in the call to `notifyListeners`. All we need to do is put in a call to `policy.notifyListeners()` in the body of the advice:

```
after() returning : policyStateUpdate() {
  policy.notifyListeners();
}
```

If we enter this into the editor buffer, and save, the compiler tells us that there is a small problem with our implementation as it stands (see Figure 2.30). "policy" cannot be resolved, the variable is not defined. How can the advice get ahold of the policy object whose state has just been updated?

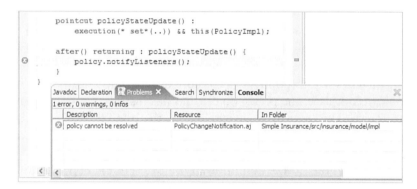

Figure 2.30   "policy cannot be resolved."

We need to pass the policy object into the advice as a parameter, which is done in the same way as specifying parameters for methods:

```
after(PolicyImpl policy) returning : policyStateUpdate() {
  policy.notifyListeners();
}
```

Let's try that out in the editor. Figure 2.31 shows the result: a "formal unbound in pointcut" error.

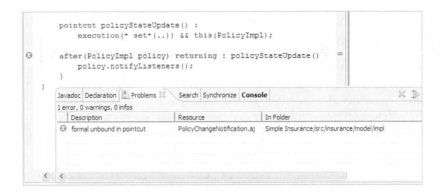

Figure 2.31   Formal unbound in pointcut.

What could that mean? Recall that unlike a method, there are no explicit calls to advice. So if you do not call the advice explicitly, passing in the parameters it needs, from where does the advice get its parameter values? The answer is that the advice parameter values have to be provided by the pointcut: When the pointcut matches a join point, it needs to extract some information from that join point (in our case, the policy object that has just been updated), and pass it into the advice. The error message is telling us that the "formal" (advice parameter) is not "bound" in the pointcut—or to put it another way, the pointcut is not giving the advice the parameter it needs yet.

Take another look at the definition of the `policyStateUpdate` pointcut:

```
pointcut policyStateUpdate() :
   execution(* set*(..)) && this(PolicyImpl);
```

This matches any join point that is the execution of a method whose name begins with "set," where the currently executing object (the object bound to "this" within the method body) is an instance of `PolicyImpl`. What we need is for the pointcut to tell us not just whether the currently executing object is an instance of `PolicyImpl`, but which instance it is. The set of values provided by a pointcut when it matches a join point is specified in its parameter list:

```
pointcut policyStateUpdate(PolicyImpl aPolicy) : ...
```

(So that's what those parentheses after the pointcut name are for!) Now it just remains to specify where the value of the policy parameter comes from. This is done via name binding in the pointcut expression:

```
pointcut policyStateUpdate(PolicyImpl aPolicy) :
  execution(* set*(..)) && this(aPolicy);
```

This revised pointcut expression matches the same join points as the previous version (the execution of any method whose name begins with "set," and where the object executing the method is an instance of `PolicyImpl`), but also makes available the actual `PolicyImpl` object at each join point it matches.

We are nearly there now; we just need a way to say that the policy object provided by the pointcut when it matches a join point should be matched to the `policy` parameter we specified in the advice definition. This is done by name binding, too:

```
after(PolicyImpl policy) returning :
  policyStateUpdate(policy)
{
  policy.notifyListeners();
}
```

If we make these changes in the editor buffer, the aspect compiles successfully. Figure 2.32 shows the completed aspect in the editor.

```
 PolicyListener.java    PolicyImpl.java    PolicyChangeNotification.aj    HousePolicyImpl.java

  package insurance.model.impl;

  public aspect PolicyChangeNotification {

      pointcut notifyingListeners() :
          call(* PolicyImpl.notifyListeners(..));

      declare warning :
        notifyingListeners() && !within(PolicyChangeNotification)
        : "Only the PolicyChangeNotification aspect should be notifying list

      pointcut policyStateUpdate(PolicyImpl aPolicy) :
          execution(* set*(..)) && this(aPolicy);

      after(PolicyImpl policy) returning : policyStateUpdate(policy) {
          policy.notifyListeners();
      }
  }
```

Figure 2.32   The completed *PolicyChangeNotification* aspect.

The next section shows you how you can use the tools to understand the effect of the advice that we just wrote.

2.7   Showing Advice In AJDT

AJDT contains a lot of features designed to help you understand and be aware of the effects of advice in your program. The primary means are the editor and Outline view, but there is also a visualization view and the capability to generate documentation.

2.7.1 The Outline View

Let's look at the Outline view for the `PolicyChangeNotification` aspect. This is shown in Figure 2.33, with the node for the after returning advice fully expanded. Notice how the Outline view shows us all the places that the advice advises. To be slightly more precise, the Outline view is showing us all the places in the program source code that will give rise to a join point at runtime that will be matched by the pointcut expression associated with the advice. Just like the declare warning matches in the Outline view, these matches are links, too. If you click one, it will take you to the corresponding source location.

Figure 2.33   Showing the effect of advice in the Outline view.

If we click the first match in the list, `HousePolicyImpl.setWorth` `(double)`, the editor opens on the source file containing the definition of the `HousePolicyImpl` class, at the `setWorth` method. The Outline view updates to display the outline for the `HousePolicyImpl` class, as shown in Figure 2.34.

The node for the `setWorth` method has been expanded, and we can see that it has been "advised by" the after returning advice in the `PolicyChangeNotification` aspect. The `setAddress` method has also been advised, the plus sign (+) next to its node in the tree view gives us a cue, and if we expanded it we would see the "advised by" relationship as we do for `setWorth`. Once again the entries shown under "advised by" are hyperlinks that can be used to navigate to the definition of the advice affecting the method, simply by clicking.

Figure 2.34   An advised method in the Outline view.

2.7.2 The Editor

Now let's look at the editor buffer we just opened on `HousePolicyImpl.java`. This is shown in Figure 2.35. There are two key points to note in this figure. First, in the left margin next to the `setWorth` and `setAddress` methods, we see an advice marker (the arrow pointing down and to the right). This tells us that there is after advice in place on these methods. In other words, after returning from the execution of the `setWorth` and `setAddress` methods, some advice will run.

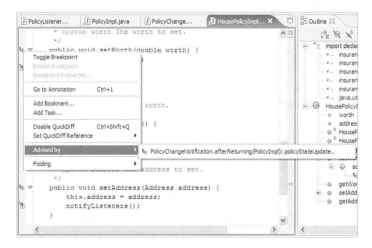

Figure 2.35   Advised methods in the editor.

In the right margin, we see the overview ruler for the whole source file. In this margin, there are check marks indicating the presence of advice (and also the warnings generated by the declare warning statement). You can click these check marks to navigate to the corresponding location in the source file.

Returning our attention to the advice markers in the left margin once more, they tell us that the method has after returning advice, but not which advice. As we have already seen, we can use the Outline view to find that out. Another option is to right-click the advice marker to bring up the context menu, as shown in Figure 2.36.

Figure 2.36   Using the context menu to discover advice.

Selecting the **Advised by** option in the menu brings up a list of all the advice affecting the method. Selecting one of the items in the list (in Figure 2.36 there is only one) opens the editor on the advice declaration.

2.7.3 Documentation and Visualization

AJDT also provides a visualization view that gives you an overview of the source files in your application and where the advice defined in aspects matches lines of source code that will give rise to advised join points at runtime. Figure 2.37 shows an example of the kind of views it produces.

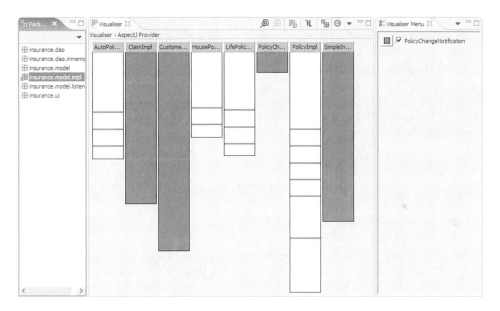

Figure 2.37   Visualization view.

Each vertical bar represents an individual source file. The highlighted bars contain lines of code that will give rise to join points matched by advice at runtime. The stripes on the highlighted bars indicate the places that advice applies. You can click these to navigate. In this example, the Visualiser is highlighting the classes in the policy hierarchy. Chapter 12 provides more detail on using the Visualiser.

A final way of understanding the effects of advice is through the documentation that AJDT produces via the ajdoc tool (ajdoc is AspectJ's version of the javadoc tool). We show you how to use AJDT to generate documentation in Chapter 4.

2.8   Evaluating the Implementation

We can see then from the tools that the advice we wrote seems to be calling
`notifyListeners()` at all the right times. We're not finished yet though because
we still have all the old calls to `notifyListeners()` scattered throughout the
policy classes, and we haven't run the test suite.

We want to know that all the tests would still pass with the
`PolicyChangeNotification` aspect in place, and all the old calls to
`notifyListeners()` removed. Ideally we would like to know that now, before
we actually go ahead and remove all those calls, because that will be a smaller step
if we find we have to backtrack. We are going to show you an AspectJ technique
you can use to do this. Remember we said that AspectJ supports several kinds of
advice, including around advice. Around advice gives you complete control over
the execution of a matched join point. One of the things you can do with around
advice is decide whether and when the computation at the matched join point
should proceed. A "no-op" around advice implementation looks like this:

```
Object around() : somePointcut() {
   return proceed();
}
```

It does nothing before proceeding with the computation at the join point,
and returns immediately that computation has completed. As a transition stage
in the development of the `PolicyChangeNotification` aspect, we can add the
following around advice to the aspect:

```
void around() : notifyingListeners() &&
                !within(PolicyChangeNotification)
{
}
```

Because it contains no call to proceed, this advice has the effect of bypassing
the computation at join points it matches. We previously defined the
`notifyingListeners` pointcut to match all calls to `notifyListeners`, so this
advice effectively removes all those calls that aren't made by our aspect from the
runtime execution of the program—it lets us run the test cases and see what
would happen if the calls weren't there. We should stress at this point that we are
only using empty around advice as a transition stage in our refactoring. We do
not advise you to create programs that use around advice to "stub out" unwanted calls as a permanent part of the design. See the next chapter for an example
of the use of around advice as part of the program design.

With this temporary around advice in place, we can run the test suite. The results are shown in Figure 2.38. A test case has failed!

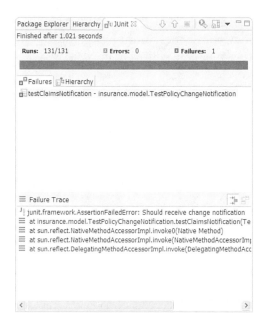

Figure 2.38 A failing test case.

What's going on? We can double-click in the JUnit view to go to the test case definition. The editor opens on the test case, with the failing assert highlighted (see Figure 2.39).

```
⊞ PolicyListene...   ⊞ PolicyImpl.java   ⊞ PolicyChang...   ⊞ HousePolicyIm...   ⊞ TestPolicyCh... ⊠   ⊟
  ▽    public void testScheduleNotification() {
           policy.setSchedule(null);
           assertTrue("Should receive change notification",listener.wasNot:
       }

  ▽    public void testClaimsNotification() {
           policy.setClaims(new HashSet());
           assertTrue("Should receive change notification",listener.wasNot:
           listener.clearNotification();
           Claim c = new ClaimImpl(new Date(),100d,"OPEN","");
           policy.addClaim(c);
           assertTrue("Should receive change notification",listener.wasNot:
           listener.clearNotification();
           policy.removeClaim(c);
           assertTrue("Should receive change notification",listener.wasNot:
       }

  ▽    protected void setUp() throws Exception {
           super.setUp();
```

Figure 2.39 The failing test case definition.

You can see that the test case adds a new claim against a policy, and then checks to see that a notification of update was received. The method called to add the new claim against the policy is addClaim. We defined the policyStateUpdate pointcut to match the execution of methods beginning with "set" on policy objects. "addClaim" does not fit this pattern—our pointcut definition is not quite correct. If we open the editor on the PolicyImpl class, we can see what's going on (see Figure 2.40).

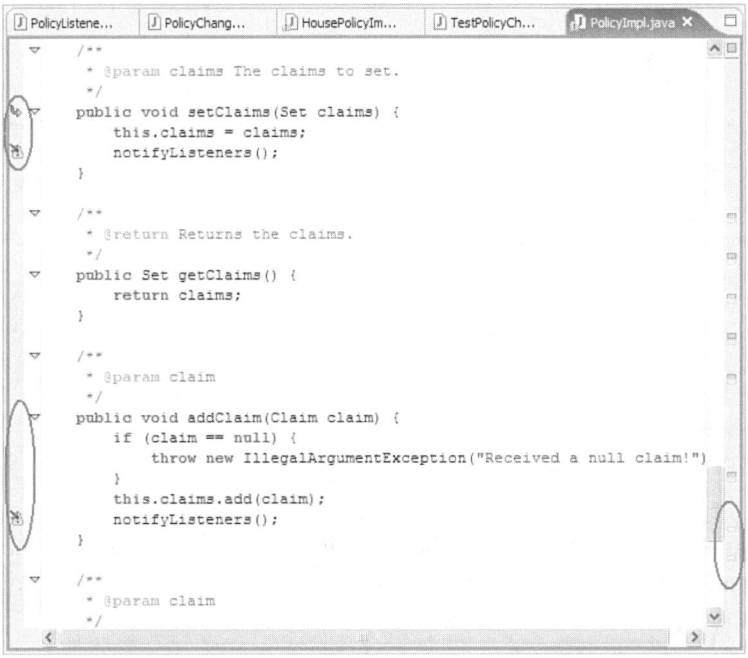

Figure 2.40 Clues in the editor.

Notice that the setClaims method has an after advice marker next to it in the left margin. The addClaim method has no such advice marker—although it does have a warning marker because the old implementation contains a call to notifyListeners. Another clue is in the ruler in the right margin. You can see that the advice markers and warning markers are nicely paired throughout the file, apart from the last two (highlighted), which have warnings but no advice markers. These warnings are against the addClaim and removeClaim methods.

Aspects aren't a silver bullet—you can use them to improve the modularity of your programs, but they don't alleviate the need for test-driven development or any of the other best practices you have learned from working with Java.

2.8.1 Updating the Pointcut Declaration

Let's go back to the `PolicyChangeNotification` aspect and update the definition of the `policyStateChange` pointcut. We want to match join points that represent either the execution of a "set" method, or the "addClaim" method, or the "removeClaim" method. Figure 2.41 shows the updated pointcut definition.

```
package insurance.model.impl;

public aspect PolicyChangeNotification {

    pointcut notifyingListeners() :
        call(* PolicyImpl.notifyListeners(..));

    declare warning :
        notifyingListeners() && !within(PolicyChangeNotification)
        : "Only the PolicyChangeNotification aspect should be notifying l:

    pointcut policyStateUpdate(PolicyImpl aPolicy) :
        (execution(* set*(..)) ||
         execution(* addClaim(..)) ||
         execution(* removeClaim(..)))
        && this(aPolicy);

    after(PolicyImpl policy) returning : policyStateUpdate(policy) {
        policy.notifyListeners();
    }

    void around() : notifyingListeners() && !within(PolicyChangeNotifica
        // this implementation deliberately left bla
    }
}
```

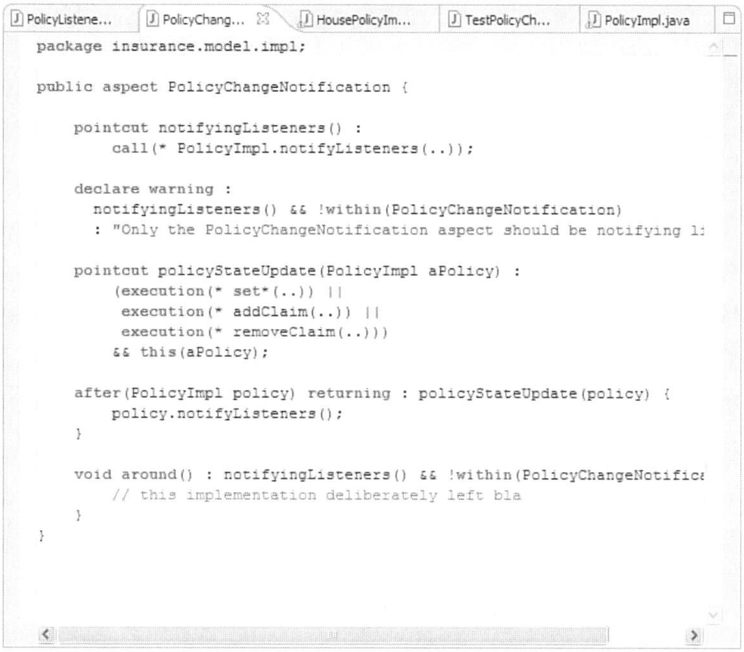

Figure 2.41   The updated pointcut definition.

We can use either the Outline view or the editor to check that we are now indeed matching the execution of the add and remove claim methods. Figure 2.42 shows how the `PolicyImpl.java` source file looks in the editor now.

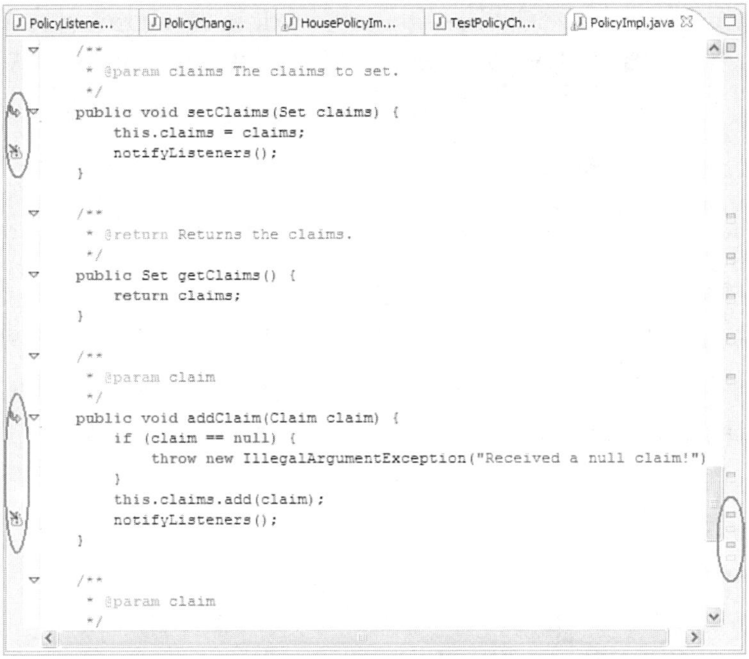

Figure 2.42   New matches as a result of the updated pointcut.

Notice that the advice markers are now appearing next to the `addClaim` and `removeClaim` methods. In the right margin you can also see that the advice markers and the warnings are now balanced: every time there is a call to `notifyListeners` coded in the `PolicyImpl` class, there is also advice in effect to achieve the same result. Now when we re-run the test cases, they all pass.

2.8.2 Removing the Old Calls to Notify

Now the time has come to remove all the calls to `notifyListeners` that are scattered throughout the classes in the policy hierarchy. We can use the warning tasks in the Problems view (see Figure 2.27) to navigate to all the offending places and remove the call. Now we can take out the around advice as well, and the job is done. Save all the files and re-run the test cases—they all pass.

Figure 2.43 shows the completed `PolicyChangeNotification` aspect.

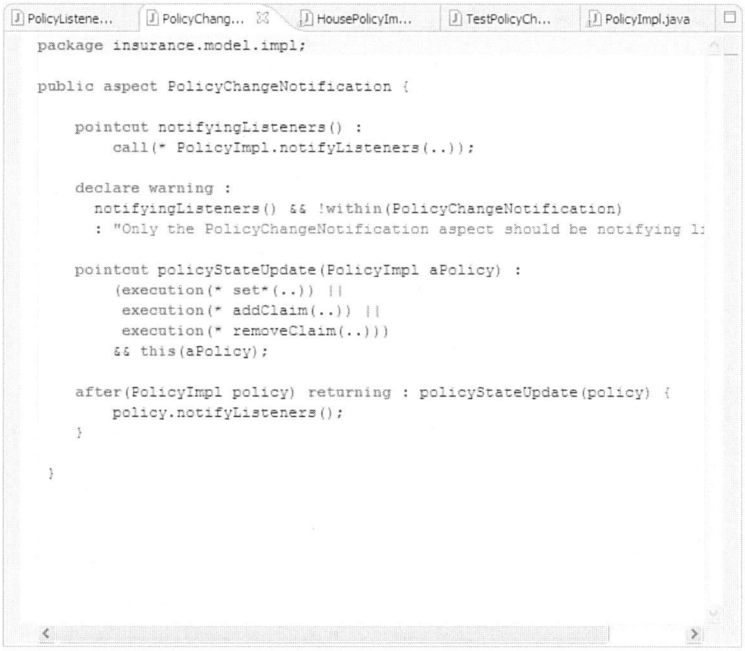

```
┌─────────────────────────────────────────────────────────────────────────────┐
│ [J] PolicyListene... │ [J] PolicyChang... ⊠ │ [J] HousePolicyIm... │ [J] TestPolicyCh... │ [J] PolicyImpl.java │ □ │
├─────────────────────────────────────────────────────────────────────────────┤
│    package insurance.model.impl;                                               │
│                                                                                │
│    public aspect PolicyChangeNotification {                                    │
│                                                                                │
│        pointcut notifyingListeners() :                                         │
│            call(* PolicyImpl.notifyListeners(..));                             │
│                                                                                │
│        declare warning :                                                       │
│          notifyingListeners() && !within(PolicyChangeNotification)             │
│            : "Only the PolicyChangeNotification aspect should be notifying l:   │
│                                                                                │
│        pointcut policyStateUpdate(PolicyImpl aPolicy) :                         │
│            (execution(* set*(..)) ||                                           │
│             execution(* addClaim(..)) ||                                       │
│             execution(* removeClaim(..)))                                       │
│            && this(aPolicy);                                                   │
│                                                                                │
│        after(PolicyImpl policy) returning : policyStateUpdate(policy) {         │
│            policy.notifyListeners();                                            │
│        }                                                                       │
│                                                                                │
│    }                                                                           │
└─────────────────────────────────────────────────────────────────────────────┘
```

Figure 2.43   The finished aspect.

2.8.3 Comparing the Modular and Non-modular Implementations

While working through the tasks in the Problems view removing all the unwanted calls to `notifyListeners`, we noticed an interesting case in the
`LifePolicyImpl` class. This is shown in Figure 2.44.

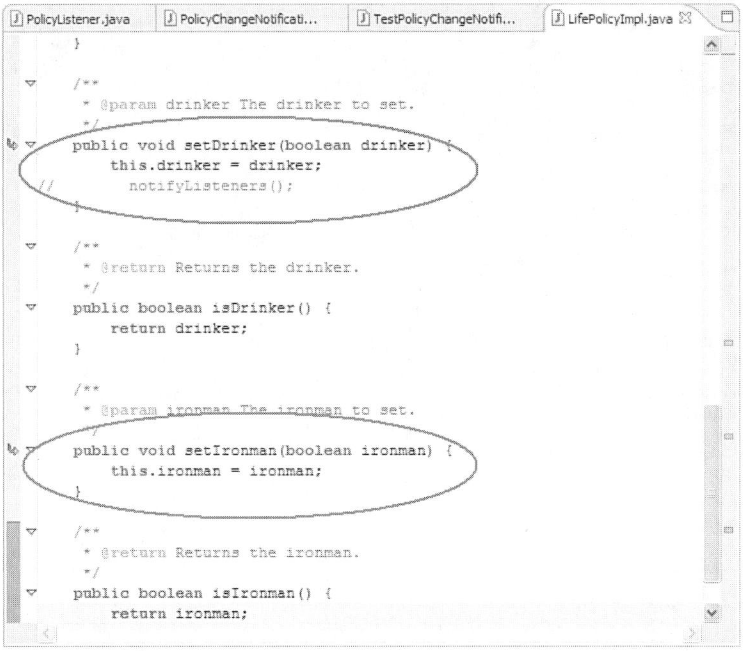

Figure 2.44 Ironman.

Notice that the `setDrinker` method contained a call to `notifyListeners`, but the call to `setIronman` a little farther down in the source file did not. This was a bug in the original implementation. How did this happen? Originally Simple Insurers Inc. just sold ordinary life policies pretty much like every other insurance company. Sometime after the original `LifePolicyImpl` class was written, the marketing department decided that anyone fit enough to compete in an Ironman competition ought to be a pretty good prospect for life insurance, and decided to go after the market niche with special discounts. The programmer that added the `ironman` field into the `LifePolicyImpl` class forgot to add in the call to `notifyListeners`.

The `PolicyChangeNotification` aspect *does* notify listeners after the ironman field has been updated. Because the pointcut specifies by property (all the set methods) rather than by exhaustive enumeration when a notification should be issued, it gets it right. In our experience, it is fairly common for an aspect-based implementation such as this to be more accurate than the scattered, hand-coded alternative.

2.9 Finishing Touches

Now that our refactoring is complete, we can make one more finishing touch. In the `PolicyChangeNotification` aspect, we can turn the declare warning statement into a declare error.

```
declare error :
  notifyingListeners() && !within(PolicyChangeNotification)
  : "Only the PolicyChangeNotification aspect should be
      notifying listeners";
```

Now if anyone inadvertently breaks the modularity we just put in place, he or she will receive a compilation error.

Finally we are now ready to go ahead and add the `PetPolicyImpl` class we need for the new pet insurance business line—the change that started us off down this road in the first place. Pet policies have attributes such as `petName`, `petType`, `vetName`, and `vetAddress`. Figure 2.45 shows the `PetPolicyImpl` class in the editor.

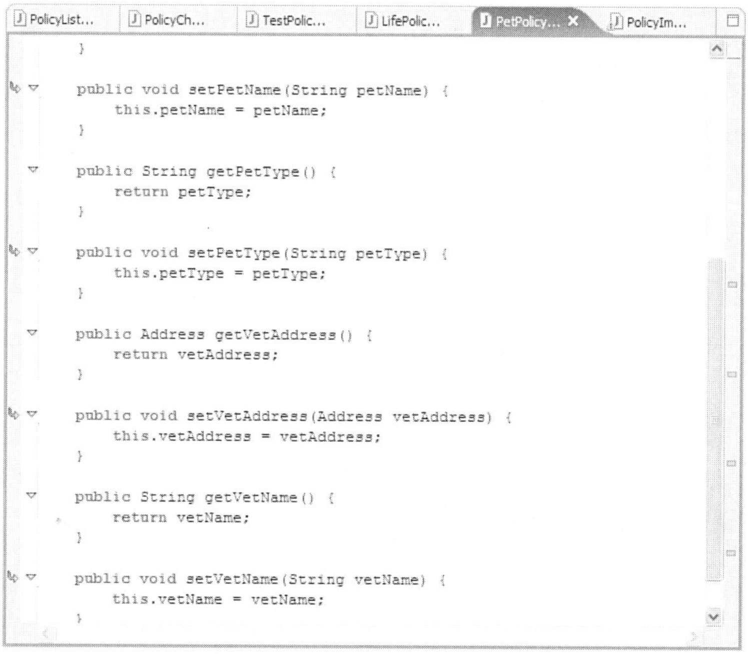

Figure 2.45   Adding in the *PetPolicyImpl* class.

Notice that all the methods that update the state of the `PetPolicyImpl` class are being advised by the `PolicyChangeNotification` aspect. The aspect continues to correctly notify changes even in code added to the system after the aspect was written. This is the power of capturing the design for change notification in the code (whenever the state of a policy changes), rather than coding by hand the implications of the design (putting calls to `notifyListeners` throughout the policy hierarchy).

If the `PetPolicyImpl` programmer somehow manages to miss the advice markers in the editor gutter and the "advised by" relationships in the Outline view, and starts to implement change notification the old way, the `PolicyChangeNotification` aspect soon tells him or her (see Figure 2.46).

Figure 2.46   Catching a violation of the change notification design.

2.10   Summary

We've come a long way in this chapter. We identified a problem in the Simple Insurance application that came to light when we decided to add support for pet insurance to the application, whereby calls to `notifyListeners` were spread throughout the policy class hierarchy. We decided to refactor this implementation to get back to a one-to-one mapping from design requirement (notify whenever the state of a policy object changes) to implementation. We applied the eXtreme programming philosophy "make sure everything is expressed once and only once," also known as the DRY principle (*don't repeat yourself*). Using

AJDT and AspectJ, we were able to implement a modular solution to change notification using an aspect. The tools helped us during the refactoring process, both to explore the code and to incrementally test the changes we were making.

When we had finished, all the test cases were passing, we had replaced 15 calls to notifyListeners with one single call, found and removed a bug, and left behind a guard (the declare error) so that our chosen design modularity would remain in place in the code during evolution and maintenance. Even better, the solution we implemented in the aspect continued working even when the new PetPolicyImpl class was added—there was no additional effort spent implementing change notification for pet policies.

There is more that we could do to modularize change notification for policies— keeping track of listeners, and adding and removing them, also really belongs in the PolicyChangeNotification aspect. Chapter 8 shows you how to do that, too.

CHAPTER 3

Extending the Application

Simple Insurers Inc. has the basic structure of their insurance application domain model completed. Right now, however, there's a fundamental problem with the application—when you start up the application it looks like the screenshot shown in Figure 3.1; you can create as many customers and policies as you like, but when the application shuts down, they are all lost. In short, there is no persistence. This is proving to be a problem when showing the end users the evolving application as part of iteration planning—it's too tedious to build up a set of customers and policies from scratch each time.

Figure 3.1   Yes, we have no persistence.

At this morning's stand-up meeting, it was agreed that a temporary persistence solution, "if it can be done in half an hour," would be very useful for a planned meeting with the end users tomorrow. In parallel, the team will kick off a work activity to determine the proper persistence solution and deliver it in the next iteration.

This chapter walks you through the implementation of both the quick-fix persistence solution and the final solution that uses Hibernate[1] for persistence. In the Introduction we talked about the desire for a modular implementation so that support for a feature would be easy to add, easy to remove, and easy to maintain. Now we get to see how that pans out when implementing the persistence support for the Simple Insurance application using AspectJ.

3.1   The Story So Far

The Simple Insurance application is constructed with a façade interface, `insurance.model.SimpleInsurance`, which provides clients with operations to create, insert, find, update, and delete objects in the business domain model. Figure 3.2 shows an excerpt from the interface.

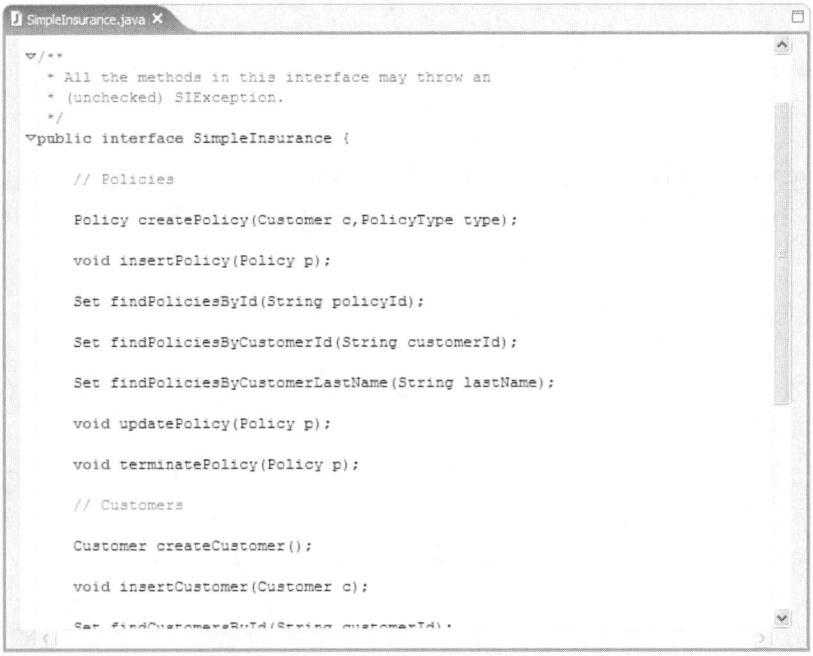

```
🗋 SimpleInsurance.java ✕                                                        ▭

▽/**
   * All the methods in this interface may throw an
   * (unchecked) SIException.
   */
▽public interface SimpleInsurance {

      // Policies

      Policy createPolicy(Customer c, PolicyType type);

      void insertPolicy(Policy p);

      Set findPoliciesById(String policyId);

      Set findPoliciesByCustomerId(String customerId);

      Set findPoliciesByCustomerLastName(String lastName);

      void updatePolicy(Policy p);

      void terminatePolicy(Policy p);

      // Customers

      Customer createCustomer();

      void insertCustomer(Customer c);

      Set findCustomersById(String customerId);
```

Figure 3.2   The *SimpleInsurance* interface.

---

1. http://www.hibernate.org

The interface is implemented by the `SimpleInsuranceImpl` class, which delegates to *data-access objects* (DAOs) to perform any operation requiring a change to the "persistent" representation of an object. The package `insurance.dao` contains DAO interfaces for `Customer`, `Policy`, and `Claim`. The `PolicyDao` interface is shown in Figure 3.3.

```
┌─ SimpleInsurance.java ─┬─ SimpleInsuranceImpl.java ─┬─ PolicyDao.java ⊠ ──────────────┐
     package insurance.dao;

   ▶ import insurance.model.Policy;☐

   ▽/**
      * All operations in this interface may throw an
      * (unchecked) SIPersistenceException.
      */
   ▽public interface PolicyDao {

        void insertPolicy(Policy p);

        Set findPoliciesById(String policyId);

        Set findPoliciesByCustomerId(String customerId);

        Set findPoliciesByCustomerLastName(String lastName);

        void updatePolicy(Policy p);

        void deletePolicy(Policy p);

   }
```

Figure 3.3 *PolicyDao interface.*

Finally, the application contains an implementation of the DAO interface that keeps all objects in memory. This implementation is in the `insurance. dao.inmemory` package. Figure 3.4 shows an excerpt from the `Customer DaoImpl` class in this package—you can see that the set of known customers is simply maintained in a `Set`.

```
┌──────────┬──────────┬──────────┬──────────┬───────────────┐
│ J SimpleInsur... │ J SimpleInsur... │ J PolicyDao.j... │ J PolicyDaoI... │ J CustomerDa... ☒ │  □
├──────────┴──────────┴──────────┴──────────┴───────────────┘
  package insurance.dao.inmemory;

▶ import java.util.HashSet;☐

▽public class CustomerDaoImpl implements CustomerDao {

      private Set customers = new HashSet();

▽      public CustomerDaoImpl() {
       }

▽      public void insertCustomer(Customer c) {
           if (!customers.add(c)) {
               throw new SIPersistenceException("Duplicate customer");
           }
       }

▽      public Set findCustomersById(String customerId) {
           Set found = new HashSet();
           customerId = customerId.replaceAll("\\*",".*");
           for (Iterator iter = customers.iterator(); iter.hasNext();)
               Customer cust = (Customer) iter.next();
               if (cust.getCustomerID().matches(customerId)) {
                   found.add(cust);
               }
```

Figure 3.4   *CustomerDaoImpl.*

3.2   Serialization-Based Persistence

To get a basic persistence capability in place for tomorrow's demonstration, it has been decided to use simple Java serialization. (Remember that the goal is to spend less that half an hour on the implementation.) Here's the design of the solution:

1. Make all the domain classes implement `Serializable`.

2. When the application starts up, look for the existence of a file called SimpleInsurance.dat. If it is found, load the set of customers and the set of policies from the file. (Claims are stored as part of the state of a policy.)

3. When the application shuts down, serialize the state of the `CustomerDao` and `PolicyDao` objects into the SimpleInsurance.dat file. These types hold the set of customers and set of policies respectively.

We want to implement this in a modular way without disturbing the rest of the application, so we will use an aspect to keep everything related to the serialization-based persistence solution in a single module.

3.2.1 Creating the SerializationBasedPersistence Aspect

Let's create an aspect called `SerializationBasedPersistence` in the `insurance.dao.inmemory` package. Select **New > Aspect** from the context menu of the package in the Package Explorer, fill in the aspect name as shown in Figure 3.5, and click **Finish**.

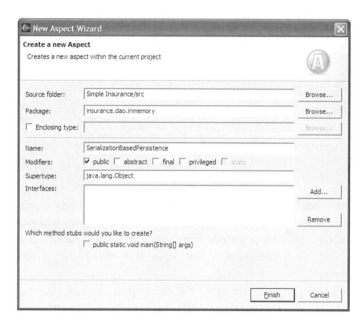

Figure 3.5   Creating the *SerializationBasedPersistence* aspect.

AJDT creates the aspect and opens the editor on the source file `SerializationBasedPersistence.aj`.

3.2.2 Making the Domain Objects Serializable

The first component of the design was to make all the domain objects serializable. We could go through all the classes in the `insurance.model` and `insurance.model.impl` packages and add `implements Serializable` next to each class definition. However, this approach would not demonstrate the modularity we are after—the implementation of the persistence solution should be transparent to the domain model.

Figure 3.6 shows an alternative implementation using AspectJ that meets our criteria. It uses an AspectJ statement known as *declare parents*.

```
SerializationBasedPersistence.aj ⊠

    package insurance.dao.inmemory;

    import java.io.Serializable;
    import insurance.model.impl.PolicyChangeNotification;

    public aspect SerializationBasedPersistence {

        declare parents: insurance.model..* &&
                         !PolicyChangeNotification implements Serializable;

    }
```

Figure 3.6 Implementing *Serializable*.

The `declare parents` statement in Figure 3.6 can be read as follows: "Every type in the `insurance.model` package, and in any subpackages (except the `PolicyChangeNotification` aspect), implements the `Serializable` interface. The and subpackages piece comes from the `..` wildcard, which matches any number of dot-separated identifiers. Notice in the editor that imports work exactly as they would for a class."

Figure 3.7 shows the Outline view for the aspect. It has been updated to show the `declare parents` member inside the aspect, and all the types that are affected by that statement. You can see that the result of this declaration is exactly as it suggests; all the classes in the `insurance.model` package and subpackages now implement `Serializable`. The test case shown in Figure 3.8 passes with the `SerializationBasedPersistence` aspect included in the build.

Figure 3.7   Outline view for declare parents.

```
[J] SerializationBasedPersistence.aj    [J] TestSerializationBasedPersistence.java ⊠                              ▯
    package insurance.dao.inmemory;

  ▽import insurance.model.Address;
    import junit.framework.TestCase;

  ▽public class TestSerializationBasedPersistence extends TestCase {

     ▽    public void testSerializable() {
              Address a = new Address("a","b","c","d","e");
              assertTrue("Should be serializable",
                         a instanceof java.io.Serializable);
          }


     }
```

Figure 3.8   Declare parents test case.

Chapter 8 provides a more complete overview of the declare parents construct.

3.2.3 Managing the DAOs

The `SerializationBasedPersistence` aspect is going to be responsible for managing the DAOs used by the application. We will keep them as state inside the aspect, which will then be responsible for creating, loading, and saving them as necessary. The serialized DAOs will be kept in a file named `SimpleInsurance.dat`. Listing 3.1 shows the additions made to the aspect to support the loading and saving of the DAOs. This is straightforward object-serialization code. Perhaps the most interesting thing to note is that we can declare methods and fields inside aspects just as we can inside classes.

Listing 3.1   Load and Save Implementations

```
package insurance.dao.inmemory;

import java.io.*;
import insurance.dao.*;
import insurance.model.impl.PolicyChangeNotification;

public aspect SerializationBasedPersistence {

    private static final String filename =
            "SimpleInsurance.dat";
    private PolicyDao policyDao;
    private CustomerDao customerDao;
    private ClaimDao claimDao;

    declare parents : insurance.model..* &&
                      !PolicyChangeNotification
                      implements Serializable;

    private boolean loadData() {
      boolean loadedSuccessfully = false;
      ObjectInputStream ois = null;
      try {
        File f = new File(filename);
        if (f.exists()) {
          FileInputStream fis = new FileInputStream(f);
          ois = new ObjectInputStream(fis);
          customerDao = (CustomerDao) ois.readObject();
          policyDao = (PolicyDao) ois.readObject();
          loadedSuccessfully = true;
        }
      } catch (IOException ioEx) {
        ioEx.printStackTrace();
      } catch (ClassNotFoundException cnfEx) {
        cnfEx.printStackTrace();
      } finally {
        if (ois != null) {
          try {ois.close();}
          catch(IOException ex) {ex.printStackTrace();}
        }
      }
      return loadedSuccessfully;
    }

    private void saveData() {
```

```
      ObjectOutputStream oos = null;
      try {
        FileOutputStream fos = new FileOutputStream(filename);
        oos = new ObjectOutputStream(fos);
        oos.writeObject(customerDao);
        oos.writeObject(policyDao);
      } catch (IOException ioEx) {
        ioEx.printStackTrace();
      } finally {
        if (oos != null) {
          try {oos.close();}
          catch(IOException ex) {ex.printStackTrace();}
        }
      }
    }

}
```

The loadData method looks for a file called SimpleInsurance.dat, and if
the file exists, it attempts to read a CustomerDao and a PolicyDao object from
it. It returns true if it managed to load the objects successfully. The saveData
method writes the CustomerDao and PolicyDao objects to the stream. Because
ClaimDao is stateless (recall claims are stored as part of the state of a policy), we
don't need to load or save it.

Implementing these methods leads us to realize that not only do the domain
objects have to be serializable, but also the CustomerDao and PolicyDao classes.
We can easily extend the aspect to cater for this with a second declare parents
statement, as shown in Figure 3.9.

Figure 3.9 Making the DAOs serializable.

Notice the way we specify the two target interfaces : (PolicyDao || CustomerDao). The declare parents construct takes a type pattern (more on type patterns in Chapter 6), and the pattern given here matches if the target type is either a PolicyDao or a CustomerDao.

3.2.4 DAO Dependency Injection

The SimpleInsurance application implementation class, SimpleInsuranceImpl, is currently creating and managing its own DAOs. A look at the source code, as shown in Figure 3.10, shows that this is done just by creating the necessary DAOs in its constructor.

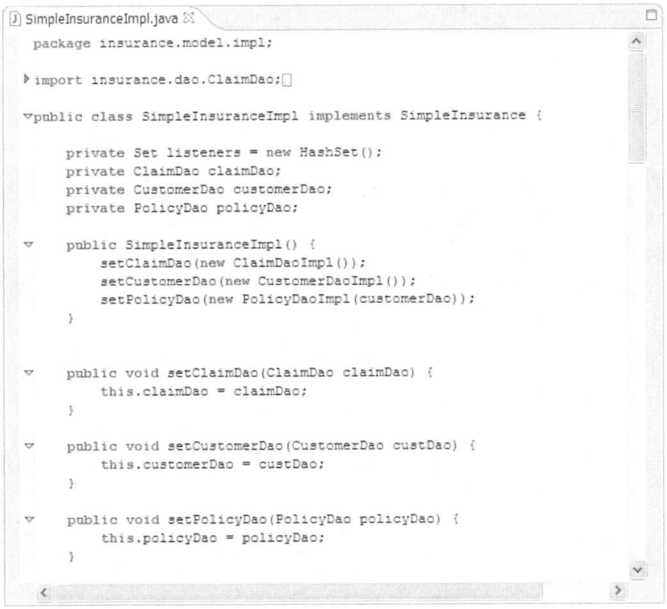

```
SimpleInsuranceImpl.java

    package insurance.model.impl;

  ▶ import insurance.dao.ClaimDao;

  ▽ public class SimpleInsuranceImpl implements SimpleInsurance {

        private Set listeners = new HashSet();
        private ClaimDao claimDao;
        private CustomerDao customerDao;
        private PolicyDao policyDao;

  ▽     public SimpleInsuranceImpl() {
            setClaimDao(new ClaimDaoImpl());
            setCustomerDao(new CustomerDaoImpl());
            setPolicyDao(new PolicyDaoImpl(customerDao));
        }

  ▽     public void setClaimDao(ClaimDao claimDao) {
            this.claimDao = claimDao;
        }

  ▽     public void setCustomerDao(CustomerDao custDao) {
            this.customerDao = custDao;
        }

  ▽     public void setPolicyDao(PolicyDao policyDao) {
            this.policyDao = policyDao;
        }
```

Figure 3.10 DAO creation in *SimpleInsuranceImpl*.

We want the SerializationBasedPersistence aspect to manage the DAOs (and later on we will want the Hibernate implementation to manage its own DAOs, too), so we need to change this implementation slightly. Instead of the SimpleInsuranceImpl class creating new DAOs, we will pass them to it via dependency injection.[2]

---

2. See Martin Fowler's article "Inversion of Control Containers and the Dependency Injection Pattern" at http://www.martinfowler.com/articles/injection.html.

The class already has setter methods that the constructor is calling. The first step is to extract them into an interface. With the type name selected in the editor, choose **Refactor > Extract Interface** from the context menu, as shown in Figure 3.11.

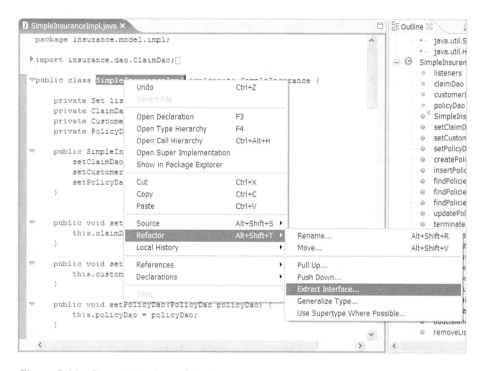

Figure 3.11   Extract interface refactoring.

The refactoring dialog box shown in Figure 3.12 appears. We have chosen to call the interface `INeedInsuranceDaos`, and have selected the three `set*Dao` methods to be part of it. Later in the aspect, we will write some code to provide DAOs to anyone who declares that `INeedInsuranceDaos`.

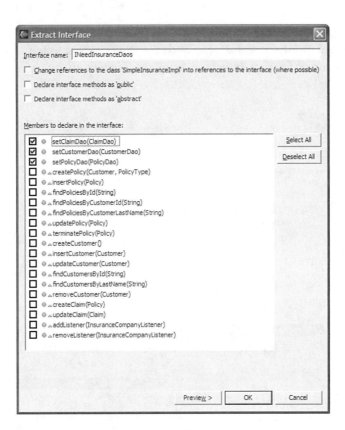

Figure 3.12   Creating the interface.

After you click **OK**, a new source file INeedInsuranceDaos.java is created in the insurance.model.impl package alongside the SimpleInsuranceImpl class, and the class definition is updated to say that it implements the interface. At this stage we can delete the three DAO constructor calls from the SimpleInsuranceImpl constructor and remove the related import declarations (refer back to Figure 3.10). The Package Explorer should look as shown in Figure 3.13.

The interface we just created better belongs in the insurance.dao package. You can drag the INeedInsuranceDaos.java file in the Package Explorer and drop it in the insurance.dao package. The confirmation dialog shown in Figure 3.14 appears, and the interface is moved when you click **OK**.

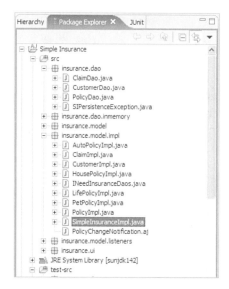

Figure 3.13   Package Explorer after Extract Interface.

Figure 3.14   Confirming the package move.

Back in the `SerializationBasedPersistence` aspect at last we are now ready to implement the logic that creates the DAOs and injects them into any class implementing the `INeedInsuranceDaos` interface. It should come as no surprise by now that we are going to use a combination of a pointcut and some advice to do it. Whenever an `INeedInsuranceDaos` object is constructed, we want to make sure that it gets them. The `daoConsumerCreation` pointcut matches join points at which `INeedInsuranceDaos` implementing objects are constructed.

```
pointcut daoConsumerCreation(
    INeedInsuranceDaos dataConsumer) :
    execution(INeedInsuranceDaos.new(..))
    && this(dataConsumer);
```

We're going to need to know which particular `INeedInsuranceDaos` object has just been constructed, so we get the pointcut to provide this information to us. If you enter this pointcut definition into the editor and press **Ctrl+S** to save, you get the result shown in Figure 3.15.

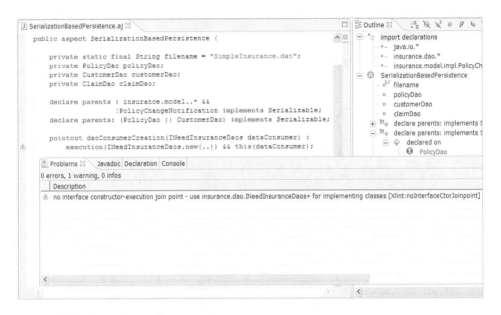

Figure 3.15   Use + for implementing classes.

The compiler warns us that there is "no interface constructor-execution join point," and that we should "use insurance.dao.INeedInsuranceDaos+" to instead match the construction of any classes that implement the interface. In other words, interfaces don't have constructors. The compiler is guessing that you meant the construction of any object implementing the interface, and is suggesting an alternative type pattern that will achieve that result. We take the compiler's suggestion and amend the pointcut definition:

```
pointcut daoConsumerCreation(
    INeedInsuranceDaos dataConsumer) :
    execution(INeedInsuranceDaos+.new(..))
    && this(dataConsumer);
```

When + is used in a type pattern, it means match this class and any class that extends it. Interface implementation is considered a form of extension. Once more, Chapter 6 provides more information on type patterns.

With the pointcut definition correct, we now need to write the advice that initializes the necessary DAOs and passes them to the newly created `INeedInsuranceDaos` object:

```
after(INeedInsuranceDaos dataConsumer) returning :
  daoConsumerCreation(dataConsumer) {
  if (!loadData()) {
    customerDao = new CustomerDaoImpl();
    policyDao = new PolicyDaoImpl(customerDao);
  }
  claimDao = new ClaimDaoImpl();
  dataConsumer.setCustomerDao(customerDao);
  dataConsumer.setPolicyDao(policyDao);
  dataConsumer.setClaimDao(claimDao);
}
```

If the `loadData` method fails to read in existing DAO objects, new ones are created. We always create a new `ClaimDao` because the `ClaimDaoImpl` class is stateless and therefore not persisted. After the DAOs have been created, we inject them into the `dataConsumer`.

The Outline view shows that the advice is affecting just one place, the construction of a `SimpleInsuranceImpl` object, as shown in Figure 3.16.

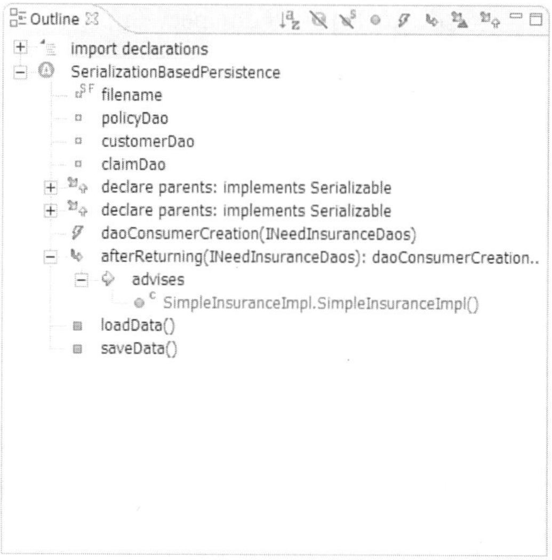

Figure 3.16 Dependency injection advice.

If we follow the link to open the `SimpleInsuranceImpl` class in the editor, you can also see the advice marker in the gutter next to the constructor (see Figure 3.17).

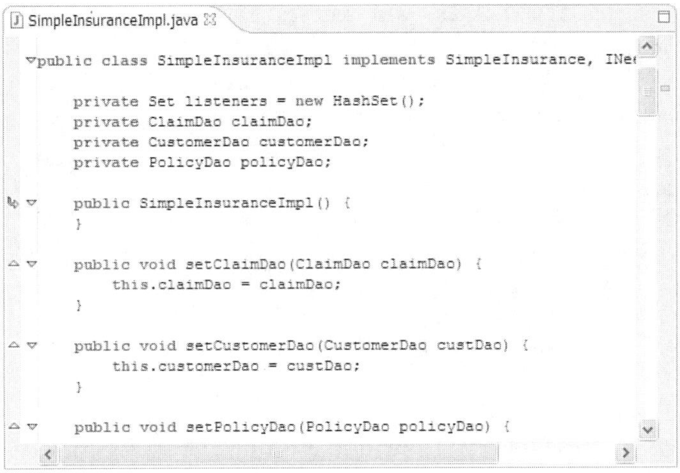

```
SimpleInsuranceImpl.java

public class SimpleInsuranceImpl implements SimpleInsurance, INe

    private Set listeners = new HashSet();
    private ClaimDao claimDao;
    private CustomerDao customerDao;
    private PolicyDao policyDao;

    public SimpleInsuranceImpl() {
    }

    public void setClaimDao(ClaimDao claimDao) {
        this.claimDao = claimDao;
    }

    public void setCustomerDao(CustomerDao custDao) {
        this.customerDao = custDao;
    }

    public void setPolicyDao(PolicyDao policyDao) {
```

Figure 3.17   Advised construction.

3.2.5 Finishing the Aspect

There's now only one thing left to do to finish the aspect implementation: We need to call the `saveData` method when the application is shutting down. There's no great way to determine when the application is finishing, so we'll just do this at the end of the `main` method:

```
pointcut applicationShutDown() :
  execution(* SimpleInsuranceApp.main(..));

after() returning : applicationShutDown() {
  saveData();
}
```

Figure 3.18 shows the result of entering this into the editor and saving.

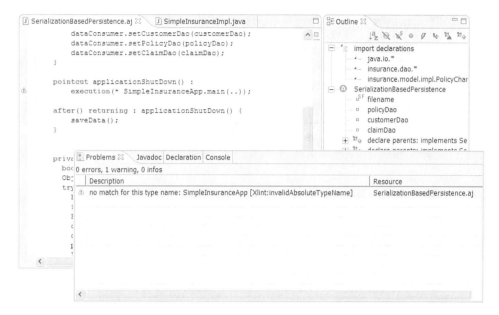

Figure 3.18   No match for this type name.

The compiler is telling us that the type pattern "SimpleInsuranceApp" used in the pointcut expression looks like it was intended to match a type name, but the type is unknown to it. We could either fully qualify the type name in the pointcut expression, or add an import statement. After adding the import statement, the aspect compiles successfully.

Now we can start up the application, add a customer, and then shut it down again. By refreshing the project in the Package Explorer (choose **Refresh** from the context menu or press **F5**), you can see that a file called `SimpleInsurance.dat` has been created. Restarting the application shows that the `SerializationBased Persistence` aspect is doing its job, as shown in Figure 3.19.

Figure 3.19   Persistence pays.

3.2.6 Evaluating the Implementation

The completed aspect is shown in Listing 3.2. It is only 90 lines long, including comments and white space. By keeping the persistence implementation modularized within the aspect, it was easy to add, and if we ever want to in the future it will be easy to remove. We refactored the `SimpleInsuranceImpl` class a little to expose a new interface, but there were no other changes outside of the aspect, and the business domain model remained untouched. Implementing the same change without AspectJ would have required modification of a dozen or so classes.

Listing 3.2 The Finished Aspect

```
package insurance.dao.inmemory;

import java.io.*;
import insurance.dao.*;
import insurance.model.impl.PolicyChangeNotification;
import insurance.ui.SimpleInsuranceApp;

public aspect SerializationBasedPersistence {

    private static final String filename =
        "SimpleInsurance.dat";
    private PolicyDao policyDao;
    private CustomerDao customerDao;
    private ClaimDao claimDao;

    declare parents :  insurance.model..* &&
                       !PolicyChangeNotification
                       implements Serializable;


    declare parents : (PolicyDao || CustomerDao)
                       implements Serializable;

    pointcut insuranceAppCreation(
        INeedInsuranceDaos dataConsumer) :
      execution(INeedInsuranceDaos+.new(..))
      && this(dataConsumer);

    after(INeedInsuranceDaos dataConsumer) returning :
      insuranceAppCreation(dataConsumer) {
      if (!loadData()) {
        customerDao = new CustomerDaoImpl();
        policyDao = new PolicyDaoImpl(customerDao);
      }
      claimDao = new ClaimDaoImpl();
      dataConsumer.setCustomerDao(customerDao);
      dataConsumer.setPolicyDao(policyDao);
      dataConsumer.setClaimDao(claimDao);
```

```
    }

    pointcut applicationShutDown() :
      execution(* SimpleInsuranceApp.main(..));

    after() returning : applicationShutDown() {
      saveData();
    }

    private boolean loadData() {
      boolean loadedSuccessfully = false;
      ObjectInputStream ois = null;
      try {
        File f = new File(filename);
        if (f.exists()) {
          FileInputStream fis = new FileInputStream(f);
          ois = new ObjectInputStream(fis);
          customerDao = (CustomerDao) ois.readObject();
          policyDao = (PolicyDao) ois.readObject();
          loadedSuccessfully = true;
        }
      } catch (IOException ioEx) {
        ioEx.printStackTrace();
      } catch (ClassNotFoundException cnfEx) {
        cnfEx.printStackTrace();
      } finally {
        if (ois != null) {
          try {ois.close();}
          catch(IOException ex) {ex.printStackTrace();}
        }
      }
      return loadedSuccessfully;
    }

    private void saveData() {
      ObjectOutputStream oos = null;
      try {
        FileOutputStream fos = new FileOutputStream(filename);
        oos = new ObjectOutputStream(fos);
        oos.writeObject(customerDao);
        oos.writeObject(policyDao);
      } catch (IOException ioEx) {
        ioEx.printStackTrace();
      } finally {
        if (oos != null) {
          try {oos.close();}
          catch(IOException ex) {ex.printStackTrace();}
        }
      }
    }

}
```

3.3   Hibernating

The Simple Insurance project team chose Hibernate for their persistence solution. Hibernate enables you to work with *plain old Java objects* (POJOs), keeping most of the information about the persistence strategy in configuration files. This fits well with our philosophy of making each class do one thing and one thing only—we won't need to mix persistence code in with our domain objects. As you will see in this section, the combination of Hibernate and AspectJ is very powerful indeed.

3.3.1 Preparing to Use Hibernate

If you are following along with the development of the Simple Insurance application in your own workspace, you need to take a few configuration steps at this point to download and install Hibernate and a database (we used MySQL). The instructions for doing this are described in the file data/Hibernate-README.txt in the Simple Insurance project. If you're just reading along in the book, you'll be pleased to know that we've done this for you.

3.3.2 Implementing Persistence with Hibernate

We are not intending to provide a Hibernate tutorial at this point, but in case you haven't used Hibernate before, let us tell you very briefly what is involved.

A lot of the work in using Hibernate goes on outside of the code. You write XML mapping files that tell Hibernate how your domain objects should be persisted in the database. Listing 3.3 shows the mapping file that we created for the `CustomerImpl` class as an example.

Listing 3.3   Mapping File for Customer

```
<?xml version="1.0"?>
<!DOCTYPE hibernate-mapping PUBLIC
    "-//Hibernate/Hibernate Mapping DTD 2.0//EN"
    "http://hibernate.sourceforge.net/hibernate-mapping-
      2.0.dtd">
<hibernate-mapping>
  <!-- insurance.model.Customer is an interface -->
  <class name="insurance.model.impl.CustomerImpl"
        table="Customer" >
    <id name="customerID" type="string" column="id"
        access="field">
      <generator class="assigned"/>
    </id>
```

```
          <property name="firstName" column="firstName"
                    type="string" access="field"/>
          <property name="lastName" column="lastName"
                    type="string" access="field"/>
          <property name="dob" column="dob"
                    type="timestamp" access="field"/>
          <many-to-one name="address" column="address_id"
                    cascade="save-update"
                    class="insurance.model.impl.AddressImpl"
                    access="field"/>

          <!-- Customer has a collection of policies -->
          <set name="policies" table="policies" access="field"
              cascade="all-delete-orphan" inverse="true">
            <key column="cust_id" />
            <one-to-many
                class="insurance.model.impl.PolicyImpl"/>
          </set>
      </class>
</hibernate-mapping>
```

In addition to the mapping files, there is a configuration file called `hibernate.properties` that tells Hibernate the name of your database, the JDBC driver you will be using, the ID and password for connecting to the database, and so on.

Within the source code of your application, you need to initialize Hibernate before carrying out any persistence operations. This involves creating a Hibernate configuration object and telling it about your mappings, and then building a `SessionFactory` that you will use later on to create `Session` objects for communicating with the database. Listing 3.4 shows an example of this for the Simple Insurance application.

Listing 3.4   Example Hibernate Initialization Code

```
SessionFactory sessionFactory = null;
try {
  Configuration cfg = new Configuration();
  cfg.addResource("mappings/address.hbm.xml");
  cfg.addResource("mappings/customer.hbm.xml");
  cfg.addResource("mappings/claim.hbm.xml");
  cfg.addResource("mappings/policy.hbm.xml");
  sessionFactory = cfg.buildSessionFactory();
} catch (HibernateException hEx) {
  // handle exception
}
```

All update interactions with the database throughout the rest of the application then follow a simple pattern: Open a Hibernate session, begin a transaction, save, update, or delete domain objects as needed, and then either commit or roll back the transaction and close the session again. Listing 3.5 shows an example code fragment for saving a `Customer` object to the database.

Listing 3.5   Saving a Customer to the Database

```
try {
  Session session = sessionFactory.openSession();
  Transaction tx = null;
  try {
    tx = session.beginTransaction();
    session.save(customer);
    tx.commit();
  } catch (HibernateException hEx) {
    if (tx != null) tx.rollback();
    throw hEx;
  } finally {
    session.close();
  }
} catch (HibernateException hEx) {
  // handle exception
}
```

Listing 3.6 shows an example of finding all the `Customer` objects where the customer has a given last name.

Listing 3.6   Retrieving Customers from the Database

```
List findCustomersByLastName(String lastName) {
  List customers = null;
  try {
    Session session = sessionFactory.openSession();
    Transaction tx = null;
    try {
      tx = session.beginTransaction();
      Criteria criteria =
        session.createCriteria(Customer.class);
      criteria.add(Expression.like("lastName", lastName));
      customers = criteria.list();
      tx.commit();
    } catch (HibernateException hEx) {
      if (tx != null) tx.rollback();
      throw hEx;
    } finally {
      session.close();
    }
```

```
  } catch (HibernateException hEx) {
    // handle exception
  }
  return customers;
}
```

3.3.3 Creating the HibernateManager Aspect

Recall that the DAO interfaces are defined in the `insurance.dao` package, and the in-memory implementation was defined in the `insurance.dao.inmemory` package. We will create a new package called `insurance.dao.hibernate` and put the Hibernate-based persistence implementation in it. The goal is that we do not need to change anything outside of this package—the persistence implementation should be completely transparent.

We can use Eclipse to quickly create the DAO implementation classes for us. Bring up the New Java Class Wizard and populate the fields as shown in Figure 3.20. You can use the **Add** button next to the Interfaces field to bring up a selection dialog box for choosing the `CustomerDao` interface.

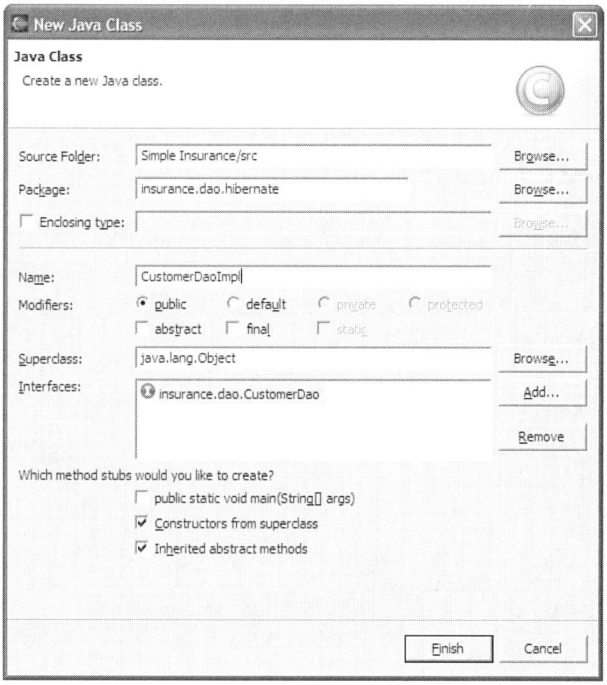

Figure 3.20   Creating a new DAO implementation class.

When the wizard completes you will have a class with empty template methods for each of the operations in the interface signature. Repeat this exercise to create `PolicyDaoImpl` and `ClaimDaoImpl` classes in the `insurance.dao.hibernate` package, too.

We are going to want to manage the creation of these DAOs, and the configuration of Hibernate itself, in a similar way to the DAO management in the `SerializationBasedPersistence` aspect. Let's create an aspect, `HibernateManager`, to do this. You can do this using the New Aspect Wizard as before. When the wizard completes, you should be looking at an empty aspect as shown in Figure 3.21.

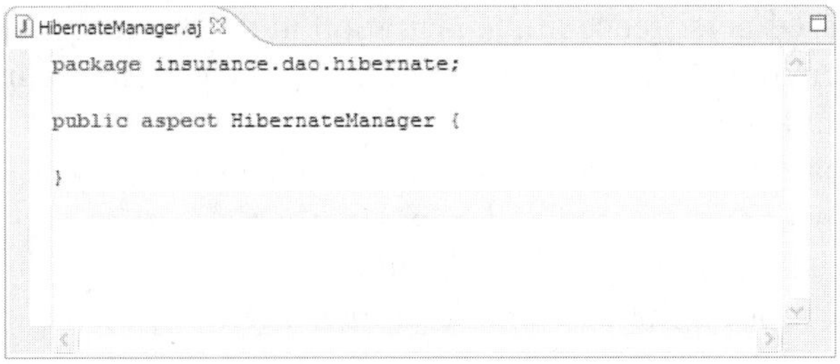

```
package insurance.dao.hibernate;

public aspect HibernateManager {

}
```

Figure 3.21   The HibernateManager aspect—ready to go.

Now we're ready to start filling in the implementation.

3.3.4 DAO Dependency Injection

The next simple step we can take is to create instances of the Hibernate DAO classes and provide them to implementers of the `INeedInsuranceDao` interface, as we did in Section 3.2.4. Here's the implementation we are going to put in the `HibernateManager` aspect:

```
// Hibernate DAO management
pointcut daoConsumerCreation(
   INeedInsuranceDaos dataConsumer) :
   execution(INeedInsuranceDaos+.new(..))
   && this(dataConsumer);

after(INeedInsuranceDaos dataConsumer) returning :
   daoConsumerCreation(dataConsumer) {
   dataConsumer.setCustomerDao(new CustomerDaoImpl());
   dataConsumer.setPolicyDao(new PolicyDaoImpl());
   dataConsumer.setClaimDao(new ClaimDaoImpl());
}
```

It's simpler than the `SerializationBasedPersistence` aspect's equivalent advice because there is no need to remember DAO instances; we just create new ones and pass them to the application. Now the application will be configured to use the Hibernate DAOs for its persistence. Of course, they don't actually do anything yet.

3.3.5 Meeting Hibernate's Requirements

Hibernate requires that each class to be mapped into a database table has a unique key. The `Customer`, `Policy`, and `Claim` objects all have natural keys in the business domain (customer number, policy number, and claim number respectively). We will also be storing addresses in an address table. `Address` does not have a natural key, so we need to add a key to the `AddressImpl` class that Hibernate can use to uniquely identify addresses. This key field is an artifact of our Hibernate persistence implementation, and not part of the business domain implementation of an `Address`. We can use an AspectJ construct known as an inter-type declaration to put the declaration of the field in the `HibernateManager` aspect where it belongs. This way, it makes it clear that the `id` field in an `AddressImpl` object is there for the benefit of Hibernate, and is not part of the business domain.

3.3.5.1 Introducing Inter-Type Declarations

An inter-type declaration looks just like a normal method, constructor, or field declaration, except that the declaration is made on behalf of a type other than the declaring one. It looks like this:

```
public aspect HibernateManager {
   ...
   public Long AddressImpl.id;
   ...
}
```

Notice that whereas the declaration of an `id` field in the `AddressImpl` class would have a signature `public Long id`, the inter-type declaration shown here has a signature `public Long AddressImpl.id`. This declaration can be read as "I'm providing the `id` field on behalf of the `AddressImpl` class."

In a similar vein, an inter-type declared method would look like this:

```
public aspect HibernateManager {
   ...
   public Long AddressImpl.getId() {
```

```
   return this.id;
  }
  ...
}
```

This can be read as "I'm providing an implementation of the getId() method on behalf of AddressImpl." At runtime, if a call is made to the getId() method on an AddressImpl object, the aspect will answer on the object's behalf. Inside the body of an inter-type declared method or constructor, this refers to the target object of the declaration (the AddressImpl object), and not the declaring aspect.

Inter-type declarations can also be used to provide implementations of constructors on behalf of other types. An inter-type constructor declaration has no return type and uses the special name new. Here's an example of defining a simple constructor on behalf of the AddressImpl class—this will come in very handy soon:

```
public aspect HibernateManager {
  ...
  public AddressImpl.new() {
    // implementation goes here...
  }
  ...
}
```

Inter-type declarations are somewhat similar to open-class mechanisms or mixin classes in languages that support those features. Chapter 8 provides more details.

3.3.5.2 Declaring the Address Key

We can use a simple inter-type field declaration to define the id key that Hibernate needs for addresses, as shown in Figure 3.22.

The Outline view as shown in Figure 3.23 can help us understand the effect of this declaration. It shows us that AddressImpl.id is a member of the aspect, and that it declares the id field on behalf of the AddressImpl class. The "declared on" nodes in the Outline view can be used for navigation just like the "advised by" nodes. Clicking AddressImpl in the outline opens the editor on the AddressImpl class, as shown in Figure 3.24.

```
package insurance.dao.hibernate;

import insurance.dao.INeedInsuranceDaos;
import insurance.model.impl.*;

public aspect HibernateManager {

    // meeting Hibernate's requirements
    public Long AddressImpl.id;

    // Hibernate DAO management
    pointcut daoConsumerCreation(INeedInsuranceDaos dataConsumer
            execution(INeedInsuranceDaos+.new(..)) && this(dataConsu

    after(INeedInsuranceDaos dataConsumer) returning : daoConsum
        dataConsumer.setCustomerDao(new CustomerDaoImpl());
        dataConsumer.setPolicyDao(new PolicyDaoImpl());
        dataConsumer.setClaimDao(new ClaimDaoImpl());
    }

}
```

Figure 3.22   A key for addresses.

Figure 3.23   Outline view for an inter-type declaration.

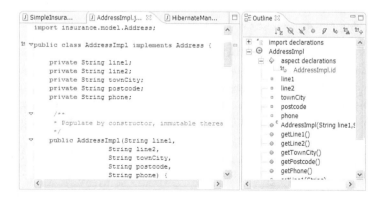

Figure 3.24   Inter-type declarations in the editor.

There are a few points to note in Figure 3.24. In the left gutter of the editor, we see the inter-type declaration marker (an arrow pointing down and to the right) next to the `AddressImpl` type declaration. In the right gutter (the overview ruler), we also see the inter-type declaration marker. The Outline view is showing that `AddressImpl` is affected by one or more aspect declarations—in this case an `id` field declared by the `HibernateManager` aspect. Hovering over the inter-type declaration markers displays hover help that tells you what the inter-type declaration is. (The hover help displays "AddressImpl: id" in this case.) You can also right-click the marker in the left gutter to bring up the context menu. This contains an "Aspect Declarations" entry that enables you to navigate to any inter-type declarations affecting the type (see Figure 3.25).

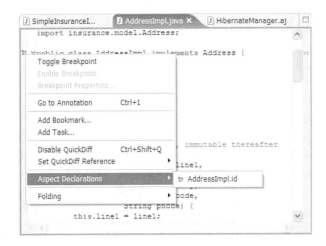

Figure 3.25   The "Aspect Declarations" context menu entries.

3.3.5.3 Declaring No-Argument Constructors

Hibernate also requires that all the classes it persists have a no-argument constructor. So far, not all of our domain objects provide this. In fact, several of the objects in our domain model are immutable (`Automobile` and `Schedule`, for example), so providing a no-argument constructor for them would be a very odd thing to do. Instead of adding no-argument constructors into all the domain objects, we can put them inside the aspect using inter-type declarations. This way, it once again makes it clear that they are there because of the Hibernate persistence implementation, and are not a true part of the business interface. Figure 3.26 shows the set of constructors we need to declare to make Hibernate happy.

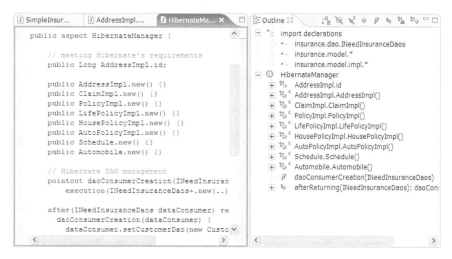

Figure 3.26   Inter-type constructor declarations.

3.3.5.4 Protecting Against Accidental Use

We said that the inter-type declared field and constructors were only for use by Hibernate, and we've been able to modularize them within the `HibernateManager` aspect—but what if other parts of the program start calling them? That would create a dependency on a part of the Hibernate implementation that we don't want. We can use the "declare warning" mechanism that we saw in Chapter 2 to guard against this. We will just declare it to be a compile time warning if any part of our program tries to access them:

```
declare warning : get(* AddressImpl.id) ||
                  set(* AddressImpl.id)
  : "this field is only for use by Hibernate";

declare warning : call(insurance.model.impl.*Impl.new()) ||
                  call(Schedule.new()) ||
                  call(Automobile.new())
  : "this constructor is only for use by Hibernate";
```

This example also illustrates the use of the `get` and `set` pointcut expressions to match field access and update join points. Chapter 6 provides more information on their usage. If we add these declarations to the aspect and save, we get the result shown in Figure 3.27.

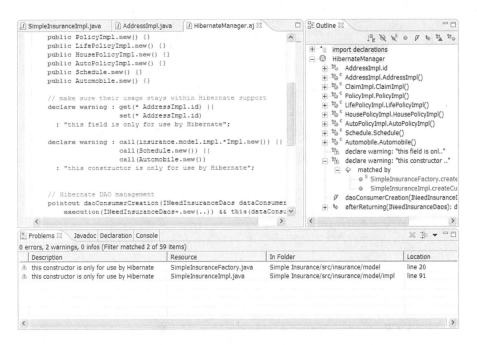

Figure 3.27 Protecting against accidental usage.

Notice that the second declare warning statement has given rise to two warnings. If we double-click the warnings in the Problems view, we will see that these are calls to the `SimpleInsuranceImpl` and `CustomerImpl` no-argument constructors that are legitimately part of our domain model. The wildcard call expression `call(insurance.model.impl.*Impl.new())` matched a little more than we wanted. We can refactor the pointcut declaration to explicitly capture only calls to constructors that the `HibernateManager` aspect itself declares:

```
declare warning : call(AddressImpl.new()) ||
                  call(ClaimImpl.new()) ||
                  call(PolicyImpl.new()) ||
                  call(LifePolicyImpl.new()) ||
                  call(HousePolicyImpl.new()) ||
                  call(AutoPolicyImpl.new()) ||
                  call(Schedule.new()) ||
                  call(Automobile.new())
     : "this constructor is only for use by Hibernate";
```

If ever a programmer inadvertently breaks our intended modularity by calling one of these, the compiler will produce a warning message like those in Figure 3.27.

3.3.6 Initial Hibernate Configuration

Listing 3.4 presented an example of the modest configuration that Hibernate requires at runtime. We need to perform this configuration in the `HibernateManager` before any use is made of Hibernate for talking to the database. A good point to do this is when the `SimpleInsuranceImpl` class is loaded. After a class has been loaded by the JVM, its static initialization block is executed. We can use this join point to trigger the Hibernate configuration:

```
private SessionFactory sessionFactory;

pointcut insuranceCompanyInit() :
  staticinitialization(SimpleInsuranceImpl);

after() returning : insuranceCompanyInit() {
   Configuration cfg = new Configuration();
   cfg.addResource("mappings/address.hbm.xml");
   cfg.addResource("mappings/customer.hbm.xml");
   cfg.addResource("mappings/claim.hbm.xml");
   cfg.addResource("mappings/policy.hbm.xml");
   sessionFactory = cfg.buildSessionFactory();
}
```

We will keep `sessionFactory` as a private member in the aspect—it will be needed every time we have to create a Hibernate session for talking to the database. This example illustrates the use of `staticinitialization` in a pointcut expression to match static initialization join points. See Chapter 6 for more details.

Entering these definitions into the editor (and adding the necessary imports for `net.sf.hibernate.*` and `net.sf.hibernate.cfg.*`) reveals a new problem, as shown in Figure 3.28. Nearly every call to a Hibernate API can throw a checked `HibernateException`. (`MappingException` is a subtype of `HibernateException`.) We're going to be making a lot of Hibernate calls, both within this aspect and within the DAOs in the `insurance.dao.hibernate` package. Is there something we can do to give a consistent treatment of `HibernateExceptions` in our application?

Figure 3.28   Unhandled exceptions.

3.3.7 Mapping Exceptions

For this iteration at least, the project team have decided to log any `HibernateException` that occurs, and then map it into a domain exception and rethrow. The mapping prevents the rest of the application from having to know about `HibernateException`, because we want only the `HibernateManager` aspect to have that knowledge. The `insurance.model` package defines an unchecked domain exception `SIException` that can be thrown by any of the methods in the `SimpleInsurance` façade. The `insurance.dao` package defines a subtype of `SIException`, `SIPersistenceException`. We will wrap any `HibernateException` that occurs in an `SIPersistenceException`.

We can use a form of advice known as `after throwing` advice to perform the mapping. Whereas the `after returning` advice that we've been using so far runs after a normal exit from any matched join points, `after throwing` advice runs after a join point is exited by throwing an exception. We can write a pointcut that will match any call made to a Hibernate API, and then use `after throwing` advice to handle any thrown exception, as shown in Figure 3.29. You can also see at the top of Figure 3.29 that we have temporarily commented out the calls in the advice that were giving us errors in Figure 3.28.

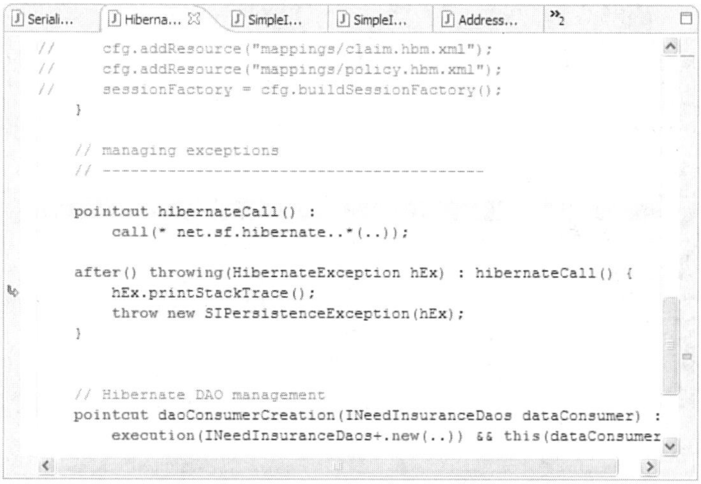

Figure 3.29 Handling Hibernate exceptions.

The Hibernate classes are defined in packages beginning with `net.sf.hibernate`, and the `hibernateCall` pointcut just matches any call made to a class defined in a package with that prefix. The `after throwing` advice gains access to the actual exception thrown by declaring an advice parameter inside the `throwing()` clause. The advice itself prints out the stack trace (it's a form of logging isn't it?) and then wraps the exception in a new `SIPersistenceException` for rethrowing. Chapter 7 has more information on `after throwing` advice and on throwing exceptions from within advice.

There's something else to notice about Figure 3.29—there's an advice marker in the gutter next to the call `hEx.printStackTrace()`. A look at the Outline view helps to explain what is going on (see Figure 3.30).

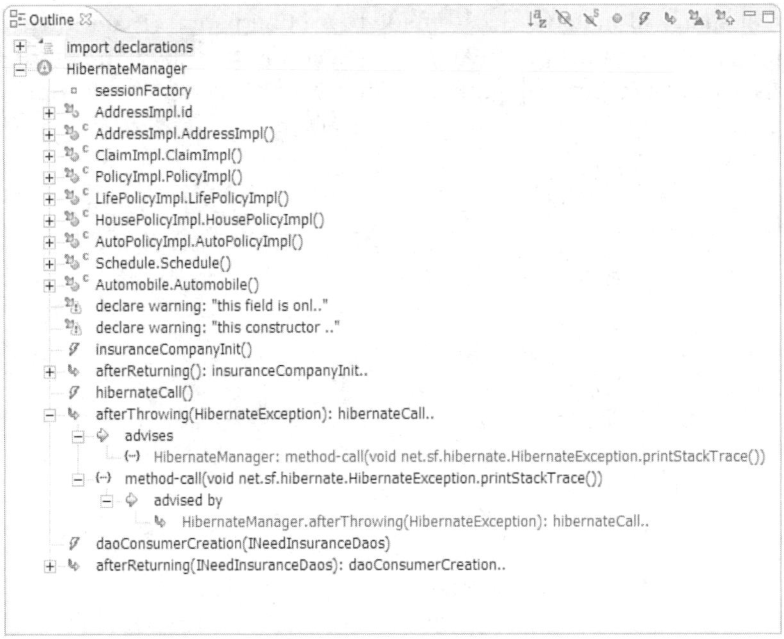

Figure 3.30   After throwing in the Outline view.

You can see that the `after throwing` advice advises the call to `HibernateException.printStackTrace`. Also note the method-call node in the outline, which is present whenever a call join point within a method or constructor has advice affecting it. The outline tells us that this method call is advised by the `after throwing` advice. In short, if `printStackTrace` were ever to throw a `HibernateException` (unlikely I grant you), we could get into trouble. We can tidy up that loose end by excluding `HibernateException` itself from list of target types we want to advise:

```
after() throwing(HibernateException hEx)
: hibernateCall() && !target(HibernateException) {
  hEx.printStackTrace();
  throw new SIPersistenceException(hEx);
}
```

There's one more thing we can do to make our code cleaner at this point. We know (because of the advice we just wrote) that any `HibernateException` thrown is going to be handled in a consistent manner—so we really do not need catch blocks all over our code anymore. AspectJ lets us *soften* checked exceptions.

Softening basically means converting a checked exception into an unchecked exception so that the compiler does not force us to place a catch block at every point it may be thrown. Softening is achieved via the `declare soft` statement, which has the following general form:

```
declare soft : ExceptionType : pointcutExpression;
```

This has the effect that any time an exception of type `ExceptionType` is thrown at a join point matched by `pointcutExpression`, it will be softened. Figure 3.31 shows the `declare soft` statement in the editor.

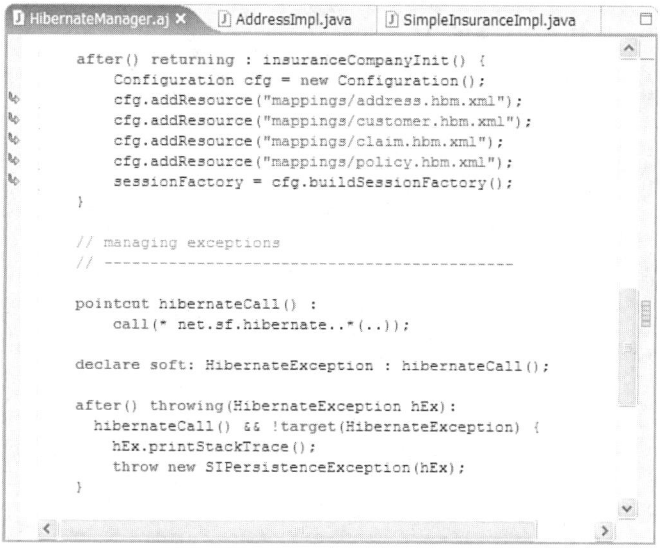

```
 HibernateManager.aj ✕      AddressImpl.java      SimpleInsuranceImpl.java

        after() returning : insuranceCompanyInit() {
            Configuration cfg = new Configuration();
            cfg.addResource("mappings/address.hbm.xml");
            cfg.addResource("mappings/customer.hbm.xml");
            cfg.addResource("mappings/claim.hbm.xml");
            cfg.addResource("mappings/policy.hbm.xml");
            sessionFactory = cfg.buildSessionFactory();
        }

        // managing exceptions
        // ---------------------------------------------------

        pointcut hibernateCall() :
            call(* net.sf.hibernate..*(..));

        declare soft: HibernateException : hibernateCall();

        after() throwing(HibernateException hEx):
          hibernateCall() && !target(HibernateException) {
            hEx.printStackTrace();
            throw new SIPersistenceException(hEx);
        }
```

Figure 3.31   Declare soft.

Notice that we no longer get compilation errors for the calls to Hibernate APIs within the configuration advice—the exceptions have been softened. You can also see the advice markers in the gutter indicating that the exception mapping `after throwing` advice is in effect on these calls.

The Outline view shows us all the places where a potential exception will be softened (see Figure 3.32). As we add more Hibernate calls, the `after throwing` and `declare soft` statements will continue to do their work. You can find more details on the `declare soft` statement in Chapter 7.

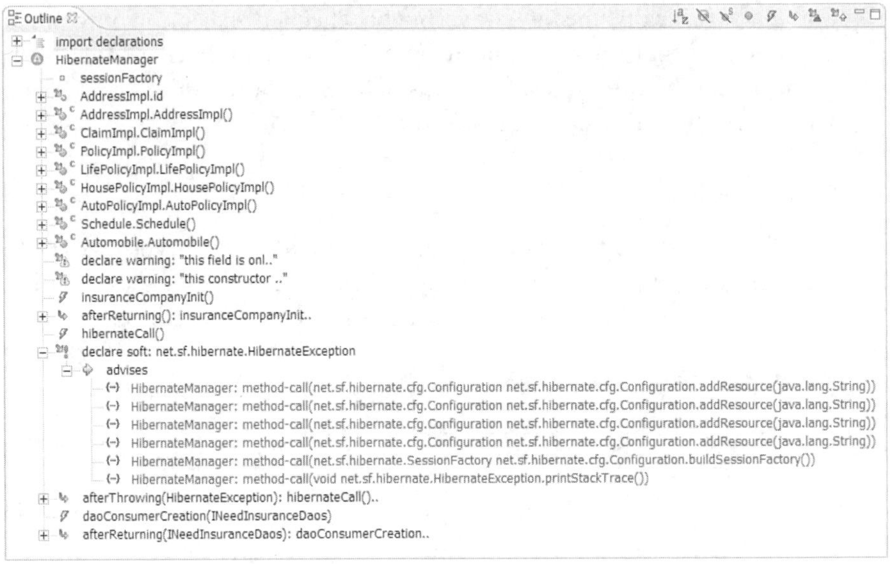

Figure 3.32 Declare soft in the Outline view.

3.3.8 Implementing the Data Access Objects

All that remains is to fill in the actual implementation of the DAO classes we created in Section 3.2.3. This follows the basic pattern shown in Listings 3.5 and 3.6 in Section 3.3.2. Listing 3.7 shows an excerpt from the `CustomerDaoImpl` class.

Listing 3.7 *CustomerDaoImpl*

```
public void insertCustomer(Customer c) {
  Session session = sessionFactory.openSession();
  Transaction tx = null;
  try {
    tx = session.beginTransaction();
    session.save(c);
    tx.commit();
  } catch (SIPersistenceException ex) {
    if (tx != null) tx.rollback();
    throw ex;
  } finally {
    session.close();
  }
}
```

```
public void updateCustomer(Customer c) {
  Session session = sessionFactory.openSession();
  Transaction tx = null;
  try {
    tx = session.beginTransaction();
    session.update(c);
    tx.commit();
  } catch (SIPersistenceException ex) {
    if (tx != null) tx.rollback();
    throw ex;
  } finally {
    session.close();
  }
}

public void deleteCustomer(Customer c) {
  Session session = sessionFactory.openSession();
  Transaction tx = null;
  try {
    tx = session.beginTransaction();
    session.delete(c);
    tx.commit();
  } catch (SIPersistenceException ex) {
    if (tx != null) tx.rollback();
    throw ex;
  } finally {
    session.close();
  }
}
```

There are a couple of points to note in this listing. First, we need to surround the transaction itself inside a try-catch block so that we can roll back if an exception occurs. Notice that we catch an `SIPersistenceException`—the `HibernateException` will already have been wrapped by the time it reaches the catch block. Second (and we hardly need to point it out), did you notice the repetition across the method implementations? Only the actual work done inside the transactions differs in each case. The situation would be even worse if it were not for the exception handling management in the `HibernateManager` aspect—at least we don't have to handle exceptions that occur while opening and closing sessions, too. We have a number of DAO classes to implement, and quite a few methods in each. Before reading any further, can you think of an easy way to remove this redundancy without using AspectJ?

The code would be much simpler and clearer if we could write something like this:

```
public void insertCustomer(Customer c) {
  session.save(c);
}
```

```
public void updateCustomer(Customer c) {
  session.update(c);
}

public void deleteCustomer(Customer c) {
  session.delete(c);
}
```

If you look again at Listing 3.7 you'll notice there's a basic pattern going on. We do some work inside of a hibernate transaction, and around that transaction is a set of boilerplate code for opening and closing the session, and for committing or rolling back the transaction. In AspectJ terms, we could express it like this:

```
Object around() : hibernateTransaction() {
  Object ret = null;
  Session session = sessionFactory.openSession();
  Transaction tx = null;
  try {
    tx = session.beginTransaction();
    ret = proceed();
    tx.commit();
  } catch(SIPersistenceException ex) {
    if (tx != null) tx.rollback();
    throw ex;
  } finally {
    session.close();
  }
  return ret;
}
```

This uses around advice at the set of join points matched by the `hibernateTransaction` pointcut to apply the session and transaction management logic. The actual work inside the transaction happens when the advice calls `proceed()`. Note that the return type of the advice is `Object` (around advice is the only kind to have a return value), and we return from the advice whatever value is returned by `proceed()`. We give more details on this mechanism in Chapter 7—for now it is enough to know that the caller of the original method will see its return value.

There is one problem with this implementation as it stands: How does the DAO executing the `hibernateTransaction()` get access to the `session` object that the around advice creates? We can use another form of dependency injection to solve this problem—the aspect can inject the session object into the DAO, not once when the DAO is constructed, but before each transaction. An easy way to do this is to make all the Hibernate DAOs we created in the `insurance.dao.` `hibernate` package extend a common superclass, `HibernateDao`. The implementation of `HibernateDao` is shown in Figure 3.33.

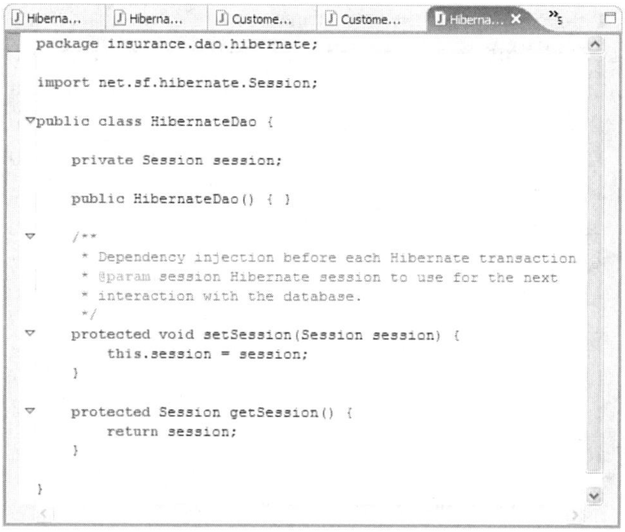

```
 J Hiberna...   J Hiberna...   J Custome...   J Custome...   J Hiberna... ×   »₅    □

  package insurance.dao.hibernate;

   import net.sf.hibernate.Session;

 ▽public class HibernateDao {

     private Session session;

     public HibernateDao() { }

 ▽   /**
      * Dependency injection before each Hibernate transaction
      * @param session Hibernate session to use for the next
      * interaction with the database.
      */
 ▽   protected void setSession(Session session) {
         this.session = session;
     }

 ▽   protected Session getSession() {
         return session;
     }

 }
```

Figure 3.33   The HibernateDao superclass.

Now the `CustomerDaoImpl`, `PolicyDaoImpl`, and `ClaimDaoImpl` classes can all call `getSession()` to access the session object they need. Figure 3.34 shows the definition of the `hibernateTransaction` pointcut and the completed around advice implementation with the dependency injection call.

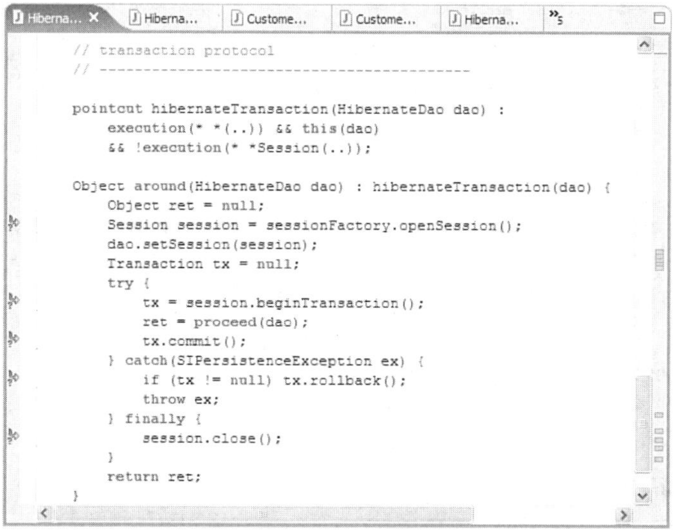

```
 J Hiberna... ×   J Hiberna...   J Custome...   J Custome...   J Hiberna...   »₅    □

     // transaction protocol
     // ----------------------------------------

     pointcut hibernateTransaction(HibernateDao dao) :
         execution(* *(..)) && this(dao)
         && !execution(* *Session(..));

     Object around(HibernateDao dao) : hibernateTransaction(dao) {
         Object ret = null;
         Session session = sessionFactory.openSession();
         dao.setSession(session);
         Transaction tx = null;
         try {
             tx = session.beginTransaction();
             ret = proceed(dao);
             tx.commit();
         } catch(SIPersistenceException ex) {
             if (tx != null) tx.rollback();
             throw ex;
         } finally {
             session.close();
         }
         return ret;
     }
```

Figure 3.34   The Hibernate transaction protocol.

The `hibernateTransaction` pointcut matches the execution of any method on a `HibernateDao`—except the `getSession` and `setSession` methods. At each join point it matches, it makes available the actual `HibernateDao` instance in the `dao` parameter. The around advice definition has been updated to take the `HibernateDao` object as a parameter, and after opening the session it calls `dao.setSession(session)` to pass the `dao` the session object it should use for the transaction. The gutter annotations in Figure 3.34 indicate the hibernate calls that are advised by the after throwing advice we wrote earlier to deal with exceptions. Figure 3.35 shows all the places that the advice applies.

Figure 3.35   Hibernate transactions.

With this advice in place the `HibernateManager` aspect is complete. The implementation of the `CustomerDaoImpl` class (for example) is now as shown in Listing 3.8, a considerable improvement.

Listing 3.8   Oh Happy DAO (*CustomerDAOImpl*)

```
package insurance.dao.hibernate;

import insurance.dao.CustomerDao;
import insurance.model.Customer;

import java.util.HashSet;
```

```
import java.util.Set;

import net.sf.hibernate.Criteria;
import net.sf.hibernate.expression.Expression;

public class CustomerDaoImpl extends HibernateDao
implements CustomerDao {

  public CustomerDaoImpl() {
  }

  public void insertCustomer(Customer c) {
    getSession().save(c);
  }

  public Set findCustomersById(String customerId) {
    Set result = null;
    customerId = customerId.trim().replace('*', '%');
    Criteria criteria =
      getSession().createCriteria(Customer.class);
    criteria.add(Expression.like("id", customerId));
    return new HashSet(criteria.list());
  }

  public Set findCustomersByLastName(String lastName) {
    Set result = null;
    lastName = lastName.trim().replace('*', '%');
    Criteria criteria =
      getSession().createCriteria(Customer.class);
    criteria.add(Expression.like("lastName", lastName));
    return new HashSet(criteria.list());
  }

  public void updateCustomer(Customer c) {
    getSession().update(c);
  }

  public void deleteCustomer(Customer c) {
    getSession().delete(c);
  }

}
```

3.3.9 Evaluating the Implementation

The completed `HibernateManager` aspect is shown in Listing 3.9. We have been able to add a Hibernate-based persistence implementation to the application, without changing a single file outside of the `insurance.dao.hibernate` package. Within the Hibernate DAOs themselves, we made significant improvements to the code clarity and eliminated a lot of duplication. We also put in place a simple consistent exception-handling policy. The solution is completely transparent to the rest of the application. We were able to do this because of a combination of factors:

- ○ The application is designed in clean layers, with good separation between interface and implementation.

- ○ We selected a persistence technology (Hibernate) that is noninvasive with respect to the classes it persists.

- ○ We used AspectJ to complement Hibernate and keep the persistence implementation modular and concise.

AspectJ works in conjunction with all the good OO design principles you already know; it is not a replacement for them.

Listing 3.9   The *HibernateManager* Aspect

```
package insurance.dao.hibernate;

import insurance.dao.INeedInsuranceDaos;
import insurance.dao.SIPersistenceException;
import insurance.model.*;
import insurance.model.impl.*;
import net.sf.hibernate.*;
import net.sf.hibernate.cfg.Configuration;

public aspect HibernateManager {

  private SessionFactory sessionFactory;

  // meeting Hibernate's requirements
  public Long AddressImpl.id;

  public AddressImpl.new() {}
  public ClaimImpl.new() {}
  public PolicyImpl.new() {}
  public LifePolicyImpl.new() {}
  public HousePolicyImpl.new() {}
  public AutoPolicyImpl.new() {}
  public Schedule.new() {}
  public Automobile.new() {}

  // make sure their usage stays within Hibernate
  declare warning : get(* AddressImpl.id) ||
                    set(* AddressImpl.id)
    : "this field is only for use by Hibernate";

  declare warning : call(AddressImpl.new()) ||
                    call(ClaimImpl.new()) ||
                    call(PolicyImpl.new()) ||
```

```
                        call(LifePolicyImpl.new()) ||
                        call(HousePolicyImpl.new()) ||
                        call(AutoPolicyImpl.new()) ||
                        call(Schedule.new()) ||
                        call(Automobile.new())
    : "this constructor is only for use by Hibernate";

// initial configuration
// ---------------------------------------

pointcut insuranceCompanyInit() :
  staticinitialization(SimpleInsuranceImpl);

after() returning : insuranceCompanyInit() {
  Configuration cfg = new Configuration();
  cfg.addResource("mappings/address.hbm.xml");
  cfg.addResource("mappings/customer.hbm.xml");
  cfg.addResource("mappings/claim.hbm.xml");
  cfg.addResource("mappings/policy.hbm.xml");
  sessionFactory = cfg.buildSessionFactory();
}

// managing exceptions
// ---------------------------------------

pointcut hibernateCall() :
  call(* net.sf.hibernate..*(..));

declare soft : HibernateException : hibernateCall();

after() throwing(HibernateException hEx) :
  hibernateCall() && !target(HibernateException) {
  hEx.printStackTrace();
  throw new SIPersistenceException(hEx);
}

// Hibernate DAO management
pointcut daoConsumerCreation(
  INeedInsuranceDaos dataConsumer) :
  execution(INeedInsuranceDaos+.new(..)) &&
  this(dataConsumer);

after(INeedInsuranceDaos dataConsumer) returning :
  daoConsumerCreation(dataConsumer) {
  dataConsumer.setCustomerDao(new CustomerDaoImpl());
  dataConsumer.setPolicyDao(new PolicyDaoImpl());
  dataConsumer.setClaimDao(new ClaimDaoImpl());
}


// transaction protocol
// ---------------------------------------
```

```
pointcut hibernateTransaction(HibernateDao dao) :
   execution(* *(..)) && this(dao)
   && !execution(* *Session(..));

Object around(HibernateDao dao) :
   hibernateTransaction(dao) {
   Object ret = null;
   Session session = sessionFactory.openSession();
   dao.setSession(session);
   Transaction tx = null;
   try {
     tx = session.beginTransaction();
     ret = proceed(dao);
     tx.commit();
   } catch(SIPersistenceException ex) {
     if (tx != null) tx.rollback();
     throw ex;
   } finally {
     session.close();
   }
   return ret;
   }

}
```

3.4   Managing Build Configurations

Now we have a project with two persistence implementations, one in the `insurance.dao.inmemory` package and one in the `insurance.dao.hibernate` package. It is hard to imagine a scenario where we would want both of them at the same time, but we're not quite ready to throw the in-memory version away—it enables us, for example, to create a single Jar run-anywhere version of the application for demos and so on.

Eclipse supports exclusion filters for source folders; these enable you to include or exclude certain files from the build. Because including and excluding aspects is a more common operation (for example, temporarily adding an aspect that gives some debugging output), AJDT makes the exclusion filter mechanism easily accessible directly from the Package Explorer.

Figure 3.36 shows the Package Explorer with the Simple Insurance project opened. Selecting the `insurance.model.inmemory` package node and right-clicking brings up a context menu from which you can select the **Exclude from build configuration** action. The result is shown in Figure 3.37. This action is also available for multiple selections and for individual source files. Notice in Figure 3.37 that the icon for the excluded source files has changed to an outlined J  rather than a solid J 🇯—this indicates that these files are not currently included in the build. The package icon is also empty, indicating that the entire package contents are excluded. A package with some included and some excluded files would show as a half-full icon.

Figure 3.36   Excluding files from the build configuration.

Figure 3.37   Excluded files in the Package Explorer.

The context menu option **Include in build configuration** enables you to add previously excluded resources back into the build.

3.5   Summary

This chapter extended the Simple Insurance application with two persistence implementations, one using Java serialization and one using Hibernate. AspectJ helped us to create modular solutions, which made them easier to add (and easier to remove) from the application. In the end, either solution could be included or excluded from the application with a single mouse click.

We saw how a number of the Eclipse tools can be used in the development of AspectJ programs—including some of the powerful refactorings that Eclipse makes available. We also introduced you to a number of new AspectJ constructs, including after throwing advice, declare parents, declare soft, and inter-type declarations. Part 2 of the book goes into all these concepts in more depth, but for now we complete Part 1 with a look at some of the basic capabilities of AJDT not yet discussed.

CHAPTER 4

More AJDT

This chapter covers some of the basic facilities in AJDT that we didn't get to during Chapters 2 and 3—including the answer to everyone's favorite question, "But what about debugging?" This chapter covers the following topics:

- ❍ Compiler settings and build options
- ❍ Debugging
- ❍ Editor templates and the Outline view toolbar
- ❍ Generating documentation (ajdoc)
- ❍ AspectJ help, examples and cheat sheets

4.1   Building an ASPECTJ Project

In the last two chapters, we were using AJDT in its default mode, in which a full build of your project occurs every time that you save a file. When working with larger projects, this can be too slow. This section shows you how to turn on incremental compilation, and how to trigger builds manually. You also learn how to configure the basic AspectJ compiler options.

4.1.1 Controlling Project Builds

The only reason to change from the default Eclipse behavior of allowing builds to occur automatically on every resource change is if you are working with a large project. This is because in the current version of AJDT at the time of writing (AJDT v1.1.11), automatic builds are always full builds: *all* of the source code for the project is compiled each time. The alternative to a full build is an incremental build, which means building as little as possible to ensure the output is consistent.

Incremental compilation of a regular Java program is relatively straightforward. When you have modified an individual source file and saved it, an incremental build usually means just compiling that single file, and any other files containing types that reference the recompiled types. Incremental compilation for an AspectJ program has additional considerations: The changed file has to be relinked with any aspects in the project. If an aspect itself is changed, all types in the program potentially need to be relinked.

The AspectJ compiler (since version 1.1.1) can correctly perform this analysis and does offer an incremental compilation mode. For an IDE environment, additional work is needed to also update the various views (such as the Outline view) that show program structure. AJDT 1.1.11 does not fully support this incremental updating of the program structure. This is why the default compilation mode is to perform a full build,[1] so that the various AJDT views stay correct at all times.

If you are working with large projects and find that the default building behavior of AJDT is degrading your productivity, you can switch to incremental compilation mode, or to manual building.

4.1.1.1 Incremental Compilation

AJDT's incremental compilation mode exploits the incremental compilation support in the AspectJ compiler itself, at the cost of not always keeping the program structure displayed in the Outline view fully current. Configuring a project to build incrementally keeps the automatic building behavior, but makes those builds faster because they are *incremental* builds rather than *full* builds.

To activate incremental compilation, select the project node in the Package Explorer and choose **Properties** from the context menu (or press **Alt+Enter**). Select the properties for AspectJ in the left pane, as shown in Figure 4.1.

Check the first option on the page, **Use incremental compilation**, and click **OK**. With incremental building turned on, AJDT behaves in the following way:

---

1. We're working on full incremental support in AJDT—by the time you read this, there may be an AJDT version available that supports it: Check the AJDT Web site at http://www.eclipse.org/ajdt for the latest updates.

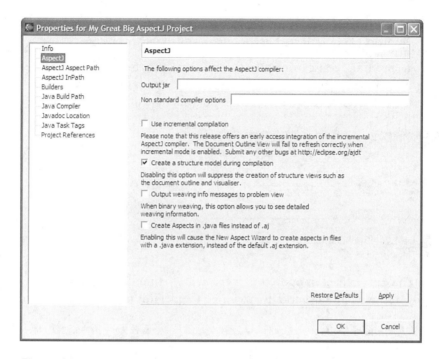

Figure 4.1   AspectJ Properties page.

Cross-reference information not fully shown   The overall structure shown by the Outline view will be maintained correctly after an incremental build, but the "advised by" nodes only show the name of the advising aspect, and the link is not navigable ("aspect declaration" nodes behave in a similar manner). In addition, the advice and inter-type declaration markers in the gutters of the editor are not shown. The output of the build—the `.class` files on the disk—will be correct, and if you run your application it *will* be in a consistent state.

Program structure not shown for other files   Having saved a source file, if you then open a different source file in the editor, its Outline view will be empty and contain the text "build to view structure." Structure information is only available for files included in the most recent incremental build.

Full build triggered if you modify an aspect   Each time you save a resource in your AspectJ project, and an automatic incremental build is started, the compiler examines the change deltas. If you have changed an aspect, a full compilation of the project will be performed to ensure any changes to pointcuts and advice in the aspect you have modified are appropriately reflected across the rest of your project.

At any time you can restore the full structure and cross-reference information by manually triggering a full build using the build button (see Figure 4.2). The cross-references display until the next incremental build occurs.

Figure 4.2 The build button.

You can expect support for incremental compilation to improve in future AJDT releases, and eventually it will be the default mode.

4.1.1.2 Manual Builds

Rather than losing structure information altogether for files not included in the most recent incremental build, you can disable the automatic building feature and work with manual builds instead. To disable automatic building, deselect Build **Automatically** from the Project menu, as shown in Figure 4.3

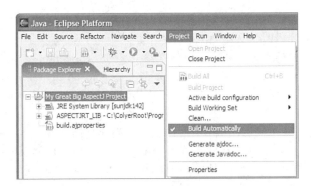

Figure 4.3 Disabling automatic builds.

With automatic building disabled, the display of the program structure and cross-reference information is based on the results of the last build, and is updated each time you trigger a manual build (but not before).

With automatic building turned off, the Java Development Tools in Eclipse add their own build button to the toolbar—so that two build buttons appear. The AspectJ build button is differentiated by its orange coloring and by the pull-down next to it (see Figure 4.4, in which the AspectJ build button is highlighted).

Figure 4.4 AspectJ build button with autobuilding disabled.

To trigger a manual build either press the AspectJ build button, or open the Project menu again and select **Build Project**.

4.1.2 Setting Compiler Options

The AspectJ compiler respects the options that can be specified in Eclipse for normal Java compilation. The property page for specifying these compiler options can be found under the workbench preferences. Open **Window > Preferences** on the Eclipse toolbar. In the dialog box that appears, open the Java node on the left and select **Compiler**. You will see the panel shown in Figure 4.5.

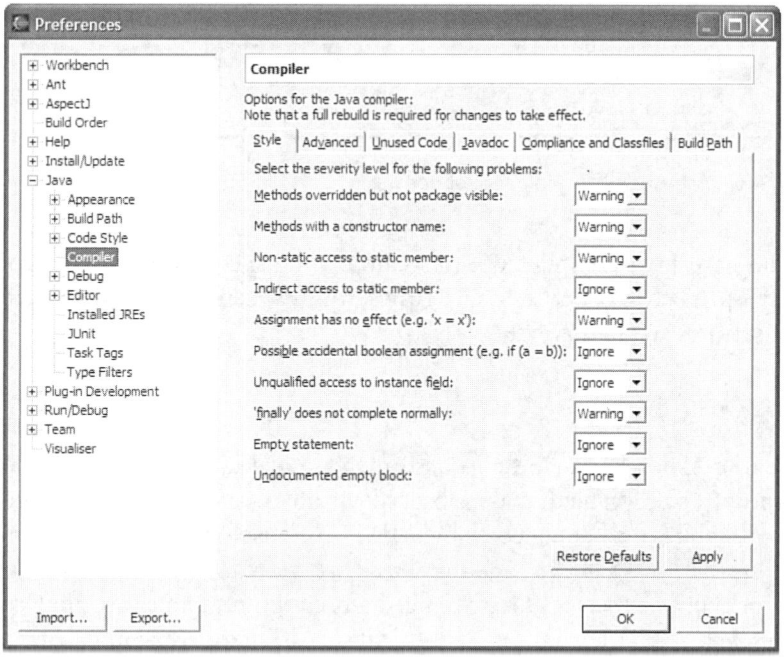

Figure 4.5 Base Java compiler options.

Any options set here will be respected by the AspectJ compiler as well as by the Java compiler. There are additional compiler options which the AspectJ compiler supports that the JDT compiler does not, and these are found in the Compiler section of the AspectJ node, as shown in Figure 4.6. The meanings of these various options are covered in Part 3 of the book.

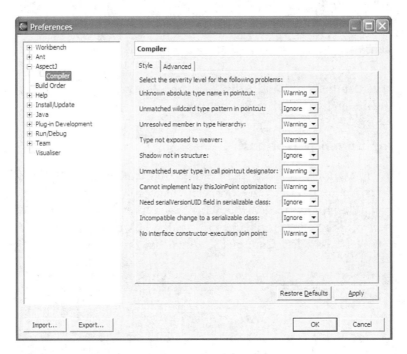

Figure 4.6 AspectJ specific compiler options.

The base Java compiler options can also be specified on a per-project basis from the project's Properties page. Any settings specified here override the workbench settings we saw above.

4.2 Debugging

Debugging AspectJ code in Eclipse is much like debugging Java code; you can set breakpoints, step through code, observe variables, and so forth. Let's go through a typical debugging sequence using AJDT. Suppose we want to confirm that the advice in the `SerializationBasedPersistence` aspect (developed in Chapter 2) is working as expected. First we need a breakpoint, and to set one you can just double-click in the left gutter of the editor. Alternatively, you can bring up the context menu and choose **Toggle Breakpoint,** as shown in Figure 4.7.

Figure 4.7   Setting a breakpoint from the context menu.

Figure 4.8 shows the aspect open in the editor with a breakpoint set on line 26 at the start of the advice body (as described in Chapter 1). In the Outline view, we can see the advice is affecting the `SimpleInsuranceImpl` class.

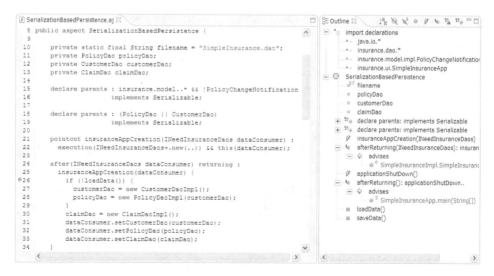

Figure 4.8   *SerializationBasedPersistence* setup for debugging.

Run the `SimpleInsuranceApp` application in Debug mode by clicking the debug button on the toolbar (see Figure 4.9). This causes the workbench to switch to the Debug perspective when program execution hits the breakpoint. Figure 4.10 shows the initial Debug view that appears.

Figure 4.9   Launching the debugger.

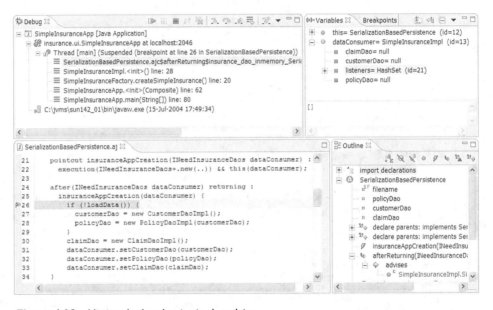

Figure 4.10   Hitting the breakpoint in the advice.

Note a couple of things about Figure 4.10:

○ In the upper-right corner, the variables view is now showing the *aspect* state. It shows the aspect instance and the advice local variable `dataConsumer`.

○ In the upper left, the thread stack is showing that we are within after returning advice in the `SerializationBasedPersistence` aspect. The next frame on the thread stack shows the advised constructor in `SimpleInsuranceImpl`.

At this point we have confirmed the advice is being invoked as expected when the constructor for `SimpleInsuranceImpl` executes. We are free to continue debugging and step through the advice, perhaps stepping into the `loadData()` method. Or we can step-return back to the `SimpleInsuranceImpl` constructor. The step-over, step-into, and step-return buttons in the debugger's toolbar work exactly as they do when debugging Java programs.

Of course, you can also set breakpoints in classes, and step into any advice affecting them. To go into the advice from the advised code you need to "step into" at the right time. Any advised method has a gutter annotation against the method declaration that tells you the kind of advice being applied. If it is *before* advice, you need to step into it when the debugger is positioned on the first line of code in the method. Figure 4.11 shows a simple class and aspect; the `printMessage()` method is advised by before advice from the aspect. We have set a breakpoint on the call to the advised `printMessage()` (line 5).

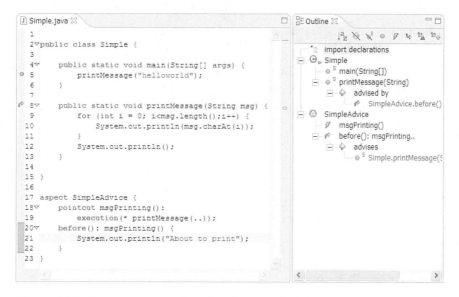

Figure 4.11   Breakpoint set on the call to the advised method.

If we now run the application in Debug mode, the debugger will stop on line 5. If we then step into the `printMessage()` call, the debugger will move to line 9, as shown in Figure 4.12.

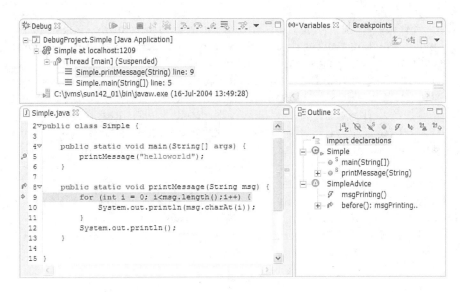

Figure 4.12   Stepping into the advised method.

Now we are at the start of the method advised by before advice. If we now click the step-into button *again*, we will go into the before advice defined in the aspect, and jump to line 19 (see Figure 4.13).

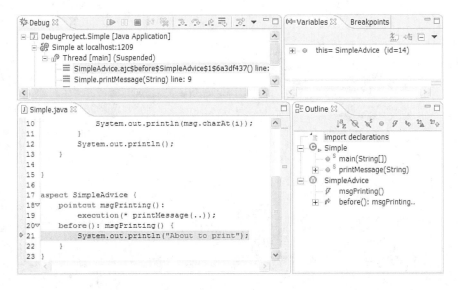

Figure 4.13   Stepping into the advice.

To step into *after* advice, you need to click the step-into button when the debugger is positioned on the last line of the method. This is not the last line of code in the method, but the last line of the method: the line containing the closing curly brace for the method. Figure 4.14 shows another simple aspect, this time with after returning advice applying to the `printMessage()` method.

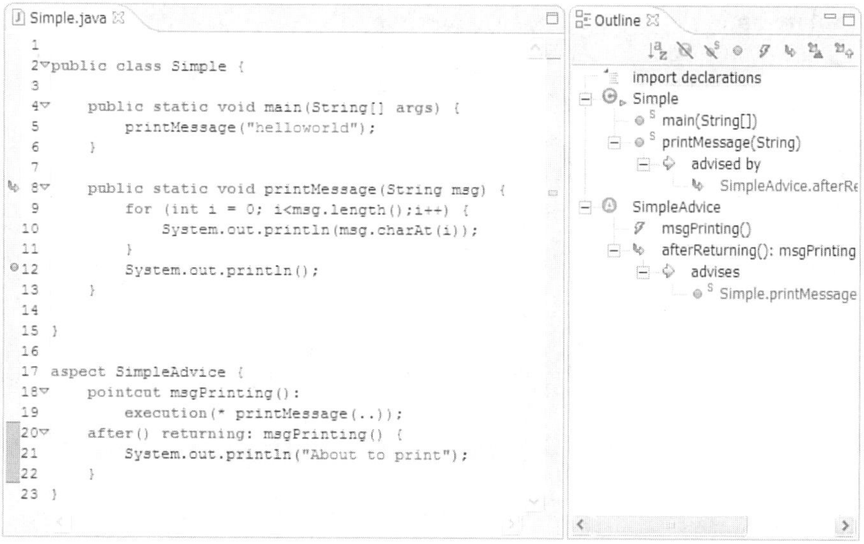

Figure 4.14   Breakpoint set for stepping into after advice.

The breakpoint has been set on the last line of code in the `printMessage()` method (line 12). The gutter annotation shows that `printMessage()` is affected by after returning advice. If we start the application in Debug mode, it will stop at line 12. Remember that to reach the after advice we have to step into the last line of the method, so the first thing to do is step over to line 13. Now, if we "step into" from there, the debugger jumps to line 21.

What we have shown here is that you need to be aware of when the advice will run in order to know when to click the step-into button. The gutter markers in the editor show you this, but it can be easier just to set the breakpoint in the advice directly.

Basically, debugging AspectJ programs works in exactly the same way as debugging Java programs; operating the debugger, observing object state, setting breakpoints, and so on all behave identically. The only remaining issue to be aware of concerns the debugging of around advice. By default the compiler inlines around advice in a manner that confuses the debugger.[2] If you put a breakpoint in such around advice, the debugger won't stop. In this situation there is an AspectJ compiler option that can help you.

Open the AspectJ compiler preferences page as described in Section 4.1.2, and then click the **Advanced** tab. In the Options page that appears, check the **No inline** option (see Figure 4.15) and click **OK**.

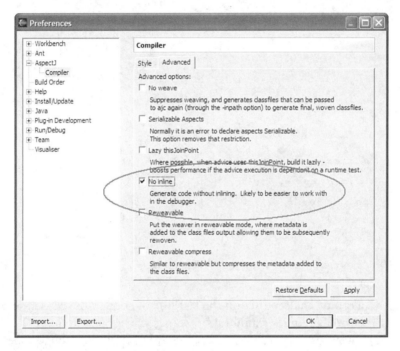

Figure 4.15   Setting the No inline option.

After the next project build, you will then be able to set breakpoints in around advice and the debugger will stop when it hits them.

---

2. This situation might have changed by the time you read this—check the AJDT home page at http://www.eclipse.org/ajdt for details of the latest releases.

4.3   Editor Templates and the Outline View Toolbar

Chapters 2 and 3 covered a lot of the basics for working with the AspectJ editor and Outline view. This section briefly describes editor templates—a form of completion for AspectJ constructs—and the options available to you in the Outline view's toolbar.

4.3.1 Editor Templates

You can type some simple shortcuts into the AspectJ editor to speed text entry (and to help you learn the AspectJ syntax more quickly). These shortcuts are expanded to templates that you can then modify as necessary. You are probably using templates for normal Java development already: If you have ever entered `sysout` or `syserr` and pressed **Ctrl+Spacebar,** you are using a template. For example, see Figure 4.16. In the top editor, the text "before" has been entered. With the cursor positioned at the end of the word *before*, **Ctrl+Spacebar** is then pressed: The template is expanded as shown in the bottom editor.

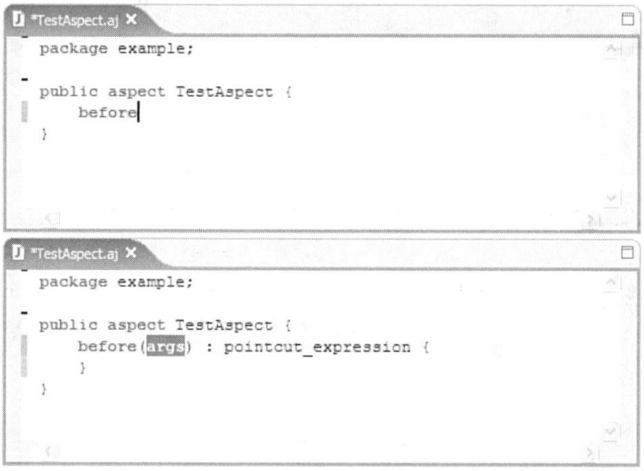

Figure 4.16   Before and after template expansion in the editor.

Many such templates are defined. You can see them in the workbench preferences page for the Java Editor. Open **Window > Preferences** and in the page that appears, select **Java, Editor and** then **Templates** in the left pane. You will see the template definitions as shown in Figure 4.17.

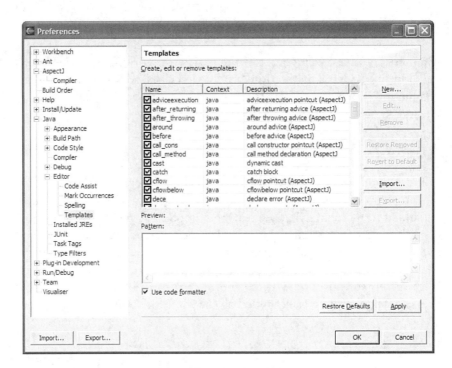

Figure 4.17   AspectJ templates defined for the editor.

4.3.2 Outline View Toolbar

The AspectJ Outline view has a toolbar that offers similar functions to those found in the normal Java Outline view. Figure 4.18 shows the toolbar for the Outline view.

Figure 4.18   Outline view actions.

These actions affect the nodes displayed in the outline tree view and from left to right, they mean

- ○ Sort alphabetically (the default order is the declaration order).
- ○ Hide fields.
- ○ Hide static members.

   ○ Hide non-public members.

   ○ Hide pointcuts.

   ○ Hide advice.

   ○ Hide inter-type declarations.

   ○ Hide declare parents.

4.4   Generating Documentation (Ajdoc)

Ajdoc is the AspectJ equivalent of the javadoc tool. It can be used to parse javadoc-style comments from AspectJ source code and produce HTML-formatted documentation. In actual usage, ajdoc is very similar to javadoc, and when using AJDT the ajdoc tool can be found in the same place as the javadoc tool. For any AspectJ project, open the Project menu and you will find the option **Generate ajdoc**. This will pop up the wizard shown in Figure 4.19.

Figure 4.19   Ajdoc wizard.

The options presented are identical to those for the javadoc tool. Usually the defaults in the wizard are fine and you can just click **Finish**; the one override you *might* want to specify is on the second page of the wizard, where you can choose to open the generated documentation immediately in a browser by checking the option **Open generated index file in browser**.

In addition to generating the standard javadoc documentation, ajdoc also generates documentation for aspects and their members (advice, inter-type declarations, pointcuts, and so on). In addition, the generated documentation also includes cross-reference information similar to that shown in the Outline view for "advises" and "advised by" relationships and so on. These references take the form of hyperlinks between, for example, an advised method and the advice that advises it. Figure 4.20 shows the generated documentation for the insurance example developed in Chapter 2. In the figure, you can see we are browsing the `PolicyImpl` class, and in the window on the right we can see that the `setStartDate()` and `setEndDate()` methods are advised by after returning advice from the `PolicyChangeNotification` aspect.

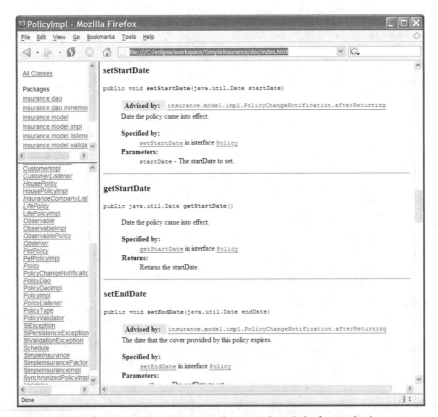

Figure 4.20 Generated documentation showing advice links for methods.

4.5 AspectJ Help, Examples, and Cheat Sheets

We finish this chapter with a look at some useful resources that will help you learn more about AspectJ programming in AJDT.

4.5.1 Getting Basic Help on AJDT and AspectJ

Chapter 1, Section 1.4 covered how to access the AJDT and AspectJ manuals installed as part of the AJDT Eclipse feature. These manuals are included as part of the standard Eclipse help. To access the help at any time, open the **Help** menu on the menu bar and select **Help Contents**.

4.5.2 AspectJ Examples

One of the simplest ways of getting to grips with any new language is by looking at existing sample code and modifying it to suit your own needs. AJDT provides some sample AspectJ projects and a simple mechanism for importing them into Eclipse. The wizard for importing examples can be found in the same place as other wizards for creating new resources. Open **File > New > Other** and in the dialog box that appears, open the **AspectJ** node and then the **AspectJ Examples** below it and you will see the examples shown in Figure 4.21.

Figure 4.21   AspectJ examples.

Just choose an example from the list, click **Next**, change the name for the imported project if you want, and then click **Finish**. You will then have a new AspectJ project in your workspace. These examples are all ready to compile and run—for more information on what they actually do, see the help on the examples included as part of the AJDT Eclipse help. They are described in Chapter 3 of the AspectJ programming guide, and Figure 4.22 shows exactly where you can find this in the help system.

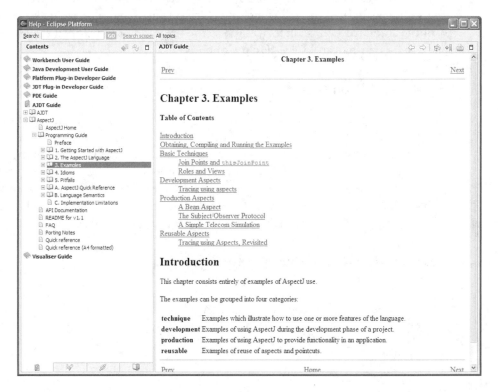

Figure 4.22   Help on the AspectJ examples.

4.5.3 AspectJ Cheat Sheets

Eclipse provides a facility called cheat sheets. A cheat sheet is a guide that helps you achieve a particular task. In the case of AJDT that task might be simply to create your first AspectJ project. The AJDT development team is currently working to create cheat sheets for all the common activities in AJDT. These cheat sheets run alongside your normal development perspective in Eclipse and guide you through the wizards, dialog boxes, and options in order to complete a task. To see those currently available, open **Help > Cheat Sheets**. Figure 4.23 shows the Simple AspectJ Application cheat sheet included in AJDT v1.1.11.

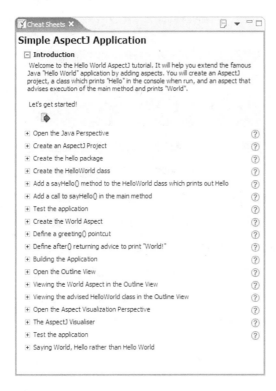

Figure 4.23   Using an AJDT cheat sheet in Eclipse.

4.6   Summary

This part of the book has introduced all the basic facilities of AJDT. You now know how to create, build, run, explore, and debug AspectJ projects in Eclipse. This part also described where to find help and some facilities to assist you in learning the language and tools.

However, there are still many additional features of AJDT that we haven't covered yet; creating and linking with aspect libraries, using shared source folders, and project visualization to name but a few. These more advanced capabilities are discussed in Part 3.

PART 2

The AspectJ Language

Part 1 introduced you to AspectJ and the AspectJ Development Tools in a tutorial fashion. Along the way, you should have picked up a basic understanding of the AspectJ language. In Part 2, we build on that and fill in some of the details that we passed over previously to give you the complete picture.

Chapter 5 presents an overview of the language, showing how the constituent parts fit together. In Chapter 6 you will find an in-depth treatment of pointcut expressions for matching join points. Chapter 7 explores the different kinds of advice that you can write in an AspectJ program and discusses their usage. Chapter 8 describes inter-type declarations in all their various forms, and Chapter 9 shows how all the parts fit together into aspects. Chapter 9 also discusses aspect lifecycle choices. We conclude this part of the book with a look at AspectJ's runtime *application programming interfaces* (APIs).

A lot of detailed material is presented in the pages that follow. It is fine to read it through quickly the first time around and press on to Part 3, where we return to a more complete example-driven style. If you decide to do this, do come back and read Part 2 carefully later—there is a lot of useful information packed into these chapters. However you decide to initially read them, we hope that you find these chapters a useful reference to turn to again and again while learning your way around the AspectJ language.

CHAPTER 5

An Overview of AspectJ

This chapter presents an overview of the AspectJ language, describing the various constructs in AspectJ and how they fit together. We cover the notion of an aspect as a unit of modularity for crosscutting concerns, and then look at the constituent parts of an aspect—pointcuts (and the join point model on which they depend), advice, and inter-type declarations. The chapters that follow provide more detail on each of these concepts.

5.1   What Is An Aspect?

So what exactly *is* an aspect? Like a class, an aspect is a unit of modularity, encapsulation, and abstraction; and although classes and aspects have many similarities, there are also some important differences. Unlike classes, aspects can be used to implement crosscutting concerns in a modular fashion. (You have seen a few examples of crosscutting concerns in Part 1 of this book.)

What makes a concern (or a feature) crosscutting? The notion of an insurance policy (as implemented, for example, by the `PolicyImpl` class from the Simple Insurance application in Part 1) is not crosscutting. The notion of issuing a change notification whenever the state of a policy is updated (as implemented for example by the `PolicyChangeNotification` aspect) *is* crosscutting. What's the difference?

Let's look at part of the implementation of the `PolicyImpl` class, the `addClaims` method:

```
public void addClaim(Claim claim) {
    if (claim == null) {
        throw new IllegalArgumentException(
          "Received a null claim!");
```

```
    }
    this.claims.add(claim);
}
```

When this method has been written, assuming there are no bugs in it, we can say that the implementation of adding a claim to a policy is completed. Now consider the following implementation of change notification:

```
protected void notifyListeners() {
    for (Iterator iter = listeners.iterator();
         iter.hasNext();) {
      PolicyListener l = (PolicyListener) iter.next();
      l.policyUpdated(this);
    }
}
```

Is this implementation complete? Have we done everything that's needed for change notification to work? No, we haven't—the implementation of change notification requires that the notifyListeners method be invoked at appropriate points in the program control flow, otherwise it would not be correct.

A crosscutting concern is one that *requires* certain behavior to occur at one or more points in the control flow of a program for its implementation to be correct. In addition, at those required points, the primary focus of the program is not on accomplishing the required behavior.

Huh?

Let's make that a little clearer by example. The implementation of the addClaim method requires that the new claim be added to the set of known claims for the policy. In the control flow of the addClaim method, this behavior needs to occur, but at that point the primary focus of the program is to do exactly this—add the claim. In contrast, the implementation of change notification also needs some behavior to occur at the point a claim is added—it needs to issue a change notification. At this point in the program, however, the primary focus is on adding a claim, not on issuing change notifications.

Here's one way of implementing the crosscutting change notification that has certain modularity characteristics:

```
public void addClaim(Claim claim) {
    if (claim == null) {
        throw new IllegalArgumentException(
            "Received a null claim!");
    }
```

```
    this.claims.add(claim);
    for (Iterator iter = listeners.iterator();
        iter.hasNext();) {
      PolicyListener l = (PolicyListener) iter.next();
      l.policyUpdated(this);
    }
}
```

Here's another way of implementing the crosscutting change notification that has better modularity characteristics:

```
public void addClaim(Claim claim) {
    if (claim == null) {
        throw new IllegalArgumentException(
            "Received a null claim!");
    }
    this.claims.add(claim);
    notifyListeners();
}
```

Part 1 of the book showed you another way to implement the crosscutting change notification that has even better modularity characteristics again: the PolicyChangeNotification aspect.

Another example of this kind of crosscutting concern is the implementation of a security feature that *requires* control to be passed to it before accessing protected resources; otherwise it cannot fulfill its obligations and its implementation would not be correct. This kind of crosscutting concern is modularized in an aspect primarily through the use of pointcuts and advice.

There's a second type of crosscutting concern, too. This type of crosscutting concern arises when you need multiple types in a program to acquire a capability (such as the ability to be printed) for some common purpose. In a language such as Java, you can often recognize this situation by a class implementing an interface such as IPrintable. In Java, however, without using up the precious inheritance slot, or performing cumbersome delegation, there's no way to reuse (even a default) Printable implementation. Another example of this kind of crosscutting was found in the HibernateManager aspect from Chapter 3—for the Hibernate persistence implementation to be complete, we needed several types in the program to acquire a new capability (a default constructor). Aspects in AspectJ can modularize crosscutting concerns such as this through a mechanism known as inter-type declarations. They work in a way that is similar to open classes or mixins in languages that support those features.

5.1.1 Modularity, Encapsulation, and Abstraction

Modularity is just the notion of dividing a system into parts (modules). Aspects provide a unit of modularity for crosscutting concerns, enabling us to separate scattered logic from the classes in which it was previously tangled, and place it in a module of its own.

Modularity is a good start, but aspects provide a second key benefit. They *encapsulate* the implementation of the feature or function that they implement. Encapsulation means that all information relating to the implementation of the feature is hidden from other modules (information hiding; Parnas 1972, 1053–1058). Aspects hide information in the same way as classes, by controlling visibility of their members. They also provide a powerful form of information hiding that classes cannot. Not only can an aspect hide the details of *how* something is done, but also *when*. Within an aspect, it is easy to implement the requirement that any error occurring within the control flow of a user interaction in a GUI should be flagged to a user in a dialog box, and any error not directly resulting from a user-initiated action should just be logged. Not only is that requirement hard to implement without aspects, but doing so also means that information about the policy for error handling (or at a minimum, the presence of a policy) has to leak into all the places that errors might occur.

The act of separating the implementation of a feature into an aspect (modularizing), and encapsulating the details of the implementation inside of it, leads us to a third key property of aspects: by *naming* the aspect, it becomes a *unit of abstraction* for that concept in the system. Together modularity, encapsulation, and abstraction are key weapons in the battle against software complexity.

5.2   Join Points and Pointcuts

So how exactly does an aspect specify "when" it wants control? Underpinning any aspect-oriented approach is something called a *join point model*. The join point model defines the set of events (join points) visible to an aspect during program execution. Aspects specify which of these events they are interested in through a *pointcut*—which is a predicate (or filter) against which join points are matched.

5.2.1 Join Points

As discussed in Chapter 2, Section 2.5.1, join points are events in the control flow of a program. They exist in any program (even those written before AO was invented). Examples of events that occur during the execution of a program are a call being made to a method, a field being updated, an expression being evaluated, the fourth line of code in the Foo.bar() method being executed, and so on. Some of these events (such as method calls) represent principled points in the program that we can refer to with some confidence. Other events (such as the execution of the fourth line of code in a certain method) are less principled, and references made to them are likely to be fragile in the face of program maintenance. A join point model determines which events will be exposed as join points (and hence can be referred to in pointcut expressions), and which will not. AspectJ exposes join points for the following:

- ○ A call to a method or constructor
- ○ The execution of a method, constructor, or advice body
- ○ The access or update of a field
- ○ The initialization of classes and objects
- ○ The execution of an exception handler[1]

Figure 5.1 shows the execution of a testTransfer method in an AccountManager class. Join points are highlighted as rounded gray rectangles, indicating where they occur in the control flow of the program execution. The sequence begins with the execution of the testTransfer method (execution join point), which calls the Account() constructor (call join point). A new Account object is initialized (initialization join point) and the constructor executes (execution join point). The testTransfer then creates a second Account object in a similar manner. Finally, it calls the transfer method (call join point), which executes (execution join point). This calls the debit method on the "from" account (call join point), which executes (execution join point) and returns by throwing an InsufficientFundsException. This is caught and handled in the transfer method (handler join point).

---

1. after() throwing advice can be used to capture the exit from any join point via a thrown exception, as discussed in Chapter 7.

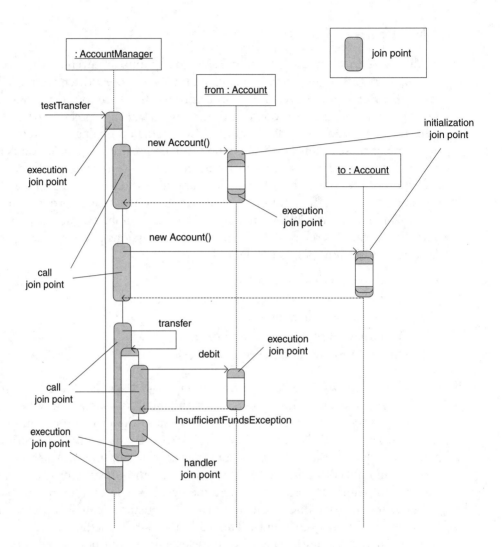

Figure 5.1 Join points in program execution.

5.2.2 Pointcuts

A pointcut is used to select join points. It acts as a filter, matching join points that meet its specification, and blocking all others. For example, the pointcut `call(String toString())` will match any call made to a method named `toString` that takes no arguments and returns a `String`. AspectJ supports three different categories of pointcuts. The first category, and the most fundamental, matches join points based on the *kind of join point* (is it a method call, the execution of an exception handler, the static initialization of a class, and so on). The second category matches join points based on *scope*. For example, does the code that gave rise to the join point reside within a certain package? Has the join point occurred within the control flow of a given operation? The final category of pointcut matches join points based on *context* information at the join point itself. For example, is the currently executing object an instance of a given type?

Pointcuts can be named or anonymous. In all but the simplest cases, naming pointcuts improves the clarity of your code. (Part 1 of this book used named pointcuts almost exclusively.) Named pointcuts are declared using the `pointcut` keyword. Pointcut declarations can occur inside both classes and aspects, but not in interfaces. The general form of a pointcut declaration is as follows:

```
[visibility-modifier] pointcut name( ParameterList ) :
PointcutExpr ;
```

Here are some concrete examples of pointcut definitions. (The next chapter explains in detail the syntax used to construct pointcut expressions.)

```
pointcut jdbcCall() :
  call(* java.sql..*(..)) ||
  call(* javax.sql..*(..));

pointcut inPersistenceLayer() : within(insurance.dao..*);

pointcut dbExceptionHandler() : handler(SQLException+);
```

The ability to name pointcuts provides for abstraction, encapsulation, and reuse. Abstraction is provided by the ability to refer to the pointcut by name (for example, `jdbcCall`) rather than by the detailed expression. Encapsulation arises because you are not aware of the detailed pointcut expression when referring to a pointcut by name. Reuse occurs because you can refer to a named pointcut in other pointcut expressions. For example:

```
pointcut leakedException() :
  dbExceptionHandler() &&
  !inPersistenceLayer();
```

This example also illustrates the powerful ability to *compose* pointcuts to create new pointcut expressions using the `&&`, `||`, and `!` operators.

A pointcut can also expose contextual information at the join points it matches (like the identity of the object being called at a call join point). The contextual information to be provided by the pointcut is specified in the `ParameterList`. Informally we sometimes refer to this as the "provides" list, because the parameter values are provided by the pointcut when it matches a join point, instead of being passed to the pointcut by some external caller.

Combining Pointcut Expressions with `&&`

We have described pointcuts as predicates matching on join points. A common trap is to use `&&` to combine pointcut expressions when you really meant `||`. Suppose you want to capture all calls to methods defined in the java.sql package, and all calls to methods defined in the javax.sql package. It is tempting to write `call(* java.sql..*(..)) && call(* javax.sql..*(..))`. This pointcut actually matches nothing: There are no join points that are both a call to a method defined in the java.sql package *and* a call to a method defined in the javax.sql package. The correct pointcut expression is `call(* java.sql..*(..)) || call(* javax.sql..*(..))`, which matches if a call is being made to a method defined in the java.sql package , *or* if a call is being made to a method defined in the javax.sql package.

5.3   Advice

Pointcuts are predicates that match join points, and advice specifies what to do at those join points. Each piece of advice is associated with a pointcut (named or anonymous) and specifies behavior that it wants to execute before, after, or around, the join points that the pointcut matches. An advice declaration may contain parameters whose values can be referenced in the body of the advice. Unlike method calls, in which parameter values are explicitly passed by the caller, the parameter values are provided by the pointcut.

Because advice is always invoked implicitly, there is no need to name it. (You cannot call advice by name, or by any other means.) For the same reason, there are no visibility modifiers for advice. The implicit invocation of advice can happen *before* the join points matched by its pointcut, *after* the join points matched by its pointcut (here AspectJ enables you to distinguish between normal return from the join point and exceptional return conditions), or *around* the join points. Before and after advice are the simplest kinds: Whereas they can read contextual information at a join point (such as arguments and return values), they cannot change it. Around advice is the most powerful form of advice; it can not only read contextual information but also change it—and can even decide whether the original join point should be executed at all. The basic forms of advice declarations for before, after, and around advice are as follows:

```
before(ParameterList) : PointcutExpr{ … };
after(ParameterList) returning : PointcutExpr { … };
after(ParameterList) throwing : PointcutExpr { … };
Type around(ParameterList) : PointcutExpr { … };
```

See Chapter 7 for more details on these forms and others. The pointcut expression may be anonymous, or may refer to a named pointcut. Because advice is not named, using a named pointcut can aid program readability. Here's a concrete example of using advice with an anonymous pointcut:

```
after(Account acc, Money amount) returning:
  execution(void Account.*(Money)) &&
  args(amount) &&
  this(acc) {
  acc.getStatement().recordTransaction(
    thisJoinPointStaticPart, amount);
}
```

Here's the same example rewritten to use a named pointcut:

```
pointcut accountUpdate(Account acc, Money amount) :
  execution(void Account.*(Money)) &&
  args(amount) &&
  this(acc);

after(Account acc, Money amount) returning :
  accountUpdate(acc,amount) {
  acc.getStatement().recordTransaction(
  thisJoinPointStaticPart, amount);
}
```

The execution of a join point in AspectJ includes not only the event represented by the join point itself (the method call or execution, for example), but also the execution of any advice associated with a pointcut that matches the join point. When we want to document the control flow of an AspectJ program using a sequence diagram, we use a rounded gray rectangle to represent the execution of join points of interest. Because advice invocation is implicit, we use a dashed arrow to show the transfer of control into an advice body. We then show the transition as guarded by the pointcut associated with the advice. Some examples of this notation are illustrated in Figure 5.2.

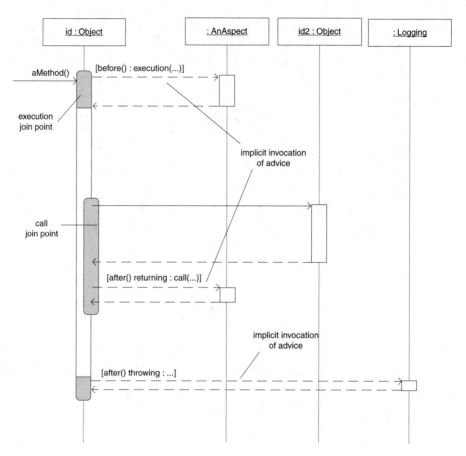

Figure 5.2   Showing advice invocations in sequence diagrams.

5.4   Inter-Type Declarations

Whereas advice is a declaration that an aspect will execute certain behavior in the program control flow at designated join points, inter-type declarations are a statement that an aspect takes complete responsibility for certain capabilities on behalf of other types (the "targets" of the inter-type declarations). The most basic forms of inter-type declarations are for methods and fields. An inter-type declaration inside an aspect looks just like the definition of a normal method or field in the aspect, except that the method or field name is preceded by a type name. Here's a simple example:

```
public aspect AccountSession{
   private SessionContext Account.context;
   public SessionContext Account.getSessionContext() {
     return context;
   }
   public void Account.setSessionContext(SessionContext ctx)
   {
     context = ctx;
   }
}
```

The AccountSession aspect declares that it will manage a javax.ejb.SessionContext context on behalf of the Account class, and that it provides getSessionContext() and setSessionContext() methods on behalf of the Account class. The visibility modifiers preserve aspect modularity—the context attribute, for example, is private to the AccountSession aspect, not to the Account class. Because the get and setSessionContext methods are declared public in the aspect, these are visible to all clients of the Account class. A client can just call one of these methods on an instance of Account, and control is implicitly transferred to the AccountSession aspect, that responds on the Account's behalf. Figure 5.3 shows a way of representing the effect of inter-type declarations in sequence diagrams. The EJBContainer explicitly calls the setSessionContext() method on an Account, at the Account instance control is implicitly transferred to the AccountSession aspect, which responds to the setSessionContext method. We have used a small circle on the sequence diagram to represent the point where control is transferred, and a dashed arrow to indicate that the call into the aspect is implicit.

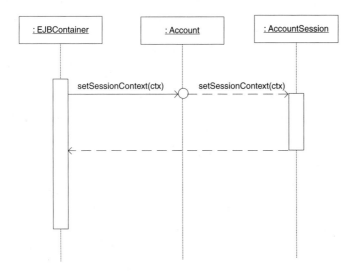

Figure 5.3   Showing inter-type declarations in sequence diagrams.

Inter-type declarations can be made on interfaces, too, in which case the aspect must supply a default implementation for any methods. This is used in the case where classes implementing the interface do not provide their own definition of the method. Inter-type declarations can also be used to declare parents (a superclass or superinterface) for classes and interfaces, and to declare that a type or set of types implement an interface. (We saw an example of this when we wrote the SerializationBasedPersistence aspect in Part 1.)

You can find a more in-depth treatment of inter-type declarations in Chapter 8.

5.5   Key Design Properties of the AspectJ Language

AspectJ is a language that has evolved through feedback from a strong and vibrant user community. AspectJ has also been very carefully designed to follow a set of principles that the language designers believed to be important. The combination of user responsiveness and a principled underpinning have made AspectJ what it is today. This section sets out some of the principles behind AspectJ, to give the reader a keener insight into the language. These principles were first developed by the AspectJ team at PARC during the early work on AspectJ.

1. **Every legal Java program is a legal AspectJ program.** AspectJ was designed as an extension of the Java language. This important property means that incremental adoption of AspectJ can begin on any existing Java project.

2. **AspectJ produces standard Java class files that execute on any Java Virtual Machine.** No special infrastructure is required to run an AspectJ program. This property ensures that AspectJ programs can be packaged and distributed in the same way as Java programs, without end users needing to install any dedicated runtime.

3. **Join points, pointcuts, and advice are orthogonal concepts.** The different kinds of join points, the different primitive pointcuts, and the different kinds of advice can be used in any combination.[2]

4. **Advice is associated with a pointcut, and pointcuts match join points.** There is no relationship in the other direction: Join points do not know what advice is applied to them, or what pointcuts match them. Pointcuts do not know what advice refers to them.

5. **Pointcuts support composition and abstraction.** Abstraction is supported through the ability to name pointcut expressions. Composition allows pointcut expressions to be combined to yield new pointcut expressions.

---

2. The current AspectJ implementation falls short of this goal in just one or two places—for example, it does not support after advice on handler join points because the end of a catch block is not well defined in bytecode.

6. **Static type checking.** AspectJ is a type-safe language, bringing the associated safety and productivity benefits.

7. **Efficient implementation.** The bytecodes produced by the AspectJ compiler should be as efficient as the compiled result of an equivalent (scattered and tangled) Java implementation written by hand.

8. **A simple kernel.** AspectJ programs can be reasoned about using a simple model, and the orthogonal principle (3) means that it is easy to start with a simple kernel of capability and slowly add to that as your experience with the language grows.

9. **Semantics remain constant regardless of weaving time.** Weaving is the task undertaken by the AspectJ compiler when linking together classes and aspects to produce a set of executable bytecodes. The AspectJ semantics remain the same whether linking happens as a source level preprocessing step, during compilation, as a postprocessing step after compilation, at class-load time, or during runtime. The current AspectJ distribution supports compilation, postcompilation and class-load time linking.

Other Approaches

AspectJ is not the only approach to AOP. Others have built AOP tools or frameworks using different goals from those we just outlined for AspectJ. One common principle is a desire to avoid changing the Java language in any way. This design principle leads to aspect frameworks that capture behavior in standard Java classes and then use extralingual specifications (XML files are popular), metadata, or a runtime API to compose the aspect behavior with the types in the program. AspectWerkz by Jonas Böner is a good example of a framework-based approach that surfaces many of the capabilities of AspectJ. Hyper/J from the IBM T.J. Watson Research Laboratory was based on a design principle of symmetry: In Hyper/J, there is no distinction between classes and aspects. Everything is a class, and classes can be composed in multiple ways. A second-generation Hyper/J tool is now being developed as part of the Eclipse CME project. The JBoss AOP framework was designed around a principle of dynamic, per-instance aspect binding. Aspects can be applied to individual objects dynamically at runtime through interceptor chains. Spring and dynaop support smaller aspect-frameworks based primarily on the concept of method interception.

* AspectWerkz : http://aspectwerkz.codehaus.org

* Hyper/J : http://www.research.ibm.com/hyperspace/

* CME : http://www.eclipse.org/cme

* JBoss : http://www.jboss.org/developers/projects/jboss/aop.jsp

* Spring : http://www.springframework.org

* dynaop : http://dynaop.dev.java.net/

5.6   Summary

Join points are events in the control flow of a program: A *join point model* determines which join points will be exposed by an aspect-oriented implementation. Pointcuts are predicates (or filters) that match join points. AspectJ supports a rich set of pointcut designators that can match join points based on their kind, the scope in which they occur, and contextual information available at the join point. Pointcuts support the important properties of abstraction and composition.

Advice is behavior that is implicitly invoked at join points matched by the pointcut expression associated with the advice, and inter-type declarations enable an aspect to take complete responsibility for messages sent to other types. Finally, aspects are the unit of modularity that encapsulate a collection of advice, pointcuts, inter-type declarations, fields, and methods, and abstract them into a coherent whole.

References

Parnas, D. L. 1972 (December). On the Criteria to Be Used in Decomposing Systems into Module. *Communications of the ACM* 15:12 1053–1058.

CHAPTER 6

Straight to the Point

This chapter examines AspectJ's support for writing pointcuts and matching join points. You have already seen a number of pointcut expressions in Part 1 of this book, so you know that pointcuts are built out of a set of basic building blocks with names such as "call" and "execution." In the AspectJ language, these building blocks are known as *pointcut designators*. This chapter introduces the pointcut designators in the order that you are likely to need/encounter them as you start working with AspectJ. Although there may be a lot of detail here, you do not need to master it all on day one to start being productive with AspectJ, as we hope the examples in the first part of the book demonstrated.

Also in this chapter, you will find information on common patterns of usage when writing pointcuts. By the end of the chapter, you should have all the power of pointcuts at your fingertips, and you will know the best practices for constructing them.

6.1 The Calculator Program

Throughout this chapter we use a rolling example of a simple calculator program. This gives us the opportunity to put the pointcut designators and their usage into some (admittedly simple) context. The calculator is a *Reverse Polish Notation* (RPN) calculator. Don't panic! You might not have heard of this kind of notation before, but it is very simple and enables us to keep the program simple but still functional. In RPN, the mathematical operator is specified after the operands to which it applies, so an expression you normally see as 1 + 2 is expressed in RPN as 1 2 +. This notation is extremely well suited to stack-based processing. Our short calculator program supports all the basic mathematical operators, and it even has a memory function. The calculator supports expressions such as the following:

```
20 10 * 5 4 + p
1 2 1 + + p
```

The additional p you see above is a command to the calculator to print the element on top of the stack (usually the result of evaluating the expression). This example is not intended to motivate the need for AspectJ or AOP; it is just a Java program that we are using to illustrate the join point matching rules of the various pointcut designators. The calculator program is available as one of the examples in the Examples plug-in introduced at the end of Chapter 1.

6.2   Introduction to Pointcut Designators

You already know that join points are events that occur during the runtime execution of a program, and that pointcuts match (or filter) join points. Pointcut expressions are built from compositions of the basic pointcut designators, and a pointcut may be either named or anonymous.[1] The general form of a named pointcut definition is as follows:

```
[visibility-modifier] pointcut name(ParameterList):
PointcutExpression;
```

The `visibility-modifier` defines the visibility of the pointcut. The options for visibility are the same as for other Java artifacts: `public`, `private`, `protected`, or `package`—the latter being assumed by the absence of any other specifier. The optional `visibility-modifier` is followed by the AspectJ keyword `pointcut` and a user-defined name for the pointcut. The pointcut name is followed by a parameter list, and then a colon (`:`), followed by the definition of what the pointcut is to match (the `PointcutExpression`).

Anonymous pointcuts consist solely of the `PointcutExpression` component and cannot be easily reused.

The `PointcutExpression` is built by combining pointcut designators using and (`&&`), or (`||`), and not (`!`) as appropriate. Pointcut designators filter events based on simple tests such as "is this a method call?" , "is this the execution of a method?", "is this join point within a certain scope?", "is this join point within a certain control flow?", and so on. By combining these simple building blocks you can create sophisticated pointcuts that match precisely the join points in your program execution that you are interested in.

AspectJ supports a comprehensive set of pointcut designators that can be grouped into three categories:

---

1. Pointcuts may also be declared abstract, a topic we return to in Chapter 9.

Designators that match based on the kind of a join point. These match a certain "kind" of join point event (for example, a method `call`, a method `execution`, a field `set` or an exception `handler`). Most pointcut definitions include a single kind designator.

Designators that match based on join point context. These match join points based on contextual information at a join point such as the values of arguments or the identity of a method caller. For example, if you are matching method calls, you might want to know the exact parameters for the call—to do this, you use a context designator. It is perfectly reasonable to have no context designators in your pointcut expression, and equally it is possible that you will use more than one if you want to expose or match on multiple pieces of information about the join point.

Designators that match based on the scope in which a join point occurs. Optional scoping designators in your pointcut expression enable you to limit the set of matched join points to only those occurring within a certain scope. If you are interested in all calls to method `foo()`, you can add a scoping designator to specify "but only when the calls are made from the xyz package."

Pointcut Style

Before we introduce the designators, a few words about good practice in writing pointcuts. Although anonymous pointcut definitions can be used, in all but the simplest cases using a well-named pointcut is preferred because it greatly aids program understanding. Try to keep individual pointcut definitions relatively simple, and build up more complex expressions from smaller, named, constituent parts. A pointcut definition would normally contain at most one type of kind designator (for example, a set of calls, or a set of method executions, but not a mixture of both—and definitely not if they are combined with &&) and optionally some context and scoping designators. The reasoning behind this guidance will become clearer as we work through the chapter.

6.3   The Method Call Pointcut Designator

One of the most basic join points you may want to match is the point at which a method call is called. Figure 6.1 shows the definition of the `call` designator.

```
Method-Call Pointcut Designator (Kind Designator)


                    call(Method-Signature)


Matches any call to a method or constructor matching Method-Signature.
```

Figure 6.1   Method call pointcut designator.

The `call` designator is a *kind* designator. (It selects join points based on the their kind.) This chapter describes the specifics of the method signature shortly.

Listing 6.1 shows the `evaluateExpression` routine from the calculator program, which is also the main functional routine in the calculator.

Listing 6.1   The Main Calculator Routine

```
01 private void evaluateExpression(String expression) {
02   System.err.print("Evaluating expression:'" +
03     expression + "' = ");
04   String token = null;
05   try {
06     StringTokenizer st = new StringTokenizer(expression);
07     while (st.hasMoreTokens()) {
08       token = st.nextToken();
09       if (token.equals("+"))        performAdd();
10       else if (token.equals("*")) performMultiply();
11       else if (token.equals("/")) performDivide();
12       else if (token.equals("-")) performSubtract();
13       else if (token.equals("p")) printStack();
14       else if (hasMemory && token.equals("ms"))
15         memoryStore();
16       else if (hasMemory && token.equals("mr"))
17         memoryRecall();
18       else {
19         try {
20           operandStack.push(token);
21         } catch (NumberFormatException nfe) {
22           System.err.println(
23             "\nERROR: This is not a number:" + token);
24         }
25       }
26     }
27   } catch (EmptyStackException ese) {
28     System.err.println(
29       "\nERROR: Invalid attempt to access empty stack"+
30       " made, token was:'"+token+"'");
31   }
32 }
```

Suppose we want to track the number of components there are in each expression that is processed. On line 6 of the listing, you can see we are using a simple `StringTokenizer` to break the input expression into pieces and then process each piece. To count the number of components in an expression, we need to know how many tokens are returned by the tokenizer. Each token is retrieved by a call to `nextToken()` (line 8), so let's create our first pointcut expression:

```
call(String nextToken())
```

This pointcut matches any join point that represents a call to a method named `nextToken()` (and is defined to return a `String`).

Figure 6.2 shows a sequence diagram for this part of the calculator routine, highlighting some of the call join points, and identifying the particular one matched by the `call(String nextToken())` pointcut expression.

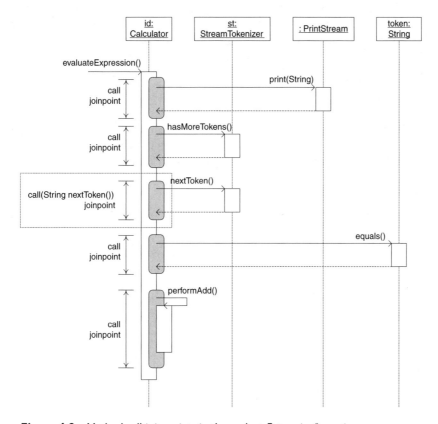

Figure 6.2   Method call join points in the *evaluateExpression()* routine.

What can we *do* with this pointcut definition? It is perfectly usable in its current form, and we could use it within an advice declaration. However, we seem to have lost something in going from the description of the requirement "count the number of parts in an expression" to the actual pointcut definition of "`call(String nextToken())`." The pointcut as it stands is anonymous; it has no name. A powerful feature of the AspectJ language is the ability to name pointcuts. Exploiting this capability here means that when we come back to review our code in six months' time, we know the semantic intent behind the expression `call(String nextToken())`. Giving pointcuts good names is an excellent way of writing self-documenting code. Let's give our pointcut a name:

```
pointcut fetchNextExpressionComponent():
  call(String nextToken());
```

Much better. You can see the power we have with this naming capability. Individual pointcuts can be composed together as discussed later, so you lose no expressive power if you keep them short and name them. We can even reuse them after they are named entities.

6.3.1 Where Do Pointcuts Live?

Now we have our first pointcut, but were do these things live? You already know that pointcut declarations can be made inside aspects, but they can also be made inside classes. The most common place to declare a pointcut is alongside the advice that uses it, in an aspect. You might choose to declare a pointcut inside a class instead if the pointcut itself is considered part of the interface of the class, and is bound to details about the class' implementation such that the pointcut will need to be updated as the class is maintained. If you use anonymous pointcuts, you *must* include them as part of your advice declaration. Let's package our pointcut in an aspect, as shown in Listing 6.2.

Listing 6.2   Calculator Statistics

```
aspect CalculatorStatistics {

  int elements = 0;

  pointcut fetchNextExpressionComponent():
    call(String nextToken());

  after() returning: fetchNextExpressionComponent() {
    elements++;
  }
}
```

```
        // Needs some further advice to print out elements
        // count...
}
```

Figure 6.3 shows how the pointcut matches manifest themselves in AJDT—
you can see the advice marker 🔖 on the nextToken() call within the evaluate Expression() routine, and the Outline view for the editor is showing that
the evaluateExpression() routine is advised by the aspect.

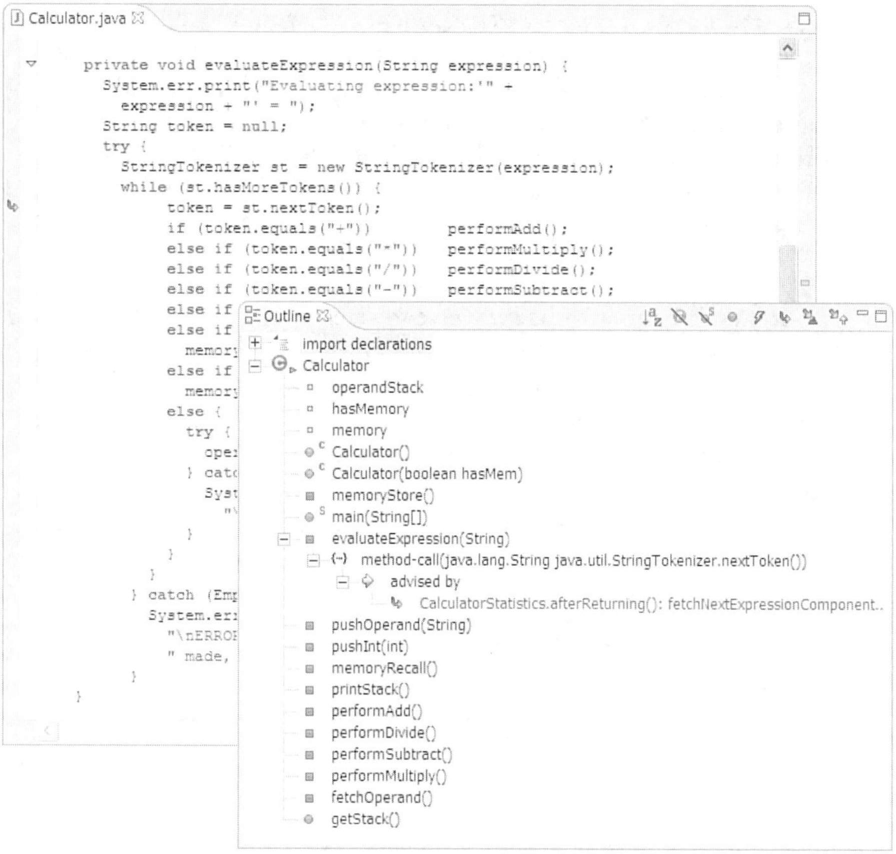

Figure 6.3   How matches are shown in AJDT.

AJDT uses the lightning bolt 🗲 icon to represent a pointcut definition. The
use of AJDT to understand pointcut matches associated with advice was covered
extensively in Chapter 2.

6.3.2 Reusing Pointcuts

You *cannot* reuse anonymous pointcuts; instead, you must carefully cut and paste the pointcut expression to a new advice declaration, ending up with two pieces of advice, each with its own copy of the pointcut. Obviously it would be better if the advice declarations could each share (reuse) a common pointcut declaration, and naming pointcuts provides a means of referring to them and therefore sharing them.

In the calculator program, if *another* aspect also wanted to apply some advice after fetching an expression component, we would ideally like it to refer to the same pointcut expression. Suppose, for example, we want to print a tape showing the stages of the calculation. We don't want to copy-and-paste the pointcut expression, and we don't have to. The pointcut in the aspect is visible (without a visibility modifier, it has default package level visibility) to other types—it can be referenced just like a static field on a class:

```
CalculatorStatistics.fetchNextExpressionComponent()
```

It is a little bit ugly that we have to refer to `CalculatorStatistics` though, isn't it? Creating a paper tape record of the calculation is really nothing to do with statistics. What we have in our `CalculatorStatistics` aspect is actually a more generally reusable pointcut. We can easily move it—we have just shown how pointcuts are as easily accessible as static fields on a type. We can capture pointcut expressions that pick out interesting join points in the calculator program in an entirely separate type that contains shared pointcut definitions. Listing 6.3 shows the reusable pointcut encapsulated in such an aspect.

Listing 6.3   A Shared Pointcut

```
aspect CalculatorEvents {
  pointcut fetchNextExpressionComponent():
    call(String nextToken());
}
```

As discussed in Section 6.1, AspectJ does not limit you to defining pointcuts only in aspects; they can also be defined in classes. (Advice, however, must be contained within an aspect.)

6.4   **Pointcut Composition**

You have seen how to match an individual method call using the `call` designator, now let's try something trickier. Suppose we want to count how many mathematical operations we perform. Using our experience so far, we can pick out the
interesting program join points with the following four pointcuts:

```
pointcut addOperation(): call(void performAdd());
pointcut subtractOperation(): call(void performSubtract());
pointcut multiplyOperation(): call(void performMultiply());
pointcut divideOperation(): call(void performDivide());
```

AspectJ supports the use of simple Boolean operators to compose pointcuts,
as we have seen in Part 1 of this book. The operators are and (`&&`), or (`||`), and
not (`!`). So we can combine the definitions above as follows:

```
pointcut mathematicalOperation():
   addOperation() || subtractOperation() ||
   multiplyOperation() || divideOperation();
```

This matches any join point that is either an `addOperation`, or a
`subtractOperation`, or a `multiplyOperation`, or a `divideOperation`. Using
pointcut composition, we have been able to create a higher-level abstraction,
`mathematicalOperation`, that can be referred to in the rest of the program. You
will see examples of using `&&` and `!` as we work through the rest of this chapter.

Figure 6.4 shows the Outline view of the aspect containing the
`mathematicalOperation()` pointcut. You can see there are four matched
method calls in the `Calculator` class. Figure 6.5 shows the `evaluate`
`Expression()` routine, with the lines making the matched method calls all
marked in the editor gutter. AJDT shows places where *advice* is in effect—strictly, it shows places in the source code that will give rise to a join point matched
by a pointcut expression associated with advice. In the case of call join point, it
shows the call site. A consequence of this is that if you want to use AJDT to
understand which join points a particular pointcut expression will match (as we
wanted to in this example), you need to associate some advice with the pointcut.
(The advice body can be empty.)[2]

---

2. Future versions of AJDT may enable you to see pointcut matches directly without the need for advice.
   Check the AJDT home page at http://www.eclipse.org/ajdt for the latest information.

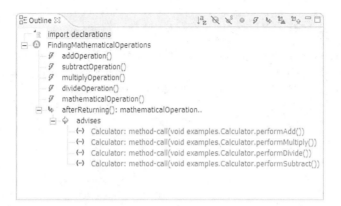

Figure 6.4 Outline view of *mathematicalOperation()* matches.

```
Calculator.java ⊠    FindingMathematicalOperations.aj
▽       private void evaluateExpression(String expression) {
            System.err.print("Evaluating expression:'" +
              expression + "' = ");
            String token = null;
            try {
              StringTokenizer st = new StringTokenizer(expression);
              while (st.hasMoreTokens()) {
                token = st.nextToken();
                if (token.equals("+"))        performAdd();
                else if (token.equals("*"))    performMultiply();
                else if (token.equals("/"))    performDivide();
                else if (token.equals("-"))    performSubtract();
                else if (token.equals("p"))    printStack();
                else if (hasMemory && token.equals("ms"))
                  memoryStore();
                else if (hasMemory && token.equals("mr"))
                  memoryRecall();
                else {
                  try {
                    operandStack.push(token);
                  } catch (NumberFormatException nfe) {
                    System.err.println(
                      "\nERROR: This is not a number:" + token);
                  }
                }
              }
            } catch (EmptyStackException ese) {
              System.err.println(
                "\nERROR: Invalid attempt to access empty stack"+
                " made, token was:'"+token+"'");
            }
          }
```

Figure 6.5 Matches in *evaluateExpression()*.

6.5 Patterns and Signatures

Programs are under continual maintenance. At some point in the future, a developer may need to add a new kind of operation to the calculator—perhaps to calculate square roots. The developer will add a `performSquareRoot()` method to the calculator and *someone* will have to go and add a new pointcut that matches calls to it, and change the definition of `mathematicalOperation()` to include it, so that we continue to count the number of mathematical operations correctly. As we have captured the counting of mathematical operations in an aspect orthogonal to the codebase, it wouldn't be surprising if the developer adding the new mathematical operation to our calculator did not know that the aspect had to be changed (although the gutter annotations in the editor might be a clue). It seems a shame that our aspect is *so* tightly dependent on the structure of the calculator program, especially given that we have a common pattern to our calculator operations: They all begin `perform<something>()`.

We can improve the situation by using wildcards. AspectJ allows wildcards to be used with many of the pointcut designators. Here is a much simpler definition of a mathematical operation that does not require a pointcut to be defined for each operation:

```
pointcut mathematicalOperation():
  call(void perform*());
```

This is just one example of where wildcards can be used. In this case, the `*` represents zero or more occurrences of any character. The pointcut definition above matches any call to a method whose name starts with the string `perform`—this will match all the currently defined perform operations, and when the developer later adds `performSquareRoot()`, the pointcut is flexible enough to pick up that change, too.[3]

6.5.1 Type Patterns

Recall from Section 6.3 that the `call` pointcut designator matches based on a method signature. Apart from the method name itself, method signatures are really all about types—the declaring type, the return type, the number and types of any arguments, and the types of any exceptions that can be thrown. An important part of AspectJ's pointcut language then, is the facilities it provides for matching types.

---

3. In Part 1 of the book, you saw how declare error and declare warning can also be used to preserve aspect modularity in the face of program evolution. There's more on these forms in the next chapter.

A type pattern is a means of matching a type or a set of types. The most exact form of type pattern is something like `java.lang.String`, which specifies a fully qualified type name. The most general form of type pattern is `*`, which means any type in any package. The following wildcards are allowed in type patterns:

`*`, which stands for zero or more occurrences of any character—when used by itself. When embedded within a sequence of characters (for example, `java.*.String`), it matches zero or more occurrences of any character except the package separator (`.`).

`+`, which can be specified as a postfix to a type pattern to indicate you mean this type and all of its subtypes (those that extend or implement the type that is post-fixed).

`..`, which can be used to specify all subpackages (so `java..String` matches `java.lang.String`). It matches any sequence of characters that starts and ends with the package separator (`.`).

There is immense freedom in combining these features when specifying a type pattern. Given the following selection of `Claim`-related types from the Simple Insurance project, Table 6.1 presents a selection of wildcarded type patterns and what they match.

```
insurance.model.Claim
insurance.model.impl.ClaimImpl
insurance.model.listeners.ClaimListener
```

Table 6.1 Type Patterns

Type Pattern	Matched Types
`Claim`	Matches `Claim`
`ClaimImpl`	Matches `ClaimImpl`
`Claim*`	Matches `Claim`, `ClaimImpl`, and `ClaimListener`
`C*m`	Matches `Claim`
`*ai*`	Matches `Claim`, `ClaimImpl`, and `ClaimListener`
`*Impl`	Matches `ClaimImpl`
`insur*.model.Claim*`	Matches `Claim`
`insurance.model..Claim*`	Matches `Claim`, `ClaimImpl`, and `ClaimListener`
`*..ClaimImpl`	Matches `ClaimImpl`
`*..*Listener`	Matches `ClaimListener`

There should be no great surprises here. . . . is able to stand in for *zero* or more package names within a type pattern, and * can be used anywhere within the type pattern to denote zero or more characters.

If you are working with array types, then [] can be used in the type pattern to match them. For example, `String[]` will match on a `String` array. Wildcards can also be used with array types, and so `String*` will also match on a `String` array.

What about +? Consider this set of types from the Simple Insurance project and their hierarchical relationships; all types are in the same package:

```
Policy
LifePolicy extends Policy
AutoPolicy extends Policy
HousePolicy extends Policy
```

Table 6.2 shows some possible type patterns and the types that they match.

Table 6.2   Using + in Type Patterns

Type Pattern	Match
Policy	Policy
Policy+	Policy, LifePolicy, AutoPolicy, HousePolicy
LifePolicy	LifePolicy
LifePolicy+	LifePolicy
Life*+	LifePolicy
*Policy+	Policy, LifePolicy, AutoPolicy, HousePolicy
*+	Policy, LifePolicy, AutoPolicy, HousePolicy

Type patterns in a pointcut that do *not* use wildcards are resolved against the set of types visible within the source file in which the pointcut is declared (that is, in the same package as the pointcut declaration, or included via an import statement). For example, suppose we have two implementations of Foo:

```
example.aop.Foo
example.aop.subpkg.Foo
```

The type pattern Foo will match at most one of them, depending on whether they are visible, and which is resolved first. This is the same as the rules for resolving types referred to within a regular Java class. Type patterns that don't explicitly refer to types but use wildcards (for example, * or F*) will be matched against the complete set of types visible to the compiler.

Type patterns can also be built up using the Boolean operators &&, ||, and !. For example, (Foo || Bar) is a combination of basic type patterns that will match either Foo or Bar. We call these combinations of type patterns *compound type patterns*.

Now that we know about type patterns, let's finally get back to the call method signatures and see where we can use them.

6.5.2 Method Signatures

Recall that the call pointcut designator takes the form call(Method-Signature). So far the method signatures we have used have been relatively simplistic. The full format of the method signature is actually as follows:

```
[modifiers] [returnTypePattern]
  [DeclaredTypePattern.]methodName([Parameters])
  [throws TypePattern]
```

The components of the signature in square brackets are optional. Let's work through the components of the method signature specification in order. Each of the following sections starts with a copy of the method signature from above but indicates in bold the element that is being described.

6.5.2.1 Modifier Patterns

```
[modifiers] [returnTypePattern]
  [DeclaredTypePattern.]methodName([Parameters])
  [throws TypePattern]
```

A modifier pattern enables us to match call join points based on particular characteristics of the method being called. The complete set of options for modifiers is as follows:

```
public, protected, private, final, static
```

Any of these can be used with the negation operator (!) to invert what you want to select. A common idiom is to use public in conjunction with a mostly wildcarded signature to catch calls to (or executions of) public methods. For example, the following will match a call to any public method in the insurance.model.impl package:

```
call(public * insurance.model.impl.*(..));
```

Modifiers can be specified in groups to select methods with a particular group of characteristics; so to match any non-public final methods, you can write !public final. There is no need to specify any Boolean operators between modifiers, because they are implicitly joined by AND.

6.5.2.2 Return-Type Pattern

```
[modifiers] [returnTypePattern]
  [DeclaredTypePattern.]methodName([Parameters])
  [throws TypePattern]
```

This is the return type of the method we are trying to identify with our call designator. It is mandatory unless matching a call to a constructor, in which case it must be omitted. We have been using this in our examples already—for example, we have specified String and void as return types. The wildcard * is often used to match any return type. The full set of wildcards (. ., *, and +) can be used in specifying the return types we are interested in. We can even use compound type patterns. The following return-type pattern matches a method returning a Policy or any subtype of Policy:

```
Policy+
```

If we have some methods that return int, and others that return Integer, we can match both sets with the pattern (int || Integer).

6.5.2.3 Declared-Type Pattern

```
[modifiers] [returnTypePattern]
  [DeclaredTypePattern.]methodName([Parameters])
  [throws TypePattern]
```

The declared-type pattern portion of the method signature can be omitted (in which case the pointcut will match a method declared in any type, as long as that method meets the other criteria specified in the method signature). If a declared type pattern is specified, the pointcut will only match calls made to methods that are declared in a type matched by the pattern, or one of its super-types. In the calculator example, we designated perform* methods as mathematical operations. That's okay in our small example because we only have one type in the system that declares methods beginning with perform. If we had other types declaring methods matching this pattern, the pointcut would have matched them, too. To correct this, we need to specify a declared type pattern:

```
call(* Calculator.perform*())
```

Like all type patterns, the wildcards +, *, and .. can be used, and so can a compound type pattern. There is a subtlety with using the method-type pattern in the call designator. (See the sidebar. Make sure you read it; you will encounter it at some point!)

Understanding the Declared-Type Pattern

Quick Java quiz: What output does the following program produce?

```
public class A {
  public void m() { System.out.println("A.m()");
}
public class B extends A {
  public void m() { System.out.println("B.m()");
}
public class Main {
  public static void main(String[] args) {
    A a = new B();
    a.m();
  }
}
```

That's right, the output is B.m()—this is the beauty of polymorphism and overriding at work.

Now let's change the Main class somewhat; what output does the program produce now?

```
public class Main {
  public static void main(String[] args) {
    A a = new B();
    a.m();
    process(a);
  }

  private static void process(A a) {
    System.out.println("Processing an A");
  }

  private static void process(B b) {
    System.out.println("Processing a B");
  }
}
```

The answer surprises some people. This program produces the following output:

```
B.m()
Processing an A
```

It is a common source of confusion among Java programmers that the choice between overridden methods is made dynamically at runtime, but the choice between overloaded methods is made statically at compile time. Even though the variable `a` is assigned to an instance of type `B`, the static type of `a` (the type used in the variable declaration), is `A`. Because the choice between overloaded methods is based on static typing, the `process(A)` method is called rather than the `process(B)` method.

So what's all this got to do with declared-type patterns in a call pointcut? Declared-type patterns are matched based on static type information, not dynamic (or runtime) type information. Suppose we have a simple shape hierarchy, in which a base class `Shape` is extended by `Square` and `Triangle`. If we write `Shape.*(..)`, this will match a call to a method declared in the `Shape` class or one of its superclasses. It does *not* match "a call to a method on a `Shape`"—meaning a call to a method where the target of the call is an instance of `Shape`. Calls to methods defined in the `Triangle` and `Square` subclasses will not be matched. AspectJ has another way to say "a call to a method on a `Shape`" using the target designator that we'll see shortly.

The closely related pattern `Shape+.*(..)` does match calls to methods defined in `Triangle` and `Square`—the + wildcard means "or any subtype," and `Triangle` and `Square` are both subtypes of `Shape`. We can read this pattern as "a call to a method declared in the `Shape` class or one of its superclasses, or a call to a method declared in any subtype of `Shape`."

There's a second matching issue because matches are made based on static rather than dynamic type information. If we write `Triangle.*(..)`, this matches a call made to a method declared in the `Triangle` class or one of its superclasses. Suppose we have the following call to a `Triangle`:

```
Shape s = new Triangle(3,4,5);
s.getNumSides();
```

Even if the `Triangle` class redefines the `getNumSides` method (which it is reasonable to expect it would), the pattern `Triangle.*(..)` does not match in this case. The reason is that the static type of s is `Shape`, not `Triangle`, so from a static-typing perspective, this is a call to a `Shape`, not a call to a `Triangle`. It might not make much difference in this simple example, but imagine that you were writing a pointcut to match a call to a secured operation, and the security checks were made in a piece of advice associated with that pointcut. Now it suddenly makes a big difference.

There's a sting in the tail too when using Java compilers prior to the 1.4 JDK level. (In Eclipse 3.0 and with AJDT 1.1.11, this issue doesn't apply unless you explicitly turn on the 1.3 compiler option). Java compilers at this level will compile a call to, say, `Triangle.getNumSides()` into a call to `Shape.getNumSides()` in bytecode. (It is converted to a call on the root-defining type of the method.) In other words, if you have the following source code:

```
        Triangle t = new Triangle();
        System.out.println( t.getNumSides() );
```

The generated bytecodes are as if you had written this:

```
        Triangle t = new Triangle();
        System.out.println( ((Shape)t).getNumSides());
```

Because AspectJ's static matching is based on bytecodes, a pointcut `call(*` `Triangle.getNumSides())` will not match (because the static type in bytecode will be `Shape`, not `Triangle`). This problem is fixed in JDK 1.4 and above for methods defined on any type other than `Object`.

Object-oriented programmers (and even aspect-oriented ones) are much more accustomed to thinking in terms of runtime types than static types. For this reason, it is best to restrict the use of a declared-type pattern in the call designator to those occasions when you are sure that static-type matches are what you really want. By default, you should omit the declared-type pattern, and instead combine the call pointcut designator with "target," which is introduced in Section 6.7.

6.5.2.4 Method Name

```
[modifiers] [returnTypePattern]
   [DeclaredTypePattern.]methodName([Parameters])
   [throws TypePattern]
```

The method name component of a method signature always has to be supplied, and only the * wildcard can be used in the name. As a simple example, `set*` matches all methods starting with the string `set`. A * on its own matches any method name. To match calls to a constructor for a type, you need to specify the special method name `new`—when using this form, you *must not* specify a return type. For example, to match a call to any `Calculator` constructor, use the following:

```
call(Calculator.new(..))
```

6.5.2.5 Parameters

```
[modifiers] [returnTypePattern]
   [DeclaredTypePattern.]methodName([Parameters])
   [throws TypePattern]
```

So far we have always specified nothing between the parentheses for the parameter element of our method signatures—this matches methods defined to take no parameters, which has been the case for the methods we have been interested in identifying so far. To match a call to a method that takes parameters, we can either explicitly specify the parameter types or use wildcarding. For example, in the calculator code we push elements onto the stack using `Stack.push(Object)`—if we want to capture this method in a pointcut, we can use `call(* push(Object))`. To match any parameter set (even the empty set), we can use the notation . . . The . . wildcard has a different meaning when used in the parameters part of a method signature, matching any number of parameters of any type. So, in the push example, `call(* push(..))` will also match.

To match methods taking at least one parameter, where the first parameter is a `String`, we can use `call(* interestingMethods(String,..))`. The .. pattern can be used in the middle of a parameter list, too. If we have a complex method such as the following

```
doComplexThing( String what, int number,
  TraceStream stream, boolean logActivity)
```

Then we can match calls to it using `call(* doComplexThing(String,int, ..,boolean))`. Similarly, `call(* doComplexThing(String,.., int,..))` will also match. The . . pattern matches zero or more parameters of any type, anywhere in the parameter set for the method.

Types specified in the parameter set can even be type patterns—including compound type patterns. This means that the following pointcut is valid:

```
call(* *(Policy+,))
```

It matches any call to a method taking at least one parameter and the first parameter is a `Policy` or a subtype of `Policy`.

6.5.2.6 Throws Clause

```
[modifiers] [returnTypePattern]
  [DeclaredTypePattern.]methodName([Parameters])
  [throws TypePattern]
```

Methods can, of course, be declared to throw exceptions. The `call` designator enables us to capture these methods by specifying a `throws` clause in the method signature. It is very similar to the return-type pattern in terms of what it will actually accept. It can take a compound type pattern, as in the following:

```
call(* *(..) throws (Exception+ && !ClassNotFoundException))
```

This matches any call to a method that is declared to throw an exception (or a subclass of exception—that's what the + means), apart from those that are declared to throw a `ClassNotFoundException`.

6.5.3 Summary

This section covered type patterns and method signatures. Type patterns can be used to specify the return type, declaring type, argument types, and thrown exception types in a method signature. Although we've only covered the `call` designator so far, everything you have learned about type patterns applies to the other designators, too.

6.6   The Method Execution Pointcut Designator

With the information on type patterns and method signatures covered in the preceding section, you now know everything you need to write `call` pointcut expressions. We are now going to look at a very closely related designator, the method execution pointcut designator.

Right after a method has been called, the next thing that usually happens is that the method executes. The method execution pointcut designator matches the point in the runtime of a program at which a method executes. Figure 6.6 shows the definition of the execution designator.

Method-Execution Pointcut Designator (Kind Designator)

execution(Method-Signature)

Execution of a method or constructor matching Method-Signature.

Figure 6.6   Method execution pointcut designator.

The method signature that can be specified follows exactly the same format that we discussed for the `call` designator. The concepts of a method call and a method execution may seem closely related. To help you understand the difference, Figure 6.7 shows a sequence diagram of the `evaluateExpression()` method as it processes part of the expression 5 3 +. We have highlighted the various `call` and `execution` join points.

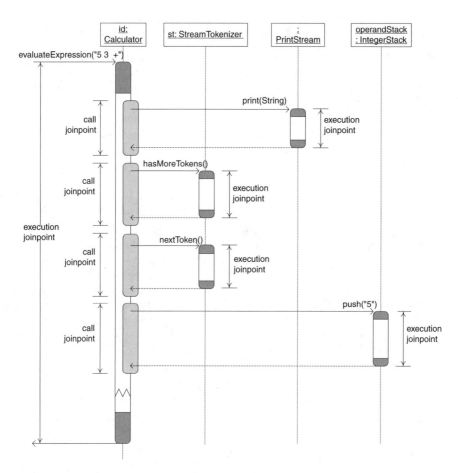

Figure 6.7   Contrasting *call* and *execution* join points in *evaluateExpression()*.

Depending on which types are passed to the AspectJ compiler for linking with aspects, there can be an important difference between `call` and `execution`, which is discussed in the sidebar "Aspect Linking and Type Availability."

Aspect Linking and Type Availability

A `call` join point occurs in the calling code at the method call site, whereas `execution` join points occur at the point of method execution. This difference can be very important when your program uses library classes for which the implementation is not available to you. Let's look at an example. Consider the `nextToken()` method that we were matching on before. We used a `call(* nextToken())` pointcut that matched the points in the program where calls were made to `nextToken()`. We want to use that pointcut in an advice declaration to increase a counter with each token. During compilation, AspectJ ensures that the increase counter advice is invoked at each call site for the `nextToken()` method.

If we change to an `execution` pointcut instead, `execution(* nextToken())`, the pointcut matches the execution of the `nextToken()` method in its declaring class. By specifying advice against this pointcut, AspectJ needs to link the aspect containing the increase counter advice with the declaring class of the `nextToken()` method ... but the `nextToken()` method is inside the `StringTokenizer` class, which is a system class. The calculator just refers to `StringTokenizer` via its class path, so the `StringTokenizer` class is not made available to the AspectJ compiler for linking. Therefore AspectJ cannot link the advice at the site of the method execution. If you have access to the call site, but not the execution site, you must use a `call` pointcut. If you have access to the execution site but not the call site, you must use an `execution` pointcut. Figure 6.8 shows how the `call` and `execution` pointcuts show their matches in AJDT. You can see in the Outline view that the call has matched the expected call site; execution has matched nothing.

There was an important sidebar earlier in this chapter about the behavior of the `call` pointcut designator when a declaring-type pattern is specified as part of a method signature. Within the `call` pointcut designator, a declared-type pattern will only match if the method specified is both defined for the type (declared in that type or one of its supertypes) and the declared type of the variable on which the call is made matches the declared-type pattern. An `execution` join point behaves slightly differently when a declared-type pattern is specified—it will only match if the method specified is defined in the type. (That is, the type either provides the first definition of that method in the type hierarchy, or it contains an overriding definition of the method from a supertype.) The expression `execution(* Triangle.getNumSides())` matches the actual execution of `getNumSides()` as declared within the `Triangle` type. If `getNumSides()` is not declared in `Triangle` but is declared on a supertype, and `Triangle` does not override the `getNumSides()` method, we don't get a match in the case of execution.

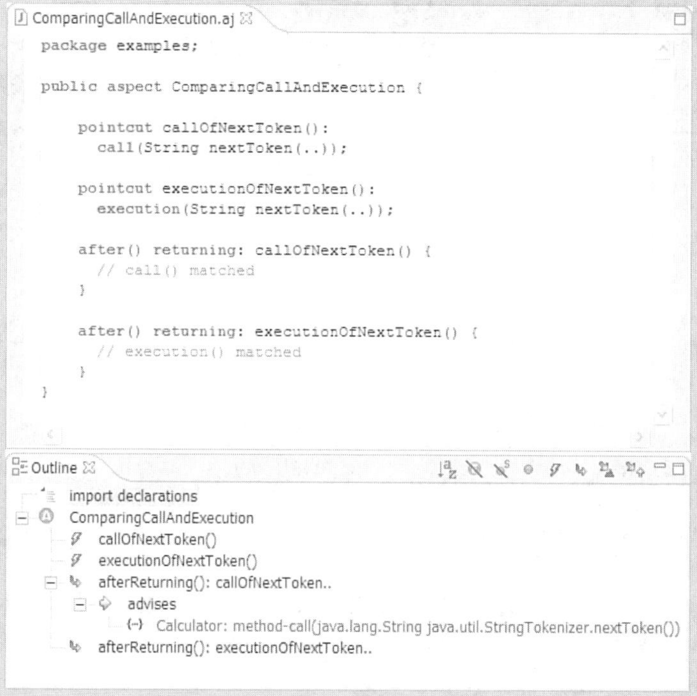

```
ComparingCallAndExecution.aj ⋈

  package examples;

  public aspect ComparingCallAndExecution {

      pointcut callOfNextToken():
        call(String nextToken(..));

      pointcut executionOfNextToken():
        execution(String nextToken(..));

      after() returning: callOfNextToken() {
        // call() matched
      }

      after() returning: executionOfNextToken() {
        // execution() matched
      }

  }
```

```
Outline ⋈                                  ⬆🔤 ⬚ ⬚ ◉ ♪ ⬚ ⬚ ⬚ ⬚ ⬚

    import declarations
   ⊖ ⓐ  ComparingCallAndExecution
      ♪   callOfNextToken()
      ♪   executionOfNextToken()
   ⊖  ◦  afterReturning(): callOfNextToken..
       ⊖ ◇  advises
              (⋅) Calculator: method-call(java.lang.String java.util.StringTokenizer.nextToken())
          ◦  afterReturning(): executionOfNextToken..
```

Figure 6.8   Contrasting *call* and *execution* join points in AJDT.

In many cases, it is not the place where a method is defined (or the declared type of a variable) that is important, but the fact that the target object is of a given type. (For example, we might be interested in execution of getNumSides() on a Triangle object, without care for where the getNumSides() method is defined, or whether we declared the program variable to be a Shape or a Triangle). This more naturally fits the way we tend to think about object-oriented programs. We can describe this kind of requirement in AspectJ by omitting the declared-type pattern, and combining the resulting pointcut with a new designator, target.

6.7   The *Target* Pointcut Designator

The general form of `target` is shown in Figure 6.9.

Target Pointcut Designator (Context Designator)

`target(Type)`

Matches a join point where the target object is an instance of Type.

Figure 6.9   The *target* designator definition.

There are *two* forms of `target`; the first form shown here matches when the target object at a join point is of a given type. The second form enables us to additionally find out the actual target instance. We cover this second usage later. For now, let's start by looking at the `target(Type)` form and how we can use it with `call` pointcuts. Only a type is allowed, not a type pattern, so we can't use `*` or `..`, and adding `+` would be irrelevant anyway—for reasons you will see shortly.

6.7.1 Call and Target

Figure 6.10 shows another sequence diagram, detailing the evaluation of a simple calculator expression 5 p, which just prints out 5.

We can see the calls to push the operand 5 onto the stack and the popping of the result when we see the p token. Suppose we want to match calls to any method that operates on the stack. This is not totally straightforward. To ensure our stack is only used for numbers, the calculator uses a subclass of `Stack` called `IntegerStack` that overrides the `push()` operation and ensures we are only allowed to push numbers. We don't have to worry about overriding `pop()` because `push()` will ensure the stack can only contain valid entries. Listing 6.4 shows the `IntegerStack` definition.

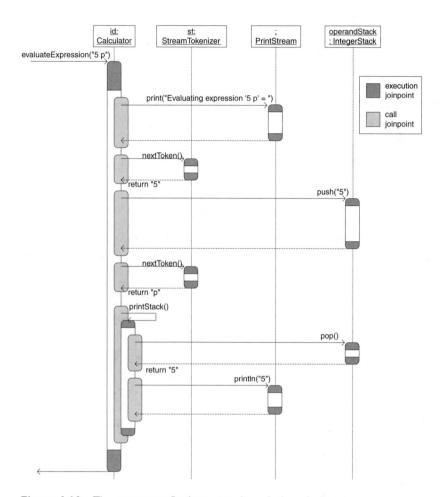

Figure 6.10   The expression *5 p* being run through the calculator.

Listing 6.4   The *IntegerStack* Class

```
public class IntegerStack extends Stack {

  public Object push(Object o) {
    Object toPush = null;
    if (o instanceof Integer) {
      toPush = (Integer)o;
    } else {
      // Other allowed option is number in string form
      Integer.parseInt((String)o);
      toPush = new Integer((String) o);
    }
    if (toPush==null) return null;
```

```
    return super.push(toPush);
}

}
```

Let's try and write a pointcut that matches the `push()` and `pop()` calls that occur in the calculator:

```
pointcut pushOrPop():
  call(* IntegerStack.push(..)) ||
  call(* IntegerStack.pop(..));
```

Figure 6.11 shows this pointcut defined in an aspect in AJDT.

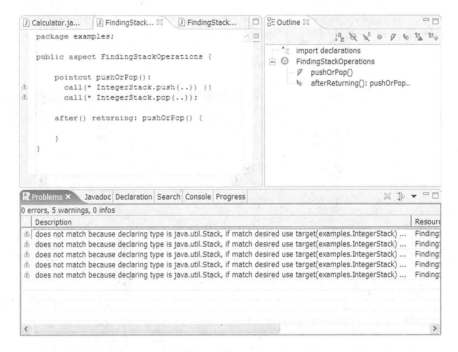

Figure 6.11 AJDT showing *push()/pops()* in calculator code.

The Outline view in Figure 6.11 is showing no matches for the advice, and the warnings against the `call()` pointcut expressions in the editor and the warnings in the Problems view tell us something is wrong. Remember that a declaring type for a `call` (or `execution`) pointcut designator is matched statically. The static type of the stack in the calculator program is `Stack`, not

`IntegerStack`, so from a static-typing perspective there are no calls to
`IntegerStack` being made. AspectJ will helpfully give you a compile-time warning in situations such as this where a pointcut does not match and you might
have expected it to. (The warning is configurable; you will see how in Part 3.)
This is what the warnings in Figure 6.11 are for. Many times static-type matching is not what you want, and this is one of them. (In fact, we go so far as to say
that you shouldn't use a declared-type pattern in a `call` or `execution` pointcut
unless you are certain that static matching is appropriate for the situation.) This
is where the target designator comes in. The target designator enables us to
match based on the actual type of an object at runtime. We recommend the use
of target in conjunction with a `call` or `execution` pointcut designator (and
without a declaring-type pattern) as the default way of writing these pointcuts.
Here is a new pointcut definition that correctly identifies calls to `push()` and
`pop()` on an `IntegerStack`:

```
pointcut pushOrPopCall() :
  call(* push(..)) || call(* pop(..));
pointcut pushOrPop():
  pushOrPopCall() && target(IntegerStack);
```

   Figure 6.12 shows this is now matching the five places it was previously
warning about. The `target(Type)` designator matches join points where the
target object passes an `instanceof <Type>` test. This is why + makes no difference for the types supplied to the `target` designator—an `instanceof` test will
always pass for the given type or any subtype of it.

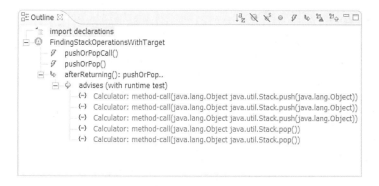

Figure 6.12   AJDT correctly matching *push()/pops()* in calculator code.

Using `target` makes pointcut definitions easier to design and understand. It is more intuitive, better matching how you think about the code. The price to pay is that we cannot statically determine every join point at which the pointcut will match (because the matching is based on runtime type information, which is only available at runtime). The AspectJ compiler *can* statically determine every join point where the pointcut *might* match. For example, a call made to an object referred to in a variable of type `Shape` *might* match a `target(Triangle)` pointcut—but a call to an object referred to in a variable of type `Square` never will. In places where a definite match cannot be made until runtime, AspectJ applies a runtime test before deeming that a given join point is matched by a pointcut.

AJDT makes it easy to tell when the execution of advice is conditional upon a runtime test. Observe in Figure 6.13 the small question mark decorator on the advice markers in the editor gutter ⚓. Figure 6.14 shows the corresponding Outline view, where you can see that any advised element (a method, constructor, and so on) includes information about whether execution of the advice is subject to a runtime test. Figure 6.12 showed that this kind of indication can also be seen in the Outline view for an aspect. There are other pointcut designators that can also cause the execution of advice to be conditional on a runtime test, as you will see later.

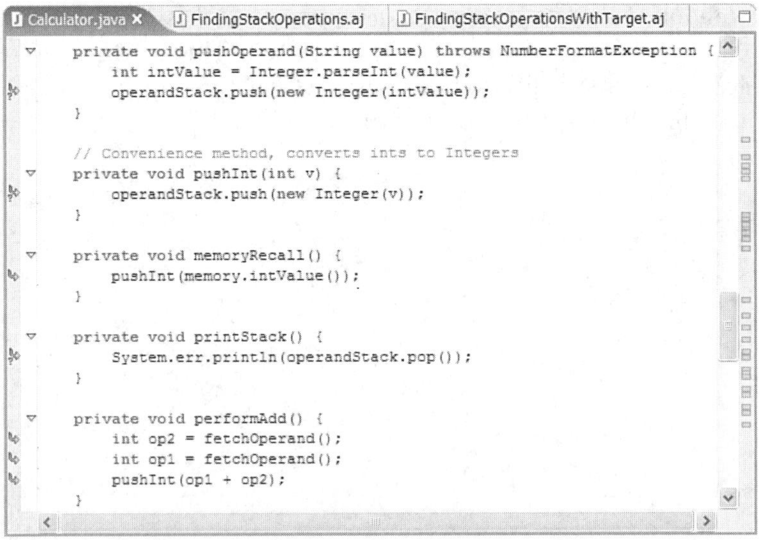

Figure 6.13 Editor showing exact matches and matches subject to a runtime test.

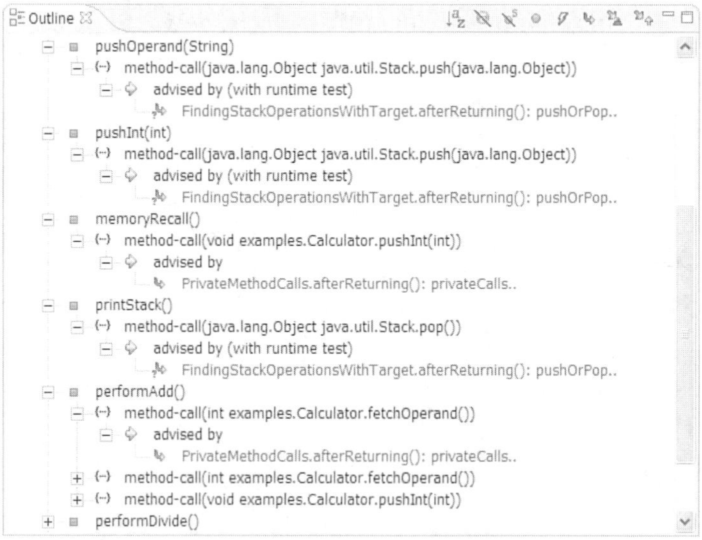

Figure 6.14   Outline view indication of conditional advice execution.

6.7.2 Static Methods

Static methods run outside of the context of any object instance. Attempting to match a call to a static method using a combination of `call` and `target` (or `execution` and `target`) will fail, because there is no target object. (We say that `target` is *unbound*.) This is a situation where you do need to use a declaring-type pattern in the `call` or `execution` pointcut.

6.7.3 Execution and Target

We have looked at what `target` means when used with `call`; what about with `execution`? The target type of a method execution is the type of the object instance in which the method executes. Let's change the pointcut used in the previous section to use `execution` and `target`:

```
pointcut pushOrPopExecution() :
  execution(* push(..)) ||
  execution(* pop(..));

pointcut pushOrPop():
  pushOrPopExecution() &&
  target(IntegerStack);
```

Look at the Outline view in Figure 6.15, which shows the places in the code that will give rise to a join point matched by this pointcut.

Figure 6.15 Matches for *target* when used with *execution*.

The figure shows that we will match the execution of the push() method in IntegerStack. The pointcut expression also matches the execution of pop() when the target object is an instance of IntegerStack, but the Outline view shows that the advice is not in effect for the execution of pop(). This is because the pop() method execution occurs in a library class (java.util.Stack), which is not made available to the compiler for aspect linking. (See the earlier sidebar "Aspect Linking and Type Availability" in Section 6.6.) Let's imagine for a moment that IntegerStack extends a class we do control the implementation of, say MyStack, and that MyStack defines an implementation of pop(). We would now advise the execution of the pop() method, too. Note that this is different from the behavior we would get if we wrote execution(* IntegerStack.pop(..)), which will never match. This is the difference between static- and dynamic-type evaluation again. The form that uses IntegerStack.pop(..) is looking for the execution of a pop() method defined in a class called IntegerStack. The form that uses target is looking for the execution of a pop() method on an instanceof IntegerStack.

6.8 The *this* Pointcut Designator

A natural complement to the target designator is this. The general form is shown in Figure 6.16.

> This Pointcut Designator (Context Designator)
>
> this(Type)
>
> Matches a join point where the currently executing object is an instance of Type.

Figure 6.16   The *this* designator.

The easiest way to understand what `this` does is to think about it in relation to the method `call` designator we have been using. Where `target` enables you to ensure the `target` of the method call is of a particular type, `this` enables you to specify that the object making the call is of a particular type. Figure 6.17 shows a sequence diagram highlighting the values of `this` and `target` for a pair of method `call` join points. For the call to `hasMoreTokens()`, `this` is the `Calculator` instance, whereas `target` is the `StreamTokenizer` instance. For the call to `push()`, `this` is again the `Calculator` instance, whereas `target` is now the `IntegerStack` instance.

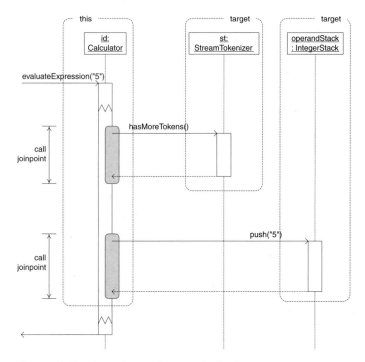

Figure 6.17   *this* and *target* for a method call.

As with `target`, there are two forms of `this`. The form shown above matches when `this` is bound to an instance of the given type. The second form enables you to additionally determine the actual object instance bound to `this`. We return to the second form later in this chapter. Like `target`, `this` only allows a type to be specified, not a type pattern.

6.8.1 Call and This

The `IntegerStack` class seems generally useful. It is likely therefore that if the `Calculator` class were part of a bigger system, there might be other classes also making calls to `IntegerStack` instances. The pointcuts we have written in the past few sections that match a call to the `push()`/`pop()` operations on the `IntegerStack` will match all these calls, too. If we are only interested in calls to `IntegerStack` made from a `Calculator`, we can use `this` to qualify the point-cut expression:

```
pointcut pushOrPopCall() :
    call(* push(..)) || call(* pop(..));
pointcut calculatorPushOrPop():
    pushOrPopCall() && target(IntegerStack) &&
                       this(Calculator);
```

Like `target`, using the `this` designator can result in advice that applies based on a runtime test; the test will determine whether the actual object making the call at runtime is of the type specified in the `this` expression. In the example here, the runtime test would make sure the object from which the calls are being made is of type `Calculator`.

6.8.2 Execution and This

For `execution` join points, `this` behaves exactly the same way as `target`. This makes sense, because the target of a method execution is defined to be the object instance in which the method executes—the value bound to "this" within the method body. The execution example from Section 6.7.3 could equally have been written as follows:

```
pointcut pushOrPopExe() :
    execution(* push(..)) || execution(* pop(..));
pointcut pushOrPop():
    pushOrPopExe() && this(IntegerStack);
```

Figure 6.18 shows the matches in AJDT for advice attached to this pointcut, exactly the same as we saw for `execution` and `target`.

Figure 6.18   Matches for pointcut including *execution* and *this*.

Like `target`, `this` is also said to be *unbound* for static methods (just as you can't refer to "this" within the body of a static method). Using `this` to identify when an instance is of a particular type will never match a join point for a static method execution because there is no object bound to "this."

6.9   The get and *set* Pointcut Designators

We have now explored all the options for methods. We can match a *call* made to a method, and the *execution* of a method. We understand the limitations of `call` and `execution` with respect to declared types, and how `target` and `this` can be used to overcome these limitations. Now it is time to look at join points that relate to accessing fields.

For selecting join points in the program flow that represent field accesses, we use the `get` and `set` designators. They are defined as shown in Figure 6.19.

Get Pointcut Designator (Kind Designator)

```
                                    get(Signature)
```

Matches a join point that is a reference to a field matching 'Signature'.

Set Pointcut Designator (Kind Designator)

```
                                    set(Signature)
```

Matches a join point that is an assignment to a field matching 'Signature'.

Figure 6.19 Field access designators.

The signature for get and set is much simpler than the method signature we looked at for call and execution. The format is as follows:

```
[modifiers] FieldTypePattern
    [DeclaredTypePattern.]fieldname
```

The following sections describe the constituent parts of a field signature.

6.9.1 Modifier Pattern

```
[modifiers] FieldTypePattern
    [DeclaredTypePattern.]fieldname
```

Used in the same way as modifiers in a method-signature pattern. The following modifiers can be specified for field signatures: public, protected, private, final, static, and transient.

6.9.2 Field-Type Pattern

```
[modifiers] FieldTypePattern
    [DeclaredTypePattern.]fieldname
```

A type pattern specifying the type of the field we are interested in. All general type pattern wildcards can be used, and compound type patterns can be used. For example, a field-type pattern of `!String` will match any field whose type is anything other than `String`.

6.9.3 Declared-Type Pattern

```
[modifiers] FieldTypePattern
    [DeclaredTypePattern.]fieldname
```

This has exactly the same use as the declared-type pattern we encountered in the method signature; it can be used to identify where the field is declared. The same issues of static type evaluation (as opposed to runtime type evaluation) apply to the declared-type pattern of a `get` or `set` designator as apply to the declared-type pattern in a `call` pointcut. The field must be defined in a type matched by the declared-type pattern, or a super-type thereof, and the static type of the variable on which the field access is made must match the declared-type pattern. As with `call`, the declared-type pattern can be omitted, and a `get` or `set` pointcut combined with `target` or `this` instead to match based on runtime type information.

Let's return to the `Shape` and `Triangle` classes for a moment. Suppose `Shape` declares a field called name. This field is inherited by `Triangle`. If we have a variable `Shape s = new Triangle()` and write the pointcut `get(* Triangle.*)` hoping to match all accesses to `Triangle` fields, we will not match gets of the name field on `s`. This is because the static type of `s` is `Shape`, not `Triangle`. To match any field access on a `Triangle` instance, use `get(* *) && target(Triangle)`.

6.9.4 Field-Name Pattern

```
[modifiers] FieldTypePattern
    [DeclaredTypePattern.]fieldname
```

Just as we could specify a method name in a method signature, in a `get/set` signature we can specify a field name or name pattern. We can use `*` on its own to match any field name.

6.9.5 Signature Examples

Examples of `get/set` signatures are shown in Table 6.3.

Table 6.3   Examples of Valid Field Signatures

Signature	Translation
`int Point.x`	The `int` field `x` in the `Point` type
`int x`	The `int` field `x` in any type
`String *`	All `String` fields in any type
`String* name`	All fields with a type starting `String`, called `name`, in any type

6.9.6 Using this and target with get and set

We have already seen one use of `target` with `get`. The `this` and `target` designators behave the same with `get` and `set` as they do with `call`: `target` matches the runtime type of the instance owning the field, and `this` matches the runtime type of the instance accessing the field.

6.9.7 Array Accesses

If a field is an array type, then join points are exposed for the `get` or `set` of the array object. Referencing individual array elements (whether to access or update them) is treated as a `get` join point on the array itself. Figure 6.20 shows a simple aspect containing some simple array accesses and some advice that affects those array accesses. Figure 6.21 shows the Outline view for this aspect, which indicates where the advice attached to the pointcut expressions containing the `get` and `set` pointcut designators match for an array type. It is showing that the initial set of the array object is matched by the `set` pointcut, whereas the assignments to the individual array elements are matched by the `get` pointcut.

```
┌─────────────────────────────────────────────────────────────┐
│ J ArraysWithGetAndSet.aj ⊠                                  □ │
├─────────────────────────────────────────────────────────────┤
│    package examples.section_6_9_7;                         ▲  │
│                                                               │
│    public aspect ArraysWithGetAndSet {                        │
│                                                               │
│        private static String[] strings;                       │
│                                                               │
│        public static void main(String[] args) {               │
│            strings = new String[4];                        □  │
│            strings[0]="andrew";                            □  │
│            strings[1]="george";                            □  │
│            strings[2]="matthew";                           □  │
│            strings[3]="adrian";                            □  │
│        }                                                      │
│                                                               │
│        pointcut arrayGet(): get(String[] *);                  │
│                                                               │
│        after() returning: arrayGet() {                        │
│            // Array field get                                 │
│        }                                                      │
│                                                               │
│        pointcut arraySet(): set(String[] *);                  │
│                                                               │
│        after() returning: arraySet() {                        │
│            // Array field set                                 │
│        }                                                      │
│                                                               │
│    }                                                       ▼  │
│  ◄                                                      ►     │
└─────────────────────────────────────────────────────────────┘
```

Figure 6.20   Simple aspect working with a simple array.

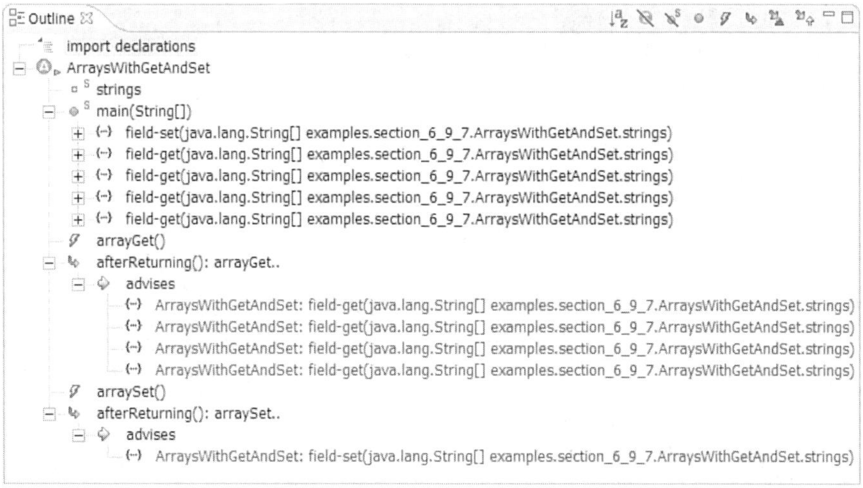

```
┌─────────────────────────────────────────────────────────────────────────┐
│ ▫ Outline ⊠                          ⫶ᴬ ⫶ ⫶ ○ ⫶ ⫶ ⫶ ⫶ ⫶ ─ □            │
├─────────────────────────────────────────────────────────────────────────┤
│  ▪ import declarations                                                    │
│ ⊟ ⊕ᴾ ArraysWithGetAndSet                                                  │
│     □ ˢ strings                                                           │
│  ⊟ ○ ˢ main(String[])                                                     │
│     ⊞ (-) field-set(java.lang.String[] examples.section_6_9_7.ArraysWithGetAndSet.strings) │
│     ⊞ (-) field-get(java.lang.String[] examples.section_6_9_7.ArraysWithGetAndSet.strings) │
│     ⊞ (-) field-get(java.lang.String[] examples.section_6_9_7.ArraysWithGetAndSet.strings) │
│     ⊞ (-) field-get(java.lang.String[] examples.section_6_9_7.ArraysWithGetAndSet.strings) │
│     ⊞ (-) field-get(java.lang.String[] examples.section_6_9_7.ArraysWithGetAndSet.strings) │
│     ⫶ arrayGet()                                                          │
│  ⊟ ⫶ afterReturning(): arrayGet..                                         │
│     ⊟ ◇ advises                                                           │
│         (-) ArraysWithGetAndSet: field-get(java.lang.String[] examples.section_6_9_7.ArraysWithGetAndSet.strings) │
│         (-) ArraysWithGetAndSet: field-get(java.lang.String[] examples.section_6_9_7.ArraysWithGetAndSet.strings) │
│         (-) ArraysWithGetAndSet: field-get(java.lang.String[] examples.section_6_9_7.ArraysWithGetAndSet.strings) │
│         (-) ArraysWithGetAndSet: field-get(java.lang.String[] examples.section_6_9_7.ArraysWithGetAndSet.strings) │
│     ⫶ arraySet()                                                          │
│  ⊟ ⫶ afterReturning(): arraySet..                                         │
│     ⊟ ◇ advises                                                           │
│         (-) ArraysWithGetAndSet: field-set(java.lang.String[] examples.section_6_9_7.ArraysWithGetAndSet.strings) │
└─────────────────────────────────────────────────────────────────────────┘
```

Figure 6.21   Matches for *get/set* on an array object.

> **Accessing Final Fields**
>
> If a field has a primitive type (for example, `int`/`float`), and is declared *final*, references to that field are not available as join points in a program—because the field is a compile-time constant, all references to the field value are inlined by the compiler, and so the `field-get` join point is no longer present in the resulting bytecodes. This limitation is a consequence of AspectJ giving consistent semantics regardless of the time at which aspect linking occurs.

6.9.8 Building Pointcuts with get and set

To demonstrate a real usage of `get` and `set`, let's look at the support for a memory that we have in the calculator. When a calculator instance is constructed, a boolean is passed to indicate whether this calculator instance should be allowed to have a memory. Listing 6.5 shows the relevant fields in the calculator class and the constructor for `Calculator`.

Listing 6.5   Calculator Fields and Constructor

```
private Stack operandStack = new IntegerStack();

// Not all calculator instances have a memory...
private boolean hasMemory = false;
private Integer memory;

public Calculator(boolean hasMem) {
  hasMemory = hasMem;
  // Initialize it if necessary
  if (hasMemory) memory = new Integer(0);
}
```

Listing 6.6 shows how the memory can be used by including the special commands `ms` (memory store) and `mr` (memory recall) in the expressions that are passed to the calculator for evaluation.

Listing 6.6   Using the Memory Support

```
...
else if (token.equals("-"))           performSubtract();
else if (token.equals("p"))           printStack();
else if (hasMemory && token.equals("ms")) memoryStore();
else if (hasMemory && token.equals("mr")) memoryRecall();
...
```

As a simple example, the expression `2 ms mr mr +` is evaluated as this: Push 2 on the stack, then store the top of the stack in memory, then retrieve the memory value and put it on the stack (do this twice), and then perform an addition—all of which leaves 4 on the stack. Let's build some pointcuts that match the join points at which the memory fields are used in our program.

The following simple pointcut will match anywhere that the memory field is updated:

```
pointcut memoryUpdate(): set(Integer memory);
```

Figure 6.22 shows how that pointcut correctly identified the memory stores in our program.

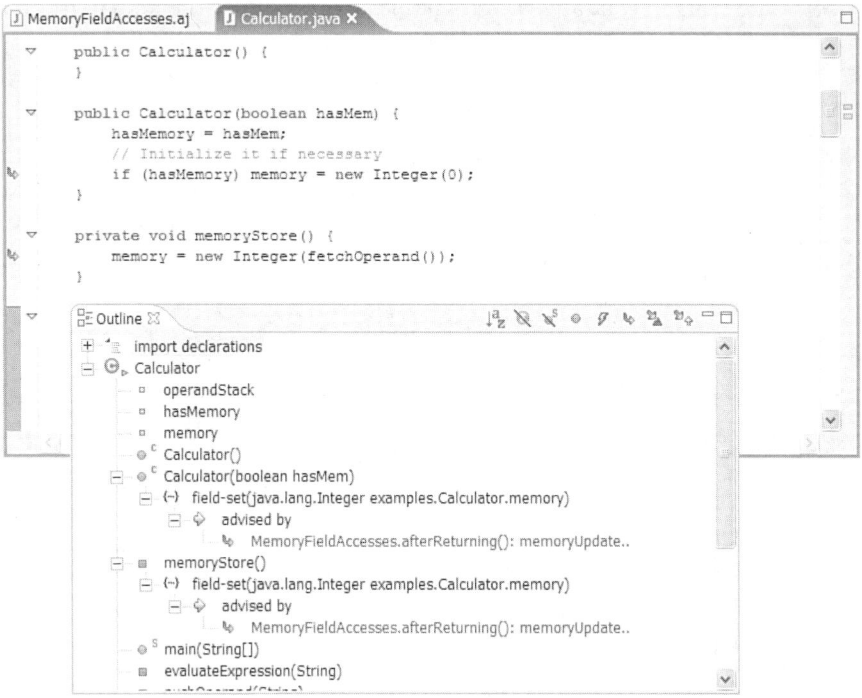

Figure 6.22   Updates to the memory field in the calculator.

The logical next question is what to do now that the memory store has been detected? It is likely that we'll want to know what is actually being stored in the field. To do that we need to use the `args` designator, which is the subject of the next section.

6.10 Capturing Context with the *args* Pointcut Designator

At most join points, there is contextual information available that you might want to use in any advice you write. For example, on a method `call` join point, you might want to know the parameters for that call; for an exception-handling join point, you might want to know the exception being handled. AspectJ defines a number of pointcut designators that enable a pointcut to provide this information to advice. The `args` designator is the first of these we are going to look at.

The `args` pointcut designator is used to match the arguments available at a join point—for example, at a `call` or `execution` join point there may be arguments passed to the method, and at a `set` join point there is the value being assigned to the field. Like `target` and `this`, the `args` designator has two forms. The first form matches arguments based on their runtime type. The second form also does this, but in addition it enables us to extract the actual argument values and provide them to any advice referring to the pointcut.

Figure 6.23 shows the two forms of `args`.

Args Pointcut Designator (Context designator)

$$args(Type, ..)$$

Matchs a join point where the arguments are instances of the specified types.

Args Pointcut Designator (Context designator)

$$args(id, ..)$$

Matchs a join point where the arguments are instances of the type of 'id' – and 'id' is bound in the pointcut definition or, for anonymous pointcuts, in the associated advice declaration.

Figure 6.23 Forms of the *args* pointcut designator.

6.10.1 *Matching Argument Types*

Let's look at the form that just matches based on runtime argument type first. A parameter type list given in a `call` or `execution` pointcut specification matches based on static type matching (that is, the declared types of the parameters in the method signature). A parameter type list given in an `args` pointcut designator matches based on the actual runtime type of the arguments passed to the method. For a field set, `args` matches based on the runtime type of the value the field is being set to. For a field get, `args` is not bound. (You cannot use `args` with `get`.)

Here's an example based on matching calls to `push()` on an `IntegerStack`:

```
pointcut push():
  call(* push(..)) && target(IntegerStack);
```

Now suppose we want to know about calls to `push()` where an `Integer` is passed. If we write:

```
pointcut pushInt():
  call(* push(Integer)) && target(IntegerStack);
```

This pointcut matches nothing! The reason being that `push()` is not declared to take a parameter of type `Integer`, but a parameter of type `Object` (static type matching). What we need is `args`:

```
pointcut pushInt2():
  call(* push(..)) && target(IntegerStack)
                && args(Integer);
```

This will match a call to a method named `push` on an instance of `IntegerStack`, where the argument passed to the `push` method is of type `Integer`. We are currently using the `IntegerStack` subclass of `Stack` to ensure that no one manages to put something other than a valid number on the operand stack for the calculator. The kind of pointcut above gives us an alternative strategy. Suppose we identify all places where a `push()` is made of a noninteger type; we could create some advice that throws a runtime exception to highlight the problem. Here is the pointcut:

```
pointcut pushOfNonIntegerType():
  call(* push(..)) && target(Stack)
                 && !args(Integer);
```

Figure 6.24 shows this pointcut being used within the calculator program. In
each of the three advised places, the gutter annotations indicate that the execution of the advice is conditional on a runtime test passing. The `args` designator
(like the `target` designator) relies on runtime type information, rather than the
type information available at compile time.

Figure 6.24 Capturing *push()* calls where the argument is not an *Integer*.

6.10.2 Extracting Argument Values

We originally started learning about the `args` designator because we wanted to
discover the value that was being placed into a field, so that we could provide
the value to advice. Let's dive in and show how we do it, and then we can walk

through the details. This pointcut will expose the value of the integer being stored in the calculator's memory:

```
pointcut memoryUpdate(Integer value):
  set(Integer memory) && args(value);
```

The `args` designator is used to bind the name `value` to the argument at the selected `set` join point. The argument value at a `set` join point is the value being assigned to the field. The type of `value` is specified as a formal parameter on the pointcut declaration. This has two effects: First, the pointcut will only match where the argument is of type `Integer` (runtime type matching); second, the actual value of the argument is bound to the `value` pointcut parameter. Formal parameters in the pointcut declaration are the mechanism by which contextual information from an actual join point match is provided by a pointcut for use in advice. The format for formals (a comma-separated sequence of `'Type name'` declarations) makes the pointcut look very much like a method declaration. Unlike the parameters on a method declaration where the parameter values are provided by the caller, the parameter values in a pointcut are provided by the pointcut itself, based on the matched join point. For this reason, instead of calling it the pointcut parameter list, we sometimes informally refer to it as the *provides* list. (It is a list of contextual values that the pointcut provides for use in advice.)

If a method takes multiple arguments, and you want to expose all the argument values, you can just specify multiple formal parameters in the pointcut definition. The `args` designator can be used to provide the values. Here is the constructor for the `CustomerImpl` class in our Simple Insurance project:

```
public CustomerImpl(String firstName, String lastName,
                    Date dob, Address address)
```

We can match a call made to this constructor using the following:

```
pointcut customerCreated():
  call(CustomerImpl.new(String,String,Date,Address));
```

We can also use the `args` designator to extract all three arguments and make them available to any advice associated with this pointcut:

```
pointcut customerCreated(
  String firstName, String lastName,
  Date dob, Address address):
  call(CustomerImpl.new(String,String,Date,Address)) &&
  args(firstName,lastName,dob,address);
```

You don't have to expose the values of all the arguments at a matched join point. It is possible to select particular arguments using `..` to stand in for zero or more arguments whose values you are not interested in. To retrieve only the address passed during customer construction, we can write this:

```
pointcut customerCreated(Address addr):
  call(CustomerImpl.new(String,String,Date,Address)) &&
  args(..,addr);
```

There are limitations on using `..`, however; in this case, it can occur at most once in an `args` designator when it is being used to expose argument values. For example, an attempt to extract the customer's last name using the following pointcut results in the error message shown in Figure 6.25:

```
pointcut customerCreated(String lastname):
  call(CustomerImpl.new(String,String,Date,Address)) &&
  args(..,lastname,..);
```

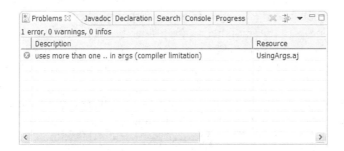

Figure 6.25 "Uses more than one .. in *args*" error message.

Why Can I Only Use .. Once with *args*?

Think about the signature of the `CustomerImpl` constructor: It takes two `String`s, a `Date` and an `Address`—`CustomerImpl(String firstname, String lastname, Date dob, Address address)`. The args pattern `..,String,..` matches zero or more arguments, followed by a `String`, followed by zero or more arguments. Suppose we are using that pattern to expose parameter values, as in the following pointcut:

```
        pointcut customerCreated(String lastname):
        call(CustomerImpl.new(String,String,Date,Address))&&
          args(..,lastname,..);
```

Should this then match once exposing the `firstname` value, once exposing the `lastname` value, or twice, exposing each value once? Multiple `..` patterns are disallowed when exposing argument values to avoid ambiguities such as this.

When we want to expose an argument value in the middle of a list such as this, we have two options. The first is to specify the type of the preceding arguments. This variant of the pointcut will match successfully:

```
pointcut customerCreated(String lastname):
  call(CustomerImpl.new(..)) &&
  args(String,lastname,..);
```

An alternative is to use the `*` wildcard to stand in for arguments we are not interested in. (`*` on its own matches a single argument.) Here's a version that uses `*`:

```
pointcut customerCreated(String lastname):
  call(CustomerImpl.new(..)) &&
  args(*,lastname,*,*);
```

In this case, it would not be sufficient to specify `args(*,lastname)` because there are four arguments to the constructor. If `*` wildcards are being used, one must be provided for each parameter you want to ignore. If a method takes five parameters and we want the second one, we have these alternatives for capturing it:

```
args(*,arg2,*,*,*)
args(*,arg2,..)
args(..,arg2,*,*,*)
```

6.10.3 Primitive Type Promotions

In the examples of context extraction with `args` shown in the previous section, we have always performed exact type matching when working with primitive types. When an argument at a join point is of type `int`, we have specified the type `int` in the formal for the pointcut. For primitive types, AspectJ also supports type promotion when exposing the primitive through the pointcut formal. Any primitive type can be promoted to its corresponding reference type. For example, values of type `int` can be promoted to type `Integer` when exposed in a particular way through the pointcut definition. The promotion mechanism enables us to treat primitive and reference types equally and write a single args designator that will work with arguments of either category. Promotion is triggered when the type of a formal parameter is declared as `Object`. It is easiest to see through an example; here is the constructor for a `Schedule` in the Simple Insurance project:

```
public Schedule(long numPayments, double paymentAmount,
                Date firstPaymentDue)
```

We can define a pointcut that matches calls to this constructor and exposes the payment amount like this:

```
pointcut scheduleCreated(double amount):
  call(Schedule.new(..)) && args(*,amount,*);
```

Alternatively, we can use the type promotion facility and express it like this:

```
pointcut scheduleCreated(Object amount):
  call(Schedule.new(..)) && args(*,amount,*);
```

This second pointcut matches exactly the same set of calls to the `Schedule` constructor that the first pointcut matched. However, this pointcut will provide the value of `amount` promoted and packaged as a `Double` type instance. To use this kind of promotion when extracting context consisting of primitive types, you *must* specify that the formal is of type `Object`. If we change the pointcut to the following, it will *not* match:

```
pointcut scheduleConstructed(Double amount):
  call(Schedule.new(..)) && args(*,amount,*);
```

This type of promotion holds for all the primitive types: `boolean`, `byte`, `character`, `short`, `int`, `long`, `float`, and `double`.

In all cases, specify the formal as of type `Object`, and the primitive will be promoted to an instance of the corresponding reference type.

6.11   Extracting Values with *this* and *target*

When we covered `this` and `target` earlier in the chapter, we mentioned in passing that they could also be used to extract the actual object instance bound to `this` or `target` at a join point. Having seen how this kind of value extraction works with `args`, let's now look at how `this` and `target` can be used in this way.

The basic mechanism is the same as for `args`: Specify a formal parameter of a given type in the pointcut signature, and then use the parameter name in place of a type name inside the `this` or `target` expression. For a method `call` join point, `target` will bind a parameter to the object instance that is the target of the call, and `this` will bind a parameter to the object instance making the call. If the method call is being made from a static context, there is no `this` and an attempt to specify that there should be a `this` of a certain type will fail to match the join point. Similarly if the call is to a static method, there will be no `target` instance, and an attempt to expose context through `target` will fail to match the join point. Figure 6.26 shows the alternative forms of `this` and `target` that are used for context extraction.

Target Pointcut Designator (Context Designator)

`target(id)`

Matches a join point where the target executing object is an instance of the type of 'id' – and 'id' is bound in the pointcut definition or, for anonymous pointcuts, in the associated advice declaration.

Target Pointcut Designator (Context Designator)

`this(id)`

Matches a join point where the executing object is an instance of the type of 'id' – and 'id' is bound in the pointcut definition or, for anonymous pointcuts, in the associated advice declaration.

Figure 6.26   Context extraction forms of *this* and *target*.

We can now revisit the `push()`/`pop()` pointcut we created earlier in Section 6.7.1 and expand it to expose context at the join point. Listing 6.7 shows a complete aspect with a pointcut that detects `push()` or `pop()` operations being performed on an `IntegerStack` object. The pointcut exposes the caller of the `push()`/`pop()` method and the object instance that will execute the method (the called object). The aspect also includes some advice referring to the pointcut, which illustrates the use of the formals in advice. (This is covered in more detail in the next chapter.) The advice just displays the object instances and their types.

Listing 6.7   Aspect to Expose Context Using *this* and *target*

```
public aspect DetectPushPopCalls {

  pointcut pushPop(Object caller,IntegerStack called):
    (call(* push(..)) || call(* pop(..))) &&
    this(caller) &&
    target(called);

  before(Object caller,IntegerStack called):
    pushPop(caller,called) {
    System.out.println("\nCaller is "+caller+
      " of type "+caller.getClass());
    System.out.println("Called object is "+called+
      " of type "+called.getClass());
  }
}
```

Compiling the aspect and executing the calculator against the expression 2 3 + p results in the following output:

```
Evaluating expression:'2 3 + p' =
Caller is examples.Calculator@cf2c80 of type class
examples.Calculator
Called object is [] of type class examples.IntegerStack

Caller is examples.Calculator@cf2c80 of type class
examples.Calculator
Called object is [2] of type class examples.IntegerStack

Caller is examples.Calculator@cf2c80 of type class
examples.Calculator
Called object is [2, 3] of type class examples.IntegerStack

Caller is examples.Calculator@cf2c80 of type class
examples.Calculator
Called object is [2] of type class examples.IntegerStack

Caller is examples.Calculator@cf2c80 of type class
examples.Calculator
Called object is [] of type class examples.IntegerStack

Caller is examples.Calculator@cf2c80 of type class
examples.Calculator
Called object is [5] of type class examples.IntegerStack
5
```

For calls to push() or pop(), the calling object instance is the calculator, and the object instance that is targeted to execute the method is the IntegerStack. Interestingly, asking the stack to print itself to standard out has resulted in it printing its contents, which enables us to see how it is growing and shrinking as the expression is evaluating—very useful!

When used with `get` and `set`, `this` is bound to the object accessing the field, and `target` is bound to the object owning the field. For `execution`, both `this` and `target` are bound to the object in which the method is executing.

6.12   The *handler* Pointcut Designator

Another well-defined point during the execution of a Java program is the execution of an exception handler.[4] Exception-handling logic is encapsulated in catch blocks, which handle exceptions of designated types. Listing 6.8 shows a sample of the calculator `evaluateExpression()` routine that deals with exception processing.

Listing 6.8   Exception Handling in *evaluateExpression()*

```
try {
  StringTokenizer st = new StringTokenizer(expression);
  while (st.hasMoreTokens()) {
    token = st.nextToken();
    if (token.equals("+"))          performAdd();
    else if (token.equals("*"))  performMultiply();
    else if (token.equals("/"))  performDivide();
    else if (token.equals("-"))  performSubtract();
    else if (token.equals("p"))  printStack();
    else if (hasMemory && token.equals("ms"))
      memoryStore();
    else if (hasMemory && token.equals("mr"))
      memoryRecall();
    else {
      try {
        operandStack.push(token);
      } catch (NumberFormatException nfe) {
        System.err.println(
          "\nERROR: This is not a number:" + token);
      }
    }
  }
} catch (EmptyStackException ese) {
    System.err.println(
      "\nERROR: Invalid attempt to access empty" +
      " stack made, token was:'"+token+"'");
}
```

---

4. See the discussion of after throwing advice in the next chapter for how to capture thrown exceptions without necessarily handling them.

This example has two exception-handling catch blocks. First, when we attempt to push a `String` onto the stack, we can fail with a `NumberFormatException` because the `IntegerStack.push()` method will verify that the `String` is a valid number. Second, if the calculator attempts to process a badly formed expression (for example, `1 + p`), we will try and pop data from an empty stack, which will cause an `EmptyStackException`.

Handling an exception via a catch block is a join point that is accessible through the AspectJ `handler` pointcut designator. The form of `handler` is shown in Figure 6.27.

Handler Pointcut Designator (Kind designator)

                    handler(TypePattern)

Matches a join point that represents the handling of an exception of a type matched by the specified TypePattern.

Figure 6.27   The *handler* pointcut designator.

Type patterns for `handler` designators are the same as for the previous designators we have looked at: We can use *, .., and + together with compound type patterns such as `Type || !Type`. The type pattern specified for `handler` matches based on static typing: So `handler(Exception)` matches a handler with signature `catch(Exception ex)`. To match handlers where the handler is an *instance of* `Exception`, you need to use `handler(Exception+)`.

The most general pointcut expression using `handler` is as follows:

```
pointcut handlingAnException(): handler(*);
```

You might use a pointcut like this if, within your application, you want to do something every time an exception is caught; perhaps you want to log that something went wrong. If you want to actually log *what* went wrong, you need to use the `args` designator to expose the exception instance being processed by the handler:

```
pointcut handlingAnException(Throwable exception):
  handler(*) && args(exception);
```

Although it is considered bad style to use exceptions as part of the normal program flow, the first thing you are likely to discover if you implement a policy such as this is that some exceptions probably occur during normal operation. Exceptions that are "expected" in normal program flow should probably be exempt from genuine exception-condition processing. For example, if you are writing a class loader, the `ClassNotFoundException` is thrown as part of the normal class-loading protocol. In this kind of situation, we can narrow the type pattern specified for `handler`. This pointcut will match the handling of any exception except for a `ClassNotFoundException`:

```
pointcut handlingANonCNFException(Throwable exception):
   handler(!ClassNotFoundException) &&
   args(exception);
```

Later in the chapter you will see the `scoping` designators that can also be used to narrow the set of matches for a pointcut.

What about using `this` and `target` with `handler`? `this` is bound to the object instance handling the exception (owning the catch block), unless of course there is no object instance because the catch block is in a static method. `target` is not bound, and an attempt to use `target` with `handler` will result in a pointcut definition that does not match anything.

In the calculator example, it is useful to print the contents of the calculator's stack every time an exception occurs because this is the key data structure that might inform us of what is going wrong. Listing 6.9 shows a simple aspect that will do this.

Listing 6.9   Printing the Operand Stack When Exceptions Occur

```
aspect PrintStackOnException {

   pointcut calcException(Calculator calculatorInstance):
      handler(*) && this(calculatorInstance);

   before(Calculator calc): calcException(calc) {
      System.err.println("\nStack contents: "+
         calc.getStack());
   }
}
```

We just extract the calculator instance handling the exception using the `this` designator and retrieve the calculator's stack and print it by making a call to the method `getStack()`. If we now ask the calculator to evaluate the expression `4 2 + ThirtySeven + p`, we get this output:

```
Evaluating expression:' 4 2 + ThirtySeven + p' =
Stack contents: [6]
ERROR: This is not a number:ThirtySeven

Stack contents: []
ERROR: Invalid attempt to access empty stack made,
    token was:'+'
```

Something else the current exception-handling code in the calculator does not do is print out the exception stack trace. This policy could easily be captured in an aspect, too, and enforced across the entire codebase: just use `args` to obtain the exception that is being handled and call `printStackTrace()` on it.

6.13 Initialization Pointcut Designators

Object initialization in Java is surprisingly complex, with rules about when field initializers run, when calls to super constructors occur (and when the field initializers in super types run), what happens when a super constructor calls a method that is overridden in a subclass, and so on. This section covers the designators specifically designed to match on initialization join points. Most of the time you only need the facilities provided by `call` and `execution`. For when it really matters, AspectJ provides additional pointcut designators that enable you to narrow in more accurately on object initialization join points. Before going on, let's quickly recap how we can capture instance construction with `call` and `execution`. A method signature for either the `call` or `execution` designators can capture the calls to, or execution of, constructors by using the "special" method name `new`. The following pointcut, for example, will match any call to a `Calculator` constructor:

```
call(Calculator.new(..))
```

When using a method signature that matches construction join points in this way, `this` and `target` are bound as follows:

1. When the method signature of a `call` expression specifies a constructor, `this` will provide the instance (if the call is being made from a nonstatic context) of the object making the constructor call. `target` is always unbound—this means attempts to use it to match on a type or expose the target of the call will leave you with a pointcut that does not match the constructor call.

2. When the method signature of an `execution` expression specifies a constructor, both `this` and `target` mean the same thing—they refer to the instance being "constructed." Before the join point (in before advice, for example), the object exposed by `this` or `target` will be completely uninitialized (instance fields will be null). After the join point (in after advice, for example), the object exposed by `this` or `target` will have been initialized by the constructor.

In addition to these uses of `call` and `execution`, AspectJ provides three other designators relating to initialization: `staticinitialization`, `preinitialization`, and `initialization`.

Figure 6.28 shows the patterns of usage for these three designators.

Staticinitialization Pointcut Designator (Kind designator)

       `staticinitialization(Typepattern)`

The execution of a static initializer of any type matching TypePattern.

Preinitialization Pointcut Designator (Kind designator)

       `preinitialization(Constructor-Signature)`

The preinitialization of an object where the first constructor called in the construction of the instance matches Constructor-Signature. The matched join point encompasses the period from the entry of the first-called constructor to the call to the super constructor.

Initialization Pointcut Designator (Kind designator)

       `initialization(Constructor-Signature)`

The initialization of an object where the first constructor called in the construction of the instance matches Constructor-Signature. The matched join point encompasses the period from the return from the super constructor call to the return of the first-called constructor.

Figure 6.28   Initialization designators.

As we said, object initialization in Java is a complex topic. We could spend the next 20 pages going through its intricacies—but you really just need to know which join points are matched by the three different initialization pointcut designators, and the best way to show that is by example. Let's take them each in turn, easiest first.

6.13.1 The staticinitialization *Pointcut Designator*

When a class is first loaded, any static initialization logic is executed. This logic comprises static initializer blocks and static variable initial assignments coded by you, and possibly also code generated by the Java compiler to automatically initialize class variables. The execution of this static initialization logic is available as a join point, which can be matched using the staticinitialization designator.

A staticinitialization pointcut expression can take either simple or compound type patterns. Here are two pointcuts that apply to the calculator program:

```
pointcut calculatorInitialization():
    staticinitialization(Calculator);

pointcut stackInitialization():
    staticinitialization(Stack+);
```

The first identifies static initialization of the Calculator class. The second identifies static initialization of Stack or any subclass of Stack—this will match the static initialization of the IntegerStack class for example.

Figure 6.29 illustrates how AJDT shows staticinitialization pointcut matches. There are two classes matched by staticinitialization pointcut. As the figure shows, whether the class actually has a static initialization code block or not, the advice marker is always shown against the class declaration itself.

For each class, static initialization only occurs once, when the class is loaded. Therefore, a pointcut that matches staticinitialization join points enables you to perform once-per-type operations in advice.

Figure 6.29   AJDT showing *staticinitialization* join point matches for two classes.

Obviously static initialization code is run in a static context, so the `target` and `this` designators are unbound. Also there are no parameters to static initialization, so `args` is unbound.

6.13.2 preinitialization *and* initialization *Pointcut Designators*

The scope of the join points matched by the `preinitialization` and `initialization` designators is slightly more difficult to get to grips with. These designators are the least frequently used. Unlike `staticinitialization`, both the `preinitialization` and `initialization` designators are related to *instance* initialization. The format of the constructor signatures accepted by these designators is the same as for method signatures, but the method name *must* be new.

The preinitialization join point is defined to be before the initialization code for an instance of a particular class runs. The scope of the join point is from the start of the execution of the first constructor in the type that was invoked for the instance, to the start of the constructor on its parent type. The initialization join point occurs just after the preinitialization join point and encompasses the time from the superclass constructor call return to the point of returning from the initially invoked constructor. This will be easier to understand with an example. Listing 6.10 shows a simple pair of classes that we will use to explain both preinitialization and initialization.

Listing 6.10   Simple Classes to Show Initialization Join Points

```
public class BaseClass {

  static int i = 1;

  BaseClass() {
    System.err.println("BaseClass constructor running");
    i = 2;
  }
}


public class SubClass extends BaseClass {

  SubClass() {
    super();
    System.err.println("Subclass constructor running");
    i = 3;
  }
}
```

We have a simple class called BaseClass that has a single int field. The constructor for BaseClass sets the int field. We then have a SubClass that extends the BaseClass, and it has a constructor that also sets the int field. Listing 6.11 shows a program that works with these classes.

Listing 6.11   Simple Class to Exercise *BaseClass* and *SubClass*

```
class InitializationTest {

  public static void main(String[] argv) {
    new SubClass();
  }

}
```

To understand where the instance initialization join points occur when running the program, let's create an aspect that will tell us. Listing 6.12 shows a simple aspect that attaches advice to each of the four join points of interest in our object hierarchy: `preinitialization` and `initialization` for the `BaseClass` and the `SubClass` types.

Listing 6.12   Exploring Initialization Join Points

```
public aspect LocateInitializationJoinpoints {

  pointcut bcpreinit() :
    preinitialization(BaseClass.new(..));

  before() : bcpreinit() {
    log("before BaseClass preinit");
  }

  after() returning  : bcpreinit() {
    log("after  BaseClass preinit");
  }

  pointcut bcinit() :
    initialization(BaseClass.new(..));

  before() : bcinit() {
    log("before BaseClass    init");
  }

  after() returning : bcinit() {
    log("after  Baseclass    init");
  }

  pointcut scpreinit() :
    preinitialization(SubClass.new(..));

  before() : scpreinit() {
    log("before SubClass  preinit");
  }

  after() returning : scpreinit() {
    log("after  SubClass  preinit");
  }

  pointcut scinit(): initialization(SubClass.new(..));

  before() : scinit() {
    log("before SubClass      init");
  }

  after() returning : scinit() {
    log("after  SubClass      init");
```

```
    }

  public void log(String msg) {
     System.err.println(msg+": i = "+BaseClass.i);
  }

}
```

Each piece of advice prints a message and the value of the field i. Knowing the value of the field helps us understand exactly where the join points are, because we know the constructors are defined to set the field to different values. The output from the InitializationTest program after the aspect has been compiled with the BaseClass and SubClass is as follows:

```
before SubClass   preinit: i = 1
after  SubClass   preinit: i = 1
before BaseClass preinit: i = 1
after  BaseClass preinit: i = 1
before BaseClass     init: i = 1
BaseClass constructor running
after  BaseClass     init: i = 2
before SubClass      init: i = 2
Subclass constructor running
after  SubClass      init: i = 3
```

To give you a better understanding of the output, Figure 6.30 shows a sequence diagram of the InitializationTest program executing and Listing 6.13 shows the code for the object hierarchy again, but this time includes comments at the location where the join points exist.

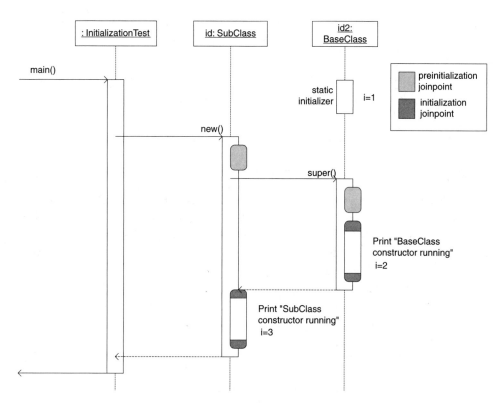

Figure 6.30   InitializationTest program executing.

Listing 6.13   Object Hierarchy Code, Annotated with Join Point Locations

```
class BaseClass {

  static int i = 1;

  BaseClass() {
    // Preinitialization of BaseClass start
    // Preinitialization of BaseClass    end
    // Initialization of BaseClass start
    System.err.println(
      "BaseClass constructor running");
    i = 2;
    // Initialization of BaseClass    end
  }
}


public class SubClass extends BaseClass {

  SubClass() {
```

```
        // Preinitialization of SubClass start
        // Preinitialization of SubClass    end
        super();
        // Initialization of SubClass start
        System.err.println("SubClass constructor running");
        i=3;
        // Initialization of SubClass    end
    }
}
```

In the listing, we are showing which code sequences the join points encompass, to give you an idea of where advice will be executed, depending on whether you choose to attach *before* or *after* advice to an initialization join point. The main difference between initialization and preinitialization is obvious from Figure 6.30, where you can see that attaching advice to `preinitialization` join points enables you to perform some operation before the superclass constructor is invoked.

With respect to `this` and `target`, at `preinitialization` join points, both `this` and `target` are unbound. At `initialization` join points, both `this` and `target` are bound to the same thing—the instance being constructed.

6.14 Static Scoping Pointcut Designators: *within, withincode*

During the discussion on kind designators, we talked about qualifying either methods or fields in order to limit the number of join points matched to just the set we are interested in. AspectJ also provides some pointcuts specifically for scoping purposes. These enable us to use a general method signature in a pointcut:

```
pointcut pushOrPop(): call(* push(..)) ||
                      call(* pop(..));
```

And then extend the pointcut expression with a scope designator so that we match only `push()` or `pop()` method calls within a certain set of packages, or within a certain piece of code. The first scope designator we will look at is `within`. The `within` designator is defined as shown in Figure 6.31.

Within Pointcut Designator (Scope designator)

`within(TypePattern)`

Matches a join point arising from the execution of logic defined in a type matching TypePattern.

Figure 6.31 The *within* designator.

The `within` designator supports compound type patterns. Examples include the following:

```
within(com.example.MyPackage)

within(com..* && !MySecretClass)

within(Calculator)
```

Figure 6.32 shows the matches in the Calculator program for a pointcut consisting of *only* `within(Calculator)`. The gutter annotations indicate just how many places are being matched by this simple pointcut expression.

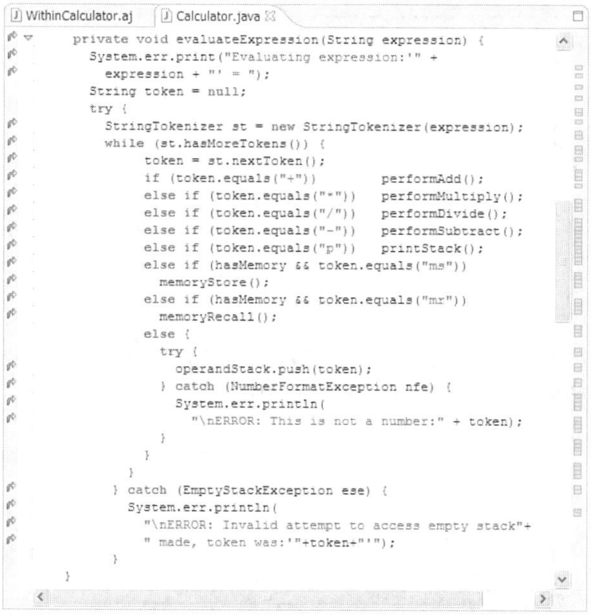
WithinCalculator.aj
Calculator.java
private void evaluateExpression(String expression) {
System.err.print("Evaluating expression:'" +
expression + "' = ");
String token = null;
try {
StringTokenizer st = new StringTokenizer(expression);
while (st.hasMoreTokens()) {
token = st.nextToken();
if (token.equals("+")) performAdd();
else if (token.equals("*")) performMultiply();
else if (token.equals("/")) performDivide();
else if (token.equals("-")) performSubtract();
else if (token.equals("p")) printStack();
else if (hasMemory && token.equals("ms"))
memoryStore();
else if (hasMemory && token.equals("mr"))
memoryRecall();
else {
try {
operandStack.push(token);
} catch (NumberFormatException nfe) {
System.err.println(
"\nERROR: This is not a number:" + token);
}
}
}
} catch (EmptyStackException ese) {
System.err.println(
"\nERROR: Invalid attempt to access empty stack"+
" made, token was:'"+token+"'");
}
}

Figure 6.32 AJDT showing the matches for *within(Calculator)*.

Remember that this will match *every single join point* in the specified scope—that's every method call, every field access, every exception handler, every initialization, and so on. This means that on its own `within` is not particularly useful. It proves *very* useful, however, when combined with some of the previous kind designators we have looked at. Expanding the `pushOrPop()` pointcut to utilize `within`, we can write the following:

```
pointcut pushOrPop():
  (call(* push(..)) || call(* pop(..))) &&
  within(Calculator);
```

This will match calls to `push()` or `pop()` methods, but only if they are made from within logic defined in the `Calculator` type. Using `within` means we will also match calls made from a static context (unlike `this(Calculator)`). The `within` designator is most often used to match join points in packages, for example:

```
pointcut inSecurityComponent() :
  within(com.xyz.security..*);
```

If you need to be more precise than the type level, you can use the `within-code` designator to narrow join point matches down to the method or constructor level. The `withincode` designator is defined as shown in Figure 6.33.

```
Within Pointcut Designator (Scope designator)

        withincode(Signature);

Matches a join point arising from the execution of logic defined in a method or constructor matching Signature.
```

Figure 6.33 The *withincode* designator.

Using `withincode`, we can specify we are interested in `push()` or `pop()` methods made from within a particular method or constructor:

```
pointcut pushOrPopFromEvaluateMethod():
  pushOrPop() &&
  withincode(* Calculator.evaluateExpression(..));

pointcut pushOrPopFromConstructor():
pushOrPop() &&
  withincode(Calculator.new(..));
```

The signature required by `withincode` is exactly the same format as that used for `call` or `execution` join points. This means we can scope by methods that have particular modifiers, or that take particular parameters.

It is worth pointing out that `within`/`withincode` also match join points in nested or anonymous types.

6.15 Dynamic Scoping Pointcut Designators: *cflow, cflowbelow*

AspectJ has two control-flow-based pointcut designators that match join points occurring within a given control flow during the runtime execution of a program. Whereas `within` and `withincode` enable us to match based on static scopes, the control-flow designators enable us to match based on what is happening at runtime. The two pointcut designators relating to control flow are shown in Figure 6.34.

---

cflow Pointcut Designator (Scope designator)

```
cflow(pointcut-expression)
```

Matches a join point in the control flow of a join point P, including P itself, where P is a join point matched by `pointcut-expression`.

---

cflow Pointcut Designator (Scope designator)

```
cflowbelow(pointcut-expression)
```

Matches a join point below the control flow of a join point P, where P is a join point matched by `pointcut-expression`; does not include P itself.

Figure 6.34 The control-flow designators.

This is the first time we have seen a designator whose parameter is itself a pointcut. The parameter can be named by reference to an already existing pointcut, or can be an anonymous pointcut. Let's look at an example. Listing 6.14 shows a simple program we can use to help us understand `cflow` and `cflowbelow`.

Listing 6.14   Greeter Program

```
class Greeter {

  public static void main(String[] args) {
    new Greeter().printGreeting();
  }

  public void printGreeting() {
    printHello();
    printGoodbye();
  }

  public void printHello() {
    printMessage("Hello");
  }

  public void printGoodbye() {
    printMessage("Goodbye");
  }

  public static void printMessage(String s) {
    System.out.println(s);
  }

}
```

The key behavior to note is that the `printMessage()` method is called by both `printHello()` and `printGoodbye()`. The `printMessage()` method then calls `System.out.println()` to output the message.

Let's start by assuming that we want to advise calls to the `println()` method. We already know how we can select the join point relating to the call of `println()`, with something like this:

```
call(* println(..))
```

Now suppose we want to be more specific. What if we want to detect the call to the `println()` method that occurred while processing the code involved in printing the "hello" message? We certainly know which join point identifies entry to the routine involved in printing "hello": `execution(* printHello())`. What we are missing is the ability to scope the set of calls to `println()` that we are interested in to just those that occur while printing "hello." The `within` and `withincode` designators cannot solve this problem: This is where `cflow` comes in. First, let's define a simple pointcut that involves `cflow`:

```
pointcut printingHello():
  cflow(execution(* printHello()))
```

Here we have used `cflow` and supplied an anonymous pointcut definition as its parameter. What does this construct mean? It will match any join point occurring in the program flow at runtime, from the point of entry to the `printHello` method, to the point of exit. This includes any join point in the call graph below `printHello`. Still confused? Figure 6.35 shows a sequence diagram for an executing instance of the Greeter program. It highlights the top-level `execution` join point selected by the `cflow(execution(* printHello()))` pointcut, and the dashed boxes show you everything (all join points) that is considered to be a match for that pointcut. The matches for `cflowbelow` are also highlighted, which we come back to later.

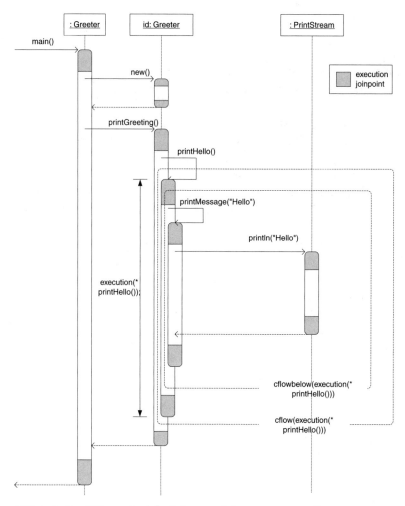

Figure 6.35   Where *cflow/cflowbelow* match for an executing Greeter program.

Listing 6.15 shows an aspect that uses the `cflow` pointcut.

Listing 6.15   *InvestigatingCflow* Aspect

```
public aspect InvestigatingCflow {

  pointcut printingHello():
    cflow(execution(* printHello())) &&
    within(Greeter);

  before(): printingHello() {
    System.out.println(
        "printingHello matched :\n  tjp is "+
        thisJoinPoint);
  }
}
```

Notice we have used a `within` designator to limit the code we are looking for join points in to just the Greeter program. We have had to do this because the `cflow` pointcut expression by itself will match on join points in the `InvestigatingCflow` aspect, too (such as the execution of the advice). It would be very unusual to write a pointcut that solely consisted of a `cflow` designator. It is nearly always found alongside another kind or scoping designator to limit the join points that are candidates for matching the `cflow`.

The actual advice we specified in Listing 6.15 is very simple: It informs us that there has been a match, and the special variable `thisJoinPoint` (discussed in the next chapter) will tell us what the matching join point is. If we compile the aspect with the Greeter program, and execute Greeter, we get the following output:

```
printingHello matched :
  tjp is execution(void Greeter.printHello())
printingHello matched :
  tjp is call(void Greeter.printMessage(String))
printingHello matched :
  tjp is execution(void Greeter.printMessage(String))
printingHello matched :
  tjp is get(PrintStream java.lang.System.out)
printingHello matched :
  tjp is call(void java.io.PrintStream.println(String))
Hello
Goodbye
```

Hopefully you can see what the `cflow` pointcut has matched is *all* the join points that occurred in the control flow of `execution(* printHello())`. After returning from the `printHello()` method (and thus beginning the flow involved in printing "goodbye"), there were no more matches. So, to solve the problem we originally set—to identify a call to `println()` made while executing the `printHello` method—we just combine the `cflow` pointcut with the pointcut that matches a call to `println()`:

```
pointcut helloPrintln():
  cflow(execution(* printHello())) &&
  call(* println(..)) &&
  within(Greeter);
```

This will match just the call `println()` that occurs during the control flow of the `printHello()` method. The example program has a very simple execution flow at runtime, just a few calls deep, but `cflow` will work on flows of any depth, enabling you to link cause and effect across disparate parts of a system.

The output of the test program showed that there were five join points that occurred within the control flow of the `execution(* printHello())` method—the first of which was the join point identified by `execution(* printHello())` itself. Sometimes when working with control-flow pointcuts, you are interested in join points that occur below (below in the sense of depth of the call stack) a specific pointcut, but *not* the particular join point your pointcut identifies. The `cflowbelow` designator enables you to express these conditions. It matches any join point in the control flow of a join point matched by the pointcut used to parameterize it, but not a join point matched by the pointcut parameter itself. Refer back to the sequence diagram in Figure 6.35 to get an idea of the difference between `cflow` and `cflowbelow`. Let's modify the `InvestigatingCflow` program from Listing 6.15 and change from using `cflow` to `cflowbelow`. Listing 6.16 shows the new program.

Listing 6.16   *InvestigatingCflowbelow* Aspect

```
public aspect InvestigatingCflowbelow {

  pointcut belowPrintingHello():
    cflowbelow(execution(* printHello())) &&
    within(Greeter);

  before(): belowPrintingHello() {
    System.out.println(
        "belowPrintingHello matched:\n  tjp is "+
        thisJoinPoint);
  }
}
```

Running the program produces the following output:

```
belowPrintingHello matched:
  tjp is call(void Greeter.printMessage(String))
belowPrintingHello matched:
  tjp is execution(void Greeter.printMessage(String))
belowPrintingHello matched:
  tjp is get(PrintStream java.lang.System.out)
belowPrintingHello matched:
  tjp is call(void java.io.PrintStream.println(String))
Hello
Goodbye
```

Comparing this output to that shown previously when we used the `InvestigatingCflow` aspect shows that `cflowbelow` matched one less join point—it did not match the execution of the `printHello()` method. This is the only difference between `cflow` and `cflowbelow`: `cflowbelow` does not match upon the join points that its supplied pointcut matches.

In AJDT, you see advice annotations for all source code lines that might give rise to a join point match for `cflow` at runtime. If you have no statically analyzable part to your pointcut, this can mean annotations against every single line of source that gives rise to a join point at runtime! In the case of the pointcut that looks for calls to `println()` within the control flow of printing the "hello" message, AJDT will show an annotation against the `System.out.println()` call ⁊ (see Figure 6.36). At runtime, a test will look at the control flow and only execute the advice if the control-flow test succeeds.

Figure 6.36 AJDT showing annotations for *cflow*.

Let's finish this section by looking at a couple of examples using the control-flow designators. For the first example, we can use the Simple Insurance project again. It represents a software system comprising multiple components (model, view, persistence), each component consisting of many Java classes. You want to take some action any time control transfers from one component to another. Without cflow this is hard to do in the case where a component uses its own services (because not all calls to the component are external). Using cflow, we can simply define these pointcuts:

```
pointcut callToInsuranceModel():
  call(public * insurance.model..*(..)) ||
  call(public insurance.model..new(..));

pointcut externalCallToInsuranceModel():
  callToInsuranceModel() &&
  !cflowbelow(callToInsuranceModel());
```

The first pointcut identifies calls made to public methods or constructors in the `insurance.model` hierarchy. The second pointcut then defines an external call to the insurance model to be "a `public` call on a `model` type, unless the call is made in the control flow of another `public` call on a `model` type." We identify the first entry point to the model component; if that routine starts to call other methods within the component, this does not create extra join point matches because these methods execute in the control flow of the originally called method.

A second use case for control flow is in program testing. We can scope advice so that when a method is executed in the control flow of a particular test, it does something different than its normal operation—perhaps it throws an unusual exception such as `OutOfMemoryException` or `IOException`, the kinds of situation that are hard to simulate but for which we usually have to write lots of code to deal with. This enables us to exercise many of the code paths through our error-handling logic that are usually not well tested.

6.16   The *adviceexecution* Pointcut Designator

The `adviceexecution` designator is analogous to the `execution` designator for methods and constructors—except it matches the execution of an advice body instead. The format for `adviceexecution` is shown in Figure 6.37.

adviceexecution Pointcut Designator (Kind designator)

                              adviceexecution()

The execution of an advice body.

Figure 6.37   The *adviceexecution* designator.

Figure 6.38 shows a program in AJDT and the kind of situation where `adviceexecution` is required. In the figure we have a simple class and a simple aspect. Some advice attached to the pointcut matches a call to the `println()` method (intending to match the call made by the class). Unfortunately the advice calls `println()` during its execution. This means that the pointcut also matches the `println()` call in the advice. The advice is advising itself (as you can see by the gutter annotations in Figure 6.38)—if we run this program, it will fail, recursively executing the advice until a stack overflow occurs. You will probably write some advice at some point that falls into this trap, too.

Figure 6.38   A program advising itself.

In this case we could use the scope designators `within` or `withincode` to limit the join point matches to places outside of the aspect; if we want to exclude advice defined in any aspect, however, it becomes much more difficult.

The `adviceexecution` designator matches the execution of an advice body, just as `execution` matches the execution of a method or constructor. Although it is tempting to write the following to avoid recursive advice, it does not in fact work as anticipated:

```
pointcut printlnCall() : call(* println(..)) &&
                         !adviceexecution();
```

The advice will still advise itself, and the program will still fail with a stack overflow. What has happened?

The problem is that `adviceexecution` matches the specific join point representing the execution of the advice body, *not* join points *within* the execution of the advice body. This means that `!adviceexecution()` means every join point in the entire system apart from those representing the execution of an advice body. Therefore we continue to match the `println()` call made from within the advice body.

We can solve this problem by combining `adviceexecution()` with `cflow`, as shown in Figure 6.39.

Figure 6.39 Solving the problem of recursive advice application.

The expression `cflow(adviceexecution())` matches join points that occur during the execution of an advice body (or any method in the control flow of the advice). If we negate this expression with `!`, we match any join points other than those that occur as a result of advice execution. By combining the original `call(* println(..))` pointcut with `!cflow(adviceexecution())`, we match a call to `println()` not initiated by advice execution. AJDT, as shown in Figure 6.39, *will* show an annotation against the `println()` call within the advice (cflow is determined dynamically), but at runtime a test will ensure that when running inside the advice body, we do not recursively call the advice.

The adviceexecution designator takes no parameters; it is solely used to identify join points that represent the execution of advice.

6.17   The *if* Pointcut Designator

The if designator is the final AspectJ designator to look at. It enables you to match a join point where a particular Boolean expression evaluates to true—so you can define your own join point matching conditions when the built-in designators aren't quite enough for the task at hand. The definition of if is shown in Figure 6.40.

---

if Pointcut Designator (Context designator)

            if(expression)

Matches a join point where the boolean expression evaluates to true.

Figure 6.40   The *if* designator.

The expression defined for an if designator can reference any visible static members, and any context exposed by other designators in the same pointcut expression (this, target, or args). You can even refer to thisJoinPoint, thisJoinPointStaticPart, or thisEnclosingJoinPointStaticPart to create the intended expression. (See the next chapter for more details.)

A common use of if is to enable or disable advice execution based on the value of a flag. The following two listings show a debugging aspect we can write that allows us to report the state of the stack before and after every calculator operation is performed on it. Instead of writing the aspect of Listing 6.17, we can write the aspect shown in Listing 6.18, where the test within the advice has been promoted to the pointcut, using the if designator.

Listing 6.17   Simple Debugging Aspect for the Calculator

```
public aspect DebugCalculatorOperations {
  private final static boolean debugOn = true;

  pointcut mathematicalOperation(Calculator calcInstance) :
    execution(void perform*(..)) &&
    this(calcInstance);
```

```
  before(Calculator calc): mathematicalOperation(calc) {
    if (debugOn) {
      recordInfo("Before operation, stack = "+
                 calc.getStack().toString());
      recordInfo("Executing operation: "+
        thisJoinPointStaticPart.getSignature().getName());
    }
  }

  after(Calculator calc) returning:
    mathematicalOperation(calc) {
    if (debugOn) {
      recordInfo("After operation, stack = "+
                 calc.getStack().toString());
    }
  }

  private static void recordInfo(String info) {
    System.out.println(info);
  }
}
```

Listing 6.18 Simple Debugging Aspect—Refactored with *if*

```
public aspect DebugCalculatorOperations {
  private final static boolean debugOn = true;

  pointcut mathematicalOperation(Calculator calcInstance) :
    execution(void perform*(..)) &&
    this(calcInstance) &&
    if(DebugCalculatorOperations.debugOn);

  before(Calculator calc): mathematicalOperation(calc) {
    recordInfo("Before operation, stack = "+
               calc.getStack().toString());
    recordInfo("Executing operation: "+
      thisJoinPointStaticPart.getSignature().getName());
  }

  after(Calculator calc) returning:
    mathematicalOperation(calc) {
    recordInfo("After operation, stack = "+
               calc.getStack().toString());
  }

  private static void recordInfo(String info) {
    System.out.println(info);
  }
}
```

The obvious benefit in the second listing is that both pieces of advice have become clearer, and we now only test whether debugging is on in one place.

The `if` designator is another example of a pointcut that results in a runtime test that has to pass in order for the corresponding advice to execute. Evaluation of the expression that is supplied to the `if` designator is done at runtime. This means that when using AJDT with pointcuts that contain `if` components, the tools will show all the places where the advice *might* run, depending on the result of evaluating the expression. In Figure 6.41 you can see that debugging is turned off (`DebugCalculatorOperations.debugOn` is set to false) but the Outline view still shows the calculator being advised and the possibility of that debug advice executing at runtime. It is only when the program executes that the `if(DebugCalculatorOperations.debugOn)` test will evaluate to false and the advice won't actually execute. And because the flag being tested is in fact declared `final`, it is likely that the Java JIT compiler will be able to completely optimize away the runtime test in this case.

Figure 6.41   AJDT showing matches for an *if* designator.

Let's finish by looking at a more sophisticated example. Listing 6.19 shows an `Account` class. Listing 6.20 shows an aspect that monitors accounts becoming overdrawn.

Listing 6.19 Simple *Account* Class

```
class Account {
  private int accountNumber;
  private double balance;

  public static Account openAccount(int num) {
    return new Account(num);
  }

  public int getAccountNumber() {
    return accountNumber;
  }

  public double getBalance() {
    return balance;
  }

  private Account(int num) {
    accountNumber = num;
    balance = 100.0;
  }

  public void debit(double amount) {
    balance -= amount;
  }

  public void credit(double amount) {
    balance += amount;
  }
}
```

Listing 6.20 Aspect to Detect Accounts Going Overdrawn

```
aspect AccountPolice {

  pointcut goingOverdrawn(Account acct,double amount):
    execution(* debit(..)) && this(acct) &&
    args(amount) && if((acct.getBalance()-amount<0));

  before(Account acct) : goingOverdrawn(acct,*) {
    System.err.println(
      "Account "+acct.getAccountNumber()+
      " is going overdrawn");
  }

}
```

You can see how we have used `this` and `args` to expose context around the chosen join point (execution of `debit()`); we have then used an `if` test to check whether the account will go overdrawn when that amount is taken out of it. Without using `if`, we would only have been able to create a pointcut that detected the `debit()` method was executing; the advice would have had to determine whether the account was going overdrawn. Using `if` in this way we have been able to simplify the advice and give a more meaningful name to the pointcut.

6.18 How to Write a Good Pointcut

Four steps are involved in writing a good pointcut. First, come up with a meaningful name that describes the characteristic of the join points you want to match—ideally in a way that serves to make your program self-documenting. For example, `secureOperation`.

```
pointcut secureOperation();
```

Join point names tend to be singular (`secureOperation` rather than `secureOperations`), and fit into the sentence "is this a <pointcut_name> join point?"

The second step is to decide what kind of join points you want to match, and add the appropriate kind designator to the pointcut definition (`call`, `execution`, `handler`, `get`, `set`, `adviceexecution`, or one of the initialization designators). It is rare to combine kind designators of more than one type in a pointcut; if you do, be sure to combine them using || rather than &&. An example might be `get(* x) || set(* x)` to match all references to a field named x. If you are matching `call` or `execution` join points, do not specify a declaring type in the signature pattern unless you are sure that you want static typing matches.

```
pointcut secureOperation() : execution(public *(..));
```

The third step is to decide in which context the pointcut should match (using `target`, `this`, or `args`). If the pointcut should match in any context, you can omit this stage. If the users of the pointcut need access to the contextual values at a matched join point, add these to the pointcut parameter list and bind the values in the context designators.

```
pointcut secureOperation(ISecured secured) :
  execution(public *(..)) &&
  this(secured);
```

Finally, decide on the scope in which the pointcut should match (within a certain component, for example, or a given control flow).

```
pointcut secureOperation(ISecured secured) :
  execution(public *(..)) &&
  target(secured) &&
  within(com.xyz.someapp..*);
```

Try to keep individual pointcut definitions small and simple, and build more complex pointcuts by combining named, simpler pointcuts.

6.19   Common Pitfalls

This section examines some common pitfalls when writing pointcuts that we haven't already covered elsewhere in the chapter.

6.19.1 Can't Match Calls to super/this

Listing 6.21 shows a common situation in a Java program where a constructor is delegating to an alternative constructor, using the `this()` mechanism to invoke the alternative constructor.

Listing 6.21   Delegating Constructors

```
class Account {
  private int accountNumber;
  private double balance;

  public Account(int acnum) {
    this(acnum,100.0);
  }

  private Account(int acnum,double bal) {
    this.accountNumber=acnum;
    this.balance=bal;
  }
}
```

Although you might think the call `this(acnum,100.0)` is a constructor call, it is actually handled in a special way by Java and consequently there is no join point available to select with a `call` designator. In these cases, you need to use the `execution` designator and select the execution of the constructor as your join point.

There is a similar situation when a method delegates to a superclass implementation using the `super()` call, as in the example shown in Listing 6.22, which is a piece of the logic from the `IntegerStack` class.

Listing 6.22   Using *super()* to Call a Superclass' Implementation

```
public class IntegerStack extends Stack {

  public Object push(Object o) {
    Object toPush = null;
    if (o instanceof Integer) {
      toPush = (Integer)o;
    } else if (o instanceof String) {
      Integer.parseInt((String) o);
      toPush = new Integer((String) o);
    }
    Object o2 = super.push(toPush);
  }
}
```

Calls to superclass implementations, such as the `super.push(toPush)` call in `IntegerStack`, get special treatment by the Java compiler, and so the call to `push()` is not selectable as a join point with the `call` designator.

6.19.2 Can't Match Calls Made Reflectively

Method calls can be made using the Java reflection API. Calls made in this way are not directly exposed as call join points to the target of the reflective call. Listing 6.23 shows reflection used to invoke a method on the `String` class.

Listing 6.23   Reflective Method Calls

```
class TestClass {
  public static void main(String[]argv) {
    String ajdt = new String("ajdt");
    try {
      Method compareMethod =
        String.class.getDeclaredMethod(
            "compareTo", new Class[] {String.class});
```

```
        System.err.println(
          "Comparing 'ajdt' to 'tdja' ="+
          compareMethod.invoke(ajdt,
            new Object[] {"tdja"})
        );

        System.err.println(
          "Comparing 'ajdt' to 'ajdt' ="+
          compareMethod.invoke(ajdt,
            new Object[] {"ajdt"})
        );
    } catch(Exception e) {
      e.printStackTrace();
    }
  }
}
```

This program builds a `String` instance, and then calls the `compareTo()` method on the instance to compare it with two other strings. The call to `compareTo()` is not exposed as a join point that you can select with a `call` designator (instead there is a join point for the call to `Method.invoke(..)`). There are two options for dealing with this situation. One is to use an `execution` designator to select the join point for execution of the method being reflectively called—but that won't work for us here because `compareTo()` is a method defined on the `String` system class. The AspectJ compiler will not have the `String` class available to it for advice linking, and so it will be unable to effect any execution advice for it. The second option is to use the `call` designator to select the call of the `invoke()` method and then perform a runtime test to check whether it is the invocation of the method we are interested in, `compareTo()`. Listing 6.24 shows an aspect that does this, using the `if` designator to capture the runtime check that determines whether the target of the reflective invocation is the `compareTo()` method.

Listing 6.24   Catching Reflective Calls

```
aspect CatchReflectiveCalls {

  pointcut compareToInvocation(Method method,
      String instance,Object[] parameters) :
    call(* invoke(..)) &&
    args(instance,parameters) &&
    target(method) &&
    if(method.getName().equals("compareTo"));

  before(String instance,Object[] parameters):
    compareToInvocation(*,instance,parameters) {
```

```
        System.err.println(
            "Instance on which compareTo is being called:"+
            instance);

        System.err.println(
          "Parameter for compareTo:"+parameters[0]);

    }

}
```

6.19.3 The Empty Pointcut Definition

The definition `pointcut  name();` is a valid pointcut definition. It is a named pointcut with no pointcut expression specified. An empty definition such as this will match no join points. Why is this allowed? It is actually a nice shortcut when developing/testing your pointcuts that enables you to quickly "switch them off." Perhaps you have a pointcut with some advice attached to it:

```
pointcut publicMethods(): execution(public *(..));
```

If you temporarily want to build a version of your program without advice against all your public methods, you don't have to comment out all the advice; you can just use the empty pointcut definition:

```
pointcut publicMethods();//: execution(public *(..));
```

6.20   Summary

This chapter presented a comprehensive introduction to all the available AspectJ pointcut designators. We discussed both what they do and how best to use them. Importantly, we also demonstrated the common groupings of designators you will be using day to day, and best practices in construction of your pointcuts. Appendix B is a quick reference for AspectJ that includes information on all pointcut designators.

CHAPTER 7

Take My Advice

This chapter explains in detail the use of advice in AspectJ. We examine the basic forms of advice that are supported, and the association between advice and a point-cut expression. We then cover the rules for writing logic within the body of an advice declaration, and tackle the issue of what happens when multiple pieces of advice all need to execute at the same join point. The declare soft mechanism for softening checked exceptions is also covered in this chapter, because it is best used in conjunction with advice implementing an exception-handling strategy. The chapter closes with a look at AspectJ's declare error/declare warning mechanism, which like advice uses pointcuts to determine join points of interest, only the action taken at a matched join point is to raise a compilation error or warning.

7.1 The Different Types of Advice

AspectJ supports three basic types of advice: before advice, after advice, and around advice. Recall that advice is associated with a pointcut expression, and executes at all the join point events matched by the pointcut expression. Before advice executes immediately before a matched join point. After advice executes immediately after a matched join point. Around advice executes both before and after (that is, around) a matched join point. Each form of advice declaration follows the same basic structure:

```
[strictfp] AdviceSpecification [ throws TypeList ] :
          PointcutExpression {
    body of advice…
}
```

The `strictfp` modifier is the only modifier allowed for advice: Because advice cannot be explicitly invoked, there is no need for the visibility modifiers associated with fields and methods. If the `strictfp` modifier is present, all floating-point expressions within the body of the advice will be FP-strict.

The optional `throws` clause indicates the exceptions that the body of the advice may throw. Advice may only throw exceptions compatible with the join points at which it executes. In particular, advice cannot throw a checked exception that the client executing at the join point is not expecting. We return to the handling and throwing of exceptions in advice in Section 7.3.2.

The pointcut expression associated with the advice can be any valid pointcut expression, as discussed in Chapter 6.

7.1.1 Before Advice

We didn't use before advice in Part 1 of the book, but it is arguably the simplest form of advice in AspectJ. The advice specification for before advice is simply as follows:

```
before( ParameterList )
```

The parameter list for before advice, as for all types of advice, takes the same form as the parameter list for a normal Java method declaration: a comma-separated list of type name, parameter name pairs.

Chapter 4 discussed code templates in the editor. AJDT defines a completion template for before advice, so you can type **before** within the body of an aspect (or any unique prefix, such as **bef**) and then press **Ctrl+Spacebar** (code completion). AJDT will populate a before advice template for you as shown in Figure 7.1. This can not only save you typing, but also remind you of the syntax while you are learning the language.

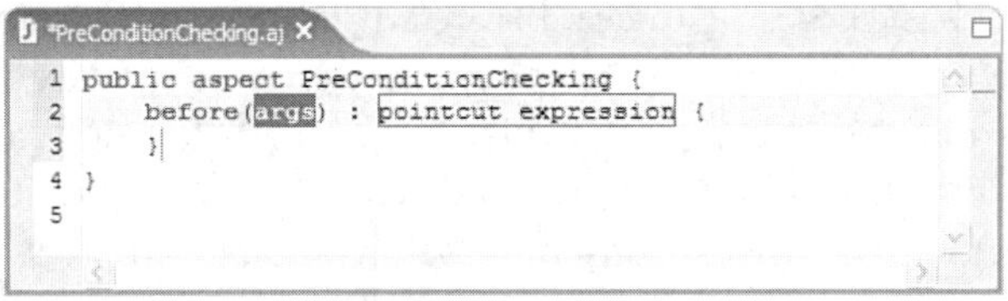

```
1  public aspect PreConditionChecking {
2      before(args) : pointcut expression {
3      }
4  }
5
```

Figure 7.1   Before advice completion in AJDT.

Listing 7.1 shows a simple aspect that uses before advice to perform precondition checking on all setters in the `insurance.model` package and sub-packages of the Simple Insurance application.

Listing 7.1   Precondition Checking with Before Advice

```
package insurance.model.impl;

/**
 * A simple aspect to validate that any object parameter
 * passed to a set method in the insurance model
 * is non-null.
 */
public aspect PreConditionChecking {

  pointcut insuranceModelSetter(Object newValue) :
    execution(* insurance.model..*set*(..)) &&
    args(newValue);

  before(Object newValue) : insuranceModelSetter(newValue) {
    if (newValue == null) {
      throw new IllegalArgumentException(
        "value must be non-null");
    }
  }
}
```

Figure 7.2 shows the effect of this aspect on the AddressImpl class. Notice that the symbol used for before advice (in both the Editor and in the Outline view) is an arrow pointing up and to the right.

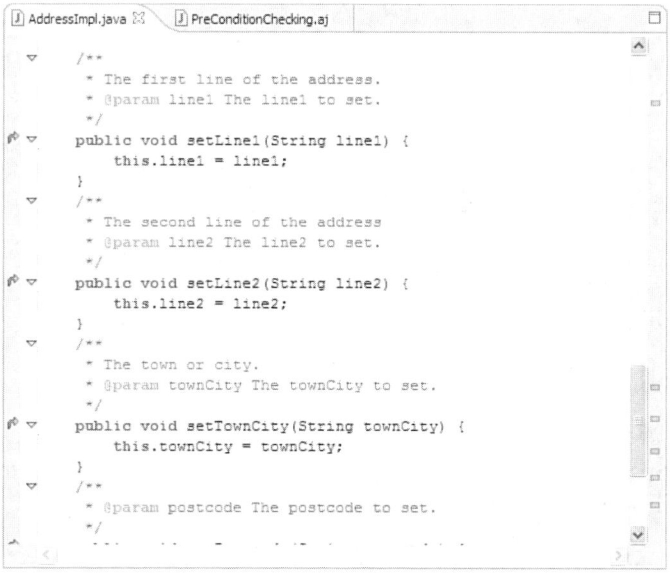

Figure 7.2   Before advice markers in the editor.

Even with the limited domain model in our simple example, this aspect is protecting nearly 30 methods from being passed a null parameter.

7.1.2. After Advice

There are three basic forms of after advice: after returning advice, which executes after the successful return from a matched join point; after throwing advice, which executes after returning from a matched join point via an exception condition; and after finally advice (also known as just "after" advice), which executes whether returning from a matched join point by either normal or exceptional return. When using AJDT, you can type **after** within the body of an aspect and then press **Ctrl+Spacebar** (code completion). AJDT offers a choice of after returning or after throwing advice, as shown in Figure 7.3. We recommend that in most cases you should use one of these two forms rather than after finally advice. After finally is only appropriate where you are fully prepared to handle both normal and exceptional return from the matched join point within the body of the advice.

Figure 7.3   Code completion options for after advice.

In the Editor and Outline view, AJDT uses an arrow pointing down and to the right to indicate after advice 📥 .

7.1.2.1 After Throwing Advice

The advice specification for after throwing advice can take one of two forms. The simple form will execute when returning from a matched join point via *any* exception condition (checked or unchecked):

```
after( ParameterList ) throwing
```

If you want advice to execute only when returning from a matched join point via a given exception condition, you can use the second form of after throwing advice:

after(*ParameterList*) **throwing** (*Formal*)

Advice specified using this form will execute only when leaving a matched join point via an exception that is an instance of the given exception type. Within the body of the advice, the exception thrown can be referred to by the name given within the `Formal`. We saw an example of after throwing advice in Chapter 3, where we used it to catch any `HibernateException` that might be thrown and map it to a `SIPersistenceException` (insulating the rest of the application from the particular persistence mechanism used):

```
after() throwing(HibernateException hEx) :
  hibernateCall() && !target(HibernateException) {
  hEx.printStackTrace();
  throw new SIPersistenceException(hEx);
}
```

7.1.2.2 After Returning Advice

Just as there are two forms of after throwing advice, there are two forms of after returning advice, depending on whether you need access to the return value within the body of the advice. The simple form of advice specification for after returning advice is as follows:

after(*ParameterList*) **returning**

This advice will execute whenever a normal return is made from a matched join point. If you need access to the actual return value, you can use the second form of after returning advice specification:

after(*ParameterList*) **returning**(*Formal*)

The `TrackFinders` aspect in Listing 7.2 uses after returning advice to log information about all the queries issued on policies in the Simple Insurance application.

Listing 7.2   Exposing Return Values in After Returning Advice

```
package insurance.logging;

import org.apache.log4j.Logger;
import java.util.Set;
import insurance.model.SimpleInsurance;

/**
 * Keep track of how many queries we are executing and
 * how many results they return...
 */
public aspect TrackFinders {

  private static Logger logger =
    Logger.getLogger(TrackFinders.class);

  pointcut findPolicies(String criteria) :
    execution(Set SimpleInsurance.findPoliciesBy*(..))
    && args(criteria);

  after(String criteria) returning(Set found) :
    findPolicies(criteria) {
    if (logger.isInfoEnabled()) {
      logger.info("Finding policies by " + criteria +
      "returned " + found.size() + " matches");
    }
  }

}
```

After returning advice specified with a formal in the `returning()` clause will only execute when the return value from the join point is an instance of the type specified in the `Formal`. Listing 7.3 shows a simple class with three methods: one that returns a `String`, one that returns a `float`, and one that returns a `char`. It also has a main method that calls each of these in turn.

Listing 7.3   Method Return Values and *after() returning()*

```
public class AClass {
  public static void main(String[] args) {
    AClass a = new AClass();
    a.myStringMethod();
    a.myFloatMethod();
    a.myCharMethod();
  }

  String myStringMethod() {
    String s = "A String";
    s.length();
```

```
      return s;
   }

   float myFloatMethod() {
      return 0.5F;
   }

   char myCharMethod() {
      return 'X';
   }
}
```

Figure 7.4 shows the matches in the Outline view when the following aspect is compiled with the class from Listing 7.3:

```
aspect AfterReturning {
   after() returning(String s) : execution(* my*Method()) {
      System.out.println("returning(String s): " + s);
   }

   after() returning(List l) : execution(* my*Method()) {
      System.out.println("returning(List l): " + l);
   }

}
```

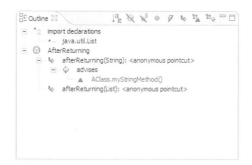

Figure 7.4 *after() returning()* matches in the Outline view.

You can see that the return type specified in the `returning()` clause is acting to further constrain the set of join points at which the advice will execute. The first piece of advice matches only the execution of the `myStringMethod`, even though the pointcut expression associated with it (`execution(* my*Method())`) matches all three methods. The second piece of after returning advice does not match at all because none of the `my*Methods` return a value of type `List`.

For *primitive* return types, if the formal also specifies a primitive return type, a type conversion will be performed in accordance with the normal Java rules for conversion among primitive types. Figure 7.5 shows the Outline view when the revised `AfterReturning` aspect below is compiled with the same class:

```
aspect AfterReturning {
  after() returning(float f) : call(int String.length()) {
    System.out.println("returning(float f): " + f);
  }

  after() returning(int i) : execution(* my*Method()) {
    System.out.println("returning(int i): " + i);
  }

  after() returning(double d) : execution(float my*Method())
  {
    System.out.println("returning(double d): " + d);
  }
}
```

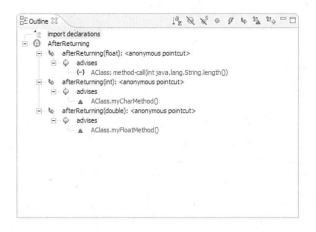

Figure 7.5 *after() returning()* matching with primitive types.

If you run this program, you see the following output:

```
returning(float f): 8.0
returning(double d): 0.5
returning(int i): 88
```

The call to `String.length` has been matched by the `returning(float f)` advice and the `int` return value converted to a `float`, the execution of `myCharMethod` has been matched by the `returning(int i)` advice and the char return value converted to an `int`, and the execution of `myFloatMethod` has been matched by the `returning(double d)` advice and the `float` return value converted to a `double`.

If you want to write after returning advice that runs for any return type and value, but still gives access to the value returned, you can specify `Object` as the type of the formal parameter. Any primitive return values will be promoted to their Object equivalents.[1] (For example, a return value of type `int` will be converted to a `java.lang.Integer`.)

Referring again to the definition of `AClass` in Listing 7.3, if we compile and run with this final version of the `AfterReturning` aspect

```
aspect AfterReturning {
  after() returning(Object o) : execution(* my*Method()) {
    System.out.println("returning(Object o): " + o);
  }
}
```

all the `my*Methods` are matched as shown in Figure 7.6, and the following output is produced when the program runs:

```
returning(Object o): A String
returning(Object o): 0.5
returning(Object o): X
```

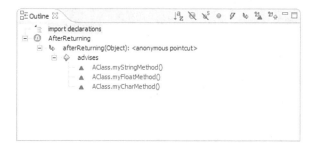

Figure 7.6   Matches with a *returning()* parameter of type *Object*.

For a matched join point that returns null or void, the returning parameter will be bound to "null."

---

1 This promotion only happens when the returning type is `Object`. A returning type of `Integer` will not match join points that return an `int`.

7.1.2.2.1 Join Point Return Values

So far we have seen how the return values from matched join points can be accessed, but we have not discussed what "return value" means for the different kinds of join points. Figure 7.7 shows a short AspectJ program inside the AJDT editor. The `ReturnValues` aspect shown in Listing 7.4 prints out the join point kind and return value for every join point in the `ExploringJoinPointReturnValues` class, which contains every kind of primitive join point (except `advice-execution`).

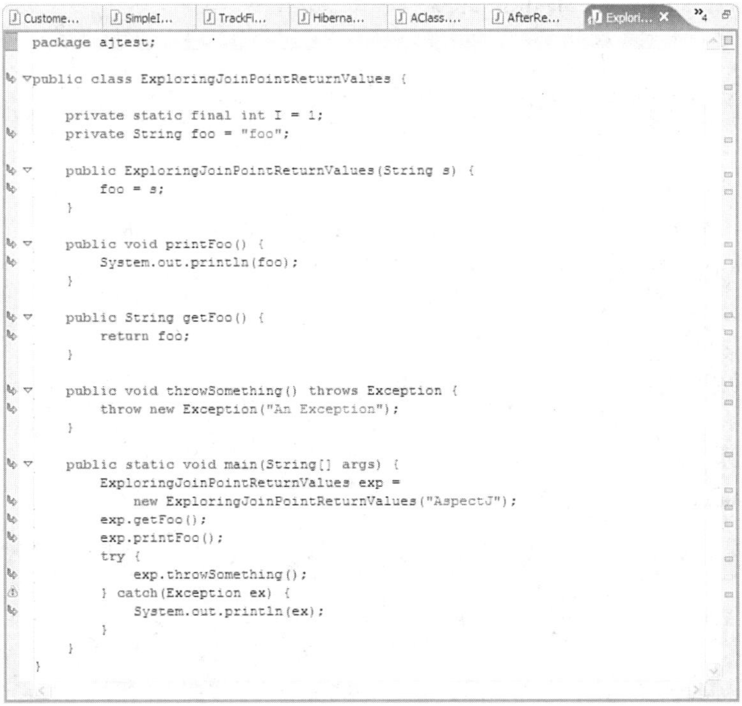

Figure 7.7   Exploring join point return values.

Listing 7.4   Aspect to Display Return Values from Join Points

```
public aspect ReturnValues {

  pointcut allJoinPoints() :
    within(ExploringJoinPointReturnValues);
```

```
after() returning(Object o) : allJoinPoints() {
  System.out.println(thisJoinPoint + ": returned " + o);
}
}
```

Perhaps the first thing to notice is the warning triangle in the gutter of the editor. The corresponding tasks view is shown in Figure 7.8. Here we see that there is no return value defined for a handler join point, because after returning advice is not supported for handler join points. We return to this topic in Section 7.7.

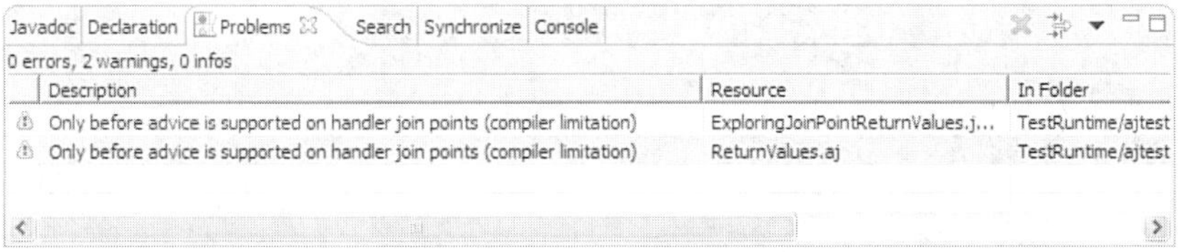

Javadoc	Declaration	Problems ⊠	Search	Synchronize	Console			× 🏗 ▼ ⬜ □
0 errors, 2 warnings, 0 infos								
Description						Resource	In Folder	
⚠ Only before advice is supported on handler join points (compiler limitation)						ExploringJoinPointReturnValues.j...	TestRuntime/ajtest	
⚠ Only before advice is supported on handler join points (compiler limitation)						ReturnValues.aj	TestRuntime/ajtest	

Figure 7.8   Tasks view.

When we run the program, we get the output shown in Figure 7.9. From this we can deduce the contents of Table 7.1, which shows the meaning of the return value for the different join point kinds.

Table 7.1   Join Point Return Values

Join Point Kind	Return Value
staticinitialization	null
preinitialization	null
initialization	null
constructor call	The created object
constructor execution	null
method call	Method return value
method execution	Method return value
Get	Value of accessed field
Set	null
handler	Not applicable

Figure 7.9   Output from join point Return Value Exploration program.

7.1.2.3 After Finally Advice

The advice specification for after finally advice is simply as follows:

```
after( ParameterList )
```

After finally advice executes however the program returns from a matched join point—whether by a normal return or by exception. Therefore if you use after finally advice you must be prepared to handle both normal and exceptional conditions. Unlike the after returning and after throwing forms, after finally advice does not provide access to the return value or exception with which a matched join point was exited. After finally advice is best used in situations where you need to take action regardless of how a join point is left (just as a finally block is executed regardless of how a block statement is left). An example might be returning a connection to a pool, or decrementing a reference count of active clients. Listing 7.5 shows an example using after finally advice to implement a multiple readers, single writer synchronization policy using Doug Lea's Concurrency library (Lea 2003).

Listing 7.5   Multiple Readers, Single Writer with After Advice

```
public abstract aspect MultipleReadersSingleWriter
perthis( readMethod() || writeMethod() ) {
    private ReadWriteLock rw =
            new WriterPreferenceReadWriteLock();

    abstract pointcut readMethod();
    abstract pointcut writeMethod();

    before() : readMethod() {
      try {
        rw.readLock().acquire();
      } catch (InterruptedException intEx) {
        throw new RuntimeException(
            "Unable to obtain R lock");
      }
    }

    after() : readMethod() {
      rw.readLock().release();
    }

    before() : writeMethod() {
      try {
        rw.writeLock().acquire();
      } catch (InterruptedException intEx) {
        throw new RuntimeException(
            "Unable to obtain W lock");
      }
    }

    after() : writeMethod() {
      rw.writeLock().release();
    }

    declare warning: readMethod() && writeMethod() :
      "A method cannot be both a read and a write method";
}
```

The aspect is abstract; it knows how to implement a multiple readers, single writer policy, but not the set of methods that are considered read methods and the set of methods considered write methods. A concrete subaspect can supply definitions of these abstract pointcuts, and the `MultipleReadersSingleWriter` aspect will create a unique `ReadWriteLock` for each instance to be protected. The after (finally) advice ensures that the locks are released regardless of how we leave a read or write method. We return to the use of abstract aspects (and the use of `perthis`) in Chapter 9.

7.1.3 Around Advice

Around advice is the most powerful form of advice. It executes both before and after (that is, around) a matched join point. Around advice can determine whether program execution should continue into the matched join point, and if so, what context the join point should execute in. It can also examine and alter the return value from the join point. Because around advice can determine the return value from the join point, around advice declarations need a return type. The advice specification for around advice takes the following form:

```
ReturnType around( ParameterList )
```

In the Editor and the Outline view, AJDT uses a double-headed arrow to indicate around advice ⟡.

Because around advice executes both before and after a matched join point, we need a way to specify when in the body of the advice we want to return control to the join point. This is achieved by calling proceed inside the body of the advice. The signature of proceed is always the same as the signature of the parameter list in the around advice specification. proceed returns a value of the same type as the return type of the around advice, which must be compatible with the return value of the matched join points (see Table 7.1). The following around advice does nothing—it just lets program flow continue into the join point:

```
void around(int age) : set(int Person.age) && args(age) {
  return proceed(age);
}
```

This is very different from other forms of advice where an empty advice body signifies no change to the program flow. An empty around advice body, as in the following example, has a quite different meaning—because the body contains no call to proceed it has the effect of never proceeding into the matched join point at all—the Person.age field will not be set:

```
void around(int age) : set(int Person.age) && args(age) {
  // advice body with no proceed bypasses matched join point
}
```

We saw an example of this usage of around advice in Chapter 2 as a temporary step in the refactoring process for PolicyChangeNotification. Normally you would decide whether to proceed based on testing some condition—we will show you an example of that later in this section with the `CleverStuffCache` aspect.

Around advice can change the context in which a matched join point proceeds, by changing the values of the arguments passed into the proceed call. The following aspect ignores the value passed into a field set join point, and uses a constant value instead:

```
aspect ForEverYoung {
  void around(int age)  : set(int Person.age) && args(age) {
    return proceed(21);
  }
}
```

For join points that have a defined return value, around advice can change the return value seen by the original caller. Here's an example of premature aging:

```
aspect PrematureAging {
  int around() : get(int Person.age) {
    int age = proceed();
    return age + 10;
  }
}
```

Here's another example of changing the context in which a matched join point proceeds—this time we have exposed the target person of a set join point:

```
aspect AlterEgo {
  Person alterEgo = new Person("Ego","Alter");

  pointcut setPersonAge(Person p, int newAge) :
    set(int Person.age) && args(newAge) &&
    target(p);

  void around(Person p, int age) : setPersonAge(p,age) {
    return proceed(alterEgo,age);
  }
}
```

The first argument in the call to the `proceed` method matches the first argument in the around advice specification—which is bound to the target of the set. By proceeding with a different value for the first argument, we change the target of the set, and end up updating the age of our alter ego.

It is a little-known fact that AspectJ does not limit you to calling `proceed` only once within the body of around advice. Here's a powerful example that exploits this fact:

```
aspect Replication {
  Server replica = ... ;
  pointcut replicatedRequested(Server s) :
    call(* Server.*(..)) && target(s);

  Object around(Server s) : replicatedRequest(s) {
    Object ret = proceed(s);
    proceed(replica);
    return ret;
  }
}
```

This example also illustrates the use of `Object` as the return type for around advice. We have written just one piece of around advice that applies to all the methods in the `Server`, regardless of their return type. When the return type of an around advice is declared as `Object`, then for join points that return a primitive type the return from a call to proceed will be promoted to its `Object` equivalent. (`int` is promoted to `Integer` and so on.) When the `Object` type is returned from the around advice, it will be converted back to the type expected by the caller. This conversion also happens for join points that return a subclass of `Object`—the `Object` return value from the around advice will be converted (cast in this case) to the appropriate type expected by the caller. The result of calling `proceed` on a call or execution join point for a method with a void return type will be `null`.

Around advice makes it very easy to implement a basic caching or pooling strategy. Listing 7.6 shows the implementation of the `CleverStuff` class, which contains a single method computing an expensive function.

Listing 7.6 Clever Stuff!

```
public class CleverStuff {

  public int computeExpensiveFunction(int a) {
    try {
      Thread.sleep(2000);
    } catch (InterruptedException intEx) {
      System.err.println("A rude awakening...");
    }
    return a*a;
  }

}
```

Because we know that computeExpensiveFunction is a true function (it always gives the same return value for the same arguments), it is amenable to caching. Let's write the test case next—CleverStuffTest shown in Listing 7.7. The test case asserts the two things we want to be true if our cache implementation is successful—clients still see the correct return values, and the program runs faster.

Listing 7.7   Testing Clever Stuff

```
public class CleverStuffTest extends TestCase {

  private static final int ERROR_MARGIN = 1000;

  public void testComputeExpensiveFunction() {
    CleverStuff cs = new CleverStuff();
    int firstPassSum = 0;
    long start = System.currentTimeMillis();
    for (int i = 0; i < 5; i++) {
      firstPassSum +=
        cs.computeExpensiveFunction(i);
    }
    long firstTime = System.currentTimeMillis()—start;
    int secondPassSum = 0;
    start = System.currentTimeMillis();
    for (int i = 0; i < 5; i++) {
      secondPassSum +=
        cs.computeExpensiveFunction(i);
    }
    long secondTime = System.currentTimeMillis()—start;

    assertEquals("caching should not affect return value",
      firstPassSum, secondPassSum);
    assertTrue("Cache speeds up computation",
      (secondTime + ERROR_MARGIN) < firstTime);
  }

}
```

If we run this test case inside Eclipse using the JUnit Test Launcher, we see the result shown in Figure 7.10.

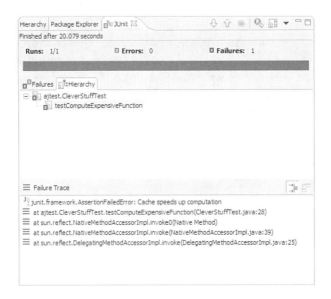

Figure 7.10   Test results.

Now we're ready to go ahead and make the test pass. The `CleverStuffCache` aspect is shown in Listing 7.8. Note how we have exploited the automatic promotion and demotion that happens when the return value of advice is declared as type `Object`—this gives us an `Object` value that the collection classes require, while still returning the primitive `int` value to the original caller.

Listing 7.8   Clever Stuff Cache

```
public aspect CleverStuffCache {
  Map cache = new HashMap();

  pointcut computeExpensiveFunction(int x) :
    execution(int CleverStuff.computeExpensiveFunction(int))
    && args(x);

  Object around(int x) : computeExpensiveFunction(x) {
    Object theAnswer;
    Integer key = new Integer(x);
    if (cache.containsKey(key)) {
      theAnswer = cache.get(key);
    } else {
      theAnswer = proceed(x);
      cache.put(key,theAnswer);
    }
    return theAnswer;
  }
}
```

If we include the `CleverStuffCache` aspect in the build, the test case passes.

Figures 7.11 and 7.12 show how we represent around advice that does (Figure 7.11) and does not (Figure 7.12) call `proceed` within a sequence diagram.

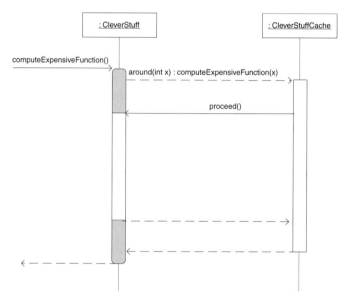

Figure 7.11 Representing *proceed* in a sequence diagram (cache miss).

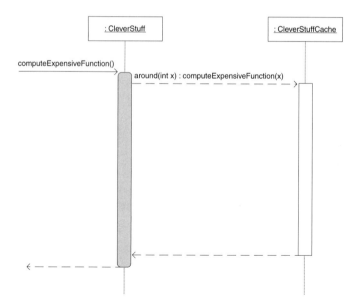

Figure 7.12 Representing around advice without *proceed* in a sequence diagram (cache hit).

7.2   Advice Parameters and Pointcuts

Chapter 2, Section 2.6.2, briefly introduced AspectJ's mechanism for binding advice parameters to values provided by pointcut expressions. In this section, we cover the rules for advice parameter binding in more depth.

Advice can take zero or more parameters, specified in the advice declaration. Because advice is invoked implicitly, there is no way for the programmer to pass parameter values on a call to the advice. Where do the values for advice parameters come from then? Recall that a pointcut declaration is a statement that the pointcut will provide contextual values of the type specified in the pointcut declaration—these provided values from the pointcut expression associated with a piece of advice are matched to the required values from the advice specification. The matching happens by name. Each parameter in an advice specification is given an identifier (a name)—and every parameter name must appear somewhere in the pointcut expression associated with the advice. Failure to "bind" every parameter in this way results in the compile time error "formal unbound in pointcut," as shown in Figure 7.13.

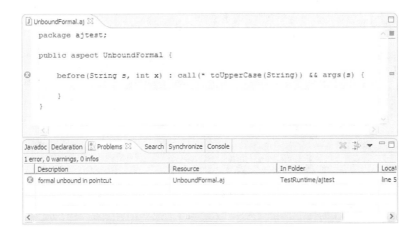

Figure 7.13   Formal unbound in pointcut.

As with writing named pointcuts, identifiers in advice formals can be bound in the primitive pointcut designators `this`, `target` and `args`, or to any parameter provided by a named pointcut. Figure 7.14 illustrates the binding process at work.

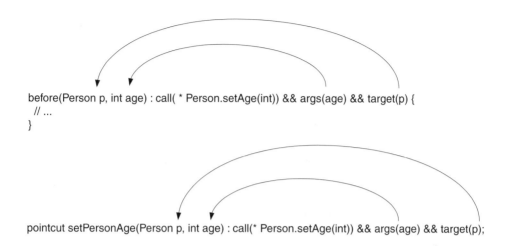

Figure 7.14   Binding advice parameters.

When an advice parameter is of type `Object`, then AspectJ applies boxing (promotion of primitive types to their object equivalents). An advice parameter of type `Object` can be matched with any primitive or object-based value. It works in the same way as boxing in pointcut declarations, as described in Chapter 6, Section 6.10.3. Using the examples from Figure 7.14, both

```
before(Person p, Object age) :
    call(* Person.setAge(..)) && args(age) && target(p) {...}
```

and

```
before(Person p, Object age) :
    setPersonAge(p,age) {...}
```

are legal expressions. In the body of the advice, `age` will have a value of type `Integer`. Boxing enables us to write one piece of advice that can apply across a wide range of join points in a type-independent manner.

If you are associating advice with a named pointcut, and you don't want or need to expose all the pointcut-provided parameters as parameters in the advice body, you can use a just type name in place of a named parameter. Here's a simple example:

```
pointcut setPersonAge(Person p, int age);

before(Person p) : setPersonAge(p, int) {...}
```

7.3   Writing Logic in the Body of Advice

As well as the contextual information provided through advice parameters, you can also gain access to contextual information through a set of special variables that AspectJ makes available. This section examines the context in which advice runs, and then looks at the rules for dealing with exceptional conditions inside advice.

7.3.1 The Context in Which Advice Runs

There are three ways for the body of advice to obtain information about the context in which it is executing. The first is through advice parameters, which we explored in the previous section. Like method parameters, parameters to advice are passed by value, so setting the value of a parameter has effect only within the body of the advice. If you want to change the context outside of the advice body, you have to use around advice as described earlier in this chapter.

The second set of contextual information available to advice is that within the aspect instance in which the advice is executing. Advice can refer to state or methods defined in the aspect or its super types in the same way that the body of a method can refer to state or methods defined in its declaring type or super types. Inside an advice body, the variable `this` is bound to the aspect instance in which the advice is executing—just as `this` inside an instance method of a class refers to the object in which the method is executing.

The third and final set of contextual information is made available through a set of special variables: `thisJoinPoint`, `thisJoinPointStaticPart`, and `thisEnclosingJoinPointStaticPart`. These variables provide reflective access to the join point that was matched for this advice execution (`thisJoinPoint`, `thisJoinPointStaticPart`), and static information about the join point lexically enclosing the matched join point (`thisEnclosingJoinPointStaticPart`). The `thisJoinPoint` variable is of type `org.aspectj.lang.JoinPoint`, and the static part variables are of type `org.aspectj.lang.JoinPoint.StaticPart`.

One useful thing to know about these variables is that they all have an informative toString() implementation—take another look at Listing 7.4 and Figure 7.9 earlier in this chapter. Using thisJoinPointStaticPart, you can access the *kind* of the join point, the *source location* that gave rise to the join point, and the *signature* of the join point. For a method-call join point, for example, the signature of the join point is the method signature. If we compile the following aspect with the ExploringJoinPointReturnValues class shown in Figure 7.7, we get the output shown in Figure 7.15 when the program runs:

```
public aspect JoinPointStaticPartExplorer {

  pointcut allJoinPoints() :
    within(ExploringJoinPointReturnValues);

  before() : allJoinPoints() {
    System.out.print(thisJoinPointStaticPart.getKind() +
      " join point at ");
    System.out.println(
      thisJoinPointStaticPart.getSourceLocation());
    System.out.println("\t signature: " +
      thisJoinPointStaticPart.getSignature());
  }

}
```

Figure 7.15   Exploring *thisJoinPointStaticPart.*

The `thisJoinPointStaticPart` variable gives access only to information about the join point that can be determined at compile time. The `thisJoinPoint` variable also gives access to runtime information—it has additional methods `getArgs()`, `getTarget()`, and `getThis()` that return the argument values, target object, and the object bound to `this` at the join point. `thisJoinPoint` proves especially useful when you want to write a piece of generic advice that applies over a widely varying set of join points. Tracing and logging aspects typically make use of `thisJoinPoint` and `thisJoinPointStaticPart`, for example.

The value of `thisEnclosingJoinPointStaticPart` in different situations is best explained by example. The simple program in Listing 7.9 should do the trick.

Listing 7.9   Exploring *thisEnclosingJoinPointStaticPart*

```
public class TEJPSPExplorer {

  private int field = 2;

  static {
    try {
      URL url = new URL("xxxxx://zz");
    } catch (MalformedURLException malEx) {
    }
  }

  public static void main(String[] args) {
    new TEJPSPExplorer().doSomething();
  }

  public int doSomething() {
    int x = field;
    field = 6;
    try {
      doSomeMore();
    } catch (Exception ex) {}
    return field;
  }

  public void doSomeMore() throws Exception {
    throw new Exception("I didn't do it...");
  }
}

aspect ThisEnclosingJoinPointExplorer {
  before() : within(TEJPSPExplorer) {
    System.out.println("JP: " + thisJoinPoint);
    System.out.println("  EJP: " +
                  thisEnclosingJoinPointStaticPart);
  }
}
```

When this program is compiled and run, it produces output like that shown in Figure 7.16.

Figure 7.16   Exploring *thisEnclosingJoinPointStaticPart*.

From the output we see that when there is no lexically enclosing join point, `thisEnclosingJoinPointStaticPart` is bound to the same value as `thisJoinPointStaticPart`. The join point kinds `staticinitialization`, `initialization`, `preinitialization`, `adviceexecution`, and `execution` fall into this category. The join point kinds `call`, `handler`, `get`, and `set` all have as their enclosing join point the static initialization join point, or constructor/method execution join point in which they occur.

The `thisJoinPoint`, `thisJoinPointStaticPart`, and `thisEnclosing JoinPointStaticPart` variables cannot be used outside of an advice body, but they can be passed as parameters to a method: `thisJoinPoint` is of type `org.aspectj.lang.JoinPoint`, and the other two variables are of type `org.aspectj.lang.JoinPoint.StaticPart`.

7.3.2 Exceptions in Advice

Advice can throw an unchecked (runtime) exception at any point. For example, the `PreConditionChecking` aspect in Listing 7.1 is free to throw an `IllegalArgumentException` (an unchecked exception) at any point it wants.

In contrast, the body of an advice may throw only those checked exceptions that are declared in the advice `throws` clause. If advice makes a call to a remote interface, for example, such as an Enterprise JavaBean, it must either handle the potential `java.rmi.RemoteException`, or declare in the `throws` clause that it may throw it. Thrown exceptions are declared in the same way as for regular method declarations:

```
after(Account acc, AuditData data) returning
throws RemoteException : auditableAccountOperation(acc,data)
{
   auditorBean.recordOperation(acc,data);
}
```

The `throws` clause comes after the advice specification, but before the point-cut expression. If you forget to add the `throws` clause to an advice body that can throw a checked exception, the compiler will give a compilation error, "`Unhandled exception type <Checked ExceptionType>`" on the line where the exception is thrown.

In addition to declaring any checked exception that may be thrown by advice in a `throws` clause, advice can only throw checked exceptions that are declared for *every* join point at which the advice executes. This is similar to the Java rule concerning the set of exceptions you can throw when overriding a method from a superclass, or implementing a method from an interface. It is there to ensure that a client is not suddenly faced with a checked exception it was not expecting. The simple program in Listing 7.10 explores this rule. The first piece of advice is acceptable because it throws a runtime exception. The second piece of advice declares that it throws a checked exception, and is advising a join point (the execution of `aRiskyMethod`) that also declares a matching checked exception, so it compiles, too.

Listing 7.10 Advice and Exceptions

```
public class AspectsAndExceptions {
  public void aMethod() {}
  public void aRiskyMethod() throws Exception {}
}

aspect AdviceThrowsException {
```

```
before() : execution(* aMethod()) {
  throw new IllegalArgumentException("No argument???");
}

before() throws Exception :
  execution(* aRiskyMethod()) {
  throw new Exception("A checked exception.");
}
}
```

If we change the pointcut expression associated with the second piece of advice slightly, so that it now matches more join points, the compilation will fail:

```
before() throws Exception : execution(* a*Method()) {
  throw new Exception("A checked exception.");
}
```

Figure 7.17 shows how the result looks in AJDT. An error marker is created both at the advice statement, and at the join point being advised. The error text explains "cannot throw checked exception 'java.lang.Exception' at this join point 'method-execution(void AspectsAndExceptions.aMethod())'."

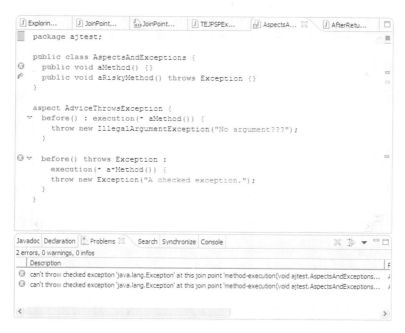

Figure 7.17   Compilation error due to incompatible *throws* clauses.

7.4   Advice Ordering

A question on most people's minds when they start to understand the advice mechanism is "what happens when more than one piece of advice needs to execute at the same join point?" The answer to that question is twofold. There are precedence rules that determine the order of advice execution for advice defined within the same aspect, and there are precedence rules that determine the ordering among sets of advice contributed by multiple aspects.

7.4.1 Precedence Within a Single Aspect

Precedence among before and around advice defined in the same aspect follows the simple rule that a piece of advice declared earlier in the source file has precedence over a piece of advice defined later in the source file. For before and around advice, advice with the highest precedence "gets to go first." The program in Listing 7.11 demonstrates the interaction between before and around advice at a shared join point.

Listing 7.11   Precedence Among Before and Around Advice

```
public aspect AdvicePrecedence {
  public static void main(String[] args) {
    System.out.println("Advice precedence test");
  }

  pointcut main() :
    execution(* AdvicePrecedence.main(..));

  // highest precedence advice
  before() : main() {
    System.out.println("Before advice #1");
  }

  // mid-precedence advice
  void around() : main() {
    System.out.println("Around advice entry");
    proceed();
    System.out.println("Around advice exit");
  }

  // lowest precedence advice
  before() : main() {
    System.out.println("Before advice #2");
  }
}
```

When run, it produces the following output:

```
Before advice #1
Around advice entry
Before advice #2
Advice precedence test
Around advice exit
```

When before advice returns normally, either the advice of the next precedence runs, or the computation under the join point if there is no further advice.
When around advice calls `proceed`, either the advice of the next precedence
runs, or the computation under the join point if there is no further advice. If
around advice does not call `proceed`, or before advice throws an exception, no
further advice is executed before the join point (and neither is the computation
at the join point itself).

When multiple pieces of advice of different kinds (for example, a mixture of
`before` and `around` advice, as in this example) match at the same join point,
AJDT uses the ➡ advice marker in the gutter of the editor.

After advice behaves differently: If two pieces of advice defined in the same
aspect want to execute at the same join point, and one or both of them are after
advice, the advice defined later in the source file has precedence over the one defined
earlier. For after advice, the advice with the highest precedence "gets the last word."
Listing 7.12 extends the program of Listing 7.11 to include after advice.

Listing 7.12   Precedence with After Advice

```
public aspect AdvicePrecedence {
  public static void main(String[] args) {
    System.out.println("Advice precedence test");
  }

  pointcut main() :
    execution(* AdvicePrecedence.main(..));

  // highest precedence before advice
  before() : main() {
    System.out.println("Before advice #1");
  }

  // mid-precedence advice
  void around() : main() {
    System.out.println("Around advice entry");
    proceed();
    System.out.println("Around advice exit");
  }
```

```
// lowest precedence before advice
before() : main() {
  System.out.println("Before advice #2");
}

// lowest precedence after advice
after() returning : main() {
  System.out.println("After advice #1");
}

// mid-precedence after advice
after() returning : main() {
  System.out.println("After advice #2");
}

// highest precedence after advice
after() returning : main() {
  System.out.println("After advice #3");
}
}
```

This time when we run it, the output is as follows:

```
Before advice #1
Around advice entry
Before advice #2
Advice precedence test
Around advice exit
After advice #1
After advice #2
After advice #3
```

As you look at Listing 7.12, notice how the advice precedence rules cause the output of the program to mirror the ordering of the advice statements in the aspect.

Advice Circularity

One side effect of the advice precedence rules is that it is possible to create situations in which circularities arise in advice precedence. Consider an aspect with three pieces of advice around1, after, and around2 in that order, all acting at the same join point. Given the pair (around1, after), the after advice should take precedence, because one of the two is after advice, and after is defined later in the source file:

after > around1

Given the pair (after, around2), around2 should take precedence, because one of the pair is after advice, and around2 is defined later in the source file:

around2 > after > around1

> Finally, given the pair (around1, around2), around1 should take precedence as neither is after advice, and around1 is defined first:
>
> around2 > after > around1 > around2 > ...
>
> When a situation such as this arises, the AspectJ compiler issues a "circular dependency" compilation error indicating the shared join point causing the error.

Let's look at a more realistic situation where advice ordering is important. Listing 7.13 shows the section of the `HibernateManager` aspect from Chapter 3 that deals with Hibernate sessions and transactions.

Listing 7.13 Hibernate Transaction Management

```
pointcut hibernateTransaction(HibernateDao dao) :
  execution(* *(..)) && this(dao)
  && !execution(* *Session(..));

Object around(HibernateDao dao) : hibernateTransaction(dao) {
  Object ret = null;
  Session session = sessionFactory.openSession();
  dao.setSession(session);
  Transaction tx = null;
  try {
    tx = session.beginTransaction();
    ret = proceed(dao);
    tx.commit();
  } catch(SIPersistenceException ex) {
    if (tx != null) tx.rollback();
    throw ex;
  } finally {
    session.close();
  }
    return ret;
}
```

If you look again at the definition of the `hibernateTransaction` pointcut, you will see that each individual operation on a `HibernateDao` executes in its own Hibernate session and transaction. What if we want to group several operations together into a single transaction? For example, suppose we have a requirement to import all the data saved in a `SimpleInsurance.dat` file, and add it to the database. After we have read in the serialized data, we will have a collection of customers and a collection of policies that need to be inserted into the database. It makes more sense to do this operation inside a single session than to open a new session for each individual insert.

To support this, we need to amend the `HibernateManager` aspect a little. What we would like is the following behavior: If we encounter a `hibernateTransaction` operation and we are not in a transaction, then start one—but if we are already in a transaction, then just use the existing session and transaction context. Using our knowledge from Chapter 6, we now know how to write some pointcuts to help us capture this protocol:

```
pointcut daoOperation(HibernateDao dao) :
  execution(* HibernateDao+.*(..)) &&
  !execution(* HibernateDao.*(..)) &&
  this(dao);

pointcut sessionBoundary() :
  hibernateTransaction() &&
  !cflowbelow(hibernateTransaction());

pointcut hibernateTransaction() :
  daoOperation(HibernateDao) ||
  execution(* ImportUtility.importDatFile(..));
```

- ❍ A `daoOperation` is the execution of any method on one of the `HibernateDao` subclasses (excluding any methods defined on `HibernateDao` itself, such as the `get-` and `setSession` methods). This matches all the data operations on the `CustomerDoaImpl`, `ClaimDaoImpl`, and `PolicyDaoImpl` classes.

- ❍ A `hibernateTransaction` is now defined to be either a `daoOperation`, or any other high-level method of our choosing. In this case we have said that the `importDatFile` method should run in a transaction.

- ❍ Finally, a `sessionBoundary` (the point of all this) is defined to be the execution of a `hibernateTransaction`, whenever we are not already in (the control flow of) a `hibernateTransaction`.

We can now amend the around advice to start a session at a `sessionBoundary`, as shown in Listing 7.14.

Listing 7.14 Protocol at Session Boundaries

```
private Session session;

Object around() : sessionBoundary() {
  Object ret = null;
  session = sessionFactory.openSession();
  Transaction tx = null;
  try {
    tx = session.beginTransaction();
```

```
    ret = proceed();
    tx.commit();
  } catch(SIException ex) {
    if (tx != null) tx.rollback();
    throw ex;
  } finally {
    session.close();
  }
  return ret;
}
```

Comparing this listing to Listing 7.13, note that we have moved the `Session` object from a local variable inside the advice to a private field in the aspect. Also note that the new around advice is no longer responsible for injecting the session dependency into a DAO. It cannot do this any longer because sessions can encompass multiple DAOs and may begin before any `HibernateDao` instance has been identified (as is the case with the `importDatFile()` method). A quick look at the Outline view for the new around advice confirms we are on the right track (see Figure 7.18). The around advice is picking out all the `sessionBoundary` points we expected, and we are also told that the execution of the around advice is conditional on a runtime test. If we call `PolicyDaoImpl.insertPolicy` on its own, the advice will execute and begin a session; if we call it in the control flow of the `importDatFile` method, however, we will not start a new session and instead will use the existing one.

Figure 7.18   Session boundaries (with runtime test).

We still need to tell the `HibernateDao` objects what `session` to use for their operations of course. This is done with a very simple piece of before advice:

```
before(HibernateDao dao) : daoOperation(dao) {
  dao.setSession(session);
}
```

Here comes the precedence piece.

If we find ourselves arriving at say `ClaimDaoImpl.updateClaim` outside of the control flow of the `importDatFile` method, we will not have an open session. If the before advice defined above executes before the around advice has opened a session, we will have a problem. It is important that the around advice gets to run first in this situation. Using what we know about the precedence rules therefore, we have to declare the around advice ahead of the before advice in the source file.

Listing 7.15 shows the revised portion of the `HibernateManager` aspect.

Listing 7.15   Revised *HibernateManager*

```
private Session session;

/**
 * Any operation invoked on a HibernateDao subclass.
 * (We don't want to match the methods in the
 * HibernateDao class itself).
 */
pointcut daoOperation(HibernateDao dao) :
  execution(* HibernateDao+.*(..)) &&
  !execution(* HibernateDao.*(..)) &&
  this(dao);

/**
 * Start a hibernate session (and transaction)
 * at these points, but only if we don't already
 * have a session active.
 */
pointcut sessionBoundary() :
  hibernateTransaction() &&
  !cflowbelow(hibernateTransaction());

/**
 * Each dao operation MUST execution in a
 * transaction. Add other, higher-level
 * transactions to this pointcut definition
 * as needed.
 */
pointcut hibernateTransaction() :
  daoOperation(HibernateDao) ||
```

```
  execution(* ImportUtility.importDatFile(..));

/**
 * The protocol for sessions and transactions.
 * It is important that this advice has precedence
 * over the DAO dependency injection advice below.
 */
Object around() : sessionBoundary() {
  Object ret = null;
  session = sessionFactory.openSession();
  Transaction tx = null;
  try {
    tx = session.beginTransaction();
    ret = proceed();
    tx.commit();
  } catch(SIException ex) {
    if (tx != null) tx.rollback();
    throw ex;
  } finally {
    session.close();
  }
  return ret;
}

/**
 * Before any DAO executes a database operation,
 * we need to tell it what session object to use.
 */
before(HibernateDao dao) : daoOperation(dao) {
  dao.setSession(session);
}
```

As an aside, note how this aspect enables us to focus on the important issue of where the appropriate session boundaries are. Just by changing the definition of the `hibernateTransaction` pointcut we can change the session boundaries for any part of the application—from including the whole program execution in a single session (add the `main` method to the pointcut definition), to the per-DAO operation model we started with, and anything in between.

7.4.2 Precedence Between Multiple Aspects

When advice declarations made in *different aspects* match at a join point, then by default the order of their execution is undefined. In certain situations, the ordering of advice execution between aspects matters. For example, you may define an aspect to perform precondition checking on arguments passed to a method and another to ensure the current user has the appropriate security permissions to access that same method. It is essential that the security checking happens first so as not to inadvertently supply information to an unauthorized caller.

In such cases, AspectJ provides a mechanism to specify an ordering through the use of a `declare precedence` statement in your program. Listing 7.16 shows how we might define a `Security` aspect to authenticate access to account details in a banking application, and a `Checking` aspect to ensure an account is always in credit. It is essential that we perform any security checks first; otherwise, an unauthorized caller could determine the account balance.

Listing 7.16   Security and Balance Checking

```
public aspect Security {

  public pointcut authenticatedOperations() :
    execution(public * Account.*(..));

  before() : authenticatedOperations() {
    authenticate();
  }

  private void authenticate() {
  }

}

public aspect Checking {

  pointcut balanceMethod (Account account, double amount) :
    execution(* debit(..)) && this(account) && args(amount);

  before (Account account, double amount) :
    balanceMethod (account, amount) {
    if (account.getBalance() < amount) {
      throw new RuntimeException("Balance of "
      + account.getBalance()
      + " is insufficient.");
    }
  }
}
```

The `declare precedence` statement could be used in either of these aspects to determine an ordering between them, but we prefer to put it in its own aspect, which keeps the `Security` and `Checking` aspects independent:

```
public aspect SystemArchitecture {
  declare precedence : Security, Checking;
}
```

If we just wish to ensure that the `Security` aspect is always called first regardless of how many aspects are used in our program, AspectJ enables us to define a partial ordering by using a simple wildcard:

```
declare precedence : Security, *;
```

This statement says that the `Security` aspect takes precedence over any-thing else. AJDT uses the ⬢ icon in the Outline view to represent a `declare precedence` statement.

The form of the `declare precedence` statement is simply this:

```
declare precedence : TypePatternList;
```

The wildcard `*`, used on its own, can appear in the list at most once and matches any aspect not matched by any other pattern in the list. The following example, taken from the Language Semantics appendix of the AspectJ Programming Guide (available in the AJDT Help), says that aspects that have "Security" as part of their name should take precedence over all other aspects, and the `Logging` aspect (and any aspect that extends it) takes precedence over all non-`Security` aspects:

```
declare precedence : *..*Security*, Logging+, *;
```

7.5   Softening Exceptions

In this section we change tack somewhat to look at a piece of the AspectJ lan-guage closely related to the issue of handling exceptions in advice. Recall that AspectJ only allows advice to throw either an unchecked exception or an excep-tion that is declared both in the `throws` clause of the advice and the signature of all join points at which the advice executes. In many cases, the body of advice may call operations that can throw checked exceptions, but the advice body is not the appropriate place to handle the exception. In these situations, you need to convert the checked exception caught in the advice body into an unchecked exception that can propagate through the system.

Other times you might put in place some advice to consistently handle excep-tions when they occur—meaning that you no longer need to put logic in catch blocks at each and every location an exception may be thrown. We saw an

example of this in Chapter 3 when we used after throwing advice to consistently convert a thrown `HibernateException` to an `SIPersistenceException`. If
you do this, the demands of the compiler to either catch a checked exception at
each place it can be thrown, or to add a throws clause to every method, can be
annoying and unnecessary.

AspectJ provides a solution to both of these problems: the `declare soft`
statement. A `declare soft` statement takes the following form:

```
declare soft: ExceptionType : PointcutExpression;
```

Any exception of `ExceptionType` thrown at any of the join points matched
by `PointcutExpression` is automatically converted (softened) into an
unchecked exception. The softened exception will be an instance of `org.aspec-
tj.lang.SoftException`. In AJDT's Outline view, the icon for a `declare
soft` statement is ▦.

We always recommend that you use declare soft in conjunction with some
advice that handles the exceptions you just softened. If you are planning to throw
the same or a converted exception, you can use after throwing advice as in the
following example:

```
after() throwing(Exception ex) {
  recordException(ex);
  throw new DomainException(ex);
}
```

If you actually want to handle the exception fully (so that it does not propagate out of the advice body), you *must* use around advice. If no exception is
thrown in the body of after throwing advice, the original exception is propagat-
ed on exiting from the advice. The pattern for handling exceptions using around
advice is as follows:

```
Object around() : mayThrowException() {
  try {
    return proceed();
  } catch( Exception ex) {
    handleException(ex);
  }
}
```

> **Checked or Unchecked Exceptions?**
>
> There's quite a debate running in the programming community about the best way to handle exceptions. Some argue that in large systems, checked exceptions do more harm than good as the majority of catch blocks are not properly filled in by programmers. (They just put in place a dummy catch block to keep the compiler happy and never remember to come back.) Proponents of this argument prefer to use unchecked exceptions everywhere. Others argue that checked exceptions should be used for conditions that a caller of an API should have checked for before calling it, and unchecked exceptions used in other cases. However, another school believes that checked exceptions should be used everywhere as they force a programmer to recognize potential errors that can occur. Whatever your philosophy on exceptions, there's no doubting that logic to handle certain kinds of exceptions can end up scattered and tangled through your codebase. (Checked exceptions really force you into this path.) AspectJ gives you the flexibility to implement the exception handling policy that is best for you in a particular situation—whatever that policy may be.

7.6   *declare warning* **and** *declare error*

AspectJ supports a compile-time mechanism that enables you to not only improve the modularity of your program, but also ensure that it stays that way as the program evolves. You have already seen examples of it at work in Chapter 2 where we made sure that no one called `notifyListeners` outside of the `PolicyChangeNotification` aspect, and in Chapter 3 where we ensured that no one inadvertently created a dependency on inter-type declarations introduced to support the Hibernate persistence implementation. The mechanism is `declare error` / `declare warning`. The form of a `declare error` or warning statement is as follows:

```
declare error : PointcutExpression : "error msg";
declare warning : PointcutExpression : "warning msg";
```

AJDT uses the ![icon] icon for a `declare warning` in the Outline view, and ![icon] for the warning marker in the editor gutter of a warning originating from a `declare warning` statement. For a `declare error`, it uses ![icon] and ![icon] respectively. The effect of a `declare warning` or `declare error` statement is that at every source statement the compiler can determine will give rise to a join point that the pointcut expression will match, it generates a warning or error with the associated text.

If you didn't read the sidebar "How Can You Match Join Points at Compile Time?" in Chapter 2 (Section 2.5.3.) at the time, now might be a good time to go back and check it out. Suppose you didn't want people to call toString() on List objects for some reason. You might write the declare warning statement shown in Figure 7.19, and then be in for a bit of a surprise when you compile it.

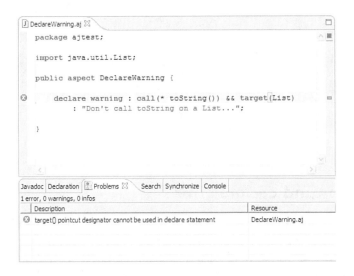

Figure 7.19 Don't call *toString* on *List* objects?

Because declare error and warning statements are evaluated at compile time, the pointcut expression is limited to those pointcut designators that can be statically evaluated—so this, target, and args, together with cflow, cflow-below, and if pointcut designators cannot be used because they all match based on runtime information. You can still enforce constraints using pointcuts that include these designators, but you have to do it using advice that throws a RuntimeException instead:

```
before() : call(* toString()) && target(List) {
  throw new RuntimeException(
    "Don't call toString on a List??");
}
```

In general we advise making the maximum use possible of declare error and warning to enforce constraints and preserve modularity in your designs. We return to this topic in Part 3 when we look at adoption strategies for AspectJ.

7.7   **Common Pitfalls**

This section lists a few of the common mistakes and pitfalls that you might run into when working with advice and `declare error` / `warning` statements.

7.7.1 *Only Before Advice at Handler Join Points*

The AspectJ compiler can work with both class files and source files as input, and gives consistent semantics in either case. One consequence of this is that the AspectJ 1.2 compiler can only support before advice on a handler join point. (After advice and around advice are not supported.) Figure 7.20 shows what happens if you try to write a program that uses after or around advice on a handler join point: You will see the compiler warning message "Only before advice is supported on handler join points (compiler limitation)."

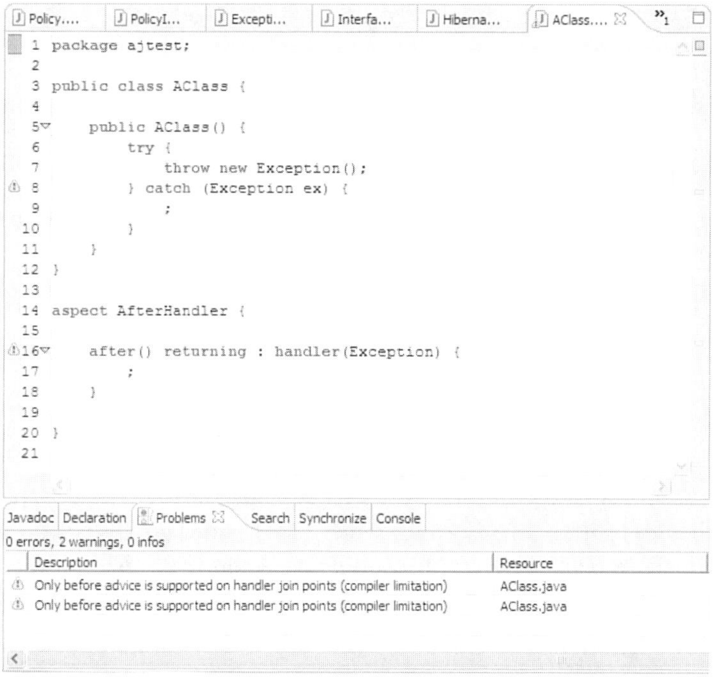

Figure 7.20   Only before advice supported at handler join points.

The reason for this limitation is that the end of a handler block is not always determinable in bytecode (so the AspectJ compiler cannot distinguish between what is "in" the handler and what is "after" the handler).

7.7.2 No get Join Points for Compile-Time Constants

A related limitation is that no join points exist at runtime for the "get" of compile-time constant final fields—so it is not possible to advise such field accesses. The reason for this is that compilers replace the field access with its constant value in the bytecodes they emit.

7.7.3 No Return Value for Constructor Execution

A common mistake is to try and use the `returning()` clause of after returning advice or the return value of a `proceed` call to access the object created by a constructor execution. As illustrated in Table 7.1, the return value of a constructor execution join point is always null. You can use `execution` in conjunction with `this()` to access the instance being constructed, or use the `call` pointcut designator to match the constructor `call` join point, which does return the constructed object.

7.7.4 No Return Value for set Join Points

As illustrated in Table 7.1, the return value for a `set` join point is always null, so you cannot use the `returning()` clause of after returning advice or the return value from a call to `proceed` to access the new field value. Instead you need to use the `args` pointcut designator in conjunction with `set`.

7.7.5 After Throwing Advice Does Not Handle Exceptions

As discussed in Section 7.5, after throwing advice does not *handle* thrown exceptions—it just gives you the opportunity to execute some additional behavior in the case where an exception is thrown. The original thrown exception will still propagate to the rest of the application after leaving the advice body (unless you throw another exception inside the advice). To handle an exception so that it does not propagate any further, you need to use around advice.

7.7.6 Restrictions on declare error / warning Pointcut Expressions

As discussed in Section 7.6, you cannot use the `this`, `target`, `args`, `cflow`, `cflowbelow`, or `if` pointcut designators in conjunction with a `declare warning` or `declare error` statement.

7.8   Summary

In this chapter we covered the three basic forms of advice:

- ○   ⚑ before advice
- ○   ⬎ after advice
- ○   ⚑ around advice

Of these three, around is the most powerful kind. Within the body of advice, both the values of any advice parameters and a set of special `thisJoinPoint` variables provide access to contextual information regarding the join point at which the advice is executing. Advice is allowed to throw only those checked exceptions both declared in the advice `throws` clause and also for all join points matched by the advice. Precedence rules ⊞ determine what happens when multiple pieces of advice need to execute at the same join point.

The ⊞ `declare soft` mechanism can be used to modularize exception handling, and allows flexible selection of exception handling policy. `declare error` ⊞ and `warning` ⚑ statements can be used to enforce design constraints and help ensure that behavior modularized in an aspect stays modularized as the program evolves.

References

Lea, D. 2003. *Overview of package util.concurrent.*
http://gee.cs.oswego.edu/dl/classes/EDU/oswego/cs/dl/util/concurrent/intro.html

CHAPTER 8

Inter-Type Declarations

Whereas advice is a declaration that an aspect will execute certain behavior in the program control flow at designated join points, inter-type declarations are a statement that an aspect takes complete responsibility for certain capabilities on behalf of other types (the "targets" of the inter-type declarations). Inter-type declarations are useful when you need one or more types in a program to acquire a capability (such as the ability to be printed) for some common purpose.

Inter-type declarations can be used to provide definitions of fields, methods, and constructors on behalf of other types. They can also be used to implement interfaces and to declare super-types. Section 8.1 shows you how to use inter-type declarations to complete the implementation of the `PolicyChangeNotification` aspect that we started in Chapter 2. Section 8.2 discusses the scoping and visibility rules for inter-type declared members, and Section 8.3 discusses the use of interfaces with inter-type declarations. We close the chapter with a short look at the ability to declare a new super-type for a target type.

The Feature Formerly Known as Introduction

In versions of AspectJ prior to 1.1, inter-type declarations were known as `intro-ductions`. Although we sometimes still refer to the process of introducing new members into a target type, the new term emphasizes the fact that the implementation of the crosscutting concern is encapsulated within the declaring aspect. The goal of this feature of AspectJ is to improve or maintain modularity, not to provide a neat way for shoving fields and methods into existing classes!

8.1   Fields, Methods, and Constructors

In Chapter 2 we began the process of refactoring policy change notification from an implementation entangled in the `PolicyImpl` class hierarchy to a modular implementation in the `PolicyChangeNotification` aspect. As we left it, all the calls to `notifyListeners` had been refactored into the aspect. The `PolicyImpl` class, however, still retained the logic to allow listeners to register for change notifications and to manage the set of subscribed listeners. Listing 8.1 is an extract from the class showing the state and behavior associated with change notification that remains in the `PolicyImpl` class. This comprises the `listeners` field and the `addPolicyListener()` and `removePolicyListener()` methods as well as the `notifyListeners()` method itself.

Listing 8.1   Extract from the *PolicyImpl* Class

```
public abstract class PolicyImpl implements Policy {

  // Other fields

  private Set listeners = new HashSet();


  // Other methods

  public void addPolicyListener(PolicyListener l) {
    if (listeners == null) listeners = new HashSet();
    this.listeners.add(l);
  }

  public boolean removePolicyListener(PolicyListener l) {
    return this.listeners.remove(l);
  }

  protected void notifyListeners() {
    if (listeners == null) return;
    for (Iterator iter = listeners.iterator();
      iter.hasNext();) {
      PolicyListener l = (PolicyListener) iter.next();
      l.policyUpdated(this);
    }
  }
}
```

This mechanism is not the primary concern of the `PolicyImpl` class, whose purpose is to represent insurance policies: the `listeners` field is not part of the state of an insurance policy, and the registration methods clutter the public interface. Consider it this way—suppose you went out and consulted with experts from all over the insurance industry, and asked them what information needed to be kept concerning an insurance policy, and what business processes were involved in processing policy documents. You would probably end up with a very wide-ranging set of requirements, but it is quite unlikely any of them would tell you that a policy must have a set of listeners. What we have here is something known as "mixed-domain cohesion." That's just a fancy way of saying that the stuff to do with the insurance domain and the stuff to do with listening don't quite belong together.

In this section, we are going to use inter-type declarations to refactor the listener support and let the `PolicyChangeNotification` aspect implement it on behalf of the policy hierarchy. The refactoring will proceed in the following steps:

1. Move the definition of the `listeners` field from the `PolicyImpl` class to the aspect.

2. Move the `addPolicyListeners` and `removePolicyListeners` methods from the `PolicyImpl` class to the aspect.

3. Move the `notifyListeners` method from the `PolicyImpl` class to the aspect, and update the `policyStateUpdate` advice to call it.

4. Make the `listeners` field private to the aspect.

8.1.1 Inter-Type Field Declarations

The general form of an inter-type field declaration is as follows:

```
[Modifiers]  FieldType TargetType.Id;
```

Inter-type declared fields can be declared with `public`, `private`, or default visibility, but may not be declared `protected`. The `FieldType` is just the type of the field (`String`, `int`, and so on), and the `TargetType` is the name of the type on whose behalf the field is being declared. Inter-type fields may also be declared static by using the `static` modifier. We saw an example of an inter-type field declaration in Chapter 3, when the `HibernateManager` aspect declared an `id` field for the `AddressImpl` class:

```
public Long AddressImpl.id;
```

This declares a public field called `id`, which the `HibernateManager` aspect manages on behalf of the `AddressImpl` class.

We begin the refactoring process for policy change notification by removing the definition of the `listeners` field from `PolicyImpl` and replacing it with an inter-type declared field rather than the `PolicyChangeNotification` aspect.

From:

```
public class PolicyImpl {
  ...
  private Set listeners = new HashSet();
  ...
}
```

To:

```
public aspect PolicyChangeNotification {
  ...
  private Set PolicyImpl.listeners = new HashSet();
  ...
}
```

Notice that inter-type declared fields can be initialized at their point of declaration, just as regular fields can be. When we try and compile the Simple Insurance application after making this change, we get the result shown in Figure 8.1.

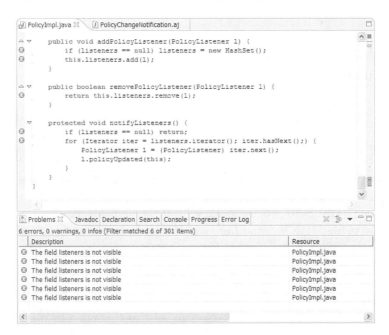

Figure 8.1   The field *listeners* is not visible.

The compiler complains that the `listeners` field cannot be seen by the remaining methods in the `PolicyImpl` class that refer to it: "The field `listeners` is not visible." The inter-type declared `listeners` field is now private to the *aspect* and not visible to the notification logic that remains in the `PolicyImpl` class. We discuss the visibility rules for inter-type declarations in Section 8.2, but for now we will temporarily declare the field as package protected to allow it to be used by both the aspect and the class. When the refactoring is complete we can come back and make the field private to the aspect once more:

```
Set PolicyImpl.listeners = new HashSet();
```

Figure 8.2 shows the Outline view for the updated `PolicyChange Notification` aspect. You can navigate to the target type of the inter-type declaration as described in Chapter 3. Notice that the ⬛ icon is used for a package protected inter-type declared field. (The icon for a regular package-protected field declaration is ▲.)

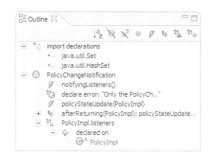

Figure 8.2 *PolicyChangeNotification* aspect in the Outline view.

Figure 8.3 shows what an inter-type declared field looks like from the point of view of the target class. The icon displayed in the gutter to show that inter-type declarations are in effect is this: ⬛.

Figure 8.3 *PolicyImpl* class showing an inter-type declaration.

What About Just Declaring the *listeners* Field Directly in the Aspect?

Instead of using an inter-type declaration, we could have defined the `listeners` field directly within the aspect itself. This would mean that there would only be one set of listeners shared among all the `PolicyImpl` instances (unless we used a `perthis` aspect—see the next chapter). Alternatively we could have maintained an internal mapping between policies and listeners, but this approach is unnecessarily complex when compared to a simple inter-type field declaration.

8.1.2 Inter-Type Method Declarations

The general form of an inter-type method declaration is as follows:

```
[Modifiers] ReturnType TargetType.Id(Formals)
[throws TypeList] { Body };
```

Like inter-type declared fields, inter-type declared methods can be declared with `public`, `private`, or default visibility, but may not be declared `protect-ed`. An inter-type method declaration looks just like a regular method declaration apart from the specification of a `TargetType`. You can declare a static inter-type method by specifying the `static` modifier. Inter-type methods can also be declared abstract, in which case they have no body.

Let's continue with the refactoring and move the methods associated with listener registration and notification from `PolicyImpl` to the `PolicyChange Notification` aspect. First we define inter-type declared methods for `addPolicyListener` and `removePolicyListener`:

```
private Set PolicyImpl.listeners = new HashSet();

public void PolicyImpl.addPolicyListener(
   PolicyListener l) {
   this.listeners.add(l);
}

public boolean PolicyImpl.removePolicyListener(
   PolicyListener l) {
   return this.listeners.remove(l);
}
```

Notice that within the body of the addPolicyListener and removePolicyListener listener methods, this is bound to the PolicyImpl object in which the method is executing (and not the PolicyChangeNotification aspect instance). The example also shows that we can refer to the inter-type declared listeners field in exactly the same way as we would a regular field declared in the PolicyImpl class. Because the addPolicyListener and removePolicyListener methods are declared public, they are visible outside of the aspect, allowing an observer to call them on any PolicyImpl instance.

Now we can move the notifyListeners method into the aspect in a similar fashion:

```
private void PolicyImpl.notifyListeners() {
   if (listeners == null) return;
   for (Iterator iter = listeners.iterator();
        iter.hasNext();)
   {
      PolicyListener l = (PolicyListener) iter.next();
      l.policyUpdated(this);
   }
}
```

We have declared the notifyListeners method to be private because it is only called within the aspect. (In the PolicyImpl class it was protected, from when subclasses needed to call it after a change in their state.) Notice again that in the call to policyUpdated(this), this refers to the PolicyImpl object and not to the PolicyChangeNotification aspect instance.

As a finishing touch, we can declare the listeners field to be private to the aspect, because all the policy change notification logic is now encapsulated in the aspect:

```
private Set PolicyImpl.listeners = new HashSet();
```

Listing 8.2 shows the completed `PolicyChangeNotification` aspect. Note that we have commented out the `declare error` statement—it is no longer possible to call `notifyListeners` outside of the aspect because we declared it to be private.

Listing 8.2   Completed *PolicyChangeNotification* Aspect

```
package insurance.model.impl;

import insurance.model.listeners.PolicyListener;
import java.util.Set;
import java.util.HashSet;
import java.util.Iterator;

public aspect PolicyChangeNotification {

  pointcut notifyingListeners() :
    call(* PolicyImpl.notifyListeners(..));

  // declare error :
  //    notifyingListeners() &&
  //    !within(PolicyChangeNotification)
  //    : "Only the PolicyChangeNotification aspect
               should be notifying listeners";

  pointcut policyStateUpdate(PolicyImpl aPolicy) :
    (execution(* set*(..)) ||
     execution(* addClaim(..)) ||
     execution(* removeClaim(..)))
    && this(aPolicy);

  after(PolicyImpl policy) returning :
    policyStateUpdate(policy) {
      policy.notifyListeners();
  }

  private Set PolicyImpl.listeners = new HashSet();

  public void PolicyImpl.addPolicyListener(
    PolicyListener l) {
    if (listeners == null) listeners = new HashSet();
    this.listeners.add(l);
  }

  public boolean PolicyImpl.removePolicyListener(
    PolicyListener l) {
    return this.listeners.remove(l);
  }

  private void PolicyImpl.notifyListeners() {
    if (listeners == null) return;
    for (Iterator iter = listeners.iterator();
```

```
        iter.hasNext();) {
    PolicyListener l = (PolicyListener) iter.next();
    l.policyUpdated(this);
    }
  }

}
```

Figure 8.4 shows the new inter-type method declarations in the Outline view.

Figure 8.4   Inter-type method declarations in the Outline view.

The icon used for a public inter-type method declaration is ![icon], and for a private inter-type method declaration the icon is ![icon]. Now that the `listeners` field is private, its icon has changed to ![icon].

8.1.3 Inter-Type Constructor Declarations

The general form of an inter-type constructor declaration is as follows:

```
[Modifiers] TargetType.new(Formals)
[throws TypeList] { Body };
```

Inter-type declared constructors can be declared with `public`, `private`, or default visibility, but may not be declared `protected`. Inter-type constructor declarations differ from inter-type method declarations in that they have no return type, and use the identifier `new` to indicate that this is a constructor declaration.

We saw examples of inter-type constructor declarations when developing the `HibernateManager` aspect in Chapter 3. Listing 8.3 is an extract from that aspect showing how we defined default constructors for all persistent types that did not previously have one.

Listing 8.3   Inter-Type Constructor Declarations

```
package insurance.dao.hibernate;

...

public aspect HibernateManager {

    ...

    // meeting hibernate's requirements
    // -----------------------------------

    public Long AddressImpl.id;

    public AddressImpl.new() {}
    public ClaimImpl.new() {}
    public PolicyImpl.new() {}
    public LifePolicyImpl.new() {}
    public HousePolicyImpl.new() {}
    public AutoPolicyImpl.new() {}
    public Schedule.new() {}
    public Automobile.new() {}

    ...

}
```

8.2   Scope and Visibility

This section discusses the visibility and scoping rules for inter-type declarations, how inter-type declarations interact with inheritance, and what happens when conflicting inter-type declarations are made by multiple aspects.

8.2.1 Visibility of, and from, Inter-Type Declarations

Inter-type declarations can be declared with public, private, or default (package-protected) visibility. The visibility modifier acts with respect to the defining aspect. (That is, a `private` inter-type field is private to the declaring aspect, not to the target type.) The private `listeners` field is visible only within the `PolicyChangeNotification` aspect (and not within the `PolicyImpl` class).

The public `addPolicyListener` and `removePolicyListener` methods can be called from anywhere. An inter-type declaration with default visibility can be seen by any type in the same package as the *declaring aspect* (not the package of the target type).

Within the body of an inter-type declared method or constructor, `this` refers to the instance of the target type on which the method was called. Even so, the aspect cannot call methods or access fields in the target type that are not visible from the aspect. As a concrete example, the `addPolicyListener` inter-type declared method can refer to the `listeners` field because it is private with respect to (and therefore visible from) the aspect. It could also call a public method on the `PolicyImpl` class, such as `this.addClaim()`, because the `addClaim` method is visible from outside of the `PolicyImpl` class. An attempt to refer to a private field within the `PolicyImpl` class (such as `this.claims`) would result in a compilation error. Although inter-type methods and constructors execute in the *context* of the target type, they inherit the *scope* of the declaring aspect.

Because an inter-type declared method or constructor executes in the context of the target class, it can only directly access *static* methods and fields in the aspect (of any visibility). As discussed in the next chapter, aspects support a static method, `aspectOf()`, which can be used to obtain the aspect instance itself.

Wildcards on Member Declarations No Longer Supported

In versions of AspectJ prior to 1.1, a wildcard expression could be used to allow a field or method to be directly introduced into more than one class. However, there was no clearly defined type for a reference to `this` within an inter-type declaration. For this reason, wildcards were dropped for fields and methods in AspectJ 1.1.

8.2.2 Inter-Type Declarations and Inheritance

An inter-type declaration made on behalf of a parent target class (such as `PolicyImpl`) is inherited by all of its subclasses (`LifePolicyImpl`, `AutoPolicyImpl`, `HousePolicyImpl`) in just the same way as a regular method declared in the parent class. If a subclass overrides a public method defined on its parent via an inter-type declaration, you get the same behavior as if you had declared the methods in the parent class directly. The simple program in Listing 8.4 illustrates this behavior.

Listing 8.4 Inheritance and Inter-Type Declarations

```
public class A {

  public static void main(String[] args) {
    new A().doSomething();
    new B().doSomething();
  }

}

class B extends A {
  public void doSomething() {
        super.doSomething();
        System.out.println("B is doing something");
  }
}
aspect ITD {
  public void A.doSomething() {
        System.out.println("A doing something (via ITD)");
  }
}
```

The method doSomething in the class B overrides the inter-type method declaration of A.doSomething made by the aspect. The output of this program is as follows:

```
A doing something (via ITD)
A doing something (via ITD)
B is doing something
```

When the doSomething method in B calls super.doSomething, the inter-type declared method executes.

8.2.3 Dealing with Conflicting Declarations

In the PolicyChangeNotification aspect we managed to avoid a collision between the name of an existing field or method defined within the target class and one chosen for the inter-type declaration. What would happen if a second aspect also tried to make an inter-type declaration of a listeners field on the PolicyImpl class? The answer is absolutely nothing. By using a private inter-type declaration, we ensure there is no collision with an existing field (because the field is private to the declaring type, that is, the aspect).

If a second aspect also tried to make a `public` inter-type declaration of an `addPolicyListener` method on the `PolicyImpl` class, we would get a compilation error. Likewise a compilation error will occur if an aspect tries to make a non-`private` inter-type declaration with the same name as an existing target type member, and that is visible in the same scope. If the target of an inter-type declaration is an interface, the rules differ slightly, as discussed in the following section.

8.3 Inter-Type Declarations and Interfaces

This section examines what happens when you use an interface as the target of an inter-type declaration, and the use of `declare parents` to declare that a set of target types implement a given interface.

8.3.1 Using an Interface as the Target of an Inter-Type Declaration

In the previous section we implemented the `PolicyChangeNotification` aspect such that it made inter-type declarations on behalf of the `PolicyImpl` class. This worked because the `Policy` interface that `PolicyImpl` implements (and that the UI is written to) includes the `addPolicyListener` and `removePolicyListener` methods:

```
public interface Policy {
    ...
    void addClaim(Claim c);
    void removeClaim(Claim c);
    void addPolicyListener(PolicyListener l);
    boolean removePolicyListener(PolicyListener l);
}
```

Of course, the same issues of modularity exist with respect to the `Policy` interface as they did with the `PolicyImpl` class—the listener registration methods don't really belong there.

AspectJ allows interface types to be the target of inter-type declarations. You can use inter-type declarations to define both methods and fields on interfaces. When you make an inter-type method declaration on an interface, you must also provide the method implementation (or alternatively declare it abstract)—this is used as the default implementation of the method in all implementing classes. If a class provides its own definition of the method in the same scope, then that class' method will be used instead (in contrast to the compilation error that will be raised if the target of the inter-type declaration is a class). The net of this is that inter-type declarations on interfaces look exactly the same as inter-type declarations on classes. Listing 8.5 shows an extract from an improved version of the `PolicyChangeNotification` aspect that makes inter-type declarations on the `Policy` interface rather than on `PolicyImpl`. The only changes from the version in Listing 8.2 are the changes to the target type of the inter-type declarations.

Listing 8.5   An Improved *PolicyChangeNotification* Aspect

```
private Set Policy.listeners = new HashSet();

public void Policy.addPolicyListener(PolicyListener l)
{
  if (listeners == null) listeners = new HashSet();
  this.listeners.add(l);
}

public boolean Policy.removePolicyListener(
  PolicyListener l) {
  return this.listeners.remove(l);
}

private void Policy.notifyListeners() {
  if (listeners == null) return;
  for (Iterator iter = listeners.iterator();
       iter.hasNext();) {
    PolicyListener l = (PolicyListener) iter.next();
    l.policyUpdated(this);
  }
}
```

With these declarations in place, we can remove the `addPolicyListener` and `removePolicyListener` methods from the `Policy` interface. The effect of these inter-type declarations is that clients can call `addPolicyListener` and `removePolicyListener` on any `Policy`, and that the aspect will manage a `listeners` field and provide default implementations of the `add`, `remove`, and `notify` methods on behalf of every class that implements the `Policy` interface.

A common idiom in AspectJ is to make inter-type declarations on an interface, and then use the `declare parents` mechanism to make a number of classes implement that interface—thus all acquiring the defined abilities. The following subsection shows you an example of this at work by adding business validation of changes to domain objects.

8.3.2 *Using* declare parents *with Interfaces*

Currently there's a piece of functionality missing from the Simple Insurance application. When the user interface makes changes to a domain object (like a Policy, or a Customer, or a Claim), it performs simple validation of the data entered by the user—for example, can the text in a field that represents a date be parsed as a valid date, and do numeric fields only contain numeric data? What's missing is any business validation of changes to a domain object—for example, is the start date of Policy earlier than the end date? It is not appropriate to perform this kind of validation in the user interface—these are business rules and belong with the domain logic.

We want to keep the validation logic separate from the classes that currently implement the domain interfaces (such as PolicyImpl and ClaimImpl). This enables us to use the same policy validation class with any implementer of the Policy interface. We can use the **New Java Interface** wizard, shown in Figure 8.5, to create a new interface for validation classes to implement in the insurance.model.validation package.

Figure 8.5   Creating the *Validator* interface.

Listing 8.6 shows the completed `Validator` interface.

Listing 8.6   *Validator* Interface

```
package insurance.model.validation;
import java.util.List;

public interface Validator {

  /**
   * Does the domain object obey all the
   * business constraints?
   */
  boolean validate(Object domainObject);

  /**
   * The reasons for failing validation on
   * the most recent call to validate.
   */
  List /* of String*/ getValidationErrors();

  /**
   * The set of types for which I can perform
   * validation
   */
  Class[] getValidatedTypes();
}
```

Now we can write classes `PolicyValidator`, `ClaimValidator`, and `CustomerValidator` that implement this interface and perform the appropriate business validation of a `Policy`, `Claim`, and `Customer` respectively. We might also need to implement validation classes for `LifePolicy`, `HousePolicy`, and `AutoPolicy`. Listing 8.7 shows an extract from the `PolicyValidator` class as an example.

Listing 8.7   Extract from *PolicyValidator*

```
public class PolicyValidator implements Validator {

  private static final Class[] validatedTypes =
    new Class[] {Policy.class};
  private List validationErrors = Collections.EMPTY_LIST;
  private Policy policy;

  public boolean validate(Object domainObject) {
    if (! (domainObject instanceof Policy) ) {
      throw new IllegalArgumentException(
                "I can't validate that!");
```

```
      }
      validationErrors = new ArrayList();
      policy = (Policy) domainObject;
      boolean ok = true;
      if (!validateDates()) ok = false;
      // other validation tests...
      return ok;
    }

    public List getValidationErrors() {
      return validationErrors;
    }

    public Class[] getValidatedTypes() {
      return validatedTypes;
    }

    private boolean validateDates() {
      boolean ok = true;
      if (policy.getStartDate().after(policy.getEndDate())) {
        ok = false;
        validationErrors.add(
          "Start date cannot be after end date");
      }
      return ok;
    }

    // other validation tests...
}
```

We have validation classes for the domain objects that need them. Now we need a clean way to determine whether a given business object requires validation, and to trigger that validation. We will use a simple interface, RequiresValidation, to indicate whether a business object requires validation and to allow uniform access to validation of any business object. If an object implements the RequiresValidation interface, a client can call the validate() and getValidationErrors() methods on it. The RequiresValidation interface looks like this:

```
interface RequiresValidation {
  boolean validate();
  List getValidationErrors();
}
```

For any object that needs it, we will perform the business validation before allowing that object to be inserted or updated. Recall from Chapter 3 that the insert and update methods are defined in the SimpleInsurance façade interface (see Figure 8.6).

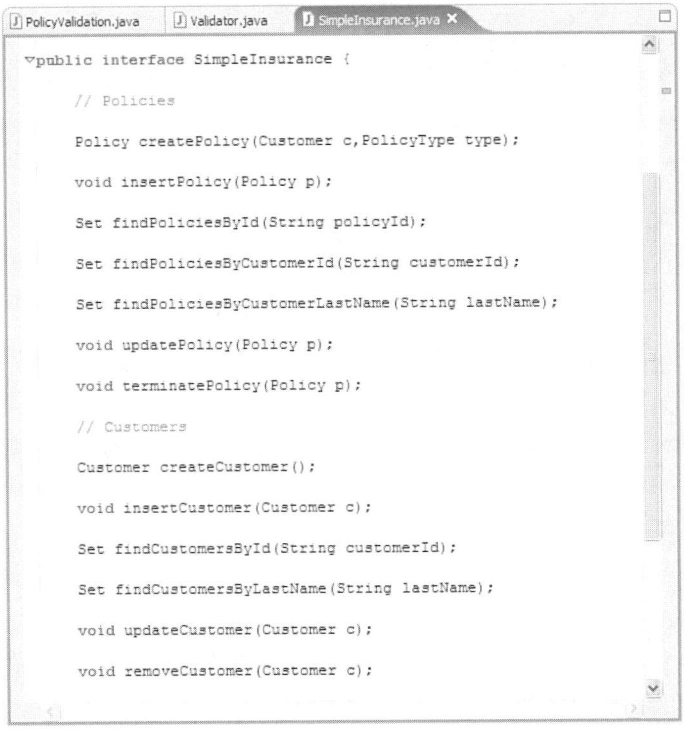

Figure 8.6   The *SimpleInsurance* façade.

Finally we get to the part about the aspect (bet you were beginning to won-der!). We will encapsulate everything to do with driving business validation in an aspect, `BusinessRulesValidation`, which we will declare in the `insurance.model.validation` package alongside the `Validator` interface and the validation classes. The first step is to define the `RequiresValidation` interface, which we chose to declare as an inner-interface in this case:

```
public aspect BusinessRulesValidation {

  public interface RequiresValidation {}

}
```

We can now use inter-type declarations to add the `validate` and
`getValidationErrors` methods to the interface, and also to declare a field,
`validationErrors`, on behalf of all implementers of the interface. We will come
back and fill in the implementation of the validate method shortly:

```
public aspect BusinessRulesValidation {

  public interface RequiresValidation {}

  public boolean RequiresValidation.validate() {
    return true;
  }

  public List RequiresValidation.getValidationErrors() {
    if (this.validationErrors == null) {
      this.validationErrors = new ArrayList();
    }
    return validationErrors;
  }

  private List RequiresValidation.validationErrors;

}
```

Both the interface itself and the two methods we have declared on it have
been made public. This was an implementation choice in case someone outside
of the `BusinessRulesAspect` wants to drive validation at some point. They
could equally have been declared private to the aspect for everything that follows
in the rest of this section.

At this point we have some shared behavior that the aspect implements on
behalf of any type that `RequiresValidation`, but no implementers of that
interface. You may remember the `declare parents` construct from Chapter 3,
which we used as part of the implementation of the `SerializationBased`
`Persistence` aspect. We can use `declare parents` here to state that all of our
domain implementation classes require some form of validation:

```
declare parents : PolicyImpl implements RequiresValidation;
declare parents :
  CustomerImpl implements RequiresValidation;
declare parents : ClaimImpl implements RequiresValidation;
```

Figure 8.7 shows the results of the `declare parents` statements in the Outline view. AJDT uses the icon for a `declare parents` member.

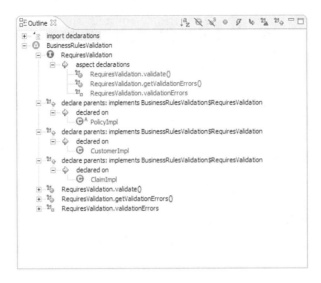

Figure 8.7 Declaring parents.

The general form of a `declare parents … implements` clause is as follows:

```
declare parents : TypePattern implements InterfaceList;
```

So another way of writing the `declare parents` statements in the aspect is to use a type pattern:

```
declare parents : (PolicyImpl || CustomerImpl || ClaimImpl)
    implements RequiresValidation;
```

Really though, the validation classes are not about validating a particular set of implementations (the `*Impl` classes), but any `Policy`, `Customer`, or `Claim` object. Just as we made `Policy` be the target of `PolicyChangeNotification` inter-type declarations, so we can target the interface types with a `declare parents` statement, too. In this case, we want to declare that the `Policy`, `Customer`, and `Claim` interfaces all extend `RequiresValidation`. By doing this, we will support validation for any implementation of those interfaces. The declaration can be made using a variation of the `declare parents` statement:

```
declare parents : Policy extends RequiresValidation;
declare parents : Customer extends RequiresValidation;
declare parents : Claim extends RequiresValidation;
```

The general form of a `declare parents ...` extends clause is as follows:

```
declare parents : TypePattern extends Type;
```

This form can also be used with classes, as shown in the following section.

Let's recap what we have achieved so far. We defined an interface inside the aspect, and made inter-type declarations on the interface so that the aspect could provide state and behavior on behalf of all the implementers of the interface. Then we used `declare parents` to make a set of existing interfaces extend our new interface. The net effect is that every implementation of the domain interfaces will now have validation supported by the `BusinessRulesValidation` aspect.

Now we just need to complete the rest of the `BusinessRulesValidation` aspect implementation. The following pointcut and advice ensure that any time we try to insert or update a domain object that requires validation, we first validate the object to make sure it satisfies the business constraints:

```
pointcut insertOrUpdate(RequiresValidation domainObject) :
  (execution(* SimpleInsurance.insert*(..)) ||
   execution(* SimpleInsurance.update*(..)))
  && args(domainObject);

before(RequiresValidation domainObject) :
  insertOrUpdate(domainObject) {
  if (!domainObject.validate()) {
    throw new SIValidationException(
      domainObject,
      domainObject.getValidationErrors());
  }
}
```

Note the use of `args` in the `insertOrUpdate` pointcut to both constrain matches to join points where the domain object implements `RequiresValidation`, and to provide the domain object itself to the advice. The advice itself calls `validate` on the domain object, and throws an `SIValidationException` if the validation fails.

All that remains is to fill in the body of the `RequiresValidation.validate` method:

```
01 public boolean RequiresValidation.validate() {
02   BusinessRulesValidation validationAspect =
03       BusinessRulesValidation.aspectOf();
04   boolean ok = true;
```

```
05   this.validationErrors = new ArrayList();
06   Set validators =
07     validationAspect.getValidatorsFor(this.getClass());
08   for (Iterator it=validators.iterator(); it.hasNext();) {
09         Validator v = (Validator) it.next();
10         if (!v.validate(this)) {
11           ok = false;
12           validationErrors.addAll(v.getValidationErrors());
13         }
14       }
15       return ok;
16 }
```

There are a few interesting things to note about this implementation. Because the context in which the inter-type declared method runs is the `RequiresValidation` object, if we want to access non-static methods and fields in the aspect itself we have to get hold of the aspect instance. (We cannot just use `this`.) Lines 02 and 03 show how we do this by calling the `aspectOf` method. (See Chapter 9 for a full discussion of this method.) The `validationErrors` field accessed on lines 05 and 12 is the inter-type declared field from the aspect—there is one copy for each `RequiresValidation` object. The rest of the implementation is straightforward: We call a helper method defined in the aspect to get all the registered validators for the domain object (line 07), and then ask each in turn to validate it. The validation errors are accumulated (line 12), and if any validation returns false, the validate method will return false, too (line 11).

The full aspect, including the definition of the helper methods, is shown in Listing 8.8. Notice how inter-type declarations and advice are working together to implement a complete solution.

Listing 8.8   The *BusinessRulesValidation* Aspect

```
public aspect BusinessRulesValidation {

  private Map validatorsByType = new HashMap();

  // RequiresValidation interface

  public interface RequiresValidation {}

  declare parents : Policy extends RequiresValidation;
  declare parents : Customer extends RequiresValidation;
  declare parents : Claim extends RequiresValidation;

  public boolean RequiresValidation.validate() {
    BusinessRulesValidation validationAspect =
      BusinessRulesValidation.aspectOf();
```

```
    boolean ok = true;
    this.validationErrors = new ArrayList();
    Set validators =
      validationAspect.getValidatorsFor(this.getClass());
    for (Iterator it = validators.iterator();
          it.hasNext();) {
      Validator v = (Validator) it.next();
      if (!v.validate(this)) {
        ok = false;
        validationErrors.addAll(v.getValidationErrors());
      }
    }
    return ok;
  }

  public List RequiresValidation.getValidationErrors() {
    if (this.validationErrors == null) {
      this.validationErrors = new ArrayList();
    }
    return validationErrors;
  }

  private List RequiresValidation.validationErrors;

  // Triggering validation

  pointcut insertOrUpdate(RequiresValidation domainObject) :
    (execution(* SimpleInsurance.insert*(..)) ||
     execution(* SimpleInsurance.update*(..)))
     && args(domainObject);

  before(RequiresValidation domainObject) :
    insertOrUpdate(domainObject) {
    if (!domainObject.validate()) {
      throw new SIValidationException(
        domainObject, domainObject.getValidationErrors());
    }
  }

  // Registration and management of Validators

  public BusinessRulesValidation() {
    addValidator(new PolicyValidator());
    // register other validators here…
  }

  private Set getValidatorsFor(Class c) {
    Set s = new HashSet();
    getValidatorsFor(c,s);
    return s;
  }

  private void getValidatorsFor(Class c, Set s) {
    Validator classValidator = (Validator)
      validatorsByType.get(c);
```

```
    if (classValidator != null) s.add(classValidator);
    Class[] interfaces = c.getInterfaces();
    for (int i = 0; i < interfaces.length; i++) {
      getValidatorsFor(interfaces[i],s);
    }
    Class superclass = c.getSuperclass();
    if (superclass != null) {
      getValidatorsFor(superclass,s);
    }
  }

  private void addValidator(Validator v) {
    Class[] validatedTypes = v.getValidatedTypes();
    for (int i = 0; i < validatedTypes.length; i++) {
      validatorsByType.put(validatedTypes[i],v);
    }
  }
}
```

When we add this aspect to the Simple Insurance application, and validate any business object that RequiresValidation before attempting to save it, we get the result shown in Figure 8.8 if a policy object business constraint is violated. If the user interface did not validate the object for some reason, we would still protect the database from ill-formed business objects by throwing an SIValidationException on an insertOrUpdate call.

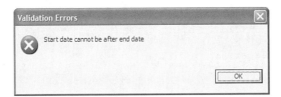

Figure 8.8 Business validation at work.

By the way, if you're looking at the implementation in Listing 8.8 (see the aspect constructor declaration) and thinking it would be much better to configure the BusinessRulesValidation aspect with a set of validators using a lightweight container and dependency injection, don't worry—so are we. We show you how to do that in Part 3.

> ### What About Multiple Inheritance?
>
> Those of you who are familiar with languages such as C++ might be asking the question "Why can't you just use multiple inheritance?" The answer is that the approach has a number of problems, including the fact that it is not supported by the Java language. First, when using multiple inheritance the crosscutting concern is only partially modularized within the additional parent class: Each affected class must also be explicitly modified to extend the parent class. We can encapsulate the behavior, but not the knowledge of which types should acquire that behavior. Second, there is the issue of nondeterministic behavior when members of inherited classes collide.
>
> AspectJ allows us to capture both the "where" and the "what" of these concerns while providing a robust solution to the problem of duplicate members.

8.4 Extending Classes

In the previous section we saw the use of `declare parents ... extends` for interfaces. You can also use this construct to change the super-type of a set of *classes* matching a type pattern. For example:

```
declare parents : insurance.model.impl.PolicyImpl
    extends java.util.Observable;
```

When declaring a new super-type for a class in this way, the declared super type must be a subclass of the existing super-type of the target object. Given three classes:

```
class A {}
class B extends A {}
class C {}
```

Then `declare parents : A extends C;` is a valid statement because `C` is a subtype of `A`'s parent (`Object`). `declare parents : B extends C;` will result in a compilation error because `C` is not a subtype of `B`'s parent (`A`).

This form of declare parents is used much less frequently than `declare parents ... implements`.

Inter-Type Declarations for Aspects

An inter-type declaration can be made on any target type including an aspect. When using an aspect as the target type of an inter-type declaration, the normal restrictions on aspect members apply (see Chapter 9).

8.5   Using Pointcuts and Advice with Inter-Type Declarations

The `call` and `execution` join points for inter-type declared methods and constructors are the same as if those methods and constructors had been declared directly in the target type. Likewise the `get` and `set` join points for inter-type declared fields are the same as if those fields had been declared directly on the target type. This important property enables you to refactor a member from a target type to an inter-type declaration and vice versa without affecting any pointcuts and advice. The only difference occurs when using the `within` scoping pointcut designator which selects join points based on the declaring type: inter-type declared members are `within` the aspect, not `within` the target type.

The following small example in Listing 8.9 shows the `CountListeners` aspect, which advises calls to the `addPolicyListener` and `removePolicy Listener` methods. The aspect works in the same way regardless of whether these methods are defined in the `PolicyImpl` class directly or as inter-type declarations in the `PolicyChangeNotification` aspect.

Listing 8.9   The *CountListeners* Aspect

```
public aspect CountListeners {

  pointcut add () :
    execution(* PolicyImpl.addPolicyListener(..));

  after () returning : add () {
    count++;
  }

  pointcut remove () :
    execution(* PolicyImpl.removePolicyListener(..));

  after () returning : remove () {
    count--;
  }

  private int count;

}
```

8.6   **Summary**

This chapter described the inter-type declaration of fields, methods, and constructors. We looked at the difference between making an inter-type declaration on a class target type and on an interface target type, and at the use of the `declare parents` statement. We also completed the implementation of the `PolicyChangeNotification` aspect and implemented a `BusinessRules Validation` aspect using a combination of inter-type declarations and advice.

We saw how inter-type declarations are represented in the Outline view using the following icons:

○ Package protected inter-type declared field:

○ Private inter-type declared field:

○ Public inter-type declared method:

○ Private inter-type declared method:

○ `declare … parents`

AJDT also uses the marker in the gutter of the editor to show the presence of inter-type declarations.

CHAPTER 9

Aspects

You have seen lots of examples of aspects so far in this book, and so you already know quite a lot about them. This chapter fills in the missing pieces that we haven't touched on so far: aspect instantiation and lifecycle, abstract aspects and aspect inheritance, inner aspects, and privileged aspects. Before we get into that, the next section presents a short overview of the basic form of an aspect declaration.

9.1 Aspect Definition and Initialization

An aspect declaration looks very much like a class declaration, with the keyword `class` replaced by the keyword `aspect`. A bare-bones aspect declaration looks like this:

```
aspect AnAspect {

}
```

AJDT uses the Ⓐ icon to represent an aspect. Aspects may be declared either with default visibility (as above), or they may be declared `public`. Just like a class, an aspect may also be declared `abstract` or `final` (see the section on aspect inheritance), or `static` (see the section on inner aspects).

The general form of an aspect declaration is as follows:

```
[ privileged ] [ Modifiers ] aspect id
[extends Type] [implements TypeList]
[PerClause] { Body }
```

The use of the keyword `privileged` is discussed in Section 9.5, and the use of a *PerClause* is discussed in the following section, Section 9.2.

Just like a class, an aspect may contain definitions of constructors, fields, methods, and pointcuts. It may also contain inner classes, aspects, and interfaces. In addition to these features that are shared with classes, aspects can also contain advice and inter-type declarations. You saw examples of an aspect containing fields and methods in Part 1 when we wrote the `Serialization BasedPersistence` aspect. What we haven't talked about so far are aspect constructors.

Just like a class, every aspect has a default constructor. You can, however, define your own constructor and use it to initialize the state of the aspect. Figure 9.1 shows the result of adding a couple of constructors to a simple aspect.

Figure 9.1   Aspect constructors.

The compiler informs us that aspects may only have no-argument constructors. As you will see in the next section, aspects are instantiated implicitly so there is no need for the programmer to pass any arguments—and hence only a no-argument constructor is supported.

Constructors give us a way of performing some initialization each time an aspect instance is constructed. If you want to perform once-per-aspect-type initialization, you can declare a static initializer in the aspect just as you would for a class:

```
aspect AnAspect {

    static {
        // once per type initialization
    }

    public AnAspect() {
        // once per instance initialization
    }

}
```

9.2 Aspect Instantiation

At runtime AspectJ creates instances of aspects, and all methods and advice within an aspect run in the context of an aspect instance (available via this in the body of the method or advice). The one exception is an inter-type declared constructor or method, which, as discussed in Chapter 8, executes in the context of the target type. AspectJ guarantees to instantiate an aspect instance for you before it is first needed. If you try to instantiate an aspect programmatically by calling its constructor, you will get a compile-time error.

So far in this book, we have used singleton aspects almost exclusively—singleton aspects are the default (you can optionally specify issingleton() for the per-clause of a singleton aspect but it is not required), and result is the creation of a single aspect instance of an aspect type within the JVM.[1] Singleton aspects are not the only model supported by AspectJ, however—it is also possible to specify alternative aspect instantiation models by using per-clauses in the aspect definition.

We can get AJDT to tell us the alternative options for aspect instantiation by using code completion in the editor. In Figure 9.2, we have positioned the cursor after the characters "per" following the aspect declaration and pressed Ctrl+Spacebar.

---

1. Strictly speaking, there will be one singleton aspect instance per class loader namespace; this is the same as the rules for ordinary singletons in Java, too.

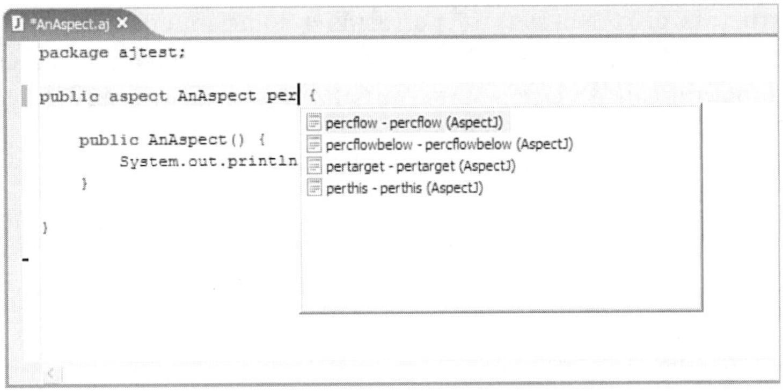

Figure 9.2   The available aspect instantiation models.

You will see that there are four additional aspect instantiation models available: `perthis`, `pertarget`, `percflow`, and `percflowbelow`. Each form takes a pointcut expression as an argument, as shown in Figure 9.3, which is the result of accepting the `perthis` code completion from Figure 9.2.

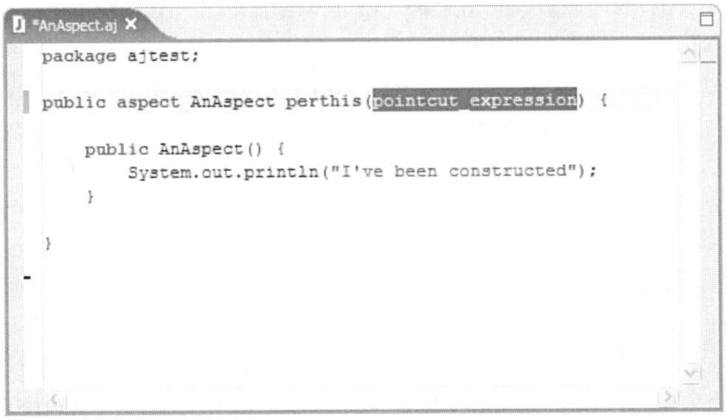

Figure 9.3   Per clauses are configured with a pointcut expression.

The `perthis` instantiation model creates an aspect instance for each unique object bound to `this` at join points matched by the pointcut expression. The `pertarget` instantiation model is similar, but creates an aspect instance for each unique object bound to `target` at matched join points. The `percflow` and `percflowbelow` instantiation models create aspect instances that live for the duration of the control flow, or the control flow below, join points matched by the pointcut. The subsections that follow explore each of these instantiation models in turn.

The pointcut expression associated with a per-clause can be built from any combination of pointcut designators, and can also refer to pointcuts defined within the aspect, pointcuts in other types (assuming they have appropriate visibility), or even methods and fields by exploiting the `if()` pointcut designator. The following example creates a unique aspect instance for each `Policy` that has a `Claim` raised against it:

```
public aspect ClaimTracking perthis(claimAddition()) {

  pointcut claimAddition() :
    execution(* Policy.addClaim(..));

    ...
}
```

Every time the `claimAddition` pointcut matches a join point, AspectJ will look at the object bound to `this` (the `Policy` to which the claim is being added), and create a new aspect instance if there is not already a `ClaimTracking` aspect in existence for that `Policy`.

If the per-clause refers to a pointcut that has parameters, you can use either the type name or `*` as a placeholder for each parameter. For example:

```
public aspect ClaimTracking perthis(claimAddition(*)) {

  pointcut claimAddition(Claim claim) :
    execution(* Policy.addClaim(claim));

    ...
}
```

The selection of an aspect instantiation model is centered around the state that you need to maintain in the aspect. If you have a state that needs to be held for each object instance, use `perthis` or `pertarget` in preference to maintaining a `Map` inside a singleton aspect. Likewise, if you have an aspect that needs to maintain state on a per-control flow basis (for example, some kind of request context), use `percflow` or `percflowbelow` rather than `ThreadLocals` or a `Map` keyed by `Thread`. If none of these conditions apply, just use a singleton.

The fact that AspectJ manages aspect instantiation for you has a number of benefits:

1. The instantiation model is clearly defined rather than buried in the logic of your aspect.

2. The code generated by the AspectJ compiler will probably be more efficient and certainly more consistent than your own efforts.

3. You can change your mind about which model to use without rewriting your aspect, or defer the decision to a sub-aspect, as discussed in the "Aspect Inheritance" section.

4. Garbage collection. AspectJ will ensure that your aspect is available for garbage collection when it is no longer needed.

Whatever aspect instantiation model you choose, AspectJ supports two special static methods that you can call on any concrete aspect type: hasAspect and aspectOf. These tell you whether an aspect instance has been created, and if so, enable you to access that aspect instance. The signature of these methods varies slightly according to the instantiation model being used, and we highlight this as we look at each model in turn.

9.2.1 Singleton Aspects

This is the default behavior and the most commonly used form. The aspect instance is created on first active use and exists for the lifetime of the program execution. For singleton aspects, the aspectOf and hasAspect methods take no arguments:

```
public static <AnAspect> aspectOf();
public static boolean hasAspect();
```

The hasAspect() method determines whether an instance of a particular aspect is available and always returns true for singleton aspects. The aspectOf() method returns the singleton instance. For example, to access the SerializationBasedPersistence aspect instance from Chapter 3, we could write the following:

```
SerializationBasedPersistence sbpAspect =
  SerializationBasedPersistence.aspectOf();
```

9.2.2 Per-This Aspects

The perthis(pointcut_expression) model creates new aspect instances as follows: For each join point matched by the pointcut expression, if this is bound to an object instance, and an aspect has not already been created for that instance, a new aspect is created and associated with it. The aspect instance is eligible for garbage collection at the same time as the object it is associated with.

The multiple readers, single writer example from Chapter 7 used a `perthis` aspect instantiation model. Listing 9.1 shows a concrete version of that aspect.

Listing 9.1   Multiple Readers, Single Writer Aspect

```
public aspect MultipleReadersSingleWriter
perthis( readMethod() || writeMethod() ) {

  private ReadWriteLock rw =
    new WriterPreferenceReadWriteLock();

  pointcut readMethod() :
    execution(* MyResource.*(..)) && !writeMethod();
  pointcut writeMethod() :
    execution(* MyResource.update*(..));

  before() : readMethod() {
    try {
      rw.readLock().acquire();
    } catch (InterruptedException intEx) {
    throw new RuntimeException(
      "Unable to obtain R lock");
    }
  }

  after() : readMethod() {
    rw.readLock().release();
  }

  before() : writeMethod() {
    try {
      rw.writeLock().acquire();
    } catch (InterruptedException intEx) {
      throw new RuntimeException(
        "Unable to obtain W lock");
    }
  }

  after() : writeMethod() {
    rw.writeLock().release();
  }

  declare warning: readMethod() && writeMethod() :
    "A method cannot be both a read and a write method";
}
```

The `perthis` pointcut expression is defined as `(readMethod() || writeMethod())`. This means that a new aspect instance will be created for each unique object bound to `this` when executing a method on `MyResource`—in other words, for each instance of `MyResource`. In this case, this is exactly what we need, because part of the state of the aspect is the `ReadWriteLock` used to protect the resource—and we want to lock individual `MyResource` instances, and not the whole collection of instances. The state held in the aspect has driven our selection of aspect instantiation model.

Figure 9.4 shows the definition of the `MyResource` class used to test the aspect, with the Outline view showing the advice in effect.

Figure 9.4   The *MyResource* class.

Listing 9.2 shows a simple test program that illustrates the use of `aspectOf` and `hasAspect` for `perthis` aspects.

Listing 9.2   A Test Program

```
01 package ajtest;
02 import org.aspectj.lang.NoAspectBoundException;
03 public class MyResourceAccessTest {
04
05   public static void main(String[] args) {
06     MyResource myFirstResource = new MyResource();
07     MyResource mySecondResource = new MyResource();
08
09     showAspectOf(myFirstResource);
10     showAspectOf(mySecondResource);
11
12     myFirstResource.getA();
13     showAspectOf(myFirstResource);
14
```

```
15        mySecondResource.getB();
16        showAspectOf(mySecondResource);
17    }
18
19    private static void showAspectOf(MyResource resource) {
20      try {
21        boolean hasAspect =
22          MultipleReadersSingleWriter.hasAspect(resource);
23        if (hasAspect) {
24          System.out.println(resource + " has aspect.");
25        } else {
26          System.out.println(resource +
27            " does not have an aspect");
28        }
29        MultipleReadersSingleWriter resourceProtection =
30          MultipleReadersSingleWriter.aspectOf(resource);
31        System.out.println("Aspect for " + resource + " is "
32            + resourceProtection);
33      } catch (NoAspectBoundException noAspectEx) {
34        System.out.println("No aspect bound for " +
35          resource);
36      }
37    }
38 }
```

Looking at the definition of the showAspectOf method on lines 19 through 37, we can see that for a perthis aspect, the hasAspect method takes a single argument—the object for which we want to know whether or not an aspect exists (line 22). Likewise, the aspectOf method takes a single argument (the object whose aspect we want to obtain—line 30). If we run this program, we get the output shown in Figure 9.5.

Figure 9.5   Results of running the test program.

There are a few things to note from running the program. First, when we call showAspectOf on line 9, we can see that hasAspect(myFirstResource) has returned false, and calling aspectOf(myFirstAspect) threw an org.aspectj.lang.NoAspectBoundException. At this stage in the program, we have not executed any methods on myFirstResource, so there have been no join points matched by the perthis pointcut expression, and hence no aspect instance has been created.

On line 12, we call a method on myFirstResource. This causes an execution join point matched by the perthis pointcut, and because we do not already have an aspect instance for myFirstResource, one is created. The console output in Figure 9.5 shows that after this call, hasAspect(myFirstResource) returns true, and aspectOf(myFirstResource) returns an instance of the MultipleReadersSingleWriter aspect. After calling a method on mySecondResource, notice in Figure 9.5 that a second aspect instance has been created.

There is one last important thing to note about this example. If you look closely at Figure 9.4, you will see that the advice markers in the gutter have a question mark against them ⟳ indicating the presence of a runtime test. The Outline view is also showing "advised by (with runtime test)." Why is there a runtime test? The definition of the readMethod() and writeMethod() pointcuts as written means that they are fully statically determinable, but there's something else going on, something caused by declaring the aspect to use the perthis instantiation model.

Whenever you use a per-clause to specify an aspect instantiation model other than singleton, every piece of advice declared within the aspect has an implicit condition associated with its execution. For a perthis aspect, the implicit condition is that the object bound to this at any matched join point be the object that the aspect is an aspectOf. In other words, where the aspect in Listing 9.1 says

```
after() : readMethod() {
  rw.readLock().release();
}
```

the actual execution of the after advice will occur only at join points that match a pointcut more like this: readMethod() && this(myObject). It is the presence of the additional this test that the advice markers and Outline view are indicating to us.

Why does AspectJ apply this additional condition when using a per clause? Think about the MultipleReadersSingleWriter aspect we have been working with. Each aspect has its own lock that it uses to protect its associated resource. Without the implicit && this(myObject) test, the before and after advice in each aspect instance would match the execution of read and write methods on any resource instance: Each aspect instance we created would be applying its own lock to *all* resource instances, not what we want at all. Instead we want the aspect to protect only its associated resource object, and that's what the implicit per-clause does for us.

9.2.3 Per-Target Aspects

The `pertarget(pointcut_expression)` model works in a very similar manner to `perthis`. It creates new aspect instances as follows: For each join point matched by the pointcut expression, if `target` is bound to an object instance, and an aspect has not already been created for that instance, a new aspect is created and associated with it. The aspect instance is eligible for garbage collection at the same time as the object it is associated with.

As an example of how you might use a `pertarget` aspect, Listing 9.3 shows a simple `Connection` class and associated `ConnectionManager`. The `ConnectionManager` maintains a pool of connections, which improves performance by allowing clients to reuse connections, and limits the total number to prevent resource exhaustion. However, the program as it stands has no notion of connection leasing: We cannot prevent a client from hogging a connection thereby preventing other clients from using it.

Listing 9.3   *Connection and ConnectionManager*

```
public class Connection {

  private boolean isOpen;

  Connection () {
  }

  void open () {
    isOpen = true;
  }

  public void write (String data) {
    if (!isOpen) {
      throw new RuntimeException("Connection closed.");
    }
  }

  void close () {
    isOpen = false;
  }
}
```

```
public class ConnectionManager {

  public static final int POOL_SIZE = 10;
  private List pool;

  public ConnectionManager () {
    initializePool();
  }

  public Connection openConnection () {
    Connection conn = borrowConnection();
    conn.open();
    return conn;
  }

  public void closeConnection (Connection conn) {
    conn.close();
    returnConnection(conn);
  }

  private void initializePool () {
    pool = new LinkedList();
    for (int i = 0; i < POOL_SIZE; i++) {
      pool.add(new Connection());
    }
  }

  void returnConnection (Connection c) {
    pool.add(c);
  }

  Connection borrowConnection () {
    return (Connection)pool.remove(0);
  }
}
```

The Reaper aspect in Listing 9.4 is used to implement connection leasing. It starts a timer task when a connection is opened, and if the connection is not returned to the pool within a set time (for this example just one second), it is closed. By using a pertarget() aspect, we ensure that a separate Reaper instance is created for each Connection object—and therefore a different timer used.

The aspect declares that a new instance should be created for every unique object bound to target at join points matched by the openConnection pointcut. Looking at the definition of the openConnection pointcut, you can see that this corresponds to one aspect instance for every opened Connection.

Listing 9.4 *Reaper* Aspect

```
public aspect Reaper pertarget(openConnection(Connection)) {

  pointcut openConnection (Connection c) :
    call(* open(..)) && target(c);

  after (Connection c) : openConnection (c) {
    this.conn = c;
    start();
  }

  pointcut closeConnection (Connection c) :
    call(* close(..)) && target(c);

  after () : closeConnection (*) && !within(Reaper) {
    stop();
  }

  public static final long TIMEOUT = 1000;
  private static Timer timer = new Timer();

  private Connection conn;
  private TimerTask task;

  private void start () {
    System.out.println("Start timer ...");
    task = new TimerTask() {
      public void run() {
        reap();
      }
    };
    timer.schedule(task,TIMEOUT);
  }

  private void reap () {
    System.out.println("Closing connection ...");
    conn.close();
  }

  private void stop () {
    System.out.println("Cancel reaper ...");
    task.cancel();
  }

}
```

Also note that by defining the `timer` object as a static variable, it can be shared by all instances of the `Reaper` aspect.

The simple client application in Listing 9.5 shows what happens when the `Reaper` aspect is used. The client opens two different connections, and then goes to sleep for a period longer than the timeout for the reaper.

Listing 9.5 A *Client* Application

```
public class Client {

  public static void main(String[] args) throws Exception {
    ConnectionManager connMgr = new ConnectionManager();
    System.out.println("Opening connections ...");
    Connection conn1 = connMgr.openConnection();
    Connection conn2 = connMgr.openConnection();
    connMgr.returnConnection(conn2);
    Thread.sleep(2000);
    System.out.println("Writing to connection ...");
    conn1.write("Hello");
  }
}
```

Running the program shows that two `Reaper` instances are created and each starts a timer when a connection is opened. When the timer expires, the connection is closed. An exception is then thrown when the client tries to use one of them. This prevents resource exhaustion or even deadlock in the system as a whole.

```
Opening connections ...
Start timer ...
Start timer ...
Closing connection ...
Closing connection ...
java.lang.RuntimeException: Connection closed.
Writing to connection ...
  at chapter9.Connection.write(Connection.java:28)
  at chapter9.Client.main(Client.java:25)
```

For `pertarget` aspects, the `hasAspect` and `aspectOf` methods are defined to take a single object argument, as is the case with `perthis`. For two `Connection` objects, `c1` and `c2`, where `c1` has been opened and `c2` has not, `Reaper.hasAspect(c1)` will return true, and `Reaper.hasAspect(c2)` will return false. `Reaper.aspectOf(c1)` returns the aspect instance associated with `c1`.

Per-target aspects also have an implicit condition associated with the execution of any advice defined within them—the condition is equivalent to adding `&&` `target(myTarget)` to the pointcut expressions associated with advice in the aspect. Without this implicit condition, each `Reaper` aspect would start a timer to reap every `Connection` object as it was opened, rather than just the `Connection` the `Reaper` was responsible for.

> ## When Should I Use *perthis* or *pertarget* Rather Than Inter-Type Declarations?
>
> Both `perthis` and `pertarget` can be used to maintain state that is managed on a per-object basis. An inter-type declaration could also be used to add an aspect-private field to target types, which is another way of maintaining state on a per-object basis. How do you know which approach to use in a given situation?
>
> The main difference between a per-object aspect and an inter-type declaration is that an inter-type declaration affects *every* instance of a target type, whereas an aspect defined with a per-clause only affects those instances matched by its pointcut expression. In fact, by using an `if()` test in the pointcut expression, you can even decide at runtime whether to create an aspect instance.
>
> Another factor that can help you decide is the affinity of the state you want to maintain—is it more logically a part of the target class, but managed by the aspect, or is it really part of the state of the aspect itself? In Chapter 8, we used inter-type declarations to manage a set of listeners on behalf of a target class, whereas in the `Reaper` example the timers used are more logically a part of the aspect state.
>
> A final factor is that advice in per-object aspects is limited by the implicit `&&` `this(myObject)` or `&& target(myTargetObject)` conditions. If you need to write advice in the aspect that applies at join points where `this` or `target` are bound to some other value, you have to use a different mechanism.

9.2.4 Per-Cflow and Per-Cflowbelow Aspects

The `percflow(pointcut_expression)` instantiation model works as follows: At each join point matched by the pointcut expression, if an aspect instance does not already exist for the current control flow (in the current thread of execution), a new aspect instance will be created. The aspect instance stays bound to the control flow until the control flow is exited, and then it is available for garbage collection.

The `percflowbelow(pointcut_expression)` instantiation model works in a similar way, except an aspect instance is created for each thread of control at join points in the control flow *below* the join points matched by the pointcut expression.

The per-control-flow instantiation models are most often used to associate contextual information with a control flow. The `HibernateManager` aspect we developed in Chapter 3 and extended in Chapter 7 needs to manage a `Hibernate` session for each `hibernateTransaction()`. An alternative implementation of the session management, which would work correctly in a multithreaded environment, would be to use a `percflow` aspect. The `HibernateSessionManager` aspect would look like the one shown in Listing 9.6.

Listing 9.6   Per-Control Flow *HibernateSessionManagement*

```
public aspect HibernateSessionManager
percflow(sessionBoundary()) {

  /**
   * Get a session factory from somewhere - maybe
   * the HibernateManager aspect?
   */
  private static SessionFactory sessionFactory = ...;

  /**
   * Session to use for this control flow
   */
  private Session session;


  /**
   * Any operation invoked on a HibernateDao subclass.
   * (We don't want to match the methods in the
   * HibernateDao class itself).
   */
  pointcut daoOperation(HibernateDao dao) :
    execution(* HibernateDao+.*(..)) &&
    !execution(* HibernateDao.*(..)) &&
    this(dao);

  /**
   * Start a hibernate session (and transaction)
   * at these points, but only if we don't already
   * have a session active.
   */
  pointcut sessionBoundary() :
    hibernateTransaction() &&
    !cflowbelow(hibernateTransaction());

  /**
   * Each dao operation MUST execution in a
   * transaction. Add other, higher-level
   * transactions to this pointcut definition
   * as needed.
   */
  pointcut hibernateTransaction() :
    daoOperation(HibernateDao) ||
    execution(* ImportUtility.importDatFile(..));

  /**
   * The protocol for sessions and transactions.
   * It is important that this advice has precedence
   * over the DAO dependency injection advice below.
   */
  Object around() : sessionBoundary() {
    Object ret = null;
    session = sessionFactory.openSession();
```

```
        Transaction tx = null;
        try {
          tx = session.beginTransaction();
          ret = proceed();
          tx.commit();
        } catch(SIException ex) {
          if (tx != null) tx.rollback();
          throw ex;
        } finally {
          session.close();
        }
        return ret;
      }

      /**
       * Before any DAO executes a database operation,
       * we need to tell it what session object to use.
       */
      before(HibernateDao dao) : daoOperation(dao) {
        dao.setSession(session);
      }

    }
```

If you compare this to Listing 7.15 in Chapter 7, you can see how little we
had to change to make the session management work in a multithreaded
environment.

For `percflow` and `percflowbelow` aspects, `hasAspect()` and `aspectOf()`
both take no parameters. (They respond according to whether or not an aspect
instance is bound in the current control flow.) As with all per-clause instantiation
models, `percflow` and `percflowbelow` both have implicit conditions associated
with the execution of any advice defined in them: The condition amounts to adding
`&& cflow(pointcut_expression)` or `&& cflowbelow(pointcut_expression)`,
respectively.

9.2.5 Summary of Instantiation Models

AspectJ supports five different aspect instantiation models:

- ❍ Singleton
- ❍ `perthis(pointcut_expression)`
- ❍ `pertarget(pointcut_expression)`
- ❍ `percflow(pointcut_expression)`
- ❍ `percflowbelow(pointcut_expression)`

Table 9.1 shows the implicit advice execution condition for each of these instantiation models.

Table 9.1   Effect of Per Clauses on Advice Execution

Per Clause	Implicit Condition
`issingleton()`	None
`per`**`this`**`(pointcut expression)`	`&&` **`this`**`(myObject)`
`per`**`target`**`(pointcut expression)`	`&&` **`target`**`(myTargetObject)`
`per`**`cflow`**`(pointcut expression)`	`&&` **`cflow`**`(pointcut expression)`
`per`**`cflowbelow`**`(pointcut expression)`	`&&` **`cflowbelow`**`(pointcut expression)`

The signature of `hasAspect` and `aspectOf` for each of these instantiation models is shown in Table 9.2.

Table 9.2   Signature of *hasAspect()* and *aspectOf()*

Per Clause	Signatures
Singleton	`hasAspect(), aspectOf()`
Perthis	`hasAspect(anObject), aspectOf(anObject)`
Pertarget	`hasAspect(aTargetObject), aspectOf(aTargetObject)`
Percflow	`hasAspect(), aspectOf()`
Percflowbelow	`hasAspect(), aspectOf()`

> **Per-Type Instances**
>
> AspectJ 1.2 does not offer a per-type instantiation model. This model is still being considered for future versions of AspectJ, but so far there have not been sufficiently compelling use cases to justify its inclusion in the language.

9.3   Aspect Inheritance

Just as you can define hierarchies of classes, you can define hierarchies of aspects. Aspects can extend classes, implement interfaces, and even extend other aspects. Classes may not extend aspects, however. Aspect inheritance is more restricted than class inheritance though, as explored in this section.

9.3.1 Extending Aspects

One aspect may extend another just like one class may extend another. The only restriction is that you can only extend an abstract aspect; that is, only "leaf" aspects can be concrete. In addition, aspects must be declared `public` if they are to be extended by aspects in another package. Figure 9.6 shows what you can and cannot do with aspect inheritance.

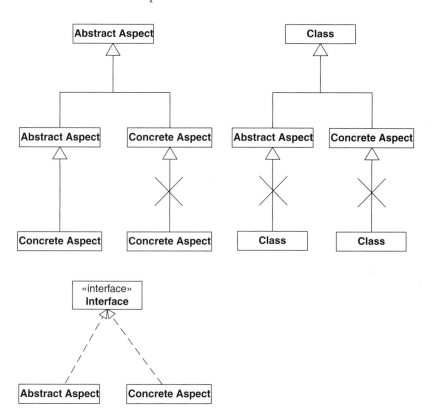

Figure 9.6   Abstract inheritance.

But what use are abstract aspects? An abstract aspect enables you to define the shape of a solution to a problem, but leave the details that will vary from case to case to be provided by a concrete sub-aspect. When one aspect extends another, not only does it inherit any fields or methods but also any pointcuts and advice. A sub-aspect can also define its own instantiation model (singleton, perthis, and so forth) as described earlier in this chapter, which allows it to override the one specified by its parent. For example, a sub-aspect may use a `perthis` instantiation model when extending a singleton aspect:

```
public abstract aspect AbstractSingletonAspect {

  ...

}

public aspect PerthisConcreteAspect
extends AbstractSingletonAspect perthis(...){

  ...

}
```

Or a sub-aspect may override a `percflow` instantiation model inherited from its parent using `issingleton()`:

```
public abstract aspect AbstractPercflowAspect
percflow(pcf()) {
  ...
}

public aspect ConcreteSingletonAspect
extends AbstractPercflowAspect issingleton() {
  ...
}
```

The `MultipleReadersSingleWriter` aspect from Listing 9.1 is a prime candidate for an abstract aspect. The aspect can encapsulate the protocol for allowing multiple reader, single writer, access to a resource, but without knowing the details of the actual resource it is protecting. Listing 9.7 shows the changes that need to be made to turn `MultipleReadersSingleWriter` into an abstract aspect.

Listing 9.7 Multiple Readers, Single Writer Abstract Aspect

```
public abstract aspect MultipleReadersSingleWriter
perthis( readMethod() || writeMethod() ) {

  private ReadWriteLock rw =
    new WriterPreferenceReadWriteLock();

  protected abstract pointcut readMethod();
  protected abstract pointcut writeMethod();

  before() : readMethod() {
    try {
      rw.readLock().acquire();
    } catch (InterruptedException intEx) {
```

```
        throw new RuntimeException(
          "Unable to obtain R lock");
      }
    }

    after() : readMethod() {
      rw.readLock().release();
    }

    before() : writeMethod() {
      try {
        rw.writeLock().acquire();
      } catch (InterruptedException intEx) {
        throw new RuntimeException(
          "Unable to obtain W lock");
      }
    }

    after() : writeMethod() {
      rw.writeLock().release();
    }

    declare warning: readMethod() && writeMethod() :
      "A method cannot be both a read and a write method";
}
```

First the keyword `abstract` is used before the `aspect` keyword—just as you would do for an abstract class. Second, we declare the `readMethod()` and `writeMethod()` pointcuts to be abstract. An abstract pointcut has the abstract modifier, and a name and parameters, but no associated pointcut expression. Because the pointcuts are declared abstract, any concrete aspect inheriting from `MultipleReadersSingleWriter` is forced to provide a definition. Listing 9.8 shows how the access protection for instances of `MyResource` from Listing 9.1 can be achieved by extending the abstract aspect.

Listing 9.8 Extending the Abstract Aspect

```
public aspect MyResourceAccessProtection
extends MultipleReadersSingleWriter {

  protected pointcut readMethod() :
    execution(* MyResource.*(..)) && !writeMethod();

  protected pointcut writeMethod() :
    execution(* MyResource.update*(..));

}
```

That's all you need to do. This example illustrates the power of creating reusable abstractions in aspect libraries (more on that in Part 3), and then reusing those abstractions in concrete sub-aspects. The advice from the parent aspect applies to the join points matched by the concrete pointcut definitions in the child aspect. If we created a second concrete sub-aspect of `MultipleReaders SingleWriter` to protect some other kind of resource, there would be two aspect instances (assuming the singleton model), one for each concrete aspect type, and the two would be completely independent.

As discussed in Chapter 6, pointcuts can be defined in classes as well as in aspects. An abstract pointcut though can only be declared in abstract aspect and can only be referred to in a concrete sub-aspect.

Although advice can be inherited from a super-aspect, it cannot be extended or overridden. A sub-aspect can add new advice but cannot modify what it inherits. However, we can use normal virtual methods to achieve the same result. If the body of an advice declaration delegates to a protected or abstract template method, then sub-aspects can override it to perform custom processing.

> **Beware**
>
> Take care when declaring concrete advice in an abstract aspect. This is advice that is bound to a concrete pointcut declared within the abstract aspect rather than an abstract pointcut made concrete within a sub-aspect. The reason for this is that every aspect that extends the abstract aspect will inherit the advice with potentially unexpected results: the advice will be invoked once for each sub-aspect at each matched join point.

9.3.2 Extending Classes

An aspect may extend a class. You would choose to do this for the same reason you might define one class to extend another: to inherit some desired behavior from the superclass. For example, an observable aspect may choose to extend `java.util.Observable`.

There are a couple of things to remember when extending a class. First, you must define a no-argument constructor for your aspect if the superclass does not have one. Second, an aspect cannot inherit from a class that implements `java.io.Serializable`. The reason for this will be explained next.

9.3.3 Implementing Interfaces

Just as classes can implement interfaces, so can aspects. This is useful if you want
to pass an aspect reference to a method that requires a particular type. Interface
implementation works in exactly the same way for aspects as for classes, with a
couple of restrictions described in a moment. Listing 9.9 below shows an example of an aspect that implements the `Runnable` interface so that it can register to
participate in JVM shutdown processing.

Listing 9.9   Implementing an Interface

```
public aspect TheTerminator implements Runnable {

  public TheTerminator () {
    Thread hook = new Thread(this);
    Runtime.getRuntime().addShutdownHook(hook);
  }
  public void run () {
        // shutdown processing…
  }
}
```

Because of the instantiation process described earlier in this chapter, an aspect
may not implement either `java.io.Serializable`[2] or `java.lang.Cloneable`.
Both of these interfaces concern explicit instance creation which is not permitted
for aspects. Trying to define an aspect that implements one of these interfaces will
result in a compilation error.

9.4   Inner Aspects

An aspect can be defined within the scope of a class, an interface, or another
aspect. The only restriction is that it must be declared as *static*. This is because
non-static inner types have their own instantiation model which is incompatible
with that used by aspects.

Inner aspects are typically used to capture concerns that crosscut a single class.
Given the abstract `MultipleReadersSingleWriter` aspect from Listing 9.7, and
the `MyResource` class from Figure 9.4, you might choose to implement protection
for `MyResource` instances with an inner aspect, as shown in Listing 9.10.

---

2. In Part 3, we will discuss briefly the `-XserializableAspects` option that gets around this restriction.

Listing 9.10   Using an Inner Aspect to Protect *MyResource*

```
public class MyResource {

  private static aspect Synchronization
  extends MultipleReadersSingleWriter {

    protected pointcut readMethod() :
      execution(* MyResource.*(..)) && !writeMethod();

    protected pointcut writeMethod() :
      execution(* MyResource.update*(..));
  }

  private Integer a;
  private Integer b;

  public MyResource() {
    a = new Integer(100);
    b = new Integer(200);
  }

  public Integer getA() { return a; }

  public Integer getB() { return b; }

  public void updateAandB(Integer a, Integer b) {
    this.a = a;
    this.b = b;
  }

}
```

Inner aspects are often useful when the definition of the aspect is tightly coupled to its enclosing class. In this example, as we maintain the class and add write methods, we will want to update the pointcut definitions in the inner aspect at the same time.

9.5   Aspect Privilege

The normal Java visibility rules apply when an aspect attempts to access members defined in another type. However, an aspect can gain additional access through the `privileged` keyword. Privileges should not be abused, and privileged aspects should be used with caution, but in certain situations they can prove very useful.

Join points never have restricted visibility; all join points occurring in the running system are available to be matched by pointcuts—even if a join point represents the set of a private field, for example. Therefore, privileged access is not required for pointcuts. Furthermore, any use of context provided by a point-cut to advice is also unrestricted.

To show you how privileged access works, we use an example of adding JavaBeans support to an existing class. Listing 9.11 shows a `HelloWorld` class and a `BeanEventSupport` aspect that fires a property change event when the value of the private `message` field is modified. The aspect does not need to be privileged because this mechanism can be implemented through the use of point-cuts and advice.

Listing 9.11   *BeanEventSupport Aspect*

```
public class HelloWorld {

  private String message = "Hello World!";

  private void println () {
    System.out.println(message);
  }

  public static void main(String[] args) {
    new HelloWorld().println();
  }
}

public aspect BeanEventSupport {

  pointcut messageChanged (String newMessage) :
    set(String message) && args(newMessage)
    && within(HelloWorld);

  after (String newMessage) : messageChanged (newMessage) {
    firePropertyChanged(newMessage);
  }

  private void firePropertyChanged (String s) {
    // ...
  }
}
```

The `privileged` keyword only controls direct access to private fields and methods from within Java code blocks; that is, it only applies to the bodies of advice and methods within an aspect

Listing 9.12 shows the `BeanPropertySupport` aspect, which adds `getter` and `setter` methods for the `message` field. The aspect needs to be privileged because we are accessing the private `message` field directly from Java code.

Listing 9.12 *BeanPropertSupport* Aspect

```
public privileged aspect BeanPropertySupport {

  public String HelloWorld.getMessage() {
    return message;
  }

  public void HelloWorld.setMessage (String s) {
    message = s;
  }
}
```

Should Private *Mean* Private?

The opinion of the AOSD community is split over whether the author of a Java class should control how and whether its behavior can be modified using aspects. Just as the use of `private` or `final` modifiers when declaring classes and methods determines how they may be used or extended by other classes, many believe the same should apply to aspects. However, one of the most powerful applications of AOSD is to facilitate unanticipated software evolution, which by its very definition cannot be foreseen by the original author of a Java program. The use of `private` and `protected` methods and fields can sometimes be required to achieve this.

Aspects can make their own use of access controls to ensure the new modularity they create is maintained. As our JavaBeans examples show, private state and structure exposed to allow the implementation of a crosscutting concern as an aspect is not automatically made available to the rest of the system. State can be private to classes, but not private to an aspect.

9.6   Common Pitfalls

9.6.1 Forgetting the Implicit Conditions on Advice Execution in Per-xxx Aspects

Advice within an aspect that uses a model other than the singleton instantiation model has its execution controlled by an additional implicit condition, as shown in Table 9.1 in this chapter.

9.6.2 Types Must Be Available for Aspect Linking

When using a `perthis` or `pertarget` object, the type that is the subject of the aspect association must be made available to the AspectJ compiler for linking. For example, you cannot easily implement a `pertarget` aspect to create one aspect instance for every `String` object that is the target of a call.

9.7 Summary

This chapter covered aspect initialization and construction, and explored the various aspect instantiation models that AspectJ provides: `issingleton`, `perthis`, `pertarget`, `percflow`, and `percflowbelow`. Using aspect inheritance, you can define behavior in an abstract aspect and reuse it in concrete sub-aspects. It is also possible to define inner aspects to encapsulate crosscutting behavior within a single type. When needed, an aspect can be granted privilege to access members defined in other types that it would not normally be able to see.

CHAPTER 10

Using the AspectJ API

Chapter 7, Section 7.3.1, discussed the use of the special variables thisJoinPoint, thisJoinPointStaticPart, and thisEnclosingJoinPoint StaticPart inside advice bodies. In this chapter, we explore the API provided by AspectJ's runtime library (aspectjrt.jar), and show how you can make full use of these variables.

Listing 10.1 shows a very simple application, MyApp, which we will use as the basis of the exploration.

Listing 10.1 *MyApp*

```
package business;

public class MyApp {

  private String mostRecentCmd;

  private void repeat() {
    repeat(1);
  }

  private void repeat(int attempts) {
    if (this.mostRecentCmd != null) {
      doSomething(mostRecentCmd, attempts);
    }
    else {
      System.out.println("Nothing to repeat.");
    }
  }

  private void doSomething(String cmd) {
    System.out.println("Ladies and gentlemen, I will now " +
cmd);
    mostRecentCmd = cmd;
```

```
  }
  private void doSomething(String cmd, int attempts) {
    System.out.println("Ladies and gentlemen, I will now "
      + cmd + " " + attempts + " times!");

    for (int i = 0; i < attempts; i++) {
      System.out.println(cmd);
    }
    mostRecentCmd = cmd;
  }

  public static void main(String[] args) {
    try {
      MyApp m = new MyApp();
      m.doSomething("move");
      m.doSomething("stand up", 3);
    } catch (BusinessException be) {
      System.out.println("Handling exception gracefully...");
    }
  }
}
```

The program creates a new instance of MyApp, and then calls both variants of the doSomething() method, each time with a different requested action. To enable convenient repetition, the class stores the most recent command in a private field each time it is asked to do something. The simple BusinessException type is defined as in Listing 10.2.

Listing 10.2 *BusinessException*

```
package business;

public class BusinessException extends RuntimeException {
  public BusinessException(String message) {
    super(message);
  }
}
```

Now we're ready to look at the contents of the org.aspectj.lang and org.aspectj.lang.reflect packages.

10.1 Package *org.aspectj.lang*

The main focus of this package is on making information about matched join points available within the body of advice through the special variables thisJoinPoint, thisJoinPointStaticPart, and thisEnclosingJoinPoint

`StaticPart`. These variables are the entry points to a rich reflective API. Also defined in this package are the AspectJ runtime exceptions.

10.1.1 org.aspectj.lang.JoinPoint

Purpose

This interface provides both statically and dynamically determined contextual information at a join point. If you only need the static information about a join point, use an instance of `org.aspectj.lang.JoinPoint.StaticPart` instead (`thisJoinPointStaticPart`).

Methods

Table 10.1   Available Methods on *org.aspectj.lang.JoinPoint*

JoinPoint Methods	
`Object[]`	`getArgs()`
`String`	`getKind()`
`Signature`	`getSignature()`
`SourceLocation`	`getSourceLocation()`
`JoinPoint.StaticPart`	`getStaticPart()`
`Object`	`getTarget()`
`Object`	`getThis()`
`String`	`toLongString()`
`String`	`toShortString()`
`String`	`toString()`

Obtaining

The special variable `thisJoinPoint` is bound to an instance of this type when within any advice body. This includes code lexically within the advice (for example, an anonymous inner class).

Using

Use of the `JoinPoint` interface is demonstrated in Listing 10.3, by an aspect used to monitor method executions in `business.MyApp` (introduced in Listing 10.1).

Listing 10.3 Monitoring Aspect That Exercises the *thisJoinPoint* Variable

```
package monitor.aspects;

import org.aspectj.lang.*;
import org.aspectj.lang.reflect.*;
import java.lang.reflect.Array;

public aspect AppMonitor {
  pointcut activity() : execution(* *(..)) &&
    !within(AppMonitor);

  before() : activity() {
    StringBuffer buff = new StringBuffer(
      "\nMONITOR::thisJoinPoint :\n" +
      "-----------------------\n");

    // First, the 'simpler' methods ...
    buff.append(
      "MONITOR::\ttoString() --> " +
      thisJoinPoint.toString() + "\n");
    buff.append(
      "MONITOR::\ttoShortString() --> " +
      thisJoinPoint.toShortString() + "\n");
    buff.append(
      "MONITOR::\ttoLongString()   --> " +
      thisJoinPoint.toLongString() + "\n");
    buff.append(
      "MONITOR::\tgetThis() --> " +
      thisJoinPoint.getThis() + "\n");
    buff.append(
      "MONITOR::\tgetTarget() --> " +
      thisJoinPoint.getTarget() + "\n");
    buff.append(
      "MONITOR::\tgetKind() --> " +
      thisJoinPoint.getKind() + "\n");

    // The following methods return values that
    // require some degree of processing...
    processArgs(
      thisJoinPoint.getArgs(), buff);
    processSignature(
      thisJoinPoint.getSignature(), buff);
    processSourceLocation(
      thisJoinPoint.getSourceLocation(), buff);

    // Finally, send the cumulative information gleaned
    // out to the console
    System.out.println(buff.toString());
  }

  private void processArgs(Object[] arguments,
                    StringBuffer buff) {
    buff.append("MONITOR::\tgetArgs() -->");
```

```
    for (int i = 0; i < arguments.length; i++) {
      Object o = arguments[i];
      Class clazz = o.getClass();

      if (clazz.isArray()) {
        clazz = clazz.getComponentType();
        int elementCount = Array.getLength(o);
        if (elementCount == 0) {
          buff.append("\nMONITOR::\t\targ " +
          i + " : <zero length array>");
        } else {
          for (int j = 0; j < elementCount; j++) {
            buff.append(
              "\nMONITOR::\t\targ " +
              i + " [" +
              j + "] : value=" +
              Array.get(o, j));
          }
        }
      } else {
        buff.append(
          "\nMONITOR::\t\targ " +
          i + " : value=" + o);
      }
    }
  }
}

  private void processSignature(Signature sig,
                                StringBuffer buff) {
    // Later...
  }

  private void processSourceLocation(SourceLocation sloc,
                                     StringBuffer buff) {
    // Later...
  }
}
```

The majority of method returns can be sent straight out to the console, albeit with some minor formatting. The exceptions to this are the products of calls to getArguments(), getSignature(), and getSourceLocation(), which require some additional work on the returned objects. The methods to process the return from getSignature() and getSourceLocation() are left empty for now until we cover the org.aspectj.lang.Signature and org.aspectj.lang.reflect.SourceLocation types further on.

Here is the console output from a run of the business.MyApp with the three input arguments Mercury, Venus, and Earth:

```
MONITOR::thisJoinPoint :
-----------------------
MONITOR::    toString() --> execution(void
business.MyApp.main(String[]))
MONITOR::    toShortString() --> execution(MyApp.main(..))
MONITOR::    toLongString()  --> execution(public static void
business.MyApp.main(java.lang.String[]))
MONITOR::    getThis() --> null
MONITOR::    getTarget() --> null
MONITOR::    getKind() --> method-execution
MONITOR::    getArgs() -->
MONITOR::      arg 0 [0] : value=Mercury
MONITOR::      arg 0 [1] : value=Venus
MONITOR::      arg 0 [2] : value=Earth

MONITOR::thisJoinPoint :
-----------------------
MONITOR::    toString() --> execution(void
business.MyApp.doSomething(String))
MONITOR::    toShortString() -->
execution(MyApp.doSomething(..))
MONITOR::    toLongString()  --> execution(private void
business.MyApp.doSomething(java.lang.String))
MONITOR::    getThis() --> business.MyApp@1172e08
MONITOR::    getTarget() --> business.MyApp@1172e08
MONITOR::    getKind() --> method-execution
MONITOR::    getArgs() -->
MONITOR::      arg 0 : value=move
Ladies and gentlemen, I will now move

MONITOR::thisJoinPoint :
-----------------------
MONITOR::    toString() --> execution(void
business.MyApp.doSomething(String, int))
MONITOR::    toShortString() -->
execution(MyApp.doSomething(..))
MONITOR::    toLongString()  --> execution(private void
business.MyApp.doSomething(java.lang.String, int))
MONITOR::    getThis() --> business.MyApp@1172e08
MONITOR::    getTarget() --> business.MyApp@1172e08
MONITOR::    getKind() --> method-execution
MONITOR::    getArgs() -->
MONITOR::      arg 0 : value=stand up
MONITOR::      arg 1 : value=3
Ladies and gentlemen, I will now stand up 3 times!
stand up
stand up
stand up
```

Because the `activity()` pointcut matches any method execution, we get an entry for the `business.MyApp.main(String[] args)` method. Because this static method does not have a currently executing object associated with it, nor any target object, it is entirely reasonable for the `getThis()` and `getTarget()` calls to return null.

Notice that the outputs from getThis() (the currently executing object) and getTarget() (the target object) are the same. This is to be expected when an object invokes a method on itself as is the case in our simple example.

It is worthwhile considering that the this and args pointcut designators can provide, respectively, the same information that methods thisJoinPoint. getThis() and thisJoinPoint.getTarget() yield but without the overhead of a reflective call. For that reason, you should always try and use the pointcut designators if you can. Likewise, in situations where the number and type of arguments does not vary, the args pointcut designator is a better choice than thisJoinPoint.getArgs().

10.1.2 org.aspectj.lang.JoinPoint.StaticPart

Purpose

As its name suggests, this is an inner interface declared statically within org.aspectj.lang.JoinPoint. This interface is intended as a convenience to provide access to the statically determinable (available at compile time) set of context information obtainable at a join point. The use of JoinPoint. StaticPart (thisJoinPointStaticPart) is more efficient than the runtime determined information in thisJoinPoint.

Methods

Table 10.2   Available Methods on *org.aspectj.lang.JoinPoint.StaticPart*

JoinPoint.StaticPart *Methods*	
String	getKind()
Signature	getSignature()
SourceLocation	getSourceLocation()
String	toLongString()
String	toShortString()
String	toString()

Obtaining

You can obtain an instance of this type in three ways. The first way is as the return value from a call to the getStaticPart() method of an org.aspectj.lang. JoinPoint reference (that is, the thisJoinPoint variable). The second way is by

far the simpler and merely involves using the special AspectJ variable
`thisJoinPointStaticPart` in your advice code. In the same way that variable
`thisJoinPoint` is bound to the `org.aspectj.lang.JoinPoint` type, so
`thisJoinPointStaticPart` is bound to `org.aspectj.lang.JoinPoint.`
`StaticPart`. The third, and probably least common, means of obtaining one of
these is in using the special AspectJ variable `thisEnclosingJoinPoint`
`StaticPart`, as discussed in Chapter 7.

Using

All the information that you can obtain from a `org.aspectj.lang.`
`JoinPoint.StaticPart` is also available to you from a `org.aspectj.lang.`
`JoinPoint`. So the result of a `getKind()` call is the same whether you call it on
the `thisJoinPoint` variable or the `thisJoinPointStaticPart` variable.

10.1.3 org.aspectj.lang.Signature

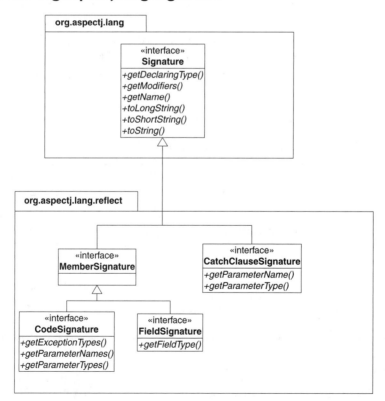

Figure 10.1   *Signature.*

Purpose

This interface represents a matched join point's signature and can be used to expose all manner of contextual details to your advice code. To provide for the different types of join-point signature that you might encounter, several interfaces extend `org.aspectj.lang.Signature` (see Figure 10.1). These subinterfaces are covered in the section devoted to the `org.aspectj.lang.reflect` package.

Methods

Table 10.3   Available Methods on *org.aspectj.lang.Signature*

Signature Methods	
Class	getDeclaringType()
String	getDeclaringTypeName()
int	getModifiers()
String	getName()
String	toLongString()
String	toShortString()
String	toString()

Obtaining

An instance of this type is returned from a call to the `getSignature()` method on the `org.aspectj.lang.JoinPoint` and `org.aspectj.lang.JoinPoint.StaticPart` types.

Using

Despite the number of interfaces that extend `org.aspectj.lang.Signature`, the parent type does still have some worth in its own right. Consider the code fragment in Listing 10.4 that contains the code for method `processSignature` (`Signature sig,StringBuffer buff`) that we left blank in Listing 10.3.

Listing 10.4   Extracting Information from a *Signature* Object

```
private void processSignature(Signature sig,
                          StringBuffer buff) {
   buff.append(
```

```
      "\nMONITOR::signature :\n" +
      "-------------------");

  buff.append(
    "\nMONITOR::\ttoString() --> " +
    sig.toString() + "\nv);
  buff.append(
    "MONITOR::\ttoLongString() --> " +
    sig.toLongString() + "\n");
  buff.append(
    "MONITOR::\ttoShortString() --> " +
    sig.toShortString() + "\n");
  buff.append(
    "MONITOR::\tgetName() --> " +
    sig.getName() + "\n");
  buff.append(
    "MONITOR::\tgetDeclaringTypeName() --> " +
    sig.getDeclaringTypeName() + "\n");
  buff.append(
    "MONITOR::\tgetDeclaringType() --> " +
    sig.getDeclaringType() + "\n");

  buff.append(
    "MONITOR::\tgetModifiers() --> ");

  int modifiers = sig.getModifiers();
  if (java.lang.reflect.Modifier.isPublic(modifiers)) {
    buff.append("is public\n");
  } else if(
    java.lang.reflect.Modifier.isProtected(modifiers)) {
    buff.append("is protected\n");
  } else if (
    java.lang.reflect.Modifier.isPrivate(modifiers)) {
    buff.append("is private\n");
  } else {
    buff.append("is default (package) access\n");
  }
}
```

With the `Signature` objects having some level of analysis carried out on them, the console output from a run of `business.MyApp` would now include the following additions:

```
MONITOR::signature :
-------------------
MONITOR::    toString() --> void
business.MyApp.main(String[])
MONITOR::    toLongString() --> public static void
business.MyApp.main(java.lang.String[])
MONITOR::    toShortString() --> MyApp.main(..)
```

```
MONITOR::      getName() --> main
MONITOR::      getDeclaringTypeName() --> business.MyApp
MONITOR::      getDeclaringType() --> class business.MyApp
MONITOR::      getModifiers() --> is public

...

MONITOR::signature :
-------------------
MONITOR::      toString() --> void
business.MyApp.doSomething(String)
MONITOR::      toLongString() --> private void
business.MyApp.doSomething(java.lang.String)
MONITOR::      toShortString() --> MyApp.doSomething(..)
MONITOR::      getName() --> doSomething
MONITOR::      getDeclaringTypeName() --> business.MyApp
MONITOR::      getDeclaringType() --> class business.MyApp
MONITOR::      getModifiers() --> is private

Ladies and gentlemen, I will now move

...

MONITOR::signature :
-------------------
MONITOR::      toString() --> void
business.MyApp.doSomething(String, int)
MONITOR::      toLongString() --> private void
business.MyApp.doSomething(java.lang.String, int)
MONITOR::      toShortString() --> MyApp.doSomething(..)
MONITOR::      getName() --> doSomething
MONITOR::      getDeclaringTypeName() --> business.MyApp
MONITOR::      getDeclaringType() --> class business.MyApp
MONITOR::      getModifiers() --> is private

...

Ladies and gentlemen, I will now stand up 3 times!
stand up
stand up
stand up
```

The handling of the integer value returned from the `getModifiers()` is only checking on the access modifier for the matched method. Numerous other static helper methods declared in `java.lang.reflect.Modifier` could have been called on to further scrutinize the join-point signature.

10.1.4 org.aspectj.lang.NoAspectBoundException

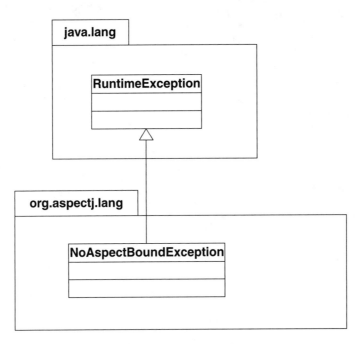

Figure 10.2   *NoAspectBoundException.*

Purpose

An exception of this type will be thrown if your AspectJ code attempts to run some advice, or obtain an aspect instance, *before an instance of the declaring aspect has been created.* We saw one way that this exception can be thrown in Chapter 9, when we called `aspectOf()` on an aspect type before an aspect instance had been created.

In Figure 10.3, a version of the monitoring aspect `AppMonitor` has been written to send a message out to the console for every method execution, including constructor executions, in the application.

```
┌─────────────────────────────────────────────────────────────────┐
│ ▣ AppMonitor.aj ✕                                              ☐  │
├─────────────────────────────────────────────────────────────────┤
│  package business;                                             ▲  │
│                                                                   │
│ ▸ public aspect AppMonitor {                                   ▫  │
│       pointcut anyMethod() :                                      │
│           execution(* *.*(..)) || execution(*.new(..));           │
│                                                                   │
│       before() : anyMethod() {                                    │
│           System.out.println(                                     │
│                   "MONITOR:: reached >" +                         │
│                   thisJoinPointStaticPart.getSignature());        │
│       }                                                           │
│   }                                                            ▼  │
│  ◁                                                       ▷        │
└─────────────────────────────────────────────────────────────────┘
```

Figure 10.3   An aspect that advises its own construction.

Unfortunately, the inclusion of the `execution(*.new(..))` part in the `anyMethod()` pointcut will try and match on the default constructor belonging to the aspect. The aspect's own `before()` advice is therefore going to try and run before the construction of the aspect itself. The result?

```
org.aspectj.lang.NoAspectBoundException: Exception while
initializing
 monitor_aspects_AppMonitor:
org.aspectj.lang.NoAspectBoundException:
 monitor_aspects_AppMonitor
   at monitor.aspects.AppMonitor.aspectOf(AppMonitor.java)
   at business.MyApp.main(MyApp.java)
Caused by: org.aspectj.lang.NoAspectBoundException:
monitor_aspects_AppMonitor
   at monitor.aspects.AppMonitor.aspectOf(AppMonitor.java)
   at monitor.aspects.AppMonitor.<init>(AppMonitor.java:3)
   at
monitor.aspects.AppMonitor.ajc$postClinit(AppMonitor.java)
   at monitor.aspects.AppMonitor.<clinit>(AppMonitor.java:3)
   ... 1 more
Exception in thread "main"
```

Notice in Figure 10.3 that the editor gutter annotation does, in fact, help indicate the presence of this self-advice. To the left of the first line of the aspect code is the before advice symbol, which can be right-clicked to reveal that this line is being advised by the `AppMonitor.before()`: `anyMethod` advice. Exploration of the Outline view is another route you can take when trying to divine the causes of an `org.aspectj.lang.NoAspectBoundException`.

10.1.5 org.aspectj.lang.SoftException

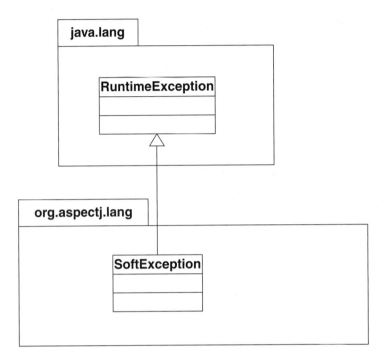

Figure 10.4   *SoftException.*

Purpose

When `declare soft` is used to soften a checked exception, the checked exception ends up being wrapped in one of these. Because this is a descendent of `java.lang.RuntimeException`, instances of this class can bubble up through the call stack all the way up to a program's `main(String[] args)` method unless your code includes the necessary handler blocks.

10.2 Package *org.aspectj.lang.reflect*

This package contains all the subtypes of `org.aspectj.lang.Signature`. Using these subtypes, it is possible to yield fine detail about the signature of any matched join point.

10.2.1 org.aspectj.lang.reflect.SourceLocation

Purpose

This interface has already been encountered in the course of the discussion on org.aspectj.lang.JoinPoint and org.aspectj.lang.JoinPoint.Static Part. Through this interface your advice can obtain details on the line of application source code that gave rise to the join point.

Methods

Table 10.4 Available Methods on *org.aspectj.lang.reflect.SourceLocation*

SourceLocation *Methods*	
String	getFileName()
int	getLine()
Class	getWithinType()

Obtaining

An instance of this type is returned from a call to the getSourceLocation() method on the org.aspectj.lang.JoinPoint and org.aspectj.lang.Join Point.StaticPart types. The returned result will be identical.

Using

Listing 10.5 contains the code for method processSourceLocation(Source Location sloc, StringBuffer buff) that was left blank in Listing 10.3.

Listing 10.5 Using the *SourceLocation* Type

```
private void processSourceLocation(SourceLocation sloc,
                                   StringBuffer buff) {
  buff.append(
    "MONITOR::sourceLocation :\n" +
    "-----------------------\n");

  buff.append(
    "MONITOR::\tgetFileName() --> " +
    sloc.getFileName() + "\n");
  buff.append(
    "MONITOR::\tgetLine() --> " +
    sloc.getLine() + "\n");
```

```
buff.append(
   "MONITOR::\tgetWithinType() --> " +
   sloc.getWithinType() + "\n");
}
```

Running `business.MyApp` with both the `Signature` and `SourceLocation` processing implemented would add the following to the original console output:

```
MONITOR::sourceLocation :
------------------------
MONITOR::     getFileName() --> MyApp.java
MONITOR::     getLine() --> 39
MONITOR::     getWithinType() --> class business.MyApp


...


MONITOR::sourceLocation :
------------------------
MONITOR::     getFileName() --> MyApp.java
MONITOR::     getLine() --> 17
MONITOR::     getWithinType() --> class business.MyApp

Ladies and gentlemen, I will now move


...


MONITOR::sourceLocation :
------------------------
MONITOR::     getFileName() --> MyApp.java
MONITOR::     getLine() --> 21
MONITOR::     getWithinType() --> class business.MyApp


...


Ladies and gentlemen, I will now stand up 3 times!
stand up
stand up
stand up
```

10.2.2 org.aspectj.lang.reflect.MemberSignature

Purpose

As presented in Figure 10.1, this interface defines no additional behavior beyond that inherited from the `org.aspectj.lang.Signature` super type. It serves to indicate that the signature at the join point is associated with members of AspectJ types, such as constructors, methods, and advice. It is unlikely that you will make direct use of this interface except possibly when testing signature instances with the Java instanceof operator.

10.2.3 org.aspectj.lang.reflect.FieldSignature

Purpose

A FieldSignature is the kind of Signature that you would use if you wanted to dynamically ascertain the type of a field at a join point matched by get and set pointcuts. The sole operation getFieldType() defined in this interface returns the java.lang.Class object for the field. Subsequent application of the methods provided by java.lang.Class can reveal to your code everything it needs to know about the field's type.

If your application can get by without needing to know the types of fields at get and set join points, there is really no need to perform the cast on the org.aspectj.lang.Signature instance. In that event, the information available from the org.aspectj.lang.Signature type would suffice.

Obtaining

When advising a field get or set join point, you can simply do a cast to FieldSignature on the return value from a call to the getSignature() method available on special variables thisJoinPoint or thisJoinPoint StaticPart.

Using

The fieldSet(Object newVal) pointcut in Listing 10.6 permits matches on field sets in the business package. By making additional use of the args primitive, it can also provide access to the new value of the field. The accompanying after advice uses both the FieldSignature type and the args value to determine both the field's type and the new value at each matched join point.

Listing 10.6   Using the *FieldSignature* Type

```
pointcut fieldSet(Object newVal) : set(* business.*.*)
   && !within(AppMonitor)
   && args(newVal);

after(Object newVal) : fieldSet(newVal) {
   Signature sig = thisJoinPointStaticPart.getSignature();
   String fieldName = sig.getName();
   String fieldType =
```

```
    ((FieldSignature) sig).getFieldType().getName();
String declaringType = sig.getDeclaringType().getName();
System.out.println(
  "Update to field "
  + declaringType
  + "."
  + fieldName
  + "("
  + fieldType
  + "). New value = "
  + newVal);
}
```

10.2.4 org.aspectj.lang.reflect.CodeSignature

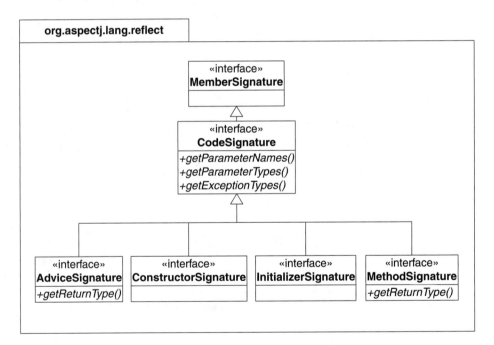

Figure 10.5   *CodeSignature.*

Purpose

This is the super interface of the `MethodSignature`, `AdviceSignature`, `ConstructorSignature`, and `InitializerSignature` types. These relationships are shown in Figure 10.5.

Methods

Table 10.5   Available Methods on *org.aspectj.lang.reflect.CodeSignature*

CodeSignature *Methods*	
Class[]	getExceptionTypes()
String[]	getParameterNames()
Class[]	getParameterTypes()

Obtaining

An instance of this type can be obtained through casting the return value from a call to the getSignature() method available on special variables thisJoinPoint or thisJoinPointStaticPart where the join point being advised is the use of a method, initializer, constructor or aspect advice.

Using

What this type adds to the API is the ability to interrogate a matched join point about its formal parameter names and types and what, if any, throwables it has stated might be thrown. In Listing 10.7, the AppMonitor aspect's aMethod() pointcut matches any method execution in the business package, and the accompanying before() advice logs the name of the method and what the names and types of its arguments are.

Listing 10.7   Using *CodeSignature* to Log Method Parameter Information

```
package monitor.aspects;
import org.aspectj.lang.reflect.*;

public aspect AppMonitor {

  pointcut aMethod() : execution(* business.*.*(..));

  before() : aMethod() {
    CodeSignature codeSig =
      (CodeSignature) thisJoinPointStaticPart.
        getSignature();

    Class[] params = codeSig.getParameterTypes();
    String[] paramNames = codeSig.getParameterNames();
    System.out.print(
      "MONITOR::\tmethod --> " + codeSig.getName());
    for (int i=0 ; i<params.length ; i++) {
      if (i == 0)
```

```
            System.out.print(" ( arguments : ");

        String name = paramNames[i];
        Class clazz = params[i];
        String clazzName =
            (clazz.isArray())
                ?
                "array of " +
                clazz.
                    getComponentType().
                        getName()
                :
                clazz.getName();

        System.out.print(" [name="
            + name
            + ", type="
            + clazzName
            + "]");

        if (i == (params.length - 1))
            System.out.print(" )");
    }// end for
    System.out.println();
  }
}
```

Compiling and running the business.MyApp program with the above aspect would produce output such as the following:

```
MONITOR::    method --> main ( arguments : [name=args,
type=array of java.lang.String] )
MONITOR::    method --> doSomething ( arguments : [name=cmd,
type=java.lang.String] )
Ladies and gentlemen, I will now move
MONITOR::    method --> doSomething ( arguments : [name=cmd,
type=java.lang.String] [name=attempts, type=int] )
Ladies and gentlemen, I will now stand up 3 times!
stand up
stand up
stand up
```

10.2.5 org.aspectj.lang.reflect.MethodSignature

An extra piece of information that we might want to log about method executions is the return type. Although it is not possible to achieve this using org.aspectj.lang.CodeSignature, it is possible if we successfully cast an org.aspectj.lang.Signature to this kind of CodeSignature (see Figure

10.5). At present, a need to know the return type of a method is the only reason you would want to use this type.

Methods

Table 10.6 Available Methods on *org.aspectj.lang.reflect.MethodSignature*

MethodSignature Methods	
Class	getReturnType()

Obtaining

As with all the children of `org.aspectj.lang.Signature`, an instance of this type can be obtained through simple casting within code that advises the use of a method.

Using

A slight modification to Listing 10.7, replacing the cast to `CodeSignature` with a cast to `MethodSignature`, would be all that is required to successfully invoke `getReturnType()` on the `codeSig` variable. The `getName()` method on `java.lang.Class` could then be used to obtain the name of each executed method's return type to the output log.

10.2.6 org.aspectj.lang.reflect.AdviceSignature

This is a direct counterpart to `MethodSignature` described in the preceding section. It provides one extra piece of behavior above that inherited from `CodeSignature`, which is again the return type. Instead of the return type of a method, however, this will enable your advice code to discover the return type of advice executions. For before and after advice, `getReturnType()` will always return `void`. It is only for around advice that a return type will be available that *might* not be void.

Methods

Table 10.7 Available methods on *org.aspectj.lang.reflect.AdviceSignature*

AdviceSignature	Methods
Class	getReturnType()

Obtaining

An instance of `AdviceSignature` is returned from `getSignature()` when the currently matched join point represents an advice execution.

Using

Consider the aspect shown in Listing 10.8. Its named pointcut `advice()` uses the `adviceexecution()` primitive pointcut to match the execution of any advice.

Listing 10.8   Using *AdviceSignature* to Determine Return Types of Advice

```
package monitor.aspects;

import org.aspectj.lang.reflect.*;

aspect AspectMonitor {
  pointcut advice() :
    adviceexecution() && within(AppMonitor);

  before() : advice() {
    AdviceSignature aSig =
      (AdviceSignature)
      thisJoinPointStaticPart.getSignature();
    String aName = aSig.getName();
    Class clazz = aSig.getReturnType();
    System.out.println(
      "MONITORMONITOR::\tadvice "
      + aName
      + " returns a "
      + clazz.getName());
  }
}
```

10.2.7 ConstructorSignature *and* InitializerSignature

The final two subtypes of `CodeSignature` only merit mentioning in passing because they currently (AspectJ 1.2) provide no additional behavior to that inherited from super types. This will not necessarily always be the case, and it is possible that extra API operations may end up here in a future release. One way in which these interfaces can help is when used in conjunction with the Java `instanceof` operator to test the type of a join point from inside advice.

10.2.8 org.aspectj.lang.reflect.CatchClauseSignature

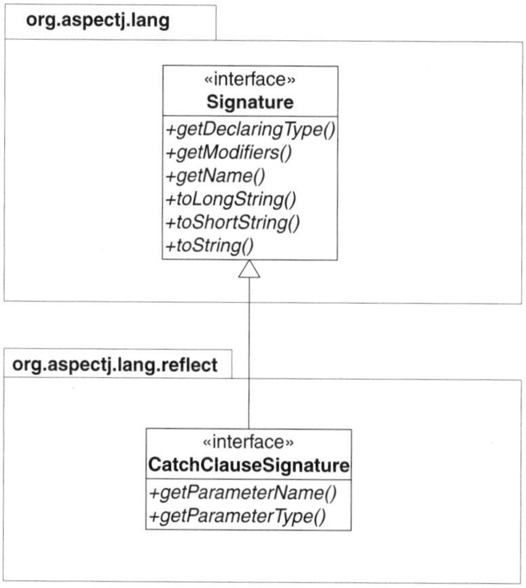

Figure 10.6   *CatchClauseSignature.*

Purpose

This type directly extends the `org.aspectj.lang.Signature`, and allows your advice code to access the type and name of the exception object being handled by a catch block. The interface makes only static information about the exception available; so if you want to interrogate an actual exception object at run-time, you must make use of the `args` primitive in your pointcut declaration.

Methods

Table 10.8   Available methods on *org.aspectj.lang.reflect.CatchClauseSignature*

CatchClauseSignature Methods	
String	getParameterName()
Class	getParameterType()

Obtaining

You can only obtain instances of this type by the appropriate casting of `org.aspectj.lang.Signature` within code advising exception handlers.

Using

Listing 10.9 shows two aspects that can be compiled with the `business.MyApp` class to demonstrate the use of `CatchClauseSignature`. Aspect `TestCatch ClauseSig` has a simple pointcut and advice that intercepts any execution of the `MyApp` class' `doSomething()` method and replaces its normal behavior with the raising of a runtime exception of type `business.BusinessException` (Listing 10.2). This approach means that the exception-handling capabilities of the `business.MyApp` class can be exercised for test purposes without the need to pollute the class' source code and so keeps testing nicely separated from core functionality. With this aspect in place, the `AppMonitor` aspect can be updated—with pointcut `problemHandling` `(Throwable t)`—to capture any handlers (that is, catch blocks) that take a `java.lang.Throwable` or any of its descendents.

Listing 10.9   Using *CatchClauseSignature* to Find the Type of a Caught Exception

```
package business;

import org.aspectj.lang.reflect.*;
import business.BusinessException;

aspect TestCatchClauseSig {
  pointcut doing() : execution(* business.*.do*(..))
    && !within(TestCatchClauseSig);

  void around() : doing() {
    throw new BusinessException("Surprise !!!!");
  }
}

public aspect AppMonitor {
  pointcut problemHandling(Throwable t) :
    handler(Throwable+) && args(t);

  before(Throwable t) : problemHandling(t) {
    CatchClauseSignature cSig =
     (CatchClauseSignature)
      thisJoinPointStaticPart.getSignature();

    System.out.println(
      "MONITOR::\tCaught a "
      + cSig.getParameterType().getName());
    System.out.println(
      "MONITOR::\t(message is \""
      + t.getMessage() + "\")");
  }
}
```

Using `args` in the declaration of the `problemHandling(Throwable)` point-cut means that advice code can get hold of the `Throwable` object during the run of the application. In our simple example, the `Throwable` has its `getMessage()` method invoked to discern the reason for its raising.

After a build and run, the following output should be expected:

```
MONITOR::    Caught a business.BusinessException
MONITOR::    (message is "Surprise !!!!")
Handling exception gracefully...
```

The `CatchClauseSignature` interface provides static type information. If the catch block in the `business.MyApp.main(String[]args)` method in Listing 10.1 handled a `java.lang.RuntimeException` instead, the output would be as follows:

```
MONITOR::    Caught a java.lang.RuntimeException
MONITOR::    (message is "Surprise !!!!")
Handling exception gracefully...
```

To determine the runtime type of the caught exception (`business.BusinessException`), you can call the `getClass()` method on the `Throwable` object provided through the `args` pointcut.

10.3 Summary

This chapter has shown how you can make use of the AspectJ runtime library in your aspects, through the types in the `org.aspect.lang` and `org.aspectj.lang.reflect` packages. The flexibility and reusability afforded to your code in adopting the runtime API needs to be weighed against the performance overhead that will inevitably be incurred because of their reliance on Java reflection.

PART 3

Putting It All Together

We hope by now you are excited about what AspectJ and AJDT can do for you, and are beginning to get to grips with the language. So how do you go about trying these ideas out on your own projects? This is the theme of the third part of the book, "putting it all together." In Chapter 11, we discuss a staged plan for adopting AspectJ that has worked well for many teams we have worked with. We also show you a few tips and tricks in AJDT that can help make the initial introduction of aspects into a project as painless as possible.

As you start working more and more with AspectJ, you will want to share aspects with your colleagues and even with other projects in your organization. In Chapter 12, we show you how to create and use aspect libraries, integrate AspectJ into Ant-based build systems, and use the Visualizer introduced briefly in Part 1 to gain a whole-project understanding of the effects of your aspects.

We close this part of the book in Chapter 13 with a brief look at how you go about finding potential aspects—in the code or in the design.

CHAPTER 11

Adopting AspectJ

Where do you begin when looking to use AspectJ on a project, and what kinds of aspects should you be writing? This chapter outlines the adoption process that we recommend for individuals and project teams new to aspect-oriented programming and to AspectJ. After a brief discussion of the different types of aspects you may encounter, the bulk of the chapter comprises examples of aspects of increasing levels of sophistication. Along the way, we also show you some features of AJDT that you haven't encountered yet.

11.1 The Adoption Process

Most project teams that we work with progress through the same set of stages in adopting AspectJ. These stages are designed to make sure that you can run before you can walk, that you have a good experience with AspectJ rather than rushing head-long into the unknown, and that risk and uncertainty are kept to manageable levels.

In the first stage, aspects are used to enforce policies (or rules) that you want to hold true in your design and implementation, but not to actually implement those policies. At the second stage of adoption, aspects are additionally used to implement common crosscutting concerns such as tracing, logging, failure han-dling, monitoring, and so on. We call these "infrastructure" or "auxiliary" aspects—it is not (normally) the primary purpose of your application to do these things, yet they are commonplace nevertheless.

The third stage of adoption uses aspects in the core of your application. We call these "core" aspects (because they are a core part of the application), or sometimes "business" aspects (when they implement business concerns).

As you and your project team progress through these stages, you will find that the way you think about the software you are developing changes, and aspect-oriented thinking will start to pervade your design and architecture.

The phases of adoption are summarized in Figure 11.1.

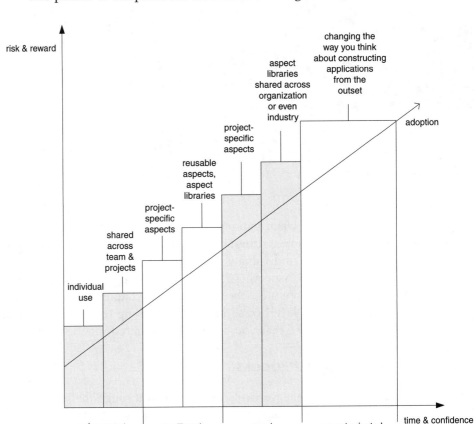

Figure 11.1   The phases of adoption.

11.1.1 Enforcement Aspects

Simple enforcement aspects—such as policing component boundaries to ensure that no inadvertent component dependencies are created, or the ubiquitous "don't use System.out"—are a great place to start using AspectJ. You can write enforcement aspects and include them in your own private builds of the project without having to sell (or tell) any of your team mates or project managers on the idea at first. Another common activity at this stage of adoption is for individual developers to write their own private aspects that assist them in debugging and problem diagnosis.

These aspects enable you to get used to the AspectJ tools, and give you a working knowledge of the core of AspectJ's pointcut language. Later on, when you have a set of aspects that you are finding useful, you can start to share them with the rest of the team, and perhaps even include them as part of the standard project build. (This is very easy to do if the project uses Ant, because AspectJ provides a set of Ant tasks ready for use out-of-the-box—these are discussed in the next chapter.) There is no need for your project to ship the AspectJ runtime library (`aspectjrt.jar`) and no runtime dependency on AspectJ. Therefore, this stage of the adoption process can be undertaken with little or no risk.

Some of the enforcement aspects you write will have applicability beyond your current project. You can take these with you to your next project, and could even consider creating a simple aspect library out of them to share with other groups in your organization.

11.1.2 Infrastructure/Auxiliary Aspects

Infrastructure aspects are a good next step for adopting AspectJ. The key hurdles to be overcome when moving from enforcement aspects to a mixture of enforcement and infrastructure aspects are that the whole project team must now become aware that some application functions are being dealt with by aspects, and that the project acquires a runtime dependency on AspectJ. Infrastructure aspects have some properties that make them ideal for making this transition— they come with an easily understood business case, and they don't require wholesale changes in the everyday tools used by project members.

Take as a simple example the implementation of application-level tracing using aspects. Most of the developers on the project team just need to be aware that tracing is being handled by an aspect, and that therefore they don't need to hand code tracing statements into their source files. Other than that, they can carry on as usual, using their normal development tools and processes. One or two people on the project team will write the tracing aspect(s) using the AspectJ tools, and these can be most conveniently packaged as an aspect library. The project's build needs to be altered (if you didn't do it already in the enforcement stage) to either compile all the project source files using AspectJ, or more commonly at this point, to build the project's Jar files as normal, and then add an additional build step that uses AspectJ's binary weaving capabilities (see Chapter 12). The additional step links the application Jar files with the aspects in the aspect library, to produce the final application including the tracing support.

Your application will need to include the AspectJ runtime library, `aspectjrt.jar`, in its distribution after you have done this.

Implementing something like application-level tracing with aspects means that you are using the technology in a low-risk portion of the application. (Tracing is seldom a business-critical function.) It is also easy to make the case for the investment. Assume that over the duration of your project, implementing tracing by hand, each developer spends 10 minutes per source file adding in the initial tracing implementation, and that subsequent maintenance (changing the way you call tracing, or just keeping up with normal refactoring of methods and parameters as the application develops) takes an additional 10 minutes per source file to address. Now multiply that effort by the number of source files in your project, and you will find that even on a relatively small project with 100 source files, you're spending nearly a person-week adding tracing. You can certainly write a tracing aspect and make the necessary changes to your build scripts in that time or less. Do the sums for larger projects with 500, 1,000, or even 10,000 source files (we have used AspectJ with projects that big and then some) and you will quickly see that the return on investment for the aspect-based approach is excellent. Moreover, in our own tests of application code with handwritten and maintained tracing statements, we found that they are at best 80 percent accurate (with cut-and-paste errors, missing entry or exit traces, unguarded calls to the tracing service, and so on all occurring relatively frequently). The AspectJ solution will, of course, be 100 percent accurate, not just now, but for all time as your application source evolves. If you have to service and support the application, and use the trace records as a vehicle for doing it, this improvement in accuracy can in itself make a significant contribution to reducing your service costs.

11.1.3 Business/Core Aspects

At the third stage of adoption, the project team becomes fully bought in to using AspectJ. All the team members need to be conversant with AspectJ, and are probably using AspectJ-based tools to develop and test the application. This is the reason that we recommend a gradual exposure to AspectJ through enforcement and infrastructure aspects first, because attempting to change an entire team's working practices in one fell swoop is prone to failure. In this stage, core pieces of the application's function are captured and modularized using aspects, the confidence to do this coming from the successes the project team has had in the previous two stages.

On larger projects with subteams working on individual components, the decision to progress to stage three adoption of AspectJ can often be taken on a component-by-component basis. This is another good strategy for managing risk and avoiding a whole-project change at one time.

11.1.4 Aspect-Oriented Design and Architecture

A project team that has successfully progressed through all the first three stages of adoption will gradually start to acquire the judgment and experience that enables them to produce designs including aspects from the very beginning (as opposed to refactoring an OO-based design and implementation after the fact). Such a team is sensitive to the notion of crosscutting concerns and can not only spot them early, but can also plan for their efficient implementation. We return to this idea in Chapter 13.

11.2 Different Types of Aspects

In the previous section we discussed different kinds of aspects that you might write at the different stages of adoption (or maturity) in your AspectJ usage. These were enforcement aspects, infrastructure (or auxiliary) aspects, and business (or core) aspects. Sometimes we hear people ask questions such as, "So how many aspects do you think there are? Have we found them all yet?" To us, this is indicative of a misunderstanding about the different types of aspects and the roles that they play. In this section, therefore, we briefly discuss three types of aspects that arise in each of the three stages of adoption. These are general-purpose aspects, domain-specific aspects, and application-specific aspects.

11.2.1 General-Purpose Aspects

General-purpose aspects are the kind that most people have in mind when they ask "so how many aspects do you think there are?" These are aspects that are likely to occur in any application—not just things like tracing, logging, and error and exception handling, but also aspects that solve common design problems such as how to connect subjects and observers. One day this set of aspects will grow into a JDK-like set of libraries.

A good source of examples of general-purpose aspects is the work by Jan Hannemann and Gregor Kiczales on design patterns in AspectJ (Hannemann 2002). You can view the original design patterns by Erich Gamma et al. (Gamma 1995) as describing a set of commonly occurring problems in object-oriented designs (together, of course, with a set of recommended solutions, or patterns, for solving them). What Jan Hannemann and Gregor Kiczales have done is to take that same set of problem statements and see whether aspect-orientation could offer any new (and better) solutions. The answer in many cases was yes. In some cases the improvement was reflected in a new solution structure with fewer or different participants; in other cases only the implementation of the classes in the originally proposed solution changed.

11.2.2 Domain-Specific Aspects

Domain specific aspects are aspects that are generally reusable within a given domain, but not in any arbitrary application. The domain of enterprise application development, for example, has some well-known candidate aspects such as transaction management, persistence, and security. Other aspects might be particular to the banking, insurance, or retail industries.

With a little work, the Hibernate aspects we have been looking at so far in the book could be turned into reusable aspects that could be applied in any application using Hibernate. These aspects would be particular to the domain of Hibernate-based persistence—useful in any project using Hibernate, but not for applications outside of that scope.

There are many more domain-specific aspects than general-purpose aspects, but they tend to be cited less often because unless you work in that domain, the example may not be immediately recognizable to you.

11.2.3 Application-Specific Aspects

Application specific aspects, just like application-specific classes, are the most numerous kind. We cannot tell you what kinds of aspects you will find in your application in this category, but as you become attuned to the ideas of aspect orientation, rest assured that you will find them. Application-specific aspects range in their crosscutting scope from aspects that affect a large number of types in the system, to inner aspects that handle crosscutting concerns within a single class or interface. The `PolicyChangeNotification` and `SerializationBasedPersistence` aspects that we developed in Part 1 are both application-specific aspects.

11.3   Enforcement Aspect Examples

This section presents some examples of enforcement aspects. If you are working on a project as part of a team, using the *Java Development Tools* (JDT) within Eclipse, then a good nonintrusive way to start using enforcement aspects in your own private workspace is to set up a new AspectJ project alongside the existing Java one.

Let's roll the clock back to the start of Part 1, when Simple Insurance was just a plain Java project in Eclipse, and show you how to do this. In Figure 11.2, we have launched the New AspectJ Project Wizard, and entered a project name of **Simple Insurance Aspects**. Clicking **Next** takes you to the Java Settings page, where we have clicked **Add Folder** to add a source folder to the project. Setting a source folder in this way also updates the output folder of the project so that class files are generated in the `bin` directory. Click **Finish** to close the wizard. The aspects that we write will go into the `src` folder that we just created.

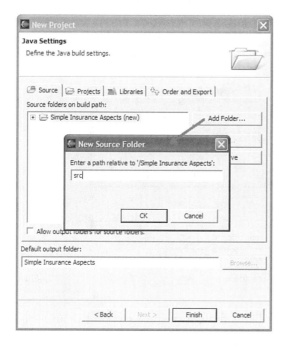

Figure 11.2 Setting a source folder.

The next step is to link the source folder from the Simple Insurance project into our newly created project, using a *linked source folder*. Bring up the Properties dialog box for the project you just created, and select the **Source** tab of the Java Build Path page. Click the **Add Folder** button once more, and in the dialog box that appears click **Create New Folder**. You should be looking at a dialog box like that shown in Figure 11.3.

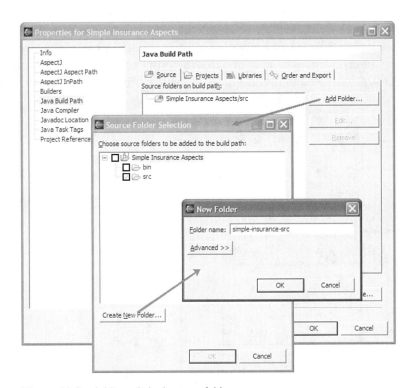

Figure 11.3   Adding a linked source folder.

Name the folder something like **simple-insurance-src**, and then click **Advanced >>**. Figure 11.4 shows that the appearance of the New Folder dialog box changes to reveal some additional options. In the example in Figure 11.4, we have done the following:

○ Checked the option **Link to folder in the file system**.

○ Clicked **Variables** to open Select Path Variable dialog box.

○ Clicked **New** and defined the new variable WORKSPACE_ROOT that points to the root directory for of the Eclipse workspace (for example, c:/eclipse/workspace).

○ Still in the Select Path Variable dialog box with WORKSPACE_ROOT selected, clicked **Extend** and specified the path to the src folder in the Simple Insurance project.

○ Clicked **OK** to close the Variable Extension and Select Path Variable dialog box.

We can then click **OK** to close the New Folder dialog box, and then click **OK** again to close the Source Folder Selection dialog box.

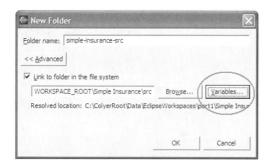

Figure 11.4   Specifying the link location.

If the source code in the folder being linked to has any library dependencies, they need to be added as library dependencies in the AspectJ project. In this case, the `insurance.ui` code in Simple Insurance depends on `swt.jar` and `jface.jar`, so they must be added as library dependencies in the Simple Insurance Aspects project. When that is done, you can close the project Properties dialog box. At this stage the Package Explorer should look like the one shown in Figure 11.5.

Figure 11.5   Linked source folder in the Package Explorer.

Notice that the `simple-insurance-src` folder has a small arrow decoration to indicate that it is a linked folder. Expanding the node we see all the content of the `src` folder from the Simple Insurance project. When you build the AspectJ project, it generates class files in its own `bin` directory. The Java project itself remains untouched by this process, so all of your CVS commits and updates can proceed as normal.

Now we're ready to go ahead and write some enforcement aspects!

11.3.1 Use of System.out

Listing 11.1 shows a very basic aspect that will catch not only usages of the common idiom `System.out.println()` or `System.err.println()`, but also anyone attempting to assign the standard error or output stream to a variable (presumably as a destination for subsequent output).

Listing 11.1   Policing *System.out*—Version 1

```
public aspect SystemOutputStreamsMonitor {

  pointcut syserrAccess() : get(* System.err);
  pointcut sysoutAccess() : get(* System.out);

  declare warning : syserrAccess() || sysoutAccess() :
    "Please don't write messages to System out or err.";
}
```

At this stage in the proceedings, we added this aspect into the Simple Insurance Aspects project (in the `src` folder) thinking, "I wonder if we will find any violations...." Figure 11.6 shows the result.

	Description	Resource	In Folder	Location
	0 errors, 18 warnings, 0 infos			
⚠	Please don't write messages to System out or err.	DeletePolicyListener.java	Simple Insurance Aspects/simple-insurance-src/in...	line 31
⚠	Please don't write messages to System out or err.	PolicyEditor.java	Simple Insurance Aspects/simple-insurance-src/in...	line 320
⚠	Please don't write messages to System out or err.	SimpleInsuranceApp.java	Simple Insurance Aspects/simple-insurance-src/in...	line 224
⚠	Please don't write messages to System out or err.	SimpleInsuranceApp.java	Simple Insurance Aspects/simple-insurance-src/in...	line 225
⚠	Please don't write messages to System out or err.	SimpleInsuranceApp.java	Simple Insurance Aspects/simple-insurance-src/in...	line 228
⚠	Please don't write messages to System out or err.	SimpleInsuranceApp.java	Simple Insurance Aspects/simple-insurance-src/in...	line 232
⚠	Please don't write messages to System out or err.	SimpleInsuranceApp.java	Simple Insurance Aspects/simple-insurance-src/in...	line 262
⚠	Please don't write messages to System out or err.	SimpleInsuranceApp.java	Simple Insurance Aspects/simple-insurance-src/in...	line 293
⚠	Please don't write messages to System out or err.	SimpleInsuranceApp.java	Simple Insurance Aspects/simple-insurance-src/in...	line 302
⚠	Please don't write messages to System out or err.	SimpleInsuranceApp.java	Simple Insurance Aspects/simple-insurance-src/in...	line 319
⚠	Please don't write messages to System out or err.	SimpleInsuranceApp.java	Simple Insurance Aspects/simple-insurance-src/in...	line 328
⚠	Please don't write messages to System out or err.	SimpleInsuranceApp.java	Simple Insurance Aspects/simple-insurance-src/in...	line 345
⚠	Please don't write messages to System out or err.	SimpleInsuranceApp.java	Simple Insurance Aspects/simple-insurance-src/in...	line 354
⚠	Please don't write messages to System out or err.	SimpleInsuranceApp.java	Simple Insurance Aspects/simple-insurance-src/in...	line 371
⚠	Please don't write messages to System out or err.	SimpleInsuranceApp.java	Simple Insurance Aspects/simple-insurance-src/in...	line 380
⚠	Please don't write messages to System out or err.	SimpleInsuranceApp.java	Simple Insurance Aspects/simple-insurance-src/in...	line 397

Figure 11.6   Warnings.

Clicking any warning or the links in the Outline view takes you directly to the offending line of code in the Simple Insurance project. Notice the warning triangles in the Package Explorer, too (see Figure 11.7), that show up under the Simple Insurance Aspects project.

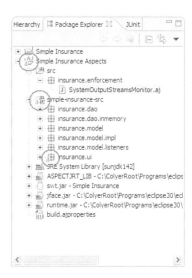

Figure 11.7   Warnings in the Package Explorer.

Try adding this aspect to one of your existing projects and see how many warnings it produces—you will be surprised. If your application has some portions where it *is* allowed to write to the System streams, such as in a message printing module, you can extend the aspect to cover those cases quite simply as shown in Listing 11.2.

Listing 11.2   Policing *System.out*—Version 2

```
public aspect SystemOutputStreamsMonitor {

    pointcut syserrAccess() : get(* System.err);
    pointcut sysoutAccess() : get(* System.out);

    pointcut inMessagePrintingModule() :
        within (insurance.logger..*);

    declare warning : (syserrAccess() || sysoutAccess()) &&
                      !inMessagePrintingModule() :
        "Please don't write messages to System out or err.";
}
```

11.3.2 Preserving Component Modularity

The Simple Insurance application is structured in a set of modules with clearly divided responsibilities, as illustrated in Figure 11.8. How can we ensure that as the program evolves we don't inadvertently create a dependency from the model on the user interface component, or start calling Hibernate APIs outside of the persistence package?

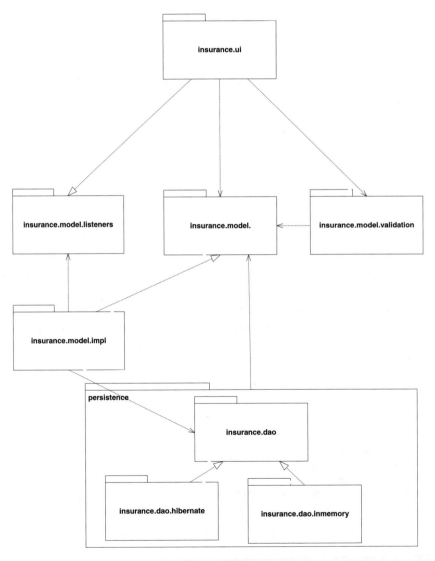

Figure 11.8 Structure of the Simple Insurance application.

AspectJ enables us to write enforcement aspects that will ensure the integrity of the design is maintained as the code evolves. When working with an application such as this, it is often a good idea to start with a "system architecture" aspect that encapsulates knowledge of how the various design components are realized in the source code. That way many aspects can refer to the system architecture, without having to redefine it in each one. Listing 11.3 shows a system architecture aspect for the Simple Insurance application.

Listing 11.3 *SystemArchitecture Aspect*

```
package insurance;

public aspect SystemArchitecture {

    public pointcut uiCall() :
      call(* insurance.ui..*(..)) ||
      call(insurance.ui..new(..));

    public pointcut modelCall() :
      (call(* insurance.model..*(..)) ||
       call(insurance.model..new(..)))
        && !javaLangObjectCall();

    public pointcut modelImplCall() :
      call(* insurance.model.impl..*(..)) ||
      call(insurance.model.impl..new(..));

    public pointcut modelListenersCall() :
      call(* insurance.model.listeners..*(..)) ||
      call(insurance.model.listeners..new(..));

    public pointcut modelValidationCall() :
      (call(* insurance.model.validation..*(..)) ||
       call(insurance.model.validation..*.new(..)))
        && !javaLangObjectCall();

    public pointcut daoCall() :
      call(* insurance.dao..*(..)) ||
      call(insurance.dao..new(..));

    public pointcut inMemoryDaoCall() :
      call(* insurance.dao.inmemory..*(..)) ||
      call(insurance.dao.inmemory..new(..));

    public pointcut hibernateDaoCall() :
      call(* insurance.dao.hibernate..*(..)) ||
      call(insurance.dao.hibernate..new(..));

    public pointcut inUI() : within(insurance.ui.*);

    public pointcut inModel() : within(insurance.model.*);
```

```
    public pointcut inModelImpl() :
        within(insurance.model.impl.*);

    public pointcut inModelListeners() :
        within(insurance.model.listeners.*);

    public pointcut inDAOLayer() : within(insurance.dao.*);

    public pointcut inInMemoryDAO() :
        within(insurance.dao.inmemory.*);

    public pointcut inHibernateDAO() :
        within(insurance.dao.hibernate.*);

    public pointcut inAnyDAO() :
        inInMemoryDAO() || inHibernateDAO();

    public pointcut inModelValidation() :
        within(insurance.model.validation..*);

    public pointcut inTestCase() :
        within(junit.framework.TestCase+);

    pointcut javaLangObjectCall() :
        call(* java.lang.Object.*(..));
}
```

We have a relatively simple mapping where each component maps to a set of packages with the same unique prefix. Your application's mapping may be more complex. It doesn't matter; the whole point of the SystemArchitecture aspect is to encapsulate those details. The SystemArchitecture aspect enables us to write pointcut expressions that refer to the components without knowing the details of their makeup.

Given these basic definitions, we can now go ahead and write an aspect to ensure that we do not inadvertently create unwanted dependencies between components and violate the intended design of the system. We will only show how to match method calls made between components, but you could easily extend this to cover field accesses if needed. Listing 11.4 shows the component dependency aspect.

Listing 11.4   Aspect to Enforce Component Modularity

```
package insurance.enforcement;
import insurance.SystemArchitecture;

public aspect PermittedComponentInteractions {
```

```
declare warning : SystemArchitecture.uiCall() &&
                  !SystemArchitecture.inUI()
  : "No calls into the user interface";

declare warning : SystemArchitecture.modelImplCall() &&
                  !SystemArchitecture.inModelImpl()
  : "Please use interfaces in insurance.model instead";

declare warning : SystemArchitecture.modelListenersCall()
                  && !SystemArchitecture.inModelImpl()
  : "Only implementors should issue notifications";

declare warning : SystemArchitecture.modelValidationCall()
              && !(SystemArchitecture.inModelValidation()
                   || SystemArchitecture.inUI())
  : "Model validation is handled by
BusinessRulesValidation aspect and UI";

declare warning : SystemArchitecture.daoCall() &&
     !(SystemArchitecture.inModelImpl() ||
       SystemArchitecture.inAnyDAO())
   : "Only model and DAO implementors should be using the
DAO interface";

declare warning : SystemArchitecture.hibernateDaoCall()
                  && !SystemArchitecture.inHibernateDAO()
   : "Please use interfaces in insurance.dao instead";

declare warning : SystemArchitecture.inMemoryDaoCall()
                  && !SystemArchitecture.inInMemoryDAO()
   : "Please use interfaces in insurance.dao instead";

declare warning : call(* net.sf.hibernate..*(..))
                  && !within(insurance.dao.hibernate.*)
   : "No hibernate dependencies outside of
insurance.dao.hibernate package";
}
```

Take your time to read through Listing 11.4, and think just how powerful such an aspect could be in terms of preserving design integrity in your applications as they evolve over multiple iterations. Figure 11.9 shows the results the first time we added this aspect to the project. Note that we are now working directly in the Simple Insurance project, rather than in the Simple Insurance Aspects project that used a linked source folder.

Description	Resource	In Folder	Location
Please use interfaces in insurance.model instead	SimpleInsuranceFactory.java	Simple Insurance/src/insurance/model	line 20
Please use interfaces in insurance.model instead	TestAddress.java	Simple Insurance/test-src/insurance/model	line 27
Please use interfaces in insurance.model instead	TestAutoPolicy.java	Simple Insurance/test-src/insurance/model	line 59
Please use interfaces in insurance.model instead	TestAutoPolicy.java	Simple Insurance/test-src/insurance/model	line 61
Please use interfaces in insurance.model instead	TestAutoPolicy.java	Simple Insurance/test-src/insurance/model	line 72
Please use interfaces in insurance.model instead	TestAutoPolicy.java	Simple Insurance/test-src/insurance/model	line 73
Please use interfaces in insurance.model instead	TestAutoPolicy.java	Simple Insurance/test-src/insurance/model	line 74
Please use interfaces in insurance.model instead	TestAutoPolicy.java	Simple Insurance/test-src/insurance/model	line 78
Please use interfaces in insurance.model instead	TestAutoPolicy.java	Simple Insurance/test-src/insurance/model	line 82
Please use interfaces in insurance.model instead	TestAutoPolicy.java	Simple Insurance/test-src/insurance/model	line 83
Please use interfaces in insurance.model instead	TestAutoPolicy.java	Simple Insurance/test-src/insurance/model	line 87
Please use interfaces in insurance.model instead	TestAutoPolicy.java	Simple Insurance/test-src/insurance/model	line 91
Please use interfaces in insurance.model instead	TestAutoPolicy.java	Simple Insurance/test-src/insurance/model	line 92

Figure 11.9   Component modularity warnings in Problems view.

There are a lot of test case matches. We could fix this by adding
`&& !SystemArchitecture.inTestCase()` to the `declare warning` statement,
but really it points to the fact that our test cases are in the wrong package. We
have test cases for the model implementation classes in the `insurance.model`
package. Moving them to the `insurance.model.impl` package eliminates most
of the warnings. In fact, we are left with only one warning, the first one shown
in Figure 11.9. Notice as an aside how useful this view is for seeing all of the violations of the system design constraints in one place.

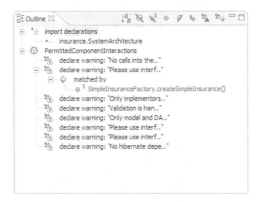

Figure 11.10   Remaining component modularity warnings.

The warning about the `SimpleInsuranceFactory` method (as shown in
Figure 11.10) is legitimate; this is the one place in the application that a call is
made to a model implementation class outside of the `insurance.model.impl`
package—to obtain an implementation of the `SimpleInsurance` façade. Later
in this chapter you learn how to remove this dependency.

Let's see what happens if a new developer joins the project who isn't familiar with the application blueprint, and writes a class something like the one
shown in Figure 11.11.

```
Someone... ×    PolicyD...    SimpleI...    SystemA...    » 15

▽public class SomeonePleaseReviewMyCode {

▽     public void editNewPolicy() {
          LifePolicyImpl policy =
              new LifePolicyImpl(new Date(),
                                 new Date(),
                                 0.0, true,
                                 null, null,
                                 false,false);
          PolicyDaoImpl dao = new PolicyDaoImpl();
          dao.insertPolicy(policy);

          Display display = new Display();
          Shell shell = new Shell(display);

          PolicyEditor editor =
              new LifePolicyEditor(shell,
                      new SimpleInsuranceImpl(),
                      policy,true);

     }

}
```

Figure 11.11   Someone please review that code.

The developer gets immediate feedback in the editor and in the Problems
view that something is wrong (see Figure 11.12).

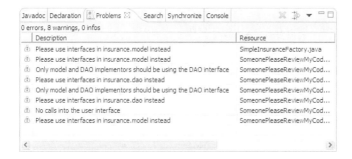

Description	Resource
Please use interfaces in insurance.model instead	SimpleInsuranceFactory.java
Please use interfaces in insurance.model instead	SomeonePleaseReviewMyCod...
Only model and DAO implementors should be using the DAO interface	SomeonePleaseReviewMyCod...
Please use interfaces in insurance.dao instead	SomeonePleaseReviewMyCod...
Only model and DAO implementors should be using the DAO interface	SomeonePleaseReviewMyCod...
Please use interfaces in insurance.dao instead	SomeonePleaseReviewMyCod...
No calls into the user interface	SomeonePleaseReviewMyCod...
Please use interfaces in insurance.model instead	SomeonePleaseReviewMyCod...

Figure 11.12   What did I do wrong?

For good measure, Figure 11.13 shows the view of the situation from the
`PermittedComponentInteractions` aspect.

Figure 11.13 Oh, that's what I did wrong then.

11.4   Infrastructure Aspect Examples

This section contains examples of infrastructure (auxiliary) aspects. We develop a tracing aspect for the Simple Insurance application, revisit exception handling, and take a look at adding support for management with JMX via an aspect.

11.4.1 Implementing a Tracing Facility

When implementing a tracing facility, there are always two primary concerns: the accuracy and completeness of the tracing information produced, and the performance overhead of the solution. The performance overhead we most care about is when tracing is turned off—this should have near-zero impact on the running system. When tracing is turned on, we assume that at least some level of reduced performance is accepted. In the examples that follow, we're just going to use log4j (http://logging.apache.org/log4j/docs/) to create our trace records, but you could use any logging framework of your choice (or even just write to standard output directly). The Hibernate framework that we have been working with throughout this book uses log4j to record trace information. This means that when the tracing facility is implemented for the Simple Insurance application, the new trace information will be seamlessly integrated with the trace information produced by Hibernate.

First we need to decide on a tracing policy. Log4j supports different levels of logging, so let's say that we will log any exception at log level WARN, entry and exit to public methods at log level INFO, and entry and exit to nonpublic methods at log level DEBUG. The first version of the tracing aspect is shown in Listing 11.5. Notice how easily the implementation follows the description of our policy.

Listing 11.5   *Tracing* Aspect—Version 1

```
package insurance.infrastructure;

import org.apache.log4j.Logger;
import org.aspectj.lang.JoinPoint;

public aspect Tracing {

  declare precedence : Tracing, *;

  private static Logger logger =
    Logger.getLogger(insurance.ui.SimpleInsuranceApp.class);

  pointcut publicMethodsAndConstructors() :
    execution(public * insurance..*(..)) ||
    execution(public insurance..new(..));

  pointcut nonPublicMethodsAndConstructors() :
    execution(!public * insurance..*(..)) ||
    execution(!public insurance..new(..));

  before() : publicMethodsAndConstructors() {
    logger.info("Entering " +
      formatTraceRecord(thisJoinPointStaticPart));
  }

  after() returning : publicMethodsAndConstructors() {
    logger.info("Exiting " +
      formatTraceRecord(thisJoinPointStaticPart));
  }

  before() : nonPublicMethodsAndConstructors() {
    logger.debug("Entering " +
      formatTraceRecord(thisJoinPointStaticPart));
  }

  after() returning : nonPublicMethodsAndConstructors() {
    logger.debug("Exiting " +
      formatTraceRecord(thisJoinPointStaticPart));
  }

  after() throwing(Throwable t) :
    publicMethodsAndConstructors() ||
    nonPublicMethodsAndConstructors()
```

```
    {
        logger.warn("Exception at " +
            formatTraceRecord(thisJoinPointStaticPart),t);
    }

    private String formatTraceRecord(JoinPoint.StaticPart sjp)
    {
        return sjp.toLongString();
    }
}
```

If you build and run the Simple Insurance application with the `Tracing` aspect included, you will find that it doesn't work, and you get a `NoAspectBoundException` as shown in Figure 11.14.

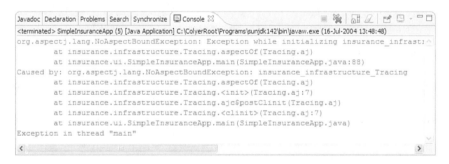

Figure 11.14   *NoAspectBoundException.*

Why is this? We have fallen into one of the most basic aspect traps. The `Tracing` aspect traces entry to all public methods and constructors. The `Tracing` aspect itself, just like all Java classes, has a default public constructor. So the `Tracing` aspect is trying to advise its own creation, before it has been created. If we got past that hurdle, we would be in trouble when the `Tracing` aspect called its `formatTraceRecord` method, too—this time because that would trigger an infinite recursion as it tried to trace entry to the `formatTraceRecord` method. You can see this clearly from the Outline view, as show in Figure 11.15.

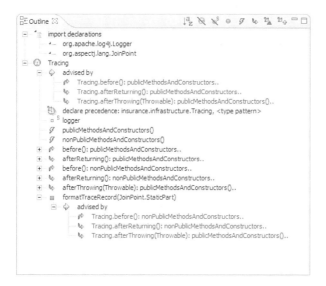

Figure 11.15   The *Tracing* aspect is advised by ... the *Tracing* aspect!

We can easily solve this problem by excluding join points in the `Tracing` aspect themselves from the trace. The changes are highlighted in Listing 11.6, where you can see we have added one new pointcut `excluded()` and used it as an extra match condition on all five pieces of advice in the `Tracing` aspect.

Listing 11.6   Revised *Tracing* Aspect

```
...
pointcut excluded() : within(Tracing);

before() : publicMethodsAndConstructors() && !excluded(){
  logger.info("Entering " +
    formatTraceRecord(thisJoinPointStaticPart));
}

after() returning : publicMethodsAndConstructors() &&
                    !excluded()
{
  logger.info("Exiting " +
    formatTraceRecord(thisJoinPointStaticPart));
}

before() : nonPublicMethodsAndConstructors()&&
          !excluded()
{
  logger.debug("Entering " +
    formatTraceRecord(thisJoinPointStaticPart));
```

```
}

after() returning : nonPublicMethodsAndConstructors()&&
                    !excluded()
{
  logger.debug("Exiting " +
    formatTraceRecord(thisJoinPointStaticPart));
}

after() throwing(Throwable t) :
  (publicMethodsAndConstructors() ||
   nonPublicMethodsAndConstructors())&&
   !excluded()

{
    logger.warn("Exception at " +
      formatTraceRecord(thisJoinPointStaticPart),t);
}
...
```

Logging of the insurance application can then be switched on by setting

```
log4j.logger.insurance=debug
```

in the `log4j.properties` file. Listing 11.7 shows an extract from the results of running the application with logging level DEBUG.

Listing 11.7   Logging at *DEBUG* Level

```
2004-07-16 14:03:31,642 [main] INFO
insurance.ui.SimpleInsuranceApp - Exiting
execution(public void insurance.model.impl.CustomerImpl.
setAddress(insurance.model.Address))
2004-07-16 14:03:31,642 [main] DEBUG
insurance.ui.SimpleInsuranceApp - Exiting
execution(protected boolean insurance.ui.CustomerEditor.
applyChanges())
2004-07-16 14:03:31,642 [main] INFO
insurance.ui.SimpleInsuranceApp - Entering
execution(public void insurance.model.impl.
SimpleInsuranceImpl.
updateCustomer(insurance.model.Customer))
2004-07-16 14:03:31,642 [main] INFO
insurance.ui.SimpleInsuranceApp - Entering
execution(public boolean insurance.model.validation.
BusinessRulesValidation.RequiresValidation.validate())
2004-07-16 14:03:31,642 [main] DEBUG
insurance.ui.SimpleInsuranceApp - Entering
```

```
execution(static java.util.Set insurance.model.validation.
BusinessRulesValidation.
access$0(insurance.model.validation.BusinessRulesValidation,
java.lang.Class))
2004-07-16 14:03:31,642 [main] DEBUG
insurance.ui.SimpleInsuranceApp - Entering
execution(private java.util.Set insurance.model.validation.
BusinessRulesValidation.getValidatorsFor(java.lang.Class))
2004-07-16 14:03:31,642 [main] DEBUG
insurance.ui.SimpleInsuranceApp - Entering
execution(private void insurance.model.validation.
BusinessRulesValidation.getValidatorsFor(java.lang.Class,
java.util.Set))
```

Looking at the log outputs, we realize it would nice if we could also see parameter and return values for methods called on the central façade interface, `SimpleInsurance`. Listing 11.8 shows the changes we need to make to do this. In this listing we have modified the `Tracing` aspect in the following ways:

❍ Added a new pointcut `simpleInsuranceMethods()` that matches the execution of methods defined in the `SimpleInsurance` interface.

❍ Added two new pieces of advice that will provide extra detail when tracing methods matched by the `simpleInsuranceMethods()` pointcut. The extra detail is obtained using `thisJoinPoint`.

❍ Modified the existing before and after advice attached to the `publicMethodsAndConstructors()` pointcut to exclude the `simpleInsuranceMethods()` that the new advice covers.

❍ Replaced the `formatTraceRecord()` with some new methods that provide better formatting.

Listing 11.8   Logging Parameters and Return Values

```
...
pointcut simpleInsuranceMethods() :
  execution(public * insurance.model.SimpleInsurance.*(..));

before() : simpleInsuranceMethods() && !excluded(){
  logger.info("Entering " +
    formatTraceRecord(thisJoinPoint));
}

after() returning(Object ret) : simpleInsuranceMethods() &&
                                !excluded() {
  logger.info("Exiting " +
    formatTraceRecord(thisJoinPointStaticPart,ret));
}
```

```
before() : publicMethodsAndConstructors() &&
          !simpleInsuranceMethods() && !excluded() {
  logger.info("Entering " +
    formatTraceRecord(thisJoinPointStaticPart));
}

after() returning : publicMethodsAndConstructors() &&
                    !simpleInsuranceMethods() && !excluded() {
  logger.info("Exiting " +
    formatTraceRecord(thisJoinPointStaticPart));
}

private String formatTraceRecord(JoinPoint.StaticPart sjp) {
  return sjp.getSignature().toLongString();
}

private String formatTraceRecord(
    JoinPoint.StaticPart sjp, Object ret) {
  return formatMethod(sjp) + "() " + ret;
}

private String formatTraceRecord(JoinPoint jp) {
  return formatMethod(jp.getStaticPart()) +
                      formatArgs(jp.getArgs());
}

private String formatMethod (JoinPoint.StaticPart sjp) {
 StringBuffer sb = new StringBuffer();
 sb.append(sjp.getSignature().getDeclaringType().getName());
 sb.append(".");
 sb.append(sjp.getSignature().getName());
 return sb.toString();
}

private String formatArgs (Object[] args) {
  StringBuffer sb = new StringBuffer();
  sb.append("(");
  for (int i = 0; i < args.length; i++) {
        sb.append(args[i]);
    if (i < args.length-1) sb.append(", ");
  }
  sb.append(")");
  return sb.toString();
}
```

Listing 11.9 shows an extract of the new log entries.

Listing 11.9   The Updated Log Output

```
2004-07-16 14:17:42,395 [main] INFO
insurance.ui.SimpleInsuranceApp-
Entering insurance.model.impl.SimpleInsuranceImpl.
updateCustomer(C1089983832212.3 EverEnd,Willit)
2004-07-16 14:17:42,395 [main] INFO
insurance.ui.SimpleInsuranceApp - Entering
public boolean insurance.model.validation.
BusinessRulesValidation.RequiresValidation.validate()
...
2004-07-16 14:17:42,395 [main] INFO
insurance.ui.SimpleInsuranceApp - Exiting
public boolean insurance.model.validation.
BusinessRulesValidation.RequiresValidation.validate()
2004-07-16 14:17:42,395 [main] INFO
insurance.ui.SimpleInsuranceApp - Entering
public void insurance.dao.inmemory.
CustomerDaoImpl.updateCustomer(insurance.model.Customer)
2004-07-16 14:17:42,395 [main] INFO
insurance.ui.SimpleInsuranceApp - Exiting public void insur-
ance.dao.inmemory.CustomerDaoImpl.updateCustomer(insurance.mo
del.Customer)
2004-07-16 14:17:42,395 [main] INFO
insurance.ui.SimpleInsuranceApp - Exiting
insurance.model.impl.SimpleInsuranceImpl.
updateCustomer() null
```

The aspect seems to be working, but it is not very efficient yet. We do all the hard work of formatting a trace record and concatenating strings to pass to the logger, regardless of whether the logger is actually logging messages at that level or not. The overhead when tracing is turned off will be too high. Imagine if you had realized this after you had just painstakingly added all those logger calls to your application by hand. Using the aspect-based approach, the solution is easy. We're going to add a single test to see whether logging is enabled at all—remember that we're interested in getting maximum performance in the case when tracing is turned off. You could imagine adding custom tests for each logging level instead if so desired. The changes are highlighted in Listing 11.10. Basically, we have

○ Added a `traceEnabled` flag that is set during static initialization of the aspect to record whether any kind of logging is enabled.

○ Defined a `shouldLog()` pointcut that checks for exclusion (using the `excluded()` pointcut) and tests the `traceEnabled` flag using an `if()` pointcut expression.

○ Modified all seven pieces of advice so that instead of using `!excluded()`, they use `shouldLog()`.

Listing 11.10   Guarding Trace Calls

```
...
private static Logger logger;
public static boolean traceEnabled;

static {
  logger =
    Logger.getLogger(insurance.ui.SimpleInsuranceApp.class);
  traceEnabled =
    (logger.getEffectiveLevel() !=
    org.apache.log4j.Level.OFF);
}

pointcut shouldLog() : !excluded() &&
  if(traceEnabled);

before() : simpleInsuranceMethods() && shouldLog(){
  logger.info("Entering " +
    formatTraceRecord(thisJoinPoint));
}

after() returning(Object ret) : simpleInsuranceMethods()
                                        && shouldLog() {
  logger.info("Exiting " +
    formatTraceRecord(thisJoinPointStaticPart,ret));
}

before() : publicMethodsAndConstructors() &&
          !simpleInsuranceMethods() && shouldLog() {
logger.info("Entering " +
    formatTraceRecord(thisJoinPointStaticPart));
}

after() returning : publicMethodsAndConstructors() &&
                    !simpleInsuranceMethods() && shouldLog()
{
  logger.info("Exiting " +
    formatTraceRecord(thisJoinPointStaticPart));
  }

before() : nonPublicMethodsAndConstructors() && shouldLog()
{
  logger.debug("Entering " +
    formatTraceRecord(thisJoinPointStaticPart));
}

after() returning : nonPublicMethodsAndConstructors()
                      && shouldLog() {
  logger.debug("Exiting " +
    formatTraceRecord(thisJoinPointStaticPart));
}

after() throwing(Throwable t) :
  (simpleInsuranceMethods() ||
```

```
    publicMethodsAndConstructors() ||
       nonPublicMethodsAndConstructors())
    && shouldLog() {
  logger.warn("Exception at " +
    formatTraceRecord(thisJoinPointStaticPart),t);
}
...
```

We have added a Boolean variable, `traceEnabled`, and initialized it to be true only when the logging level is not set to `OFF`. Notice how we test the variable using an `if()` pointcut designator (in the `shouldLog()` pointcut). Putting the test into the `shouldLog` pointcut is more efficient than including it in the body of the advice, because this avoids the need to create the `thisJoinPoint` object used by the advice body. To exploit this optimization, you also need to turn on the AspectJ Lazy thisJoinPoint compiler option.

Recall from Chapter 4 that AspectJ compiler-specific options are found under **Window > Preferences** from the workbench menu bar. Expand the AspectJ node in the left panel and click **Compiler**, and then select the **Advanced** tab. In the Preferences pane that appears, select the **Lazy thisJoinPoint** option, as shown in Figure 11.16.

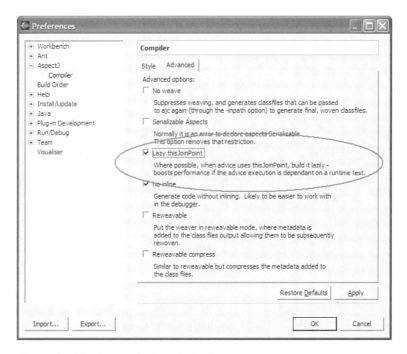

Figure 11.16   Setting the Lazy thisJoinPoint option.

What Do All the Other AspectJ Compiler Options Do?

The **No inline** option was discussed in Chapter 4—it disables the inlining of advice which enables you to breakpoint in around advice.

The **Serializable Aspects** option allows aspects to implement the `java.io.Serializable` interface. By default, this is not permitted, as discussed in Chapter 9.

Normally a class woven by AspectJ cannot be subsequently woven again to link in new aspects. Selecting the **Reweavable** option removes this restriction. It generates class files that are larger than their nonreweavable counterparts.

The **Reweavable compress** option is similar to the Reweavable option, but in addition it compresses the additional information held in the class files to reduce their size. This adds a small overhead during reweaving for decompression.

The **No Weave** option should be used with care. It generates class files that may fail verification if they are not subsequently woven. With the addition of the Reweavable option in AspectJ 1.2, there should be no real need to use the No Weave option anymore, and it may be removed in a future version of AspectJ.

If you were writing an aspect to perform tracing in a larger application, a good next step from here would be to make the `Tracing` aspect abstract, and define an abstract tracing scope pointcut that constrains all of the tracing advice. Now each component owner in the application can define a concrete subaspect and provide a specification for the tracing scope pointcut. This enables component owners to tailor tracing for their own needs, and use a custom logger if they want.

Efficient Logging

To get the minimum possible overhead in your application when a logging style aspect is used, three conditions must be met:

1. You need to test the `enabled` flag inside an `if()` pointcut expression (not in the body of the advice).

2. You need to enable the **Lazy thisJoinPoint** compiler option.

3. You need to ensure that `thisJoinPoint` is only used in before advice. (`thisJoinPointStaticPart` can be used freely anywhere.)

Before we move on, let's look at the effect of the `Tracing` aspect in the Aspect Visualiser. To open the Visualiser, choose **Window > Open Perspective,** and then select **Aspect Visualization,** as shown in Figure 11.17

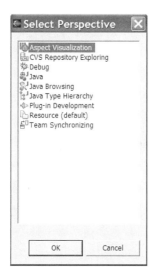

Figure 11.17   Opening the Aspect Visualization perspective.

The Visualiser will open as shown in Figure 11.18. There's more on using the Visualiser in the next chapter. For now it is enough to know that each bar represents one of the source files in the project, and the length of the bar is proportional to the number of lines in the file. Each horizontal stripe represents a point in the source file where advice is in effect. You can easily see just how much work the `Tracing` aspect is doing for us.

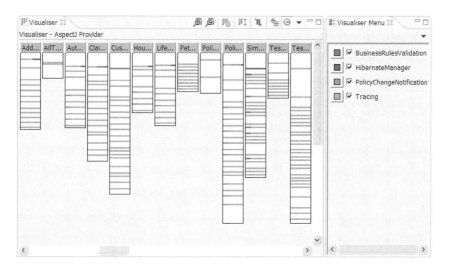

Figure 11.18   Visualization.

11.4.2 *Managing Exceptions*

The Simple Insurance application has a straightforward exception hierarchy, as shown in Figure 11.19.

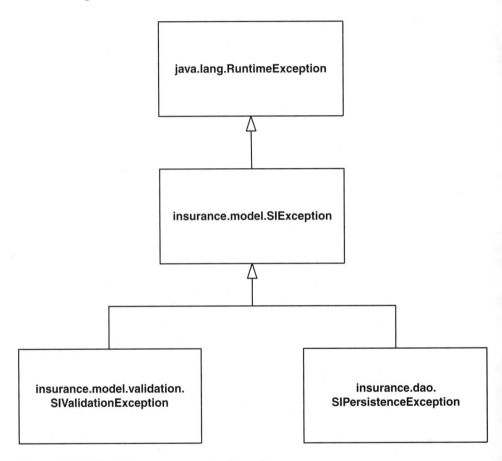

Figure 11.19   Simple Insurance exception hierarchy.

In Part 1 of this book, we showed you how to use `declare soft` and `after throwing` advice to wrap any `HibernateException` that may be thrown in the persistence layer in an `SIPersistenceException`:

```
pointcut hibernateCall() :
  call(* net.sf.hibernate..*(..));

declare soft : HibernateException : hibernateCall();

after() throwing(HibernateException hEx) : hibernateCall()
    && !target(HibernateException) {
  hEx.printStackTrace();
  SIPersistenceException siEx =
    new SIPersistenceException(hEx);
  throw siEx;
}
```

These 12 lines of source implement the entire `HibernateException` handling for the whole persistence layer. In the business logic layer, the `SimpleInsurance` façade documents that an `SIException` may be thrown by any of its methods—this could be a persistence exception throw by the persistence layer, a validation exception thrown by the validation package, or any other `SIException` thrown by one of the classes in the business logic layer. In the previous section we showed you how to make sure that any such exception gets logged. There's still a missing piece to the puzzle, however: If an `SIException` is thrown by the business layer, it will bring the whole application grinding to a halt (see Figure 11.20). In this section we complete the exception-handling strategy for the application to give a solution that spans all the tiers.

Figure 11.20   Unhandled exception.

We implement a simple scheme in the user interface layer that catches any exception thrown by a method in the `insurance.model` interface and displays a dialog box to the user (as opposed to just crashing). We're going to use a test-driven-development approach to the construction of the exception-handling aspect. This is good practice anyway, and gives us a chance to show you an example both of testing an aspect, and of how we can use aspects in testing. Listing 11.11 shows the beginnings of a test suite, `TestExceptionHandling`.

Listing 11.11   *TestExceptionHandling* Test Case

```
package insurance.ui;

import insurance.model.SIException;
import insurance.model.SimpleInsurance;
import insurance.model.SimpleInsuranceFactory;
import org.eclipse.jface.dialogs.MessageDialog;
import junit.framework.TestCase;

public class TestExceptionHandling extends TestCase {

  private SimpleInsurance simpleIns;

  public void testExceptionHandling() {
    try {
      simpleIns.createClaim();
    } catch (SIException siEx) {
     fail("This exception should already have been dealt
          with: " + siEx);
    }
    assertTrue("Dialog should be displayed to end user",
      ExceptionHandlingMonitor.aspectOf().dialogDisplayed);
  }

  protected void setUp() throws Exception {
    super.setUp();
    simpleIns =
      SimpleInsuranceFactory.createSimpleInsurance();
  }

  private static aspect ExceptionHandlingMonitor {
    public boolean dialogDisplayed = false;
  }
}
```

The test case is declared in the `insurance.ui` package. It calls a method on the `SimpleInsurance` interface (which is required to throw an exception in this case). If the test case catches an exception, it fails. (Because when the exception handling aspect that we are about to write is working correctly, the exception will have already been handled.) If a dialog box is not displayed to the user, the test case also fails. Right now the test case fails—there is no exception thrown, and no dialog box displayed. To complete the test case, we need to fill in the definition of the ExceptionHandlingMonitor inner aspect from Listing 11.11. We do this as shown in Listing 11.12.

Listing 11.12   *ExceptionHandlingMonitor Inner Aspect*

```
...
29 private static aspect ExceptionHandlingMonitor {
30       public boolean dialogDisplayed = false;
31
32       pointcut testCaseExecution() :
33           execution(* TestExceptionHandling.
34                   testExceptionHandling());
35
36       pointcut duringTestCaseExecution() :
37           cflow(testCaseExecution());
38
39       before() : testCaseExecution() {
40           dialogDisplayed = false;
41       }
42
43       pointcut createClaimCall() :
44           call(* SimpleInsurance.createClaim(..));
45
46       before() : createClaimCall() &&
47           duringTestCaseExecution() {
48             throw new SIException("Test case exception");
49       }
50
51       pointcut openMessageDialog() :
52           call(* MessageDialog.openError(..));
53
54       void around() : openMessageDialog() &&
55           duringTestCaseExecution() {
56           dialogDisplayed = true;
57       }
58
59    }
```

There are a few points to note about this aspect:

○ On lines 39 through 41, we set the dialogDisplayed flag to false every time we enter the test case.

○ On lines 46 through 49, we use before advice to simulate the throwing of an exception by the business logic. If a call is made to createClaim, *but only within the control flow of this test case* (lines 36 through 37), then an SIException is thrown.

○ On lines 54 through 57, we use around advice to achieve two goals. The first is to set the `dialogDisplayed` flag to true if a call is made to `MessageDialog.openError` *during the control flow of the test case*. The second thing the advice does is omit the call to `proceed`—this prevents dialog boxes from popping up during test case execution. We trust the `openError()` routine to do the right thing after we have called it.

When we run the test case now, we see that an exception is indeed thrown, but it is not handled. The test case fails as shown in Figure 11.21.

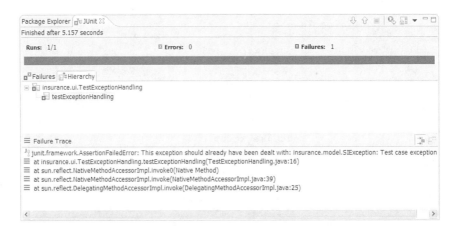

Figure 11.21   Failing test case.

Now we can write the `ExceptionHandling` aspect and see whether we can make the test case pass. Listing 11.13 shows the aspect (which is actually shorter than the test case).

Listing 11.13   *ExceptionHandling Aspect*

```
package insurance.ui;

import insurance.model.*;
import org.eclipse.jface.dialogs.MessageDialog;

public aspect ExceptionHandling {

  private static final String title =
    "Simple Insurance Exception";

  pointcut simpleInsuranceCall() :
    call(* insurance.model..*(..)) &&
    within(insurance.ui..*);
```

```
Object around() : simpleInsuranceCall()
  &&!within(ExceptionHandling) {
  Object ret = null;
  try {
    ret = proceed();
  } catch (SIException ex) {
    MessageDialog.openError(
      SimpleInsuranceApp.getShell(),title,
      "Call to "+ thisJoinPoint +" threw exception\n\n" +
      ex.getMessage()
    );
  }
  return ret;
}
}
```

It uses around advice to catch any exceptions thrown by a call to a
SimpleInsurance method (recall from Chapter 7 that after throwing advice
does not *handle* the exception) and display a dialog box to the user. When we
first run the test case with this aspect included, it still fails in the same way shown
in Figure 11.21. AspectJ treats the computation at the simpleInsuranceCall
join points as including not just the call to the model method, but also the execution of any advice before or after that call. If the ExceptionHandling
Monitor aspect in the test case has higher precedence than the Exception
Handling aspect, it will throw its exception and abort processing at the join
point before the call to the model method has even been made. We want to make
sure that our exception handling can never be circumvented by other advice in
this way, so we add a line in the ExceptionHandling aspect to declare that it
always takes highest precedence:

```
declare precedence : ExceptionHandling, *;
```

Now the test case passes (see Figure 11.22).

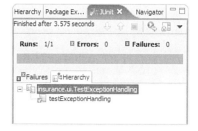

Figure 11.22 Success!

With the exception-handling aspect in place, we can run the application and shut down the database while the application is still open. Previously this crashed the application, but now you see the dialog box shown in Figure 11.23. Perhaps not the most user-friendly message, but a lot better than we had before.

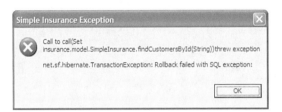

Figure 11.23   Dialog shown on error.

Before we leave this section, let's recap what we have achieved. We have a complete exception-handling strategy that spans from a `HibernateException` being thrown down in the persistence layer, all the way to a business exception being caught in the user interface. The basic exception handling policies were captured in only two aspects, `HibernateManager` and `ExceptionHandling`. We used test-driven development to write the second aspect, and also used aspects to assist in writing the tests themselves.

11.4.3 Management

The final example in this section illustrates the use of aspects to add a management capability to a simple Hello World program. The Hello World program itself is shown in Listing 11.14.

Listing 11.14   Hello World

```
package hello;

public class HelloWorld {

  private String text = "Hello World!";

  public void println() {
    System.out.println(text);
  }

  public static void main(String[] args) {
    new HelloWorld().println();
  }
}
```

We want to add the ability to manage the `HelloWorld` application via JMX, but do so in a way that is unobtrusive so that we can build variants of the application with and without the management support. The most basic form of JMX management takes place through direct implementation of MBean interfaces. Listing 11.15 shows the management interface we would like to support for `HelloWorld`.

Listing 11.15 The *MBean* interface for *HelloWorld*

```
package hello;

public interface HelloWorldMBean {
  public String getText ();
  public void setText (String newText);
  public void println ();
}
```

This time we present the management aspect in full, and then walk you through the various parts. The full listing is given in Listing 11.16. If you study it carefully you will see that the implementation is in three parts. Lines 12 through 24 are concerned with the implementation of the `HelloWorldMBean` interface by the `HelloWorld` class. We use a `declare parents` statement (lines 15 through 16) to make `HelloWorld` implement the interface. Notice, however, that although the `HelloWorld` class has an existing `println()` method, it does not support the `getText` and `setText` operations defined in the interface. Lines 18 through 24 provide implementations of these methods on behalf of `HelloWorld`. Because these methods need to access the private `text` field in `HelloWorld`, and because the class and the aspect are so tightly coupled in this case, we have made the aspect privileged (line 8).

Listing 11.16 The *Management* Aspect

```
01 package hello.management;
02
03 import hello.*;
04 import javax.management.*;
05 import com.sun.jdmk.comm.*;
06 import java.net.*;
07
08 public privileged aspect Management {
09
10   private MBeanServer server;
11
12   /*
```

```
13    * HelloWorldMBean implementation
14    */
15   declare parents :
16     HelloWorld implements HelloWorldMBean;
17
18   public String HelloWorld.getText () {
19     return text;
20   }
21
22   public void HelloWorld.setText (String newText) {
23     text = newText;
24   }
25
26
27   pointcut newHelloWorld(HelloWorld hw) :
28     execution(HelloWorld.new(..)) && this(hw);
29
30   /*
31    * Register resource with MBeanServer
32    */
33   after (HelloWorld hw) returning : newHelloWorld(hw){
34     ObjectInstance instance = null;
35     try {
36       String domain = server.getDefaultDomain();
37       ObjectName name =
38         new ObjectName(domain +
39                        ":type=HelloWorld,id=" +
40                        Integer.toString(hw.hashCode(),16));
41       instance = server.registerMBean(hw,name);
42     }
43     catch (Exception ex) {
44       ex.printStackTrace();
45     }
46   }
47
48   /*
49    * Create an MBeanServer and start the HTML adaptor
50    */
51   public Management () {
52     try {
53       server = MBeanServerFactory.createMBeanServer();
54       HtmlAdaptorServer hSvr = new HtmlAdaptorServer();
55       ObjectName html_name =
56         new ObjectName("Adaptor:name=html,port=8082");
57       server.registerMBean(hSvr, html_name);
58       hSvr.start();
59       System.out.println("hw.Management=" +
60           InetAddress.getLocalHost() + ":" +
61           hSvr.getPort());
62     }
63     catch (Exception ex) {
64       ex.printStackTrace();
65     }
66   }
67 }
```

Lines 48 through 66 are just boilerplate JMX code, in which we construct an HTML-based JMX management server (using the reference JMX implementation[1]) and start it up. We do this when the `Management` aspect is constructed. Lines 27 through 46 define a pointcut that matches the construction of `HelloWorld` objects, and then use `after()` returning advice to register any newly created `HelloWorld` objects with the `MBeanServer`.

If you build this application with the aspect included, and run `HelloWorld`, you will see output like that shown in Figure 11.24. Notice that the application has not terminated (as it would without the aspect), because the `MBeanServer` is still executing.

Figure 11.24   Running *HelloWorld*.

Because the `MBeanServer` is running, we can open up a Web browser on port 8082, and we see a page like that shown in Figure 11.25. Notice that an instance of `HelloWorld` is available for management. Selecting that link gives the page shown in Figure 11.26.

---

1. http://java.sun.com/products/JavaManagement/index.jsp.

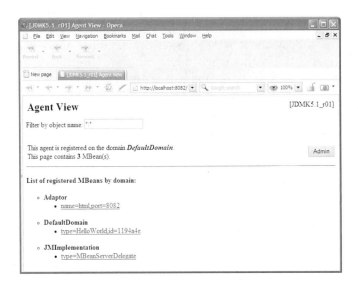

Figure 11.25   Management home page.

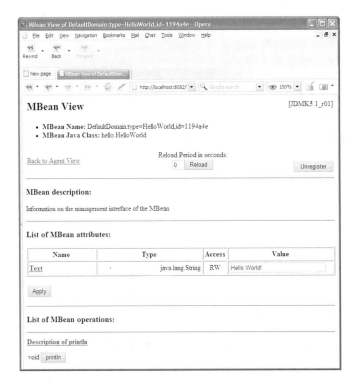

Figure 11.26   Managing *HelloWorld*.

We can update the value of the text attribute, and click **Apply**. If we then select the `println` operation, the Web browser shows the page in Figure 11.27, and if we look back at the Eclipse console window, we see the results of `println` operation (see Figure 11.28).

Figure 11.27   Applying the *println* operation.

Figure 11.28   Hello Readers.

So, with one simple aspect that can be added or removed from the system with ease, and without touching the original `HelloWorld` class in any way, shape, or form, we have been able to remotely manage the `HelloWorld` application via a Web browser. The aspect that we wrote was particular to the `HelloWorld` class, but the approach we took will be applicable in many situations.

We mentioned in Part 1 the ability to easily include or exclude files or packages from the build configuration by using the **Include/Exclude from Build Configuration** context menu options in the Package Explorer. AJDT also enables you to create named build configurations so that you can easily switch between them. Let's see how to create HelloWorld and Managed HelloWorld configurations for this simple project. Because we have currently got all of the source files included, we can save the current configuration as Managed Hello World. To do this, select **Project > Active build configuration > Save as** from the workbench menu (see Figure 11.29).

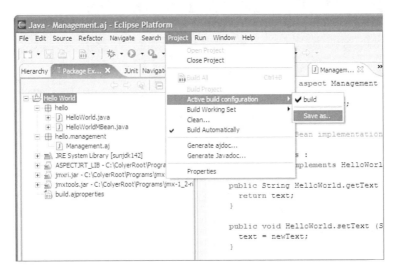

Figure 11.29   Saving a build configuration.

In the dialog box that appears, enter the name **Managed Hello World** and click **OK**. Now we need to create the plain Hello World configuration. Click the drop-down next to the AspectJ build button (bet you have been wondering what that was for), and select **build** (see Figure 11.30). This returns you to the standard build configuration.

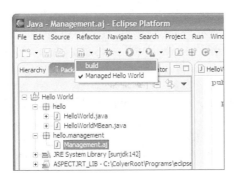

Figure 11.30   The build button.

Now select the `Management.aj` file in the Package Explorer and choose **Exclude from 'build' configuration** from the context menu. The icons in the Package Explorer change to indicate that these files are excluded from the configuration, as shown in Figure 11.31. You can now use the Project menu to save this build configuration as **Hello World** in the same way that we did before with the managed configuration.

Figure 11.31   Management aspect excluded from configuration.

From either the build button pull-down or the Project menu, you can now easily select among the saved build configurations at any time, as shown in Figure 11.32.

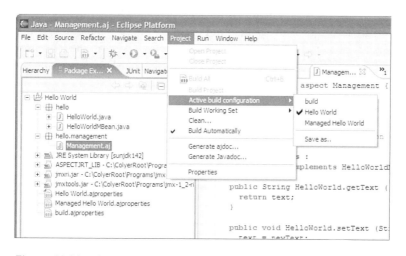

Figure 11.32   Choosing a build configuration.

You might have noticed the .ajproperties files that appear in the Package Explorer for each build configuration in the project. In addition to including and excluding files from a build using the Package Explorer's context menus, you can use these files to edit a build configuration. Just double-click one to open the Build Configuration Editor. In Figure 11.33, we have opened the editor on the Hello World.ajproperties file.

Figure 11.33   The Build Configuration Editor.

You can see that in this configuration, the management folder and all its contents are excluded. You can select and deselect files in the editor, and when you save the file the build configuration will be updated. Notice that the editor is tabbed, with tabs at the bottom of the Editor page. In Figure 11.33 you see the default build configuration page. In Figure 11.34 we have selected the **Hello World.ajproperties** tab and can see the underlying file contents. Because the files are actually stored as flat text, they are suitable for sharing among team members using CVS, and for use from Ant build scripts.

Figure 11.34   Textual view of configuration.

11.5   Core Aspect Examples

We have a confession to make. There's not a clear delineated distinction between auxiliary aspects and core aspects. Instead, there's a continuum. Something like the logging aspect we looked at in the last section is clearly auxiliary, and the business rules validation aspect we developed in Chapter 8 is clearly a part of the business (core) logic. Is exception handling an auxiliary aspect, or a core piece of your system? It depends on how you look at it. In this chapter, we chose to put it in the auxiliary section, but it could have gone the other way. Likewise the policy change notification aspect we began in Chapter 2 and completed in Chapter 8 could also be considered in either category. It doesn't implement any business logic, but it is certainly critical to the correct functioning of the application (and in that sense could be considered core). The fact that there is no clean break between the two categories is a good thing. It means that your adoption can smoothly progress into more and more critical and central pieces of your system's design, without hitting a bump in the road.

This section examines one further aspect example that is drawn from our work developing Eclipse plug-ins. We then look at how aspects and classes can be knitted together using dependency injection and a lightweight container (Spring[2]) to give you a feel for how easily aspects can be integrated into a modern, modular application design.

11.5.1 Calling Untrusted Code

Contributions to the Eclipse platform are written as Eclipse *plug-ins*. (AJDT itself comprises a set of Eclipse plug-ins.) When one plug-in wants to provide a service or facility that other plug-in developers can use and extend, it implements what is known as an *extension point*.

We have experimented with a future potential addition to AJDT, known as the *Cross-Reference view*. The Cross-Reference view will display cross-references (such as advises, advised by, implements, extends, and so on) for any item selected in the workbench. The plug-in that provides the Cross-Reference view knows nothing about the particular cross-references it will be asked to manage. Instead, it publishes an extension point, so that other plug-ins can provide cross-references for the view to display. To contribute cross-references for display in this manner, a plug-in needs to provide an implementation of the `IXReferenceProvider` interface shown in Listing 11.17.

---

2. http://www.springframework.org.

Listing 11.17 *IXReferenceProvider* Interface

```
/**
 * <p>
 * IXReferenceProvider is used to contribute cross
 * references.
 * </p>
 * <p>
 * To connect a cross reference provider into the reference
 * service use the
 * <code>org.eclipse.contributions.xref.core.providers
 * </code> extension point. The
 * following example shows the plugin.xml fragment used to
 * connect the TypeProvider reference provider that displays
 * "extends" and "implements" references for all ITypes:
 * </p>
 * <pre>
 * ...
 */
public interface IXReferenceProvider {

    /**
     * The set of classes/interfaces for which this
     * provider will contribute references.
     */
    public Class[] getClasses();

    /**
     * Get the collection of IXReferences for the Object o.
     */
    public Collection getXReferences(Object o);

    /**
     * Returns a description of the provider suitable for
     * display in a user interface.
     */
    public String getProviderDescription();

}
```

The cross-reference plug-in itself uses the Eclipse plug-in registry to obtain instances of the IXReferenceProvider objects implemented by contributors. It then calls them as necessary to display cross-reference information in the view.

Eclipse has a "safe platform rule" (Gamma 2003) that says that as the provider of an extension point, you must protect yourself against misbehavior on the part of the extenders. This is to stop a rogue plug-in (which might, for example, throw a runtime exception) from denying service to all the other implementers of the extension point. Because extension points are so common in Eclipse, Eclipse has an interface, ISafeRunnable, that you can use to run code in a safe environment. Every time that the cross-reference plug-in wants to call one of the `IXReferenceProvider` interface methods, it should wrap the call in an instance of `ISafeRunnable` and pass it to the Eclipse `Platform` object to be executed. Remembering to do this at each call site is problematic, and the logic involved in doing so is also quite verbose.

With AspectJ, we have a better solution. The solution is shown in Listing 11.18. We declare an inner aspect inside the interface that captures right alongside the interface (where it belongs) the policy that any calls made to it should be done inside an `ISafeRunnable`.

Listing 11.18   *SafeExecution* Aspect

```
public interface IXReferenceProvider {
  /**
   * ...
   */
  public Class[] getClasses();

  /**
   * ...
   */
  public Collection getXReferences(Object o);

  /**
   * ...
   */
  public String getProviderDescription();

  /**
   * Providers are contributed by other plugins, and should
   * be considered untrusted code. Whenever we call such
   * code, it should be wrapped in an ISafeRunnable.
   */
  static aspect SafeExecution {
    pointcut untrustedCall() :
      call(* IXReferenceProvider+.*(..));

    Object around() : untrustedCall() {
      ISafeRunnableWithReturn safeRunnable =
        new ISafeRunnableWithReturn() {
          Object result = null;
          public void handleException(Throwable e) {
            // don't log the exception....
            // it is already being logged by the platform
          }
          public void run() throws Exception {
            result = proceed();
          }
          public Object getResult() {
            return result;
          }
        };
```

```
      Platform.run(safeRunnable);
      return safeRunnable.getResult();
   }

   interface ISafeRunnableWithReturn extends ISafeRunnable
   {
      Object getResult();
   }
  }

}
```

The `SafeExecution` inner aspect defines an untrusted call to be any call made to an implementer of the `IXReferenceProvider`. It then uses around advice to wrap such a call in an `IsafeRunnable`, which is executed by the call to `Platform.run()`. Note the use of `proceed()` within the run method, and the exploitation of the `Object` return type for around advice. This demonstrates how `proceed` can be used as a continuation and invoked from a separate thread of execution. We declared our own extension of the `ISafeRunnable` interface, `ISafeRunnableWithReturn`, that provides access to the result so that we can return it to the original caller. With this aspect in place, all calls to the interface can be coded in conventional fashion, and the aspect transparently takes care of the safe dispatch.

Note that the only part of the `SafeExecution` aspect that is particular to the `IXReferenceProvider` extension point is the definition of the `untrustedCall` pointcut. It would be a small step from here to create a reusable abstract aspect for use across the Eclipse platform, and then let concrete subaspects provide their own definitions of untrusted calls. We look at creating an aspect library in the next chapter.

11.5.2 Configuring Aspects with Spring

There are several points in the Simple Insurance application where we could decrease coupling even further and simplify the application design by externalizing configuration details using a lightweight container.

We can eliminate the need for the `SimpleInsuranceFactory` class (and with it the one remaining design-integrity warning from Section 11.3.2) by configuring the main user interface class, `SimpleInsuranceApp`, with a `SimpleInsurance` instance rather than requiring it to create one.

We can configure the `BusinessRulesValidation` aspect from Chapter 8 with the set of validation classes, instead of hard coding knowledge of them all within its constructor.

We can externalize the configuration of data-access objects for the `SimpleInsuranceImpl` class, moving the code-based dependency-injection pattern we followed in Chapter 3 into a configuration-driven dependency-injection pattern.

Finally, we can configure the `HibernateManager` aspect from Chapter 3 with details of the Hibernate mapping files from Chapter 9 with a Hibernate `SessionFactory` object, without it needing to know where this comes from.

Figure 11.35 shows the main objects that get instantiated when the Simple Insurance application runs, and how they fit together

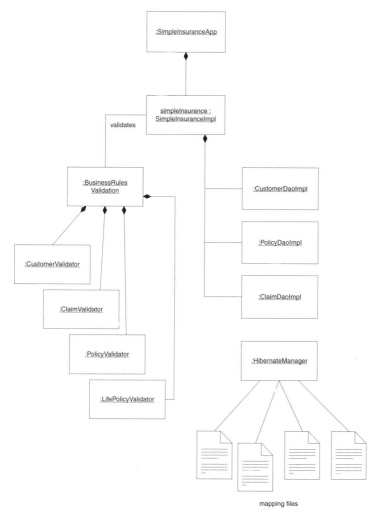

Figure 11.35   Simple Insurance Application objects.

Using Spring, we can encode all the knowledge in this diagram in a simple
configuration file, and take the configuration knowledge out of the code itself.
Each object we need at runtime is represented as a bean in the configuration file.

Let's begin at the top of the diagram and eliminate the need for the `Simple`
`InsuranceFactory`. Listing 11.19 shows the `beans.xml` configuration file.

Listing 11.19   Beginnings of a Spring Configuration File

```xml
<?xml version="1.0" encoding="UTF-8"?>
<!DOCTYPE beans PUBLIC "-//SPRING//DTD BEAN//EN"
"http://www.springframework.org/dtd/spring-beans.dtd">

<!--
  Configuration file for Simple Insurance Application
  -->
<beans>

  <bean id="simpleInsuranceApplication"
        class="insurance.ui.SimpleInsuranceApp">
    <property name="insuranceCompany">
      <ref bean="insuranceCompany"/>
    </property>
  </bean>

  <bean id="insuranceCompany"
        class="insurance.model.impl.SimpleInsuranceImpl">
  </bean>
</beans>
```

We define one bean to represent the Simple Insurance application,
`simpleInsuranceApplication`, and indicate that its `insuranceCompany` property should be set to the second bean, `insuranceCompany`. With a few simple
changes in the `SimpleInsuranceApp` class itself, we can eliminate the factory.
Listing 11.20 shows the new `main` method for the application.

Listing 11.20   The New *main* Method

```java
public static void main(String[] args) {
  Resource configFile =
    new FileSystemResource("config/beans.xml");
  XmlBeanFactory factory = new XmlBeanFactory(configFile);
  factory.preInstantiateSingletons();
  SimpleInsuranceApp app = (SimpleInsuranceApp)
    factory.getBean("simpleInsuranceApplication");
  app.run();
  app.dispose();
}
```

```
public void setInsuranceCompany(SimpleInsurance ins) {
  company = ins;
  customersTab.setData(company);
  policiesTab.setData(company);
  company.addListener(this);
}
```

Previously the `main` method used to explicitly create an instance of `SimpleInsuranceApp`, and then use the `SimpleInsuranceFactory` to create a `SimpleInsurance` instance for it to work with. Now it starts up the lightweight Spring container and simply asks it for the `simpleInsuranceApplication` bean. When Spring creates the bean, it also creates the `insuranceCompany` bean and passes it to the `SimpleInsuranceApp` by calling the `setInsuranceCompany` method. Now we can delete the `SimpleInsuranceFactory` class and with it the single remaining design-integrity warning raised by the `PermittedComponent Interactions` aspect from Section 11.3.2.

With this basic mechanism in place, we can proceed to simplify the rest of the configuration. Currently the `HibernateManager` aspect is creating DAOs and passing them to any `INeedInsuranceDaos` object that gets instantiated. We can move from this code-driven dependency injection to a configuration-driven model instead. First we extend the `beans.xml` configuration file, as shown in Listing 11.21.

Listing 11.21 Configuring the DAOs

```
<?xml version="1.0" encoding="UTF-8"?>
<!DOCTYPE beans PUBLIC "-//SPRING//DTD BEAN//EN"
"http://www.springframework.org/dtd/spring-beans.dtd">

<!--
  Configuration file for Simple Insurance Application
  -->
<beans>

  <bean id="simpleInsuranceApplication"
        class="insurance.ui.SimpleInsuranceApp">
    <property name="insuranceCompany">
      <ref bean="insuranceCompany"/>
    </property>
  </bean>

  <bean id="insuranceCompany"
        class="insurance.model.impl.SimpleInsuranceImpl">
    <property name="policyDao">
      <ref bean="policyDao"/>
    </property>
    <property name="customerDao">
      <ref bean="customerDao"/>
```

```
      </property>
      <property name="claimDao">
        <ref bean="claimDao"/>
      </property>
    </bean>

  <bean id="policyDao"
        class="insurance.dao.hibernate.PolicyDaoImpl"/>
  <bean id="customerDao"
        class="insurance.dao.hibernate.CustomerDaoImpl"/>
  <bean id="claimDao"
        class="insurance.dao.hibernate.ClaimDaoImpl"/>

</beans>
```

Now we can just comment out the portion of the `HibernateManager` aspect
that was creating DAOs and passing them to `INeedInsuranceDaos` objects on
construction because Spring is taking care of this for us:

```
// Hibernate DAO management
// pointcut insuranceAppCreation(
//            INeedInsuranceDaos dataConsumer) :
//   execution(INeedInsuranceDaos+.new(..)) &&
//   this(dataConsumer);
//
// after(INeedInsuranceDaos dataConsumer) returning :
//   insuranceAppCreation(dataConsumer) {
//     dataConsumer.setCustomerDao(new CustomerDaoImpl());
//     dataConsumer.setPolicyDao(new PolicyDaoImpl());
//     dataConsumer.setClaimDao(new ClaimDaoImpl());
// }
```

So far, we have just used Spring in the same way as you would for any Java
application. Now we're going to show you how to use Spring to configure
AspectJ aspects, too. Currently the `HibernateManager` has hard-coded knowledge of the mapping files. We want to move that configuration knowledge into
the `beans.xml` configuration file. Here's the relevant code from the current version of `HibernateManager`:

```
pointcut insuranceCompanyInit() :
  staticinitialization(SimpleInsuranceImpl);

after() returning : insuranceCompanyInit() {
  Configuration cfg = new Configuration();
  cfg.addResource("mappings/address.hbm.xml");
  cfg.addResource("mappings/customer.hbm.xml");
  cfg.addResource("mappings/claim.hbm.xml");
  cfg.addResource("mappings/policy.hbm.xml");
  sessionFactory = cfg.buildSessionFactory();
}
```

We replace both the pointcut and the advice with a simple setter method:

```
public void setMappingFiles(List mapFiles) {
  Configuration cfg = new Configuration();
  for(Iterator it= mapFiles.iterator(); it.hasNext();) {
    String configResource = (String) it.next();
    cfg.addResource(configResource);
  }
  sessionFactory = cfg.buildSessionFactory();
}
```

To make this work, we now have to define the aspect as a bean to Spring, and get Spring to call the setMappingFiles method when the bean is configured. You need Spring 1.1 or later for this step. Here's the relevant portion of the beans.xml file:

```
<bean id="hibernateManager"
      class="insurance.dao.hibernate.HibernateManager"
      factory-method="aspectOf">
  <property name="mappingFiles">
      <list>
        <value>mappings/address.hbm.xml</value>
        <value>mappings/policy.hbm.xml</value>
        <value>mappings/customer.hbm.xml</value>
        <value>mappings/claim.hbm.xml</value>
      </list>
    </property>
</bean>
```

Note that bean definition looks just like any other bean definition, except that instead of Spring creating a new instance of the HibernateManager class by calling a default constructor, we specify a factory method, aspectOf(), for Spring to call. Recall from Chapter 9 that AspectJ does not allow you to construct aspects directly (hence the default constructor is not appropriate), but does provide the aspectOf() method to obtain an instance that has been implicitly created by AspectJ. Getting Spring to call this method means that it will obtain and configure the single instance of the HibernateManager aspect. It really is as easy as that.

Now that you know how to configure aspects with Spring, let's finish off by getting Spring to configure the BusinessRulesValidation aspect, too. As we left it in Chapter 8, the constructor of the aspect looked like this:

```
public BusinessRulesValidation() {
  addValidator(new PolicyValidator());
  // add other validators here too…
}
```

The aspect has no knowledge of any of the model implementation classes, and apart from its constructor, no knowledge of the set of validation classes either. We can eliminate this last piece of coupling, and move the configuration of the validators into the `beans.xml` file:

```
<bean id="businessRulesValidation"
   class="insurance.model.validation.BusinessRulesValidation"
   factory-method="aspectOf">
   <property name="validators">
     <list>
       <ref bean="policyValidator"/>
       <!-- ... -->
     </list>
   </property>
</bean>

 <bean id="policyValidator"
     class="insurance.model.validation.PolicyValidator"/>
```

We can now replace the aspect constructor with a simple setter method:

```
public void setValidators(List /*Validator*/ validators) {
  for (Iterator it = validators.iterator(); it.hasNext();) {
    addValidator((Validator)it.next());
  }
}
```

We have simplified the code, eliminated the last few pieces of undesired coupling, and turned the diagram in Figure 11.35 into a simple configuration file that wires the application together, including the configuration of aspects. Listing 11.22 shows the complete configuration file for the application.

Listing 11.22   The Finished *beans.xml* Configuration File

```
<?xml version="1.0" encoding="UTF-8"?>
<!DOCTYPE beans PUBLIC "-//SPRING//DTD BEAN//EN"
"http://www.springframework.org/dtd/spring-beans.dtd">

<!--
  Configuration file for Simple Insurance Application
  -->
<beans>

   <bean id="simpleInsuranceApplication"
       class="insurance.ui.SimpleInsuranceApp">
     <property name="insuranceCompany">
       <ref bean="insuranceCompany"/>
```

```xml
      </property>
    </bean>

    <bean id="insuranceCompany"
          class="insurance.model.impl.SimpleInsuranceImpl">
      <property name="policyDao">
        <ref bean="policyDao"/>
      </property>
      <property name="customerDao">
        <ref bean="customerDao"/>
      </property>
      <property name="claimDao">
        <ref bean="claimDao"/>
      </property>
    </bean>

    <bean id="policyDao"
       class="insurance.dao.hibernate.PolicyDaoImpl"/>
    <bean id="customerDao"
       class="insurance.dao.hibernate.CustomerDaoImpl"/>
    <bean id="claimDao"
       class="insurance.dao.hibernate.ClaimDaoImpl"/>

    <bean id="hibernateManager"
       class="insurance.dao.hibernate.HibernateManager"
       factory-method="aspectOf">
      <property name="mappingFiles">
        <list>
           <value>mappings/address.hbm.xml</value>
           <value>mappings/policy.hbm.xml</value>
           <value>mappings/customer.hbm.xml</value>
           <value>mappings/claim.hbm.xml</value>
        </list>
      </property>
    </bean>

    <bean id="businessRulesValidation"
      class=
        "insurance.model.validation.BusinessRulesValidation"
      factory-method="aspectOf">
      <property name="validators">
         <list>
           <ref bean="policyValidator"/>
           <!-- ... -->
         </list>
      </property>
    </bean>

    <bean id="policyValidator"
       class="insurance.model.validation.PolicyValidator"/>

</beans>
```

11.6   Evaluating the Simple Insurance Application

We said in the Introduction that aspect-oriented programming was all about modularity: having each part of the system do one thing and one thing only. So how does the Simple Insurance application stack up?

Simple Insurance is a rich client application constructed in three logical tiers. The central business logic in the `insurance.model.impl` knows nothing about the user interface, the validation logic, the persistence mechanism, or change notification. It could be reused in any context.

The user interface uses only public interfaces defined by the model layer. It obtains an instance of the `SimpleInsurance` interface through dependency injection via Spring.

Validation of business objects is self-contained in the `insurance.model.validation` package. The package defines both a simple interface (`RequiresValidation`) that clients can use to perform validation of any business object (transparently to those business objects) and a safety mechanism that ensures an ill-formed business object never gets written to the database. The validation mechanism knows nothing of any model implementation classes, and makes no assumption about which business classes might implement which business interfaces. It also knows nothing about the set of `Validators` that are present in the system—these are again passed to it via dependency injection from Spring.

Change notification is encapsulated in the `PolicyChangeNotification` aspect, the policy being completely transparent to the business objects. Management of listeners on behalf of all business objects is also encapsulated in the aspect.

Persistence is completely encapsulated in the `insurance.dao` subpackages. The rest of the application knows nothing about the mechanism used to persist business objects. In fact, we have two implementations (Hibernate and the in-memory implementation) that we can freely switch between. Within the Hibernate implementation, the DAOs themselves are freed from nearly all the Hibernate considerations (session management, transactions, exception handling) with a simple aspect handling all those concerns. The set of data-access objects to use are once again configured via Spring dependency injection. (And if you don't want to use a lightweight container, we showed you how to achieve the same end via code, too.)

Both the logging and exception-handling policies are neatly encapsulated, too, and are transparent to the rest of the application. In addition, we have an aspect, `PermittedComponentInteractions`, ensuring that the system modularity stays in place throughout the subsequent evolution of the application.

All the aspects that we used to help achieve this modularity were quite simple and short—we just let the expressive power of the AspectJ language do its work.

11.7 Summary

AspectJ adoption typically proceeds in phases—enforcement aspects that don't impact your program at runtime, then infrastructure aspects that augment the application's capabilities, and finally core (or business) aspects that implement parts of its core functionality.

This chapter provided examples of aspects in each of the three categories. Along the way, you learned about preserving design integrity, writing efficient aspects, configuring aspects, testing aspects, using aspects during testing, and more. We also introduced you to several new features of AJDT.

References

Gamma, E. et. al. 1995. *Design Patterns: Elements of Reusable Object-Oriented Software*. Addison-Wesley.

Gamma, E. and Beck, K. 2003. *Contributing to Eclipse*. Addison-Wesley.

Hannemann, J. and Kiczales, G. 2002 (November). *Design Pattern Implementation in AspectJ*. Proceedings of the 17th Annual ACM conference on Object-Oriented Programming, Systems, Languages, and Applications (OOP-SLA), pages 161–173. See also http://www.cs.ubc.ca/~jan/AODPs/ for the latest information.

CHAPTER 12

Advanced AJDT

This chapter shows you how to use some of the more advanced features of AJDT, specifically covering the following topics:

- ○ How to create (and use) an aspect library
- ○ How you can use AJDT to link (weave) aspects with prebuilt class files in Jars and directories
- ○ Using AspectJ and AJDT with Ant
- ○ Aspect visualization

12.1 Aspect Libraries

An aspect library is just a Jar file containing compiled aspects (.class files) and any supporting types and resources. Using an aspect library avoids the need to compile from source any aspects you may be using in your project, and facilitates independent development of reusable aspects.

The aspects that we have been using to work with Hibernate throughout the book feel like they should be generally reusable in any Hibernate application. This section shows you how we approach making a reusable aspect, and how to use AJDT to both create and use an aspect library. We do this by creating a new AspectJ project, Hibernate Aspect Library, in which we will take a copy of the Hibernate aspects from Simple Insurance and rework them into reusable abstract aspects. Finally, we update the Simple Insurance application to use the newly created library.

The first step is to create a new AspectJ project, called Hibernate Aspect Library. We want to make the session and exception management part of the library, but we will leave the configuration of Hibernate itself (the mapping files and creation of a `SessionFactory`) to users of the library. The exception management is the simplest piece to work with first. In the `HibernateManager` aspect we developed in Part 2, this was handled by the extract shown in Listing 12.1.

Listing 12.1   Exception Softening and Wrapping in *HibernateManager*

```
pointcut hibernateCall() :
  call(* net.sf.hibernate..*(..));

declare soft : HibernateException : hibernateCall();

after() throwing(HibernateException hEx) : hibernateCall()
  && !target(HibernateException) {
  hEx.printStackTrace();
  SIPersistenceException siEx =
    new SIPersistenceException(hEx);
  throw siEx;
}
```

If we are to turn this into a reusable library aspect, we need to consider the points of variance among different users of the aspect. One obvious thing we need to parameterize is the creation of the domain exception that wraps the Hibernate exception—not every user will want an `SIPersistenceException`. We capture this point of variance by defining an abstract method, `createDomainException`, that the library aspect can call:

```
protected abstract RuntimeException
     createDomainException(HibernateException hEx);
```

A second consideration is the scope in which we want a `HibernateException` to be softened. The current implementation softens a `HibernateException` on any call to Hibernate. In general for a library aspect, we would want to give users some way of limiting the scope of advice, or in this case the use of `declare soft`. We can meet this requirement by defining an abstract pointcut, `inExceptionManagement Scope`, that subaspects can define. Listing 12.2 shows the completed `Hibernate ExceptionManagement` abstract aspect.

Listing 12.2   *HibernateExceptionManagement* Library Aspect

```
package com.simpleinsurers.hibernate;

import net.sf.hibernate.*;

public abstract aspect HibernateExceptionManagement {
```

```
protected abstract pointcut inExceptionManagementScope();

protected abstract RuntimeException
  createDomainException(HibernateException hEx);

pointcut hibernateCall() :
  call(* net.sf.hibernate..*(..)) &&
  inExceptionManagementScope();

declare soft : HibernateException : hibernateCall();

after() throwing(HibernateException hEx) :
 hibernateCall() && !within(HibernateExceptionManagement)
{
  RuntimeException wrappedException =
    createDomainException(hEx);
  throw wrappedException;
}

}
```

This aspect is created in the src folder of the Hibernate Aspect Library project. Aspect libraries are packaged as Jar files, so we need to configure the Hibernate Aspect Library project to produce a Jar file as its output. To do this, open the project Properties and go to the AspectJ page. Enter the name of the library Jar file in the Output jar field, as shown in Figure 12.1. We have chosen to name our aspect library `si-hibernate.jar`.

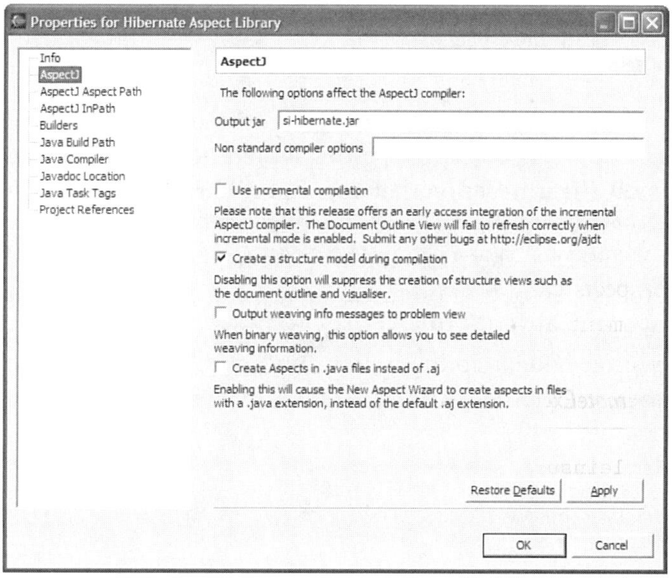

Figure 12.1 Specifying an output Jar.

Now when you build the project, you will find that a Jar file called si-hibernate.jar is created in the root project directory. The next step is to configure the Simple Insurance application project to use the library we just built. Open the project properties for the Simple Insurance project, and select the **AspectJ Aspect Path** page. Click the **Add JARs** button, as shown in Figure 12.2.

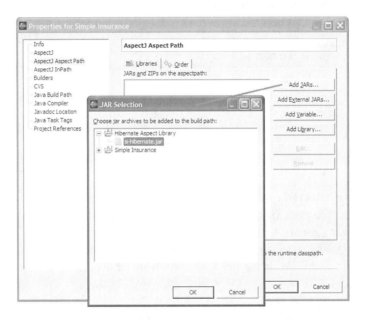

Figure 12.2   Adding a Jar to the aspect path.

Expand the Hibernate Aspect Library project node, and select si-hibernate.jar. Click **OK**. The project properties should now look like those shown in Figure 12.3. Note the instruction that any aspect libraries we use on the aspect path must also be added to the runtime classpath.

Let's add the library to the runtime classpath now before we forget. Use the pull-down next to the run button on the toolbar to open the Run dialog box and edit the launch configuration for the Simple Insurance project. Select the Simple Insurance application launch configuration, and click the **Classpath** tab. Now select **User Entries**, click **Add JARs**, as shown in Figure 12.4, and select si-hibernate.jar.

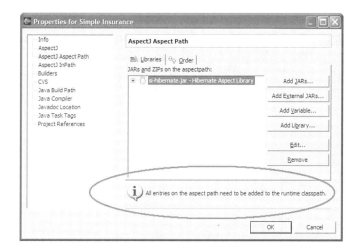

Figure 12.3   A populated aspect path.

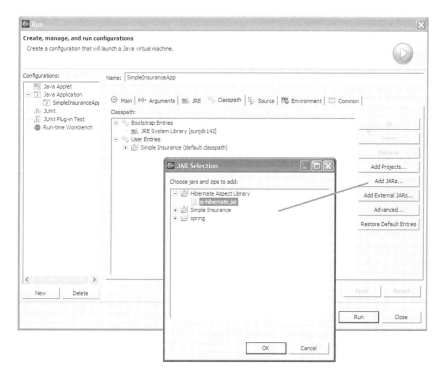

Figure 12.4   Updating the runtime classpath.

Now we're all set; the Hibernate Aspect Library project is creating an aspect library Jar file as the result of its builds, and the Simple Insurance project uses that library on its aspect path, and in its runtime classpath. Listing 12.3 shows how we can make use of the library aspect in the Simple Insurance project.

Listing 12.3   Extending the *HibernateExceptionManagement* Aspect

```
package insurance.dao.hibernate;

import com.simpleinsurers.hibernate.*;
import net.sf.hibernate.HibernateException;
import insurance.dao.SIPersistenceException;

public aspect ExceptionManagement
extends HibernateExceptionManagement {

  protected pointcut inExceptionManagementScope() :
     within(insurance.dao.hibernate..*);

  public RuntimeException
  createDomainException(HibernateException ex) {
    return new SIPersistenceException(ex);
  }

}
```

The `ExceptionManagement` aspect extends the `HibernateException Management` aspect from the library. It defines the pointcut `inException Management Scope` to be anywhere within the `insurance.dao.hibernate` package (so any `HibernateException` occurring in code from that package will be softened and wrapped). It also provides an implementation of the abstract `createDomainException` method to create an `SIPersistenceException`. With this aspect in place, we can remove the exception softening and wrapping code from the `HibernateManager` aspect (Listing 12.1) because it is no longer needed.

Now we can extend the aspect library further and also create an abstract aspect to perform Hibernate session and transaction management. In the `HibernateManager` aspect we developed in Part 1, we used a common parent class, `HibernateDao`, for all of the data access objects in the `insurance.dao.hibernate` package. This enabled us to write and use the following pointcut to match the execution of DAO operations in need of a Hibernate session and transaction:

```
/**
 * Any operation invoked on a HibernateDao subclass.
```

```
 * (We don't want to match the methods in the
 * HibernateDao class itself).
 */
pointcut daoOperation(HibernateDao dao) :
  execution(* HibernateDao+.*(..)) &&
  !execution(* HibernateDao.*(..)) &&
  this(dao);
```

For our single application, the use of a parent class (`HibernateDao`) was acceptable, but for an aspect library that may be used in a wide variety of situations, requiring that users inherit from one of your classes can be restricting—especially as Java only offers single inheritance. In the aspect library, we will define `HibernateDao` as an interface that can be implemented by DAOs wanting to participate in Hibernate sessions (see Listing 12.4).

Listing 12.4   The *HibernateDao* Interface in the Library

```
package com.simpleinsurers.hibernate;

import net.sf.hibernate.Session;

public interface HibernateDao {

  public abstract void setSession(Session session);

  public abstract Session getSession();

}
```

Because the library aspects may be used in a multithreaded environment, we will base the session management on the thread-safe version of the aspect we developed in Chapter 9 that used `percflow`. Listing 12.5 shows the completed `HibernateSessionManager` aspect.

Listing 12.5   *HibernateSessionManager*

```
01 package com.simpleinsurers.hibernate;
02
03 import net.sf.hibernate.*;
04
05 public abstract aspect HibernateSessionManager
06 percflow(sessionBoundary()) {
07
08   private Session session;
09
10   protected abstract SessionFactory getSessionFactory();
11
```

```
12   protected abstract HibernateExceptionManagement
13     getHibernateExceptionManager();
14
15 /**
16  * Each dao operation will execute in a
17  * transaction. Add other, higher-level
18  * transactions to this pointcut definition
19  * as needed.
20  */
21   protected abstract pointcut hibernateTransaction();
22
23   private Session HibernateDao.session;
24   public Session HibernateDao.getSession() {
25     return session;
26   }
27   public void HibernateDao.setSession(Session session) {
28     this.session = session;
29   }
30
31 /**
31  * Any operation invoked on a HibernateDao subclass.
32  * (We don't want to match the methods in the
33  * HibernateDao interface itself).
34  */
35 pointcut daoOperation(HibernateDao dao) :
36     execution(* HibernateDao+.*(..)) &&
37     !execution(* HibernateDao.*(..)) &&
38     this(dao);
39
40 /**
41  * Start a hibernate session (and transaction)
42  * at these points, but only if we don't already
43  * have a session active.
44  */
45   pointcut sessionBoundary() :
46     requiresTransaction() &&
47     !cflowbelow(requiresTransaction());
48
49   pointcut requiresTransaction():
50     daoOperation(HibernateDao) || hibernateTransaction();
51
52 /**
53  * The protocol for sessions and transactions.
54  * It is important that this advice has precedence
55  * over the DAO dependency injection advice below.
56  */
57   Object around() : sessionBoundary() {
58     Object ret = null;
59     try {
60       session = getSessionFactory().openSession();
61       Transaction tx = null;
62       try {
```

```
63          tx = session.beginTransaction();
64          ret = proceed();
65          tx.commit();
66        } catch(HibernateException ex) {
67          if (tx != null) tx.rollback();
68          throw getHibernateExceptionManager()
69                  .createDomainException(ex);
70        } finally {
71          session.close();
72        }
73      } catch (HibernateException ex) {
74        throw getHibernateExceptionManager()
75                .createDomainException(ex);
76      }
77      return ret;
78   }
79
80   /**
81    * Before any DAO executes a database operation,
82    * we need to tell it what session object to use.
83    */
84   before(HibernateDao dao) : daoOperation(dao) {
85      dao.setSession(session);
86   }
87
88 }
```

We have highlighted a few portions of the listing. The aspect is abstract; it doesn't know how to obtain a `SessionFactory` (line 10), or what to do with a `HibernateException` should one occur (lines 12 and 13). Although every `HibernateDao` operation needs a session if there is not already one active (lines 35 through 38, 49 through 50), there may be other higher-level, application-specific, session boundaries. These will be specified in concrete subaspects using the `hibernateTransaction` pointcut (line 21).

Just because we made `HibernateDao` an interface, it doesn't mean we have to lose the functionality that the class version previously gave us. On lines 23 through 29 we use inter-type declarations to manage a `Session` on behalf of any `HibernateDao` implementing classes.

Finally, because this aspect is no longer covered by softening, we have had to put explicit exception handling back into the around advice (lines 57 through 77). If a `HibernateException` is thrown, we use the `getHibernateException Manager` method to obtain an exception manager object that can wrap it for us (lines 68 and 69, 74 and 75).

Let's see how we can use this aspect in the Simple Insurance project. Listing 12.6 shows a concrete `SessionManagement` subaspect.

Listing 12.6   Using the *HibernateSessionManager* Aspect

```
package insurance.dao.hibernate;

import com.simpleinsurers.hibernate.*;
import net.sf.hibernate.*;

public aspect SessionManagement
extends HibernateSessionManager {

  declare parents : *DaoImpl implements HibernateDao;

  protected pointcut hibernateTransaction() :
    execution(* ImportUtility.importDatFile(..));

  protected HibernateExceptionManagement
  getHibernateExceptionManager() {
    return ExceptionManagement.aspectOf();
  }

  protected SessionFactory getSessionFactory() {
    return HibernateManager.aspectOf().getSessionFactory();
  }
}
```

We have also deleted the `HibernateDao` class from the Simple Insurance project, and so made all the `*DaoImpl` classes just extend `Object`. This was replaced by the `declare parents` statement in the `SessionManagement` aspect. Because the library aspect automatically wraps every DAO operation in a session and transaction, the only join point left to specify for the `hibernate Transaction` pointcut definition is the execution of the import method from Chapter 7.

For exception management, we return the single instance of the concrete `ExceptionManagement` aspect in the Simple Insurance project. The session factory is obtained via the (now greatly reduced in size) `HibernateManager` aspect, as shown in Listing 12.7.

Listing 12.7 The Refactored *HibernateManager* Aspect

```
public aspect HibernateManager {

  private SessionFactory sessionFactory = null;

  // meeting hibernate's requirements
  // -------------------------------------
  public Long AddressImpl.id;

  public AddressImpl.new() {}
  public ClaimImpl.new() {}
  public PolicyImpl.new() {}
  public LifePolicyImpl.new() {}
  public HousePolicyImpl.new() {}
  public AutoPolicyImpl.new() {}
  public Schedule.new() {}
  public Automobile.new() {}

  public void setMappingFiles(List mapFiles) {
    Configuration cfg = new Configuration();
    for(Iterator it= mapFiles.iterator(); it.hasNext();) {
      String configResource = (String) it.next();
      cfg.addResource(configResource);
    }
    sessionFactory = cfg.buildSessionFactory();
  }

  public SessionFactory getSessionFactory() {
    return sessionFactory;
  }

}
```

The refactoring is now complete. We created a small reusable aspect library for working with Hibernate that can be shared throughout the rest of the Simple Insurers Company. We then refactored the Simple Insurance application to use the library, which we did by writing two simple subaspects and using the aspect path to pass the aspect library to the compiler. Figure 12.5 shows the resulting application structure.

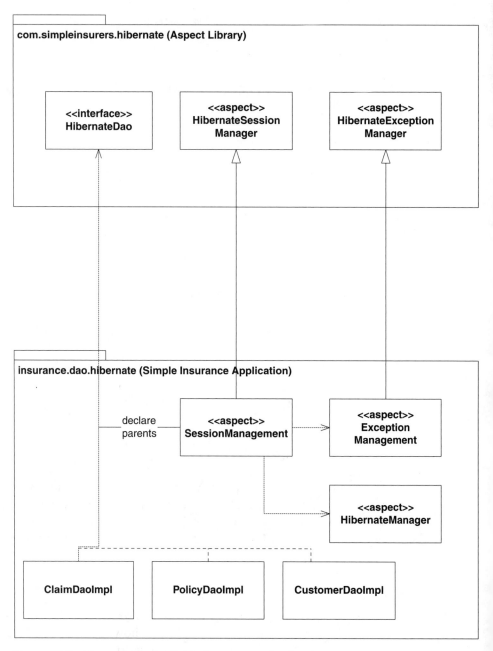

Figure 12.5 Library use in the Simple Insurance application.

Although in this case we both built and used the library, the procedure for using a third-party library supplied to you as a Jar file is exactly the same: Just add the library to the aspect path of the project, and to the runtime classpath.

What if you have a Jar file containing already built Java classes, and you want to link the contents of that Jar file with a set of aspects? AJDT can support that, too, by using the in-path option.

12.2   Linking Aspects with Compiled .class Files

Instead of compiling all of your aspects and classes together in one go, AspectJ supports the use of prebuilt aspect libraries (as discussed in the preceding section), and linking (weaving) aspects with prebuilt classes.

Simple Insurers have a reporting application that uses JDBC directly to access the database. The application is packaged as `siReporting.jar`. We have been called in to troubleshoot the application, and one of the things we would like to see is all the calls that the application makes to the database. To do this, let's create another AspectJ project, Reporting. Inside the project, define a simple aspect, `LogJDBCCalls`, as shown in Listing 12.8.

Listing 12.8   A Simple Aspect to Monitor Database Activity

```
package reporting.debug;

public aspect LogJDBCCalls {

  pointcut jdbcCall() : call(* java.sql..*(..)) ||
                        call(* javax.sql..*(..));

  before() : jdbcCall() {
    System.out.println("> " + thisJoinPoint);
  }

  after() returning : jdbcCall() {
    System.out.println("< " + thisJoinPoint);
  }

}
```

Now all we need to do is add `siReporting.jar` to the `inpath` of the Reporting project, and build. Figure 12.6 shows how to add a Jar to the inpath of an AspectJ project: Open the project properties, and select the **AspectJ Inpath** page. Then select the **Libraries and Folders** tab and use the **Add JARs** or add **External JARs** button to add the Jar file. (You use **Add JARs** if the Jar file you want to add is defined in a project somewhere in your workspace, and add **External JARs** if it is outside of the workspace.)

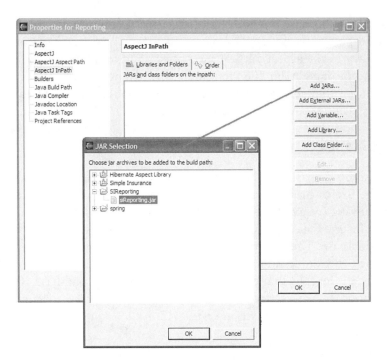

Figure 12.6 Adding a Jar file to the inpath.

After building the Reporting project, the contents of the Jar file, together with the built `LogJDBCCalls` aspect, are placed in the `bin` directory. You can run the application from there if you create a launch configuration by hand (see Figure 12.7), but it is probably more convenient to get AJDT to build you a replacement for `siReporting.jar`. To do this, just set an outjar in the project properties (as we did in the preceding section)—for example, we called the out-jar `siReportingDebug.jar`. Now you can run the reporting application as normal, but with `siReporting.jar` replaced by `siReportingDebug.jar`. The results from a sample run using `siReporting.jar` are shown in Listing 12.9. In Listing 12.10 you see the results when `siReporting.jar` is replaced by `siReportingDebug.jar`.

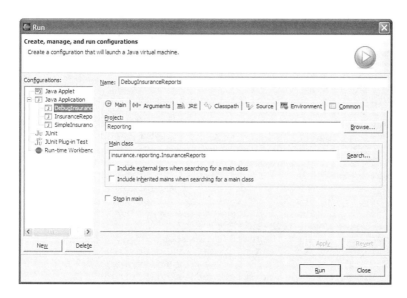

Figure 12.7   Defining a launch configuration.

Listing 12.9   Normal Run of the Reporting Tool

```
By Customer
=====================================
C1090323343799.19: Bacon, Chris. P.
   P1090323671841.5 (AutoPolicy)
C1090323360683.22: DodgyMotor, Ivar
   P1090323688324.6 (AutoPolicy)
C1090323498311.31: EverEnd, Willit
   P1090323601750.2 (LifePolicy)
   P1090323623361.3 (AutoPolicy)
C1090323302910.17: McClaim, Ivana
   P1090323645963.4 (HousePolicy)
C1090323435381.26: Penny, Arthur
   P1090323559559.1 (HousePolicy)
```

Listing 12.10   Debug Run of the Reporting Tool

```
> call(Connection
java.sql.DriverManager.getConnection(String, String, String))
< call(Connection
java.sql.DriverManager.getConnection(String, String, String))
> call(Statement java.sql.Connection.createStatement())
< call(Statement java.sql.Connection.createStatement())
By Customer
```

```
=====================================
> call(ResultSet java.sql.Statement.executeQuery(String))
< call(ResultSet java.sql.Statement.executeQuery(String))
> call(boolean java.sql.ResultSet.next())
< call(boolean java.sql.ResultSet.next())
> call(String java.sql.ResultSet.getString(String))
< call(String java.sql.ResultSet.getString(String))
> call(String java.sql.ResultSet.getString(String))
< call(String java.sql.ResultSet.getString(String))
> call(String java.sql.ResultSet.getString(String))
< call(String java.sql.ResultSet.getString(String))
C1090323343799.19: Bacon, Chris. P.
> call(Statement java.sql.Connection.createStatement())
< call(Statement java.sql.Connection.createStatement())
> call(ResultSet java.sql.Statement.executeQuery(String))
< call(ResultSet java.sql.Statement.executeQuery(String))
> call(boolean java.sql.ResultSet.next())
< call(boolean java.sql.ResultSet.next())
> call(String java.sql.ResultSet.getString(String))
< call(String java.sql.ResultSet.getString(String))
> call(String java.sql.ResultSet.getString(String))
< call(String java.sql.ResultSet.getString(String))
  P1090323671841.5 (AutoPolicy)
> call(boolean java.sql.ResultSet.next())
< call(boolean java.sql.ResultSet.next())
> call(boolean java.sql.ResultSet.next())
...
some output lines omitted...
...
> call(String java.sql.ResultSet.getString(String))
< call(String java.sql.ResultSet.getString(String))
  P1090323559559.1 (HousePolicy)
> call(boolean java.sql.ResultSet.next())
< call(boolean java.sql.ResultSet.next())
> call(boolean java.sql.ResultSet.next())
< call(boolean java.sql.ResultSet.next())
> call(void java.sql.Connection.close())
< call(void java.sql.Connection.close())
```

As well as weaving aspects with input classes in Jar files, you can add directories containing .class files to the inpath. (Inpath is like a class path in that it contains a mixture of jars and folders—but the usage of inpath is quite different.) One useful thing you can do that exploits this fact is to add the output of one project in your workspace (its bin directory) to the inpath of another project. If we have the Simple Insurance reporting project in the Eclipse workspace, an alternative to adding a Jar to the inpath of the aspect project is to add the contents of its bin directory. The procedure for doing this is shown in Figure 12.8.

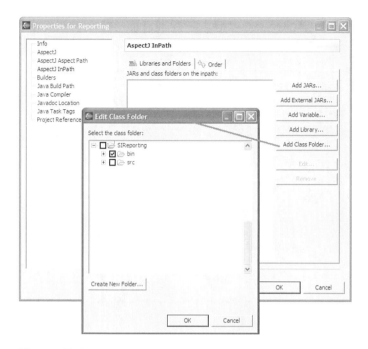

Figure 12.8   Adding a class folder.

Open the project **Properties** and select the **AspectJ InPath** page. Click the **Libraries and Folders** tab and then press **Add Class Folder**. In the dialog box that appears, select the folder containing the class files you want to add and click **OK**.

Adding the output directory of one project to the inpath of another is an alternative to the method of working with linked source folders that we showed you in Chapter 11. So which is better? There are pros and cons with both approaches.

The class folder dependency technique is better performing because the Java code is only compiled once, in the Java project. When the AspectJ project is compiled, the .class files in the output directory of the Java project are used as input, and the source is not recompiled. With linked source folders, the source is compiled a second time in the AspectJ project. However, using linked source folders enables you to see all of the advises and advised by relationships in the Editor and Outline views, which the inpath route does not.

AJDT does offer some relief in this situation. On the project Properties page, you can enable the **Output weaving messages to Problems view** option (see Figure 12.9).

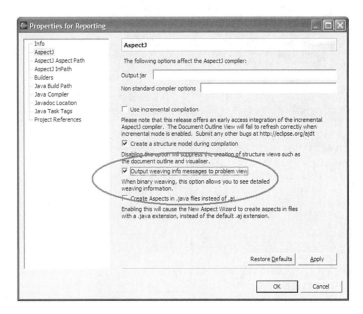

Figure 12.9   Enabling the output weave messages option.

With this option enabled, advises / advised by and other messages associated with the weaving process are output to the Problems view as information messages. Figure 12.10 shows a sample of the output for the Reporting project.

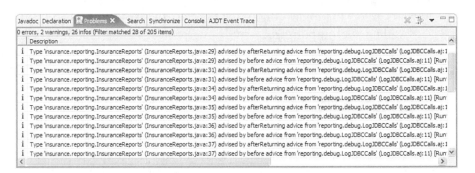

Figure 12.10   Advised by messages in the Problems view.

12.3 Ant Integration

AspectJ has good Ant support: New tasks and support classes are provided to make using the AspectJ compiler as easy as using the Java compiler. This section shows you how to convert an existing Ant build script for the Simple Insurance application into one that uses Ant.

12.3.1 Building Simple Insurance As a Java Project

Figure 12.11 shows a basic Ant script in the Eclipse Ant editor that will build the original pure Java version of the Simple Insurance project. It uses the `javac` task to build the code (see lines 16 through 18 in the figure).

```xml
1 <?xml version="1.0"?>
2 <project name="SimpleInsurance" default="compile">
3   <description>Simple Insurance application</description>
4
5   <property name="eclipse.home" value= "F:/eclipse"/>
6
7   <path id="insurance.dependencies">
8     <pathelement location="swt.jar"/>
9     <pathelement location=
10      "${eclipse.home}/plugins/org.eclipse.jface_3.0.0/jface.jar"/>
11  </path>
12
13  <target name="compile"
14         description="Build SimpleInsurance">
15    <mkdir dir="bin"/>
16    <javac srcdir="src" destdir="bin" debug="on">
17      <classpath refid="insurance.dependencies"/>
18    </javac>
19  </target>
20
21  <target name="clean"
22         description="Clean up the bin directory">
23    <delete dir="bin"/>
24    <mkdir dir="bin"/>
25  </target>
26 </project>
```

Figure 12.11   Building *SimpleInsurance* with the *javac* task.

The path `insurance.dependencies` is defined to include the `swt.jar` and `jface.jar` files that are required by the user interface code in the Simple Insurance example. There is a simple class path reference in the `javac` task to include the dependencies. Notice on line 16 that the `debug="on"` option is set. This causes Ant to generate class files that we can use in the debugger.

Executing an Ant script inside Eclipse is easy: Just select the script in the Package Explorer, open the context menu, and select **Run > Ant Build**.

Next we show you how to convert this build script to build with AspectJ in place of the Java compiler.

12.3.2 Building Simple Insurance As an AspectJ Project

AspectJ provides a plug-replacement for the `javac` task, `iajc`. Switching to building with AspectJ instead of the Java compiler involves defining the `iajc` task to Ant, and then replacing `javac` with `iajc`.

The definition of the `iajc` task is captured in

```
org/aspectj/tools/ant/taskdefs/aspectjTaskdefs.properties
```

which can be found in the `aspectjtools.jar` shipped with the AJDT plug-ins. You can define the `iajc` task directly in the Eclipse workbench preferences for Ant (see Figure 12.12), but that means any build scripts you create will not immediately work outside of Eclipse (for example, from the command line).

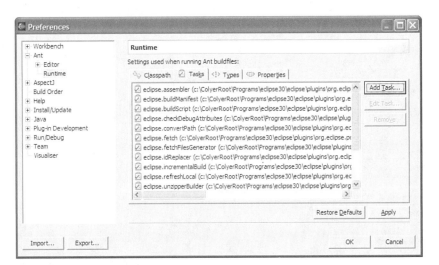

Figure 12.12   Ant runtime preferences.

We think it is preferable to create an Ant build script that will work both inside and outside of Eclipse. To do this, you need to define the `iajc` task within your build script, as shown in the following extract:

```
<property name="eclipse.home" value= "C:/eclipse"/>

<property name="aspectj.plugin.home"
    value="${eclipse.home}/plugins/org.aspectj.ajde_1.1.11"/>

<taskdef resource=
```

```
"org/aspectj/tools/ant/taskdefs/aspectjTaskdefs.properties">
    <classpath>
      <pathelement
          path="${aspectj.plugin.home}/aspectjtools.jar"/>
    </classpath>
  </taskdef>
```

The task itself is defined in the `aspectjtools.jar` library that ships as part of the AJDT distributions. The location is defined in the `aspectj.plugin.home` property and referred to when we define the `iajc` task. With these few lines of XML, `iajc` is available for use.

Figure 12.13 shows a new version of the Simple Insurance Ant script that uses the AspectJ `iajc` task to compile the project. After you convert a project to an AspectJ project, if it has an Ant build script, you should do this conversion at the same time, too.

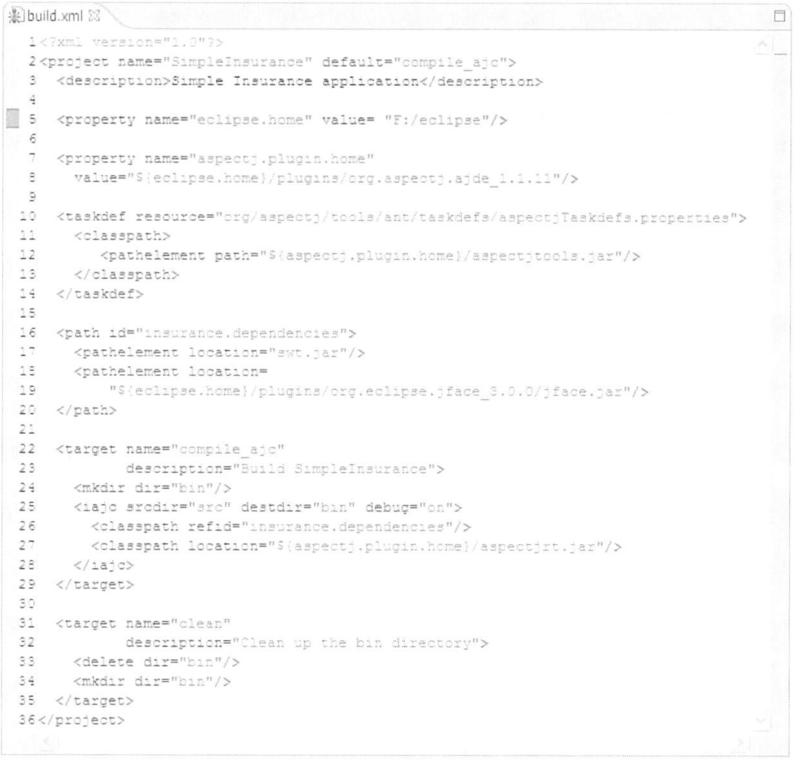

Figure 12.13   Building *SimpleInsurance* with the *iajc* task.

Let's review the changes from Figure 12.11 to Figure 12.13:

○ `iajc` task defined. (Lines 5 through 14)

○ switched `javac` to `iajc`. (Lines 25 through 28) `iajc` supports a superset of the `javac` task options. This means that we can just change from the `javac` task to the `iajc` task and know that all the options set for `javac` will continue to be valid.

○ `aspectjrt.jar` added to class path. (Line 27) The `iajc` task needs to refer to types in the AspectJ runtime library, so `aspectjrt.jar` must be added to the class path. We refer to it through the `aspectj.plugin.home` property we defined earlier because it is co-located alongside `aspectjtools.jar`.

The AspectJ help shipped with AJDT documents all the additional options that the `iajc` task supports; just search for `iajc` in the help system.

12.3.3 Limitations When Building with Ant in AJDT

You should be aware that invoking an Ant build of your AspectJ project from inside Eclipse will not give you the same kind of feedback that you get when building directly in the IDE using the standard AspectJ builder. You will not see gutter annotations at the advised lines in your source code and the outline view will not reflect your code structure or any aspects in effect.

12.4 Aspect Visualization

The markers in the editor and the relationship information in the Outline view give you a by-type and by-source file view of the effect of the aspects in your program. Sometimes it is useful to get a higher-level view of the application—perhaps to see the impact you are having across the entire codebase in capturing certain features in aspects. As discussed briefly in Part 1 and in the Chapter 11, the Aspect Visualiser can provide this view.

AJDT provides an entirely new perspective in Eclipse for visualizing the affect of aspects across your system. The Aspect Visualization perspective can be opened like other perspectives; open the **Window** menu on the menu bar, **Open Perspective > Other > Aspect Visualization**. When the perspective opens, the Eclipse workbench will look something like Figure 12.14.

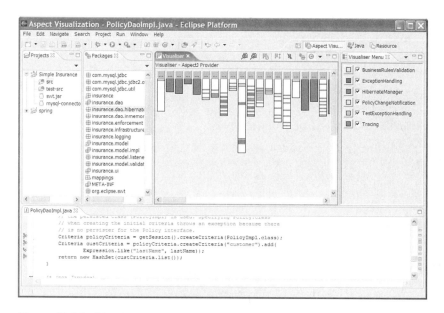

Figure 12.14   The Aspect Visualization perspective.

The Visualization perspective gives you a high-level overview of your system—it is not typically a perspective in which you would do normal code development. For this reason, the perspective is taken up with two new views: the Visualiser and the Visualiser Menu.

12.4.1 The Visualiser Menu

The menu has one entry for each aspect in your project, and can be used both to toggle the display of an aspect's effect in the main Visualiser view, and to change the color associated with that aspect's display. Figure 12.15 shows a sample menu: there are six aspects applying across the project, each is represented by a different color, and each aspect is currently visible in the main display window. The color associated with any aspect can be changed just by clicking the colored square next to it. To temporarily hide the effects of an individual aspect in the Visualiser view, deselect the check box next to it.

Figure 12.15   Visualiser menu.

12.4.2 Visualiser View

In the main Visualiser view at the center of Figure 12.14, you see a series of vertical bars. By default each bar in the view represents a source file in the project. The length of the bar is proportional to the number of lines in the file. The horizontal colored stripes across each bar show the locations of advice and inter-type declaration markers in those files. Each aspect has a different color, as indicated in the Visualiser Menu view.

The Visualiser view is linked to the Package view and Projects view (to the left of the Visualiser in Figure 12.14). As you make selections in these views, the Visualiser updates to show source files only within the scope of the selection. Click the project name in the Projects view to see the whole project at a glance. You can even click the colored stripes in the Visualiser view and the editor (at the bottom of the perspective by default) will open to the affected line of source.

There are a number of settings available on the Visualiser toolbar to influence how the bars display in the main part of the view. Figure 12.16 shows the Visualiser toolbar.

Figure 12.16   Visualiser toolbar.

From left to right, the icons represent as follows:

Zoom in   Useful when a number of colored stripes are very close together in a bar—zooms in, enabling you to see exactly what is in affect.

Zoom out   Zooms out, enabling you to look at the overall impact of your aspects.

Lock   Locks the current selection you have made to determine the bars in the Visualiser view. After the Visualiser is locked, you can select other artifacts around the Eclipse views and the Visualiser will continue to show the bars from the point you locked.

Shrink to fit   Scales bars vertically so that the longest bar fits within the visible view window.

Hide unaffected bars   The dark gray bars within the view represent types or packages that have not been affected by aspects; if you choose to hide unaffected bars, these gray bars will be removed from the view.

Package view   The normal view for the Visualiser is a class-level view where each bar represents a single source file (aspect, interface, class). Sometimes the normal view is too crowded and in these situations selecting a package level view switches to a mode where each bar represents an entire package with its members stacked on top of each other. Figure 12.17 shows a package view of the Simple Insurance project, which has too many types to fit into the display in the normal class view but fits nicely into the package view.

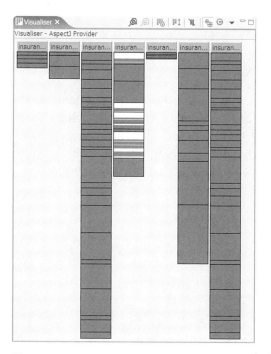

Figure 12.17   Package view of the Simple Insurance project.

Class view   Switches to the normal view where each bar represents a source file; the alternative is the package view where each bar represents a number of files.

Pull-down menu for further options   This pull-down gives you access to more advanced options for configuring the Visualiser's behavior.

As AspectJ projects get larger and larger, the Visualiser becomes more and more useful for understanding the codebase and how your aspects are affecting other types. Figure 12.18 shows a visualization of an aspect that affects many types in a program.

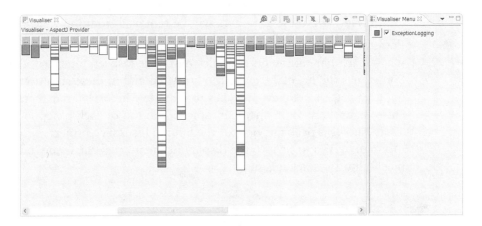

Figure 12.18   Visualizing a pervasive aspect.

A visualization showing something like this clearly validates your design—it becomes obvious that you are capturing in an aspect something that would have been completely scattered and tangled across a project. This kind of validation of your efforts can be highly motivating when you are starting out with AspectJ—and it makes a great way to impress your colleagues!

12.5 Summary

This chapter showed you how to create an aspect library using the outjar option, and how to use an aspect library via the AspectJ Aspect Path property. Aspect libraries enable you to reuse aspects that have been built by third parties rather than having to compile every aspect from source as part of your project.

AJDT also enables you to link aspects with prebuilt class files in Jar files and in folders. To do this, you use the AspectJ InPath property. Adding the output class folder of one Eclipse project to the inpath of another can be a convenient way of adding aspects to an existing project.

The `iajc` Ant task can be used as a plug-replacement for the `javac` task when migrating an Ant build script from the Java compiler to the AspectJ compiler. It is defined in the `aspectjtools.jar` file installed with the AJDT plug-ins.

Finally, AJDT provides a visualization perspective that can be used to gain a whole-system understanding of the effects of aspects in your program.

CHAPTER 13

Aspect-Oriented Design

This book has been about aspect-oriented programming. There's a whole other book to be written at some point about aspect-oriented design, and by no means does this short chapter represent a thorough treatment of the topic. What we will do, however, is leave you with a few thoughts about how to find aspects—in the design and in the code—and about judging the relative merits of an aspect-based design or implementation of some function.

13.1   Finding Aspects

Now that you have seen a selection of aspects of varying kinds, the question becomes, how can you go about discovering potential aspects in your own applications? This gets easier with experience, but in this section we have put together a few brief hints and tips to get you started. We start by looking at "top-down" aspect discovery, and then discuss things to look for in refactoring an existing code base.

13.1.1 Aspects in the Design

As you are thinking through the requirements that have to be addressed in a given iteration of your application's development, there are a number of clues in the problem statement that can suggest potential aspects to you. The aspect-oriented designer is on the lookout for adverbs and adjectives, temporal statements, and rules or policy statements.

13.1.1.1 Adverbs and Adjectives

In object orientation, we are taught to look out for nouns and verbs in the requirements. Nouns are candidate classes, and verbs are candidate operations. We have the class `BankAccount`, and now we need a *secure* `BankAccount`. Object orientation directs us to create a new type of noun, a `SecureBankAccount`, and sometimes that is the right choice. Aspect orientation opens up a new possibility; we can create an adjective "secure," the `Security` aspect. This is attractive if there are many kinds of things that need to be secure in the application, not just `BankAccount`s. The question to ask yourself is this: Is security a concept I need to deal with in its own right in this application, or is it really only ever going to be a property of `BankAccount`s? If security (or whatever adjective you are considering) is a concept that is best dealt with in its own right, you have a strong case for considering an aspect-based implementation.

Adverbs work in a similar fashion; they describe a quality or property of verbs (operations / methods). The security requirement above could equally have been couched as "all update operations on a `BankAccount` need to execute *securely*." A more-subtle example is contained in the phrase "an *audited* transfer." Is audited being used here as an adverb or an adjective? It depends on how you interpret "transfer"—if you interpret it in the sense of the action of transferring (the verb *to transfer*), then audited is playing the role of an adverb. If you interpret transfer as a noun ("a transfer"), then audited is playing the role of an adjective. The point is, it doesn't matter—you don't have to become an expert on grammar (and we don't claim to be so either)—regardless of whether it is an adverb or an adjective, it is a clue that there could be a potential aspect: Is auditing a concept to be addressed in its own right, or is it just a property of the transfer operation? The answer will either steer you toward creating an auditing aspect or toward supplementing the implementation of the transfer method.

So, nouns and verbs are candidate classes and operations, and in aspect orientation, adverbs and adjectives become candidate aspects.

13.1.1.2 Temporal Statements

Temporal statements in the requirements are a clue that suggests an advice-like solution in some cases. For example, in the statement "before executing any operation on a bank account, a user must have been authenticated," the word "before" is suggestive of before advice. Likewise the phrase "after any component writes to the database, the cache should be invalidated" is a clue suggesting after advice. Particularly be on the look out for phrases of the form "after (or before) some set of things ...."

As well as the obvious trigger words "before" and "after," you may find the following synonyms: "afterward, later, next, subsequently, thereafter, ahead of, in advance, previously," and similar.

13.1.1.3 Rules and Policy Statements

Rules or statements of policy are another clue suggesting an aspect-based implementation. For example, "All withdrawals that exceed a customer's overdraft limit must be approved by a supervisor," "Whenever a deposit, withdrawal, or money transfer is made, a record must be kept so that a bank statement can be produced at the end of the accounting period."

Some keywords to look out for here include "whenever," "anytime," "all," "always," "every," "any," "when," and so on.

13.1.2 Aspects in the Code

At the implementation level, two key clues indicate a potential aspect. Do you have (or are you about to create) the same few lines of code repeated in many scattered places throughout the source? In other words, are you doing the same thing (even if it is just a single call to a helper routine) in many places? Remember the definition of "many places" is relative—sometimes the many places can be scattered across your entire system, suggesting an aspect with global scope. Other times the many places could just be a set of methods within a single class, suggesting an inner aspect.

The second clue is if you find you have coordinated (but distinct) pieces of logic at distant places in the source code, and yet these pieces are actually all working together to achieve a single objective. Would your code be easier to read and maintain if they were pulled together into a suitably named aspect?

13.2   What Makes a Good Aspect?

What makes a good class? All the skills and experience you have built up to answer that question are equally applicable to the question of what makes a good aspect. When considering whether to make something an aspect, or what to include in an existing aspect, ask yourself the following:

   ○ Do the parts of the aspect all belong closely together (is it cohesive)?

   ○ Does the presence of the aspect reduce coupling among types in the design?

   ○ Given the kinds of changes you anticipate, will the code be easier to maintain and evolve with or without the aspect?

○ Does the aspect clarify component interactions and reduce tangling, or does it make the flow of control harder to understand?

○ Do you need to include the function encapsulated in the aspect in some versions of the application, but not in others?

○ Most important of all, is the program easier to understand with or without the aspect?

13.3   Closing Thoughts

Remember that above all, AspectJ is about improving the modularity of software systems. When modularity techniques are used well, you expect to see benefits such as less-tangled and more-natural code, easier maintenance and evolution of the software (it should be easier to understand, debug, and change the code), and more reusable components. Avoid the early temptation to make everything an aspect, and as you learn to use the technology wisely the quality of your software *will* improve.

APPENDIX A

Command-Line AspectJ

This book has focused on the use of AspectJ within the Eclipse IDE, but AspectJ is also made available as a command-line compiler by the AspectJ project. This appendix covers how to use the command-line compiler, which can prove useful for simple tests, scripting, and automated builds.

A.1   Installing AspectJ

AspectJ is distributed as an executable Jar file available from the project home page at http://www.eclipse.org/aspectj. In the Downloads section, you will find links to the latest stable release as well as previous releases going back to version 1.0.6. The Developer Resources page includes a link to access the latest source off the CVS head (including full build instructions) for those keen on working on the leading edge. This appendix discusses only officially released distributions.

After downloading the executable Jar file, you can either just double-click the Jar file (if you have the Jar Launcher configured), or run the following command from the console:

```
java -jar aspectj-1.2.jar
```

The AspectJ installer will start and you should see the Welcome screen, as shown in Figure A.1.

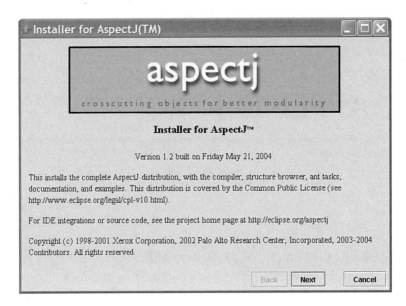

Figure A.1   Installing AspectJ.

   The installer prompts for the location of an install directory, and then proceeds with no further user intervention. In the installation directory, you will find
a `bin` directory containing the command-line compiler executable and associated
tools, a `lib` directory containing the AspectJ libraries, and a `doc` directory with
documentation and samples.
   To complete the installation, you need to add `INSTALL_ROOT/lib/aspectjrt.`
`jar` to your `CLASSPATH` environment variable, and `INSTALL_ROOT/bin` to your
`PATH`.

A.2 Using the Compiler

The AspectJ compiler is invoked by the `ajc` command. (`ajc` is to AspectJ as
`javac` is to Java.) Enter `ajc-help` to see a full list of compiler options.
   The general form of an `ajc` command is as follows :

```
ajc [options] SourceFile, SourceFile, ...
```

   Table A.1 list some of the more commonly used compiler options.

Table A.1   Selected AspectJ Compiler Options

Option	Description
`-d`	Output directory for compilation results.
`-classpath <list>`	A list of directories and archives where user class files are located. The list is delimited by the usual CLASSPATH delimiter character for the platform.
`-sourceroots <dirs>`	A PATH-delimiter separated list of directories containing source files to be compiled. All source files with the .aj or .java extension found under any of the directories supplied in the `dirs` argument will be compiled.
`-inpath <list>`	A PATH-delimiter separated list of Jar files and directories containing class files to be woven with aspects.
`-aspectpath <list>`	A PATH-delimiter separated list of Jar files containing aspects to be used in the weaving process.
`-outjar <File>`	An output Jar file in which the results of the compilation should be placed.
`-incremental`	Puts the compiler into incremental mode of operation. In this mode, the compiler continuously waits for keyboard input: Pressing the **Enter** key kicks off a build that only recompiles files changed since the last compile; pressing **Q** (for quit) ends this mode.

For example:

```
ajc *.java
```

Compiles all the .java files in the current directory.

```
ajc -sourceroots src -d bin
```

Compiles all the .java and .aj files in the `src` directory, and puts the results in the `bin` directory.

```
ajc -inpath someApp.jar -outjar debugSomeApp.jar Debug.aj
```

Weaves all the .class files in `someApp.jar` with the `Debug` aspect in `Debug.aj` and puts the result in `debugSomeApp.jar`.

A.3 Building with Ant

To use the AspectJ Ant task `iajc`, you need to add a single `taskdef` task to your Ant scripts that has a "resource" attribute pointing at the Java property file `org/aspectj/tools/ant/taskdefs/aspectjTaskdefs.properties`. This file is included in the `aspectjtools.jar` in the `lib` directory under your AspectJ installation location. So that Ant can find this `aspectjtools.jar`, you need to set the `taskdef`'s `classpath` attribute. Listing A.1 shows a sample `taskdef` task for doing this.

Listing A.1 Defining the AspectJ Compiler Tasks to Ant

```
<taskdef
    resource=
"org/aspectj/tools/ant/taskdefs/aspectjTaskdefs.properties">
  <classpath>
    <pathelement
      location=
        "c:/aspectj1.2/lib/aspectjtools.jar"/>
  </classpath>
</taskdef>
```

All the command-line options for the AspectJ compiler map to equivalent attributes for the `iajc` task. Table A.2 shows the equivalent Ant attributes and elements for the command-line options from Table A.1.

Table A.2 Common AspectJ Compile Options and Their Ant Equivalent

Command-Line Option	Ant Equivalent	Use in Ant
-d	destDir	Attribute
-classpath	classpath or classpathRef	Attribute or nested element
-sourceroots	sourceRoots or sourceRootsRef	Attribute or nested element
-inpath	inpath or inpathRef	Attribute or nested element
-aspectpath	aspectPath or aspectPathRef	Attribute or nested element
-outjar	outJar	Attribute
-incremental	incremental	Attribute. Set to value "true"

Listing A.2 shows a sample Ant script used to build sources from
${src.dir} and place the resulting .class files in ${bin.dir}.

Listing A.3   Example of Using *iajc* Task

```
<target name="compile" depends="init">
   <mkdir dir="${bin.dir}" />

   <iajc
     sourceroots="${src.dir}"
     destDir="${bin.dir}"
     fork="true"
     debug="on"
     verbose="true" >
     <classpath>
        <pathelement location=
           "${lib.dir}/aspectj/aspectjrt.jar"/>
        <pathelement location=
           "${lib.dir}/mylibs/aLib.jar"/>
     </classpath>
   </iajc>
 </target>
```

You can find the full list of attributes supported by iajc in the developer
guide shipped with the AspectJ distribution.

APPENDIX B

AspectJ Language Quick Reference

B.1 Aspect Declaration

```
[ privileged ] [ Modifiers ] aspect id
[extends Type] [implements TypeList]
[PerClause] { Body }
```

Table B.1 Per Clauses

Per Clause	Meaning
[issingleton()]	One aspect instance.
perthis(pointcut-expression)	One aspect instance for each unique object bound to this at matched join points.
	Implicit condition: && this(myObject)
pertarget(pointcut-expression)	One aspect instance for each unique object bound to target at matched join points.
	Implicit condition: && target(myTargetObject)
percflow(pointcut-expression)	One aspect instance for each control flow begun at a matched join point.
	Implicit condition: && cflow(pointcut expression)
percflowbelow(pointcut-expression)	One aspect instance for each control flow below a matched join point.
	Implicit condition: && cflowbelow(pointcut expression)

Table B.2 Signature of *hasAspect()* and *aspectOf()*

Per Clause	Signatures
[issingleton]	hasAspect(), aspectOf()
perthis	hasAspect(anObject), aspectOf(anObject)
pertarget	hasAspect(aTargetObject), aspectOf(aTargetObject)
percflow	hasAspect(), aspectOf()
percflowbelow	hasAspect(), aspectOf()

B.2   Pointcuts

```
[visibility-modifier] pointcut name(ParameterList):
PointcutExpression;
```

- ○ Pointcuts may be defined inside aspects or classes with identifiers that must be unique within the scope of the declaring type.
- ○ Pointcuts may have private, default (package), protected, or public visibility. Named pointcuts may be referred to from other aspects by prefixing the pointcut name with the name of the declaring type.
- ○ Pointcuts may be declared as abstract inside an abstract aspect. Abstract pointcuts do not have an associated pointcut expression.

Table B.3 Pointcut Designators Matching Based on Join Point Kind

Designator	Meaning and Example
call(Method-Signature)	A call to a method or constructor matching Method-Signature. call(int getCounter())
execution(Method-Signature)	Execution of a method or constructor matching Method-Signature. execution(public HelloWorld.new(..))
get(Signature)	A reference to a field matching Signature. get(int Point.x)
set(Signature)	An assignment to a field matching Signature. set(int Point.y)

Designator	Meaning and Example
handler(TypePattern)	The handling of an exception of a type matched by the specified TypePattern. handler(SIException+)
staticinitialization (TypePattern)	The execution of a static initializer of any type matching TypePattern. staticinitialization(Calculator)
initialization (Constructor-Signature)	The initialization of an object where the first constructor called in the construction of the instance matches Constructor-Signature. The matched join point encompasses the period from the return from the super constructor call to the return of the first-called constructor. initialization(public DataImpl.new(..))
preinitialization (Constructor-Signature)	The pre-initialization of an object where the first constructor called in the construction of the instance matches Constructor-Signature. The matched join point encompasses the period from the entry of the first-called constructor to the call to the super constructor. preinitialization(public DataImpl.new(..))
adviceexecution()	The execution of an advice body. cflow(adviceexecution())

Table B.4   Pointcut Designators Matching Based on Scope

Designator	Meaning and Example
withincode (Method-Signature)	A join point arising from the execution of logic defined in a method or constructor matching Method-Signature. withincode(int getCounter())
within(TypePattern)	Matches a join point arising from the execution of logic defined in a type matching TypePattern. within(insurance.ui..*)
cflow(pcut-expression)	Matches a join point in the control flow of a join point P, including P itself, where P is a join point matched by pcut-expression. cflow(execution(void printMsg(..))

Table B.4 Pointcut Designators Matching Based on Scope

Designator	Meaning and Example
`cflowbelow(pcut-expression)`	Matches a join point below the control flow of a join point P, where P is a join point matched by `pcut-expression`; does not include P itself.
	`cflowbelow(execution(void printMsg(..))`

Table B.5 Pointcut Designators Matching Based on Join Point Context

Designator	Meaning and Example
`target(Type)`	Matches a join point where the target object is an instance of `Type`.
	`target(PolicyImpl)`
`target(id)`	Matches a join point where the target object is an instance of the type of `id`—and `id` is bound in the pointcut definition or, for anonymous pointcuts, in the associated advice declaration.
	`pointcut policyActivity(Policy aPolicy):` `    call(* *(..)) && target(aPolicy);`
`this(Type)`	Matches a join point where the currently executing object is an instance of `Type`.
	`this(Policy)`
`this(id)`	Matches a join point where the executing object is an instance of the type of `id`—and `id` is bound in the pointcut definition or, for anonymous pointcuts, in the associated advice declaration.
	`pointcut callFromCalculator(Calculator calc):` `    call(* *(..)) && this(calc);`
`args(Type,..)`	Matches a join point where the arguments are instances of the specified types.
	`args(int,String)`
`args(id,..)`	Matches a join point where the arguments are instances of the type of `id`—and `id` is bound in the pointcut definition or, for anonymous pointcuts, in the associated advice declaration.
	`pointcut settingAge(String who,int age):` `    call(* setAge(..)) && args(who,age);`
`if(expression)`	Matches a join point where the Boolean expression evaluates to true.
	`if(Logger.debugEnabled)`

B.3   Wildcards

Table B.6   Type Patterns

*	By itself, represents zero or more occurrences of any character. When embedded within a sequence of characters (for example, `java.*.String`) it matches zero or more occurrences of any character except the package separator (`.`).
`..`	All subpackages of the specified package (so `java..String` matches `java.lang.String`). It matches any sequence of characters that starts and ends with a period (`.`) (the package separator).
+	Postfix to a type pattern indicates this type and all of its subtypes (those that extend or implement the type which is post-fixed).

Table B.7   Signature Patterns

*	By itself, stands for any type, method name, field name, return type, access modifier, or method argument. Embedded with other characters, represents zero or more occurrences of any character.
`..`	Any number of parameters of any type.
+	Postfix to a type pattern indicates this type and all of its subtypes (those that extend or implement the type which is post-fixed).

B.4   Advice

```
[strictfp] AdviceSpecification [ throws TypeList ] :
           PointcutExpression {
    body
}
```

Table B.8   Types of Advice

Advice Type	Description
`before(ParameterList)`	Executes before a join point matched by `PointcutExpression`.
`after(ParameterList) returning`	Executes when a normal return is made from a join point matched by `PointcutExpression`.

Table B.8   Types of Advice

Advice Type	Description
`after(ParameterList)` `returning(Formal)`	Executes when a normal return is made from a join point matched by `PointcutExpression`. Return value made accessible to advice body.
`after(ParameterList)` `throwing`	Executes when leaving a join point matched by `PointcutExpression` via any exception condition (checked or unchecked).
`after(ParameterList)` `throwing(Formal)`	Executes when leaving a join point matched by `PointcutExpression` via an exception condition where the exception is an instance of type `Formal`. Within the body of the advice, the exception thrown can be referred to by the name given within the `Formal`.
`after(ParameterList)`	Executes however the program returns from a join point matched by `PointcutExpression`—whether by a normal return or by exception.
`ReturnType` `around(ParameterList)`	Executes both before and after (i.e., around) a join point matched by `PointcutExpression`. Use `proceed()` to control execution of the matched join point.

Table B.9   Special Variables

Name	Usage
`thisJoinPoint`	Provides access to both statically and dynamically determinable contextual information at a join point.
`thisJoinPointStaticPart`	Provides access to statically determinable contextual information at a join point. Equivalent to `thisJoinPoint.getStaticPart()`.
`thisEnclosingJoinPointStaticPart`	Provides access to statically determinable contextual information about the join point lexically enclosing the current matched join point.

B.5   Inter-Type Declarations

Table B.10   Inter-Type Declarations

Declaration	Form and Example

Inter-type field declaration	`[Modifiers] FieldType TargetType.Id;`
	
	`public int HelloWorld.counter;`

Inter-type method declaration	`[Modifiers] ReturnType`
	`TargetType.Id(Formals)`
	
	`[throws TypeList] { Body };`
	
	`public int HelloWorld.getCounter() {`
	`   return counter;`
	
	`}`

Inter-type constructor declaration	`[Modifiers] TargetType.new(Formals)`
	`[throws TypeList] { Body };`
	
	`public HelloWorld.new(int counterValue) {`
	
	`   this.counter = counterValue;`
	
	`}`

Table B.11   *declare parents*

Declaration	Form and Example

Type extension	`declare parents : TypePattern`
	
	`    extends Type;`
	
	`declare parents: *DAOImpl`
	
	`    extends HibernateDAO;`

Interface implementation	`declare parents : TypePattern`
	
	`    implements InterfaceList;`
	
	`declare parents: *Bean`
	
	`    implements Serializable;`

Table B.12 *declare warning* and *declare error*

Declaration	Form and example

Compile-time warning at lines of code that give rise to matched join points	`declare warning: PointcutExpression:`
	`  "warning message";`
	
	`declare warning:`
	`  get(* System.err) || get(* System.out):`
	`  "Don't write output to System out or err";`

Compile-time error at lines of code that give rise to matched join points	`declare error : PointcutExpression :`
	`  "error message";`
	
	`declare error :`
	`  call(* net.sf.hibernate..*(..)) &&`
	`  !within(insurance.dao.hibernate..*):`
	`    "No hibernate dependencies allowed outside of`
	`      insurance.dao.hibernate package";`

Table B.13 Specifying Aspect Precedence

Declaration	Form and Example

Advice precedence among aspects	`declare precedence : TypePatternList;`
	
	`declare precedence : ExceptionManagement,*;`

Table B.14 Softening exceptions

Declaration	Form and Example

Soften exceptions at matched join points.	`declare soft: ExceptionType :`
	`              PointcutExpression;`
	
	`declare soft: HibernateException :`
	`              call(* net.sf.hibernate..*(..));`

APPENDIX C

Next Steps

In a few short pages, this book will be over, but your adventure with AspectJ is just beginning. If you have questions about using AspectJ in your own applications, a great idea about how to improve the language or the tools, or you just want to keep up-to-date with the latest releases and join the growing AspectJ community, this appendix is for you.

C.1 Mailing Lists and FAQ

AspectJ has two lively mailing lists of interest. Aspectj-users@eclipse.org is intended for user comments and questions, whereas aspectj-dev@eclipse.org exists primarily for developers to communicate with each other about the development of the language and future enhancements. Information on AspectJ releases, plans, and events of interest is sent out on the aspectj-announce@eclipse.org mailing list. Before posting to the user lists, you might find the answer to your question in the comprehensive FAQ linked from the AspectJ documentation page.

AJDT has its own developer mailing list: ajdt-dev@eclipse.org. There is also an AJDT newsgroup, news://eclipse.org/eclipse.technology.ajdt.

The eclipse.org site hosts a searchable archive for each mailing list, but it usually takes a couple of days for new posts to become available. Before you can access the archives or even post to one of the mailing lists, you must register and subscribe to the lists. You can do this by clicking the **Newsgroups** link on the main eclipse.org site and then following the **Request a Password** link.

You can find list subscription information on the User Resources pages maintained by the AspectJ and AJDT projects. Figure C.1 shows the AspectJ User Resources page.

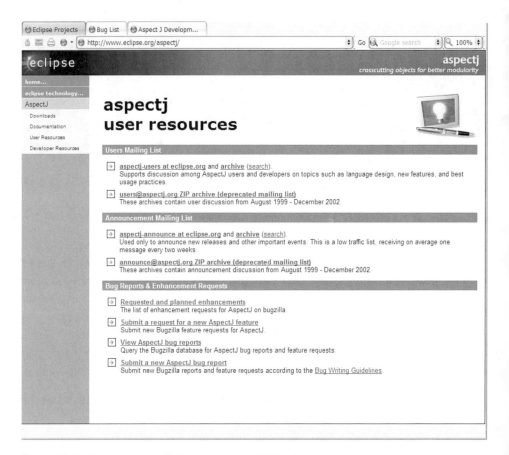

Figure C.1   User Resources links on the AspectJ Web site.

Each list has its own subscription page, such as the one shown for aspectj-users@eclipse.org in Figure C.2.

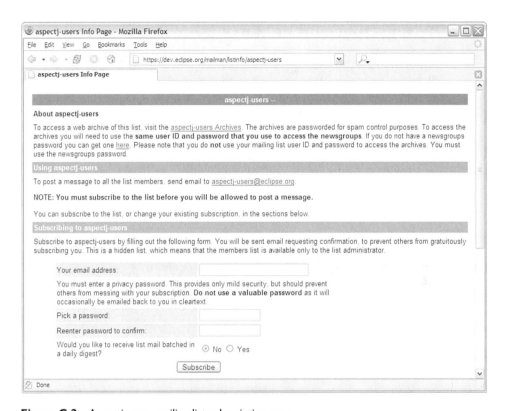

Figure C.2   Aspectj-users mailing list subscription page.

You have the option to receive posts individually or in digest form, which can be useful when traffic levels are high.

C.2   Raising Bugs and Enhancement Requests

The User Resources page on the AspectJ Web site (see Figure C.1) provides links that enable you to view existing feature requests and enter new ones for the project. You will also find a link here for raising bug reports against AspectJ. The equivalent link for AJDT is located on the AJDT project home page.

Before you raise a bug, please take a quick look through the existing bug reports to make sure that someone else hasn't already reported it. When reporting a bug, it is a tremendous help if you can narrow the problem down to a small self-contained test case. This also increases the chances of getting the bug fixed quickly. Bug reports can have test cases added as an attachment using the Create a new attachment link on the Bug Details page (see Figure C.3).

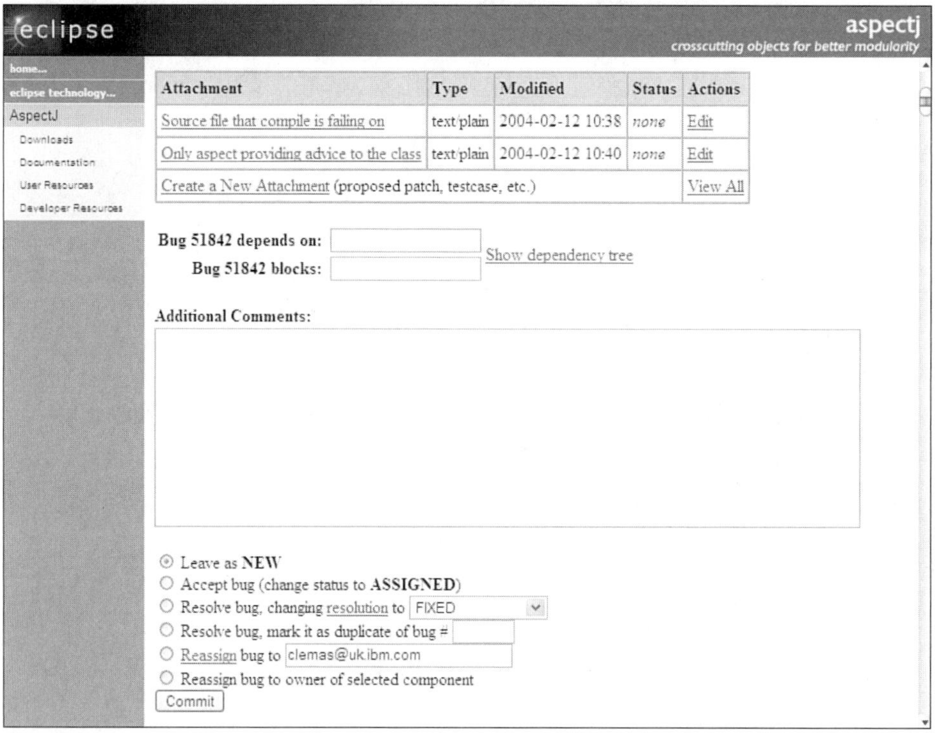

Figure C.3   Attaching a test case to a bug report.

C.3   Contributing to the Development of AspectJ and AJDT

If you want to participate in the actual development of AspectJ, the recommended way to begin is by creating test cases in the source tree, either for bugs you have raised yourself, or for some of the bugs raised by others. First you need to check out the source files for AspectJ; these are at the CVS location dev.eclipse.org:/home/technology. Full instructions for checking out and building the sources as well as the writing and submitting of test cases can be found by following the Developer FAQ link from the Developer Resources page of the AspectJ Web site (see Figure C.4).

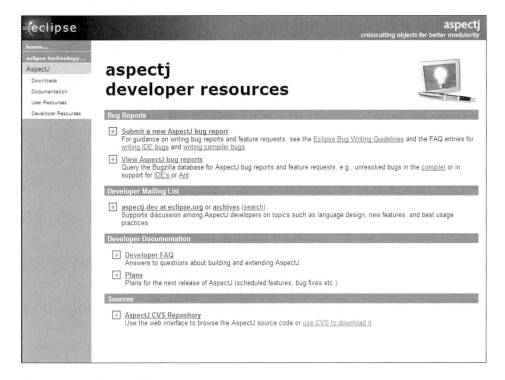

Figure C.4   Developer Resources page.

When you have successfully written one or two test cases, you might like to try your hand at debugging the problem and submitting a patch to fix it. Jim Hugunin's overview of the AspectJ implementation will help you to start finding your way around the code. In the AspectJ CVS repository, you will find it in the `docs` module as file `developer/compiler-weaver/index.html`. If you have questions as you go along, feel free to e-mail the AspectJ developer mailing list.

Options for contributing to the development of the AJDT project are very similar to those described for the AspectJ project. In addition, you have the option to write and publish your own plug-in that works alongside AJDT and complements it. We recommend Erich Gamma and Kent Beck's book *Contributing to Eclipse* (in the same series as this book) as a great place to get started with plug-in development.

APPENDIX D

AJDT Icons Reference

This chapter presents the various icons and markers used by AJDT 1.1.11.

D.1 Objects

Compilation unit (*.aj file or *.java file)

Class file

File without icon assigned to its type

Unknown object

Java scrapbook page (*.jpage file)

Jar description file

Aspect

[blue triangle decoration] Default (package) class

Public class

[blue triangle decoration] Default (package) interface

Public interface

[blue triangle decoration] Default (package) inner class

[red square decoration] Private inner class

[yellow diamond decoration] Protected inner class

Public inner class

[blue triangle decoration] Default (package) inner interface [red square decoration] Private inner interface

[yellow diamond decoration] Protected inner interface

Public inner interface

[blue hollow triangle] Default (package) field

Default (package) inter-type field declaration

[red hollow square] Private field

Private inter-type field declaration

[yellow hollow diamond] Protected field

[green hollow circle] Public field

Public inter-type field declaration

[blue solid triangle] Default method (package visible)

Default (package) inter-type method declaration

[red solid square] Private method

Private inter-type method declaration

[yellow solid diamond] Protected method

[green solid circle] Public method

Public inter-type method declaration

Advises/Declared on/aspect declarations

Before advice

Before advice with runtime test

Around advice

Around advice with runtime test

After advice

After advice with runtime test

[red solid circle with white cross] Declare error

[yellow solid triangle with exclamation mark] Declare warning

[pale blue solid arrow pointing upward] Declare parents

⏳ Declare precedence

⏳ Declare soft

⫰ Pointcut[1]

D.2   Object Adornments

AJ   Marks project as an AspectJ project

J   Marks project as a Java project

?   Marks advice execution as depending on a runtime test

☒   [red solid square with white cross] This element causes an error

⚠   This element causes a warning

╱   This element is deprecated

C   Constructor

A   Abstract member

F   Final member

S   Static member

🕐   Synchronized member

▷   Type with `public static void main(String[] args)` method

△   [blue hollow triangle] Implements method from interface

▲   [blue solid triangle] Overrides method from superclass

D.3   Markers

⇨   Advice

🐾   Before advice

🐾   Before advice with runtime test

Ɛ̧   Around advice

---

1. The color of the icon indicates visibility of the pointcut: red for private; blue for default (package); orange for protected; and green for public.

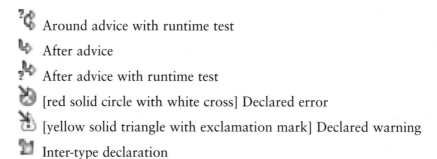

Around advice with runtime test

After advice

After advice with runtime test

[red solid circle with white cross] Declared error

[yellow solid triangle with exclamation mark] Declared warning

Inter-type declaration

D.4   Build Configuration

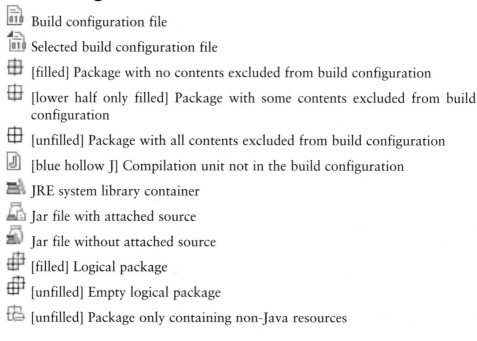

Build configuration file

Selected build configuration file

[filled] Package with no contents excluded from build configuration

[lower half only filled] Package with some contents excluded from build configuration

[unfilled] Package with all contents excluded from build configuration

[blue hollow J] Compilation unit not in the build configuration

JRE system library container

Jar file with attached source

Jar file without attached source

[filled] Logical package

[unfilled] Empty logical package

[unfilled] Package only containing non-Java resources

Index

Symbols

&& (and) operator, combining pointcuts, 140, 155
* (asterisk) wildcard, 157-158, 191
.. (double dot) wildcard, 158, 190
! (negation) operator, 155, 160
|| (or) operator, combining pointcuts, 140, 155
+ (plus sign) wildcard, 79, 158

A

abstract aspects
    and concrete advice, 322
    extending, 319-322
abstract pointcuts, 139, 321
abstraction, 136
adjectives, xxiii, 444
adopting AspectJ. *See* AspectJ, adoption process
adverbs, xxiii, 444
advice, 46, 140-142. *See also* join points; pointcuts
    adviceexecution pointcut designator, 216-219
    after advice, 46, 140, 229, 232-241, 257-258
    after finally advice, 232, 240-241
    after returning advice, 232-240, 270
    after throwing advice, 96-98, 232-233, 270
    around advice. *See* around advice
    array accesses, 182-183
    before advice. *See* before advice
    capturing context, 186-195
    circularity, 258
    concrete advice and abstract aspects, 322
    conditional upon runtime tests, 174
    contextual information, 250-253
    declaring, 457-458
    implicit conditions, 310, 318, 326
    inter-type declarations, 298
    limiting scope, 416
    parameter binding, 248-250
    parameter values, 47-49
    precedence, 256-265

    runtime tests, 310
    setting breakpoints, 117-121
    showing in AJDT, 50-53
    softening exceptions, 265-266
    strictfp modifier, 229
    thisEnclosingJoinPointStaticPart, 336
    thisJoinPoint variable, 331
    thisJoinPointStaticPart, 336
    throwing exceptions, 254-255
    throws clause, 230
    types of, 229
adviceexecution pointcut designator, 216-219
AdviceSignature interface, 349-350
after advice, 46, 140, 229, 232-241, 257-258
after finally advice, 232, 240-241
after returning advice, 232-240, 270
after throwing advice, 96-98, 232-233, 270
.aj file extension, 37
ajc command, 448-449
ajdoc tool, 125-126
AJDT (AspectJ Development Tools), xvii, 3
    advice, showing, 50-53
    ajdoc tool, 125-126
    Ant integration, 433-436
    aspect libraries, 415-423, 426-427
    cheat sheets, 128-129
    compiler options, 115-116
    Cross-Reference view, 401
    debugging, 116-122
    documentation, 18-19
    editor templates, 123-124
    examples, 127-128
    help features, 127
    icons, 467-470
    incremental compilation, 111, 114
    installing, 11-19
    Jar files, linking with aspects, 427-432
    mailing lists, 461
    manual builds, 114-115
    newsgroups, 461
    Outline view toolbar, 124-125

preferences, configuring, 32-33
project Web site, 11
ajdt-dev mailing list, 461
alternative constructors, matching calls to, 224-225
analyzing annotations, disabling, 32-33
and (&&) operator, combining pointcuts, 140, 155
annotations, disabling analyzing of, 32-33
anonymous pointcuts, 141, 148
Ant
        iajc task, 450-451
        integration with AJDT, 433-436
        running inside Eclipse, 433
AOP (aspect-oriented programming), xvii
        aspect, defined, xxiii, 28
        frameworks, list of, 145
API. *See* runtime library
application-specific aspects, 362
args pointcut designator, 186-192
argument types, matching, 187-188
argument values, extracting, 188-191
around advice, 46, 140, 229, 242-247
        debugging, 122
        implementation evaluation, 54-60
        precedence, 256-257
array accesses, 182-183
arrays, wildcards, 159
aspect discovery, 443
        adjectives and adverbs, 444
        qualities of aspects, 445-446
        rules and policy statements, 445
        scattered code, 445
        temporal statements, 444-445
aspect libraries, 415-423, 426-427
aspect linking, 168
Aspect Visualization perspective, 436-437
        Visualiser menu, 437-438
        Visualiser view, 438-440
aspect-oriented design, 361, 443. *See also* aspect discovery
aspect-oriented programming. *See* AOP
AspectJ
        adoption process, 357-358
                aspect-oriented design stage, 361
                auxiliary aspects, 359-360
                business/core aspects, 360
                enforcement aspects, 358-359
                infrastructure aspects, 359-360
        advice, 140-142
        aspects. *See* aspects
        compiler options, 383-384
        design patterns, 361
        development, 465-466
        FAQ, 461
        installing, 447-448
        inter-type declarations, 142-144
        join points, 137-138
        join point model, 136-137
        language design properties, 144-145
        mailing lists, 461-463

pointcut designators. *See* pointcut designators
pointcuts, 136-140
runtime library, 329-330
        org.aspectj.lang package, 330-342
        org.aspectj.lang.reflect package, 342-353
source folders, 363
AspectJ Development Tools. *See* AJDT
AspectJ editor, 32
        showing advice, 51-53
        templates, 123-124
AspectJ projects
        building, 111, 114-116, 434-436
        converting Java projects to, 29-31
        creating, 33-34
        debugging, 116-122
AspectJ runtime library, 30, 359
aspectj-announce mailing list, 461
aspectj-dev mailing list, 461
aspectj-users mailing list, 461
aspectjrt.jar. *See* runtime library
aspectOf() static method, 306, 454
        examples, 308
        signature, 318
aspects
        abstract aspects, 136, 322
        advice and implicit conditions, 318, 326
        application-specific aspects, 362
        array accesses, 182-183
        calling methods at shutdown, 80-81
        configuring with Spring, 404-411
        constructors, 302
        core aspects, 357, 360, 401-404
        creating, 34-36
        crosscutting concerns, 133-135
        declarations, 301-303, 453-454
        defined, xxiii, 28
        domain-specific aspects, 362
        efficient logging, 384
        encapsulation, 136
        enforcement aspects, 358-359, 362-374
        evaluating implementation, 82-83, 105-108
        fields versus inter-type declarations, 278
        general-purpose aspects, 361
        Hibernate, 362
        HibernateManager, 87-88
        infrastructure aspects, 357-360, 374-400
        inheritance, 318-323
        initialization, 303
        inner aspects, 323-324, 403
        instantiation, 303-306, 317-318, 453
        inter-type declarations. *See* inter-type declarations
        linking with Jar files, 427-432
        modularity, 136
        multiple aspects, precedence of advice in, 263-265
        per-object aspects versus inter-type
                declarations, 315
        percflow instantiation model, 304, 315-317
        percflowbelow instantiation model, 304, 315-317

pertarget instantiation model, 304, 311-314
perthis instantiation model, 304-311
points of variance, 416
precedence, 256-263, 460
private modifier, 326
privileged aspects, 324
recursion, 376
serialization-based persistence, 69
singleton aspects, 303, 306
as target of inter-type declarations, 298
testing, 388
tracing, 359
type availability for linking, 327
types of, 361
visualization, 436-440
asterisk (*) wildcard, 157-158, 191
auxiliary aspects. *See* infrastructure aspects

B

before advice, 46, 140, 229-232
    at handler join points, 269
    precedence, 256-257
boxing, 249
breakpoints, setting, 10, 116-121
bug reports, 464
Build Configuration Editor, 400
build configurations
    AJDT icons, 470
    choosing, 399
    exclusion filters, 108-110
    named configurations, 397-398
    saving, 398
builders (projects), 31
building. *See also* compilers
    AspectJ projects, 111, 114-116
    insurance application example, 433-436
business aspects. *See* core aspects

C

calculator application example, 147-148
    debugging, 219-221
    evaluateExpression routine, 150-151
    exception handling, 195-197
    IntegerStack class, 170-172
    memory support, 184-185
call pointcut designator, 149-154
    and execution poincut designator, 168-169
    and target pointcut designator, 170-175
    and this pointcut designator, 178
calling untrusted code, 401-404
CatchClauseSignature interface, 351-353
cflow pointcut designator, 209-216
cflowbelow pointcut designator, 209-216
change notification, xix

cheat sheets, 128-129
checked exceptions
    softening, 99-100
    SoftException, 342
    versus unchecked exceptions, 267
choosing build configurations, 399
circularity, advice precedence, 258
.class files. *See* compiled aspects
class folders, adding to inpath, 430-431
class path, adding aspect libraries to runtime class
    path, 418
classes
    extending, 297, 322
    running, 10
code
    mapping requirements to, xvii-xxii
    untrusted code, calling, 401-404
CodeSignature interface, 346-348
command-line compiler, 447
    ajc command, 448-449
    iajc task, 450-451
compile time, matching join points, 44
compile-time constants, get pointcut designator, 270
compiled aspects (aspect libraries), 415-423, 426-427
compiler messages (type patterns), 81
compiler options, 383-384
compilers. *See also* building
    command-line compiler, 447-451
    incremental compilation, 111, 114
    Java compiler, version 1.3 and 1.4 differences, 163
    manual builds, 114-115
    options, 115-116
compound type patterns, 160
concrete advice and abstract aspects, 322
configuring
    AJDT preferences, 32-33
    aspects with Spring, 404-411
    Hibernate, 84, 95-96
    insurance application example for aspect
        libraries, 418
conflicts, inter-type declarations, 284-285
Console view, 10
constants, compile-time constants, 270
constructors
    aspects, 302
    inter-type declarations, 281-282
    no-argument constructors, 92-93
    return value, 270
ConstructorSignature interface, 350
context, capturing
    args pointcut designator, 186-192
    this and target pointcut designators, 192-195
contextual information (advice), 250-253
control flow, percflow and percflowbelow aspect
    instantiation models, 315-317
control-flow-based pointcut designators, 209-216
converting Java projects to AspectJ projects, 29-31

core aspects, 357, 401
    adopting AspectJ, 360
    calling untrusted code, 401-404
    configuring with Spring, 404-411
Cross-Reference view, 401
crosscutting concerns, xxiii, 133-135

D

DAOs (data-access objects), 66-68
    dependency injection, 74-80, 88-89
    implementing, 100-105
    serializing, 71-74
Debug perspective, 10-11
debugging
    AspectJ projects, 116-122
    breakpoints, setting, 10
    calculator application example, 219-221
declarations. *See* declaring; inter-type declarations
declare error statement, 61-62, 267-268
    declaring, 460
    restrictions, 270
declare parents statement, 69-71, 287-296
    declaring, 459
    extending classes, 297
declare precedence statement, 264-265, 460
declare soft statement, 99-100, 265-266
    declaring, 460
    limiting scope, 416
    SoftException exception, 342
declare warning statement, 40-44, 93-94, 267-268
    declaring, 460
    restrictions, 270
declared-type patterns, 168
    field signatures, 181
    method signatures, 161-164
declaring
    advice, 457-458
    aspects, 301-303, 453-454
    inter-type declarations, 459-460
    pointcuts, 152-153
defining pointcuts, 454-456
dependency injection (DAOs), 74-80, 88-89
design. *See* aspect-oriented design
design patterns in AspectJ, 361
design properties of AspectJ, 144-145
documentation, 18-19, 125-126
domain objects, serializing, 69-71
domain-specific aspects, 362
double dot (..) wildcard, 158, 190
downloading Eclipse, 4
DRY principle, 62
dynamic scoping pointcut designators, 209-216

E

Eclipse
    Ant scripts, running, 433
    downloading, 4
    installing, 3-4
    Java project example, 6-11
    overview, 3
    plug-ins, 401
    running, 5-6
    safe platform rule, 402
    Web site, 3
editor templates (AJDT), 123-124
Editor view, 10
efficiency, logging, 384
empty around advice, 242
empty pointcut definition, 227
encapsulation, 136, 139
enforcement aspects, 362-366
    adopting AspectJ, 358-359
    preserving modularity, 368-374
    system.out, 366-367
evaluating
    aspect implementation, 82-83, 105-108
    insurance application example, 412-413
examples (AJDT), 127-128
Examples plug-in, 19-20
exception handling
    after throwing advice, 270
    handler pointcut designator, 195-198
    infrastructure aspects, 386-392
exceptions
    after finally advice, 240
    after throwing advice, 232-233
    CatchClauseSignature interface, 351-353
    checked exceptions, 99-100, 267
    mapping, 96-100
    NoAspectBoundException, 340-341
    softening, 265-266, 460
    SoftException, 342
    throwing in advice, 230, 254-255
exclusion filters, 108-110
execution pointcut designator, 166-167
    and call pointcut designator, 168-169
    and target pointcut designator, 175-176
    and this pointcut designator, 178-179
extending
    aspects, 319-322
    classes, 297, 322
extension points, 401
extensions. *See* file extensions
extract interface refactoring, 75
extracting values. *See* context, capturing

F

FAQ (AspectJ), 461
feature (AJDT), 12
feature requests, 464

field name (field signatures), 181
field signatures, 180
    declared-type patterns, 181
    examples, 182
    field name, 181
    field-type patterns, 181
    modifier patterns, 180
field-type patterns (field signatures), 181
fields
    declaring in aspects versus inter-type
        declarations, 278
    inter-type declarations, 275-278
FieldSignature interface, 345-346
file extensions, .java versus .aj, 37
final fields, 184
folders, linking source folders, 363
frameworks (AOP), list of, 145

G-H

general-purpose aspects, 361
get pointcut designator, 179-185, 270

handler join points (before advice), 269
handler pointcut designator, 195-198
Hannemann, Jan (design patterns), 361
hasAspect() static method, 306, 454
    examples, 308
    signature, 318
HelloWorld JMX application, 393
help features (AJDT), 127. *See also* AJDT, documentation
Hibernate, 84
    advice precedence, 259-263
    aspect libraries, creating, 415
    aspects, 87-88, 362
    configuring, 84, 95-96
    DAO dependency injection, 88-89
    DAOs, implementing, 100-105
    declare warning, 93-94
    evaluating aspect implementation, 105-108
    implementing persistence, 84-87
    mapping exceptions, 96-100
    unique keys, 89-94

I

iajc task, 434-436, 450-451
icons (AJDT), 467-470
if pointcut designator, 219-223
implicit conditions (advice), 310, 318, 326
incremental compilation, 111, 114
information hiding. *See* encapsulation
infrastructure aspects, 357-360, 374
    adopting AspectJ, 359-360
    exception handling, 386-392
    implementing tracing facilities, 374-386
    management, 392-400

inheritance
    aspect libraries, 421
    aspects, 318-323
    inter-type declarations, 283-284
    multiple inheritance, 297
initialization of aspects, 303
initialization pointcut designators, 198-206
    initialization, 201-206
    preinitialization, 201-206
    staticinitialization, 200-201
InitializerSignature interface, 350
inner aspects, 323-324, 403
inner interfaces (JoinPoint.StaticPart), 335-336
inpath
    adding class folders to, 430-431
    adding Jar files to, 427
installing
    AJDT, 11-19
    AspectJ, 447-448
    Eclipse, 3-4
    Examples plug-in, 19-20
    insurance application example project, 22
instances of aspects, 303-306
    list of models, 317-318
    percflow aspect instantiation model, 315-317
    percflowbelow aspect instantiation model, 315-317
    pertarget aspect instantiation model, 311-314
    perthis aspect instantiation model, 306-311
instantiation model (aspect), 453
insurance application example, 21-26
    aspect library inheritance, 423
    AspectJ projects, creating, 33-34
    building, 433-436
    configuring
        AJDT preferences, 32-33
        for aspect libraries, 418
        aspects with Spring, 404-411
    converting to AspectJ, 29-31
    DAO interfaces, 66-68
    debugging, 116-122
    declare errors, 61-62
    evaluating, 412-413
    exception hierarchy, 386
    exclusion filters, 108-110
    implementation, evaluating, 54-60
    installing project, 22
    notification policy, 37-49
    persistence, 65-66
    PolicyChangeNotification aspect, creating, 34-36
    refactoring with inter-type declarations, 274-275
    reporting application, 427
    serialization-based persistence, 68-108
    tracking policy updates, 26-28
    validation, 287-296
inter-type declarations, 89-92, 142-144, 273, 459-460
    aspects as target, 298
    conflicts, 284-285
    constructors, 281-282
    extending classes, 297

fields, 275-278
inheritance, 283-284
interfaces, 285-296
methods, 278-281
pointcuts, 298
refactoring, 274-275
versus aspect fields, 278
versus per-object aspects, 315
visibility, 282-283
wildcards, 283
interfaces
AdviceSignature, 349-350
aspects, 323
CatchClauseSignature, 351-353
CodeSignature, 346-348
ConstructorSignature, 350
DAO interfaces, 66-68
extract interface refactoring, 75
FieldSignature, 345-346
InitializerSignature, 350
inter-type declarations, 285-296
JoinPoint, 331-335
JoinPoint.StaticPart, 335-336
MemberSignature, 344
MethodSignature, 348-349
Signature, 336-339
SourceLocation, 343-344
introductions. See inter-type declarations
ISafeRunnable interface, 402

J

Jar files
as aspect library output, 417
linking with aspects, 427-432
Java classes, running, 10
Java compiler, version 1.3 and 1.4 differences, 163
Java Development perspective, 7
Java Development Tools (JDT), 362
.java file extension, 37
Java projects
building insurance application example as, 433
converting to AspectJ projects, 29-31
example, 6-11
javac task, 433
JDT (Java Development Tools), 362
JMX, HelloWorld application, 393
join points, 37-38, 137-138. See also advice; pointcuts
advice, 46
handler join points (before advice), 269
implementing policies, 45-49
inter-type declarations, 298
matching at compile time, 44
return values, 233-240
join point model, 136-137
JoinPoint interface, 331-335
JoinPoint.StaticPart interface, 335-336
JUnit view, 23

K-L

keys, unique keys (Hibernate), 89-94
Kiczales, Gregor (design patterns), 361
Lazy thisJoinPoint compiler option, 383
libraries
aspect libraries, 415-423, 426-427
runtime library. See runtime library
linked source folders, 431
linking
aspect linking, 168
Jar files and aspects, 427-432
source folders, 363
type availability for, 327
listeners
notifying, 26-28
refactoring with inter-type declarations, 274-275
logging (efficiency), 384

M

mailing lists
AJDT, 461
AspectJ, 461-463
management, infrastructure aspects, 392-400
manual builds, 114-115
mapping
exceptions, 96-100
requirements to code, xvii-xxii
mapping files (XML), Hibernate, 84
markers (AJDT icons), 469
matching join points at compile time, 44
MemberSignature interface, 344
memory support (calculator application example), 184-185
method call pointcut designator, 149-154
versus method execution pointcut designator, 168-169
and target pointcut designator, 170-175
and this pointcut designator, 178
method calls, removing, 58-59
method execution pointcut designator, 166-167
versus method call pointcut designator, 168-169
and target pointcut designator, 175-176
and this pointcut designator, 178-179
method name (method signatures), 164
method signatures, 160
aspectOf() and hasAspect(), 318
declared-type patterns, 161-164
method name, 164
modifier patterns, 160-161
parameters, 165
return-type patterns, 161
throws clause, 165-166
methods
calling at shutdown, 80-81
inter-type declarations, 278-281
on org.aspectj.lang.JoinPoint, 331

on org.aspectj.lang.JoinPoint.StaticPart, 335
on org.aspectj.lang.reflect.AdviceSignature, 349
on org.aspectj.lang.reflect.CatchClauseSignature, 351
on org.aspectj.lang.reflect.CodeSignature, 347
on org.aspectj.lang.reflect.MethodSignature, 349
on org.aspectj.lang.reflect.SourceLocation, 343
on org.aspectj.lang.Signature, 337
MethodSignature interface, 348-349
mixed-domain cohesion, 275
modifier patterns
   field signatures, 180
   method signatures, 160-161
modular implementations versus non-modular implementations, 59-60
modularity, xxii, 136, 446
   evaluating insurance application example, 412-413
   preserving, 368-374
multiple inheritance, 297

N

n-to-n mapping, xxii
n-to-one mapping, xx-xxii
named build configurations, 397-398
named pointcuts, 139-141, 148, 152
natures (projects), 31
negation (!) operator, 155, 160
New Aspect Wizard, 34-36
newsgroups, AJDT, 461
No inline compiler option, 384
No Weave compiler option, 384
no-argument constructors, 92-93
NoAspectBoundException exception, 340-341
non-modular implementations versus modular implementations, 59-60
notification policy
   implementing, 45-49
   stating, 37-44
notifying listeners, 26-28

O

object adornments (AJDT icons), 469
objects (AJDT icons), 469
one-to-n mappings, xix-xx, 28
one-to-one mappings, xviii, 28
opening Visualiser, 385
or (||) operator, combining pointcuts, 140, 155
order of advice. *See* precedence (advice)
org.aspectj.lang package, 330
   JoinPoint interface, 331-335
   JoinPoint.StaticPart interface, 335-336
   NoAspectBoundException exception, 340-341
   Signature interface, 336-339
   SoftException exception, 342

org.aspectj.lang.reflect package, 342
   AdviceSignature interface, 349-350
   CatchClauseSignature interface, 351-353
   CodeSignature interface, 346-348
   ConstructorSignature interface, 350
   FieldSignature interface, 345-346
   InitializerSignature interface, 350
   MemberSignature interface, 344
   MethodSignature interface, 348-349
   SourceLocation interface, 343-344
Outline view, 9
   showing advice, 50-51
   toolbar, 124-125

P

Package Explorer, 7, 108
package protected inter-type field declarations, 277
packages. *See* org.aspectj.lang package; org.aspectj.lang.reflect package
parameter binding (advice), 248-250
parameter values (advice), 47-49
parameters (method signatures), 165
patterns. *See* design patterns in AspectJ; type patterns; wildcards
per clauses, 453
per-object aspects versus inter-type declarations, 315
per-type instantiation model, 318
percflow aspect instantiation model, 304, 315-317
percflowbelow aspect instantiation model, 304, 315-317
persistence, 65-108
pertarget aspect instantiation model, 304, 311-314
perthis aspect instantiation model, 304-311
plain old Java objects (POJOs), 84
plug-ins, 12, 19-20, 401
plus sign (+) wildcard, 79, 158
pointcut designators, 147-149. *See also* pointcuts
   advantages of, 335
   adviceexecution, 216-219
   args, 186-192
   call, 149-154, 168-169
   categories of, 148-149
   dynamic scoping, 209-216
   execution, 166-169
   field signatures. *See* field signatures
   get, 179-185, 270
   handler, 195-198
   if, 219-223
   initialization pointcut designators. *See* initialization pointcut designators
   set, 179-185, 270
   static scoping, 206-209
   target. *See* target pointcut designator
   this. *See* this pointcut designator
   wildcards, 157-158
pointcut parameter list, 189

pointcuts, 136-140. *See also* advice; join points; pointcut designators
    abstract pointcuts, 321
    advice parameter binding, 248-250
    alternative constructors, matching calls to, 224-225
    capturing context, 186-195
    categories of, 138
    combining, 139-140, 155-156
    declare warning and declare error statements, 267-268
    declaring, 152-153
    defining, 454-456
    definition style, 149
    empty pointcut definition, 227
    final fields, 184
    implementing policies, 45-49
    inter-type declarations, 298
    method signatures. *See* method signatures
    percflow aspect instantiation model, 304, 315-317
    percflowbelow aspect instantiation model, 304, 315-317
    pertarget aspect instantiation model, 304, 311-314
    perthis aspect instantiation model, 304-311
    reflective method calls, matching, 225-227
    reuse, 154
    superclasses, matching calls to, 224-225
    type patterns, 157-160
    updating, 57-58
    writing, 38-40, 223-224
points of variance, 416
POJOs (plain old Java objects), 84
policy hierarchy
    implementing policies, 45-49
    stating policies, 37-44
policy statements, aspect discovery, 445
PolicyChangeNotification aspect, creating, 34-36
precedence (advice), 256
    between multiple aspects, 263-265
    declaring, 460
    within an aspect, 256-263
preferences (AJDT), configuring, 32-33
preinitialization pointcut designator, 201-206
preserving component modularity, 368-374
primitive type promotions, 191-192
private inter-type declarations, 282
private modifier and aspects, 326
privileged aspects, 324
Problems view, 7, 10
proceed and around advice, 242-244
projects, 31. *See also* AspectJ projects; Java projects
provides list, 189
proxy server settings (Update Manager), 14
public inter-type declarations, 283

Q-R

qualities of aspects, 445-446

recursion in aspects, 376
red squiggles, avoiding, 32-33
refactoring, 28
    creating aspects, 34-36
    extract interface, 75
    with inter-type declarations, 274-275
reflective method calls, matching, 225-227
removing method calls, 58-59
reporting application (insurance application example), 427
requirements, mapping to code, xvii-xxii
return values
    after finally advice, 240
    constructors, 270
    join points, 233-240
    set pointcut designator, 270
return-type patterns (method signatures), 161
reusable aspects. *See* compiled aspects
reuse, pointcuts, 139, 154
Reweavable compiler option, 384
Reweavable compress compiler option, 384
RPN (Reverse Polish Notation), 147
rules, aspect discovery, 445
running
    Eclipse, 5-6
    Java classes, 10
    test suite, 23
runtime class path, adding aspect libraries to, 418
runtime library, 329-330, 359. *See also* org.aspectj.lang package; org.aspectj.lang.reflect package
runtime tests, 174, 310

S

safe platform rule, 402
saving build configurations, 398
scattered code, aspect discovery, 445
scattering, xix
scope, limiting, 416. *See also* visibility
scope designators
    dynamic scoping, 209-216
    static scoping, 206-209
semantics, 145
sequence diagrams
    advice, 142
    around advice, 247
    inter-type declarations, 143
Serializable Aspects compiler option, 384
serialization-based persistence, 68-108
serializing
    DAOs, 71-74
    domain objects, 69-71
set pointcut designator, 179-185, 270
shutdown, calling methods, 80-81

Signature interface, 336-339. *See also*
    org.aspectj.lang.reflect package
signature patterns, 457
signatures. *See* field signatures; method signatures
simple insurance application example. *See* insurance
    application example
singleton aspects, 303, 306
softening
      checked exceptions, 99-100
      exceptions, 265-266, 460
SoftException exception, 342
source folders, 363
SourceLocation interface, 343-344
special variables, 458
Spring, configuring aspects, 404-411
state, maintaining, 315
static inner aspects, 323
static methods, target pointcut designator, 175
static scoping pointcut designators, 206-209
staticinitialization pointcut designator, 200-201
strictfp modifier (advice), 229
superclasses, matching calls to, 224-225
system.out, enforcement aspects, 366-367

T

tangling, xx
target pointcut designator, 170-176
      and call pointcut designator, 170-175
      capturing context, 192-195
      and execution pointcut designator, 175-176
      and get and set pointcut designators, 182
      static methods, 175
      versus this pointcut designator, 177-178
templates
      after advice, 232
      AspectJ editor templates, 123-124
      before advice, 230
temporal statements, aspect discovery, 444-445
test suite, running, 23
test-driven-development, 388
testing
      aspects, 388
      runtime tests, 310
this pointcut designator, 176-179
      and call pointcut designator, 178
      capturing context, 192-195
      and execution pointcut designator, 178-179
      and get and set pointcut designators, 182
      matching calls to, 224-225
      versus target pointcut designator, 177-178
thisEnclosingJoinPointStaticPart variable, 250-253, 336
thisJoinPoint variable, 250-2253, 331
thisJoinPointStaticPart variable, 250-253, 336
throwing exceptions in advice, 254-255
throws clause
      advice, 230
      method signatures, 165-166

tracing facilities, implementing, 374-386
tracing with aspects, 359
tracking policy updates (insurance application
    example), 26-28
type availability, 168, 327
type conversion
      after returning advice, 236
      around advice, 244
type patterns, 157-160, 457
      + (plus sign) in, 79
      compiler messages, 81
      declare parents statement, 292
type promotions, 191-192

U

unbound pointcut designators, 175, 179
unchecked exceptions versus checked exceptions, 267
unique keys (Hibernate), 89-94
untrusted code, calling, 401-404
Update Manager, 12-14
update sites, 14
updating pointcuts, 57-58

V

validation, 287-296
variables, special variables, 458
variance, points of, 416
visibility
      inter-type declarations, 277-278, 281-283
      privileged aspects, 324
Visualiser, opening, 385
Visualiser menu, 437-438
Visualiser view, 53, 438-440
visualization of aspects, 436-440

W-Z

weaving, 145, 427-432
Web sites
      AJDT project, 11
      Eclipse, 3
wildcards, 457
      arrays, 159
      inter-type declarations, 283
      in pointcut designators, 157-158
within pointcut designator, 206-209
withincode pointcut designator, 206-209
workbench, configuring AJDT preferences, 32-33
writing pointcuts. *See* pointcut designators; pointcuts

XML mapping files (Hibernate), 84

informIT

YOUR GUIDE TO IT REFERENC

Articles

Keep your edge with thousands of free articles, in-depth features, interviews, and IT reference recommendations – all written by experts you know and trust.

Online Books

Answers in an instant from **InformIT Online Book's** 600+ fully searchable on line books. For a limited time, you can get your first 14 days **free**.

POWERED BY
Safari
TECH BOOKS ONLIN

Catalog

Review online sample chapters, author biographies and customer rankings and choose exactly the right book from a selection of over 5,000 titles.